WITHDRAWN

D1253310

FAMILY, ECONOMY AND STATE

FAMILY, ECONOMY & STATE

The Social Reproduction Process Under Capitalism

EDITED BY
JAMES DICKINSON AND BOB RUSSELL

ST. MARTIN'S PRESS
New York

CALVIN T. RYAN LIBRARY
KEARNEY STATE COLLEGE
KEARNEY, NEBRASKA

©1986 James Dickinson and Bob Russell
All rights reserved. For information, write:
Scholarly & Reference Division,
St. Martin's Press, Inc., 175 Fifth Avenue, New York, NY 10010
First published in the United States of America in 1986
Printed in Great Britain

Library of Congress Cataloging in Publication Data
Main entry under title:

Family, economy and state.

  1. Marxian economics. 2. Capitalism. 3. Frankfurt
school of sociology. I. Dickinson, James, 1950–
II. Russell, Bob, 1950–   . III. Title: Social
reproduction process under capitalism.
HB97.5.F35   1986   331   85-2138
ISBN 0-312-28045-9

Contents

PART III CLASS AND SOCIAL REPRODUCTION

PART IV CONTRADICTIONS IN SOCIAL REPRODUCTION UNDER CAPITALISM

Acknowledgments

Helen Hudzina and Geraldine Holley of the Educational Support Center at Rider College typed the entire manuscript of this book with great speed and diligence, and cheerfully incorporated our seemingly endless alterations and additions. Kathryn Krepich and Anne Butera of the Sociology Department also helped to prepare parts of the manuscript. Dr. Olga Bakich of the University of Toronto rendered invaluable assistance during the final stages. We would like to thank all of them for their work in the preparation of this volume. We would also like to thank the President's Publication Fund of the University of Saskatchewan for the grant which partially offset costs.

INTRODUCTION: THE STRUCTURE OF REPRODUCTION IN CAPITALIST SOCIETY

James Dickinson and Bob Russell

The Concept of Social Reproduction

In recent years, the discipline of sociology has experienced several significant changes. Sociology has seen a revival of interest in political economy, renewed interest in the structure and functioning of the modern state and increased theoretical and empirical concern with domestic labour and the position of women in industrial capitalist society. In general, these developments are part of a movement towards the articulation of an historically-grounded structural sociology. This sociology not only seeks to ground the analysis of social institutions and processes within the logic of economic development but also takes as its central concern issues that are often neglected or ignored by conventional practices.

In no area have these interests been combined in a more fruitful way than in the current studies on social reproduction. Broadly speaking, the social reproduction literature takes the dominant relationship of our time—the wage labour/capital relationship—as its principal object of analysis and considers the institutions, mechanisms and processes associated with the economic, social, political and ideological reproduction of this relationship. Of central importance here is the social construction of the factors of material production (land, labour and capital) and in particular, the social construction of human labour power as a commodity in capitalist society.

The concept of social reproduction in turn has led to a rethinking of the traditional sociological concern with social order (and its attendant notion of equilibrium derived in large part from neoclassical economics) in terms of the dynamic and contradictory processes upon which the renewal of those elements of social production depends. In other words, while assuming the problematic status of social reproduction in common with other trends in social scientific analysis, this volume takes as its focus the social reproduction of the specific and contradictory relationships of advanced capitalism.

This reformulation, which takes the reproduction of labour power as a central concern, is in part a reaction to and an outcome of a critical engagement with the traditional sociological and economic paradigms. On the one hand, traditional economics was largely constrained to see social reproduction in terms of equilibrium between the elements that make up the economic system, particularly as regards the establishment of equilibrium prices through the interaction of supply and demand schedules. On the other hand, while Marxist political economy rejected the idea that capitalist social relations tended toward equilibrium, nonetheless reproduction was still discussed primarily at the level of the economic system as a whole in terms of the simple and expanded reproduction of capital itself.

Until comparatively recently traditional political economy failed to develop an adequate theory of the reproduction of capitalist social relations and in particular did not consider the means by which labour power was produced and maintained as a commodity. This lacuna was in marked contrast to the scope and sophistication of its theory of the capitalist accumulation process. Indeed, ever since Marx's *Capital*, the tendency in what we might describe as orthodox circles, has been to emphasize the societal moment of production and accumulation almost to an exclusion of a consideration of the processes and institutions of social reproduction which stand behind and support the circuits of capital. Despite Marx's own careful distinction between productive and individual consumption, the recognition in *Capital* that the reproduction of critical elements of production, particularly labour power, remains external to the economy, and the numerous warnings by Marx and Engels that a complete analysis of any social formation requires an appreciation of the reproductive as well as productive side of social relations, subsequent generations of Marxists generally failed to develop these insights and work out a comprehensive theory of reproduction in capitalist society.[1] Like Marx himself, his orthodox followers understood capitalism primarily as a system of the production and accumulation of surplus value, and the concept of reproduction was largely restricted to a consideration of the proportional exchange of use-values between the various 'departments' of production which would ensure the over-all capacity of the system to reproduce itself at an expanded level.[2]

Only occasionally, usually under special conditions, was it felt necessary to address the sphere of reproduction—normally under the guise of the 'woman question'. And even then, such discussions generally lacked the theoretical rigor and sophistication lavished on the other areas of contemporary society not fully elaborated on by Marx.[3] With a few notable exceptions, particularly the work of Frankfurt School members such as Horkheimer and Adorno and the psychoanalyst Wilhelm Reich, discussions of the family and state, and the significance of these structures for the reproduction of commodities, especially labour power, was ignored or passed over.[4] Generally, the reproductive side of capitalist relations was regarded as somewhat less interesting and by default was given over by and large to the cultural sciences.

The neglect of the social institutions of reproduction was to have profound consequences for the theory and practice of social change. For one thing, it set up what appeared to be a serious unresolved and often unappreciated tension between the economic and political projects of Marxism. Indeed, as the capitalist economy evolved more or less along the lines predicted by Marx, the historically liberating activities of its principal creation, the industrial working class, at least in the advanced capitalist countries either failed to materialize or be effectively consolidated at critical historical junctures.[5] Politically, this often resulted in the denouncement of economistic tendencies within the working class rather than the analysis of those structures of everyday life and experience in the reproductive sphere which might account for the presence, or at least the strength, of such a non-transcendent consciousness within the proletariat.

The failure of political economy to consider seriously the question of social reproduction meant that until fairly recently the analysis of extra-economic institutions and processes fell to conventional sociology. However, the sociology of the family—to take but one example—as it developed into a distinct subdiscipline of the field came to embody certain theoretical and empirical limitations which effectively stymied the contribution that analyses of the family might make to the broader understanding of society as an economic and political totality. Thus, in the conventional sociology that emerged in the post-World War Two era, the family was seen as part of a diffuse process of functional modernization whereby social functions find expression in the emergence of specialized institutions and an increase in the division of labour.[6] As such, the family was taken to be the locus of affective and non-instrumental ties and relationships and hence was regarded as qualitatively different and divorced from the instrumentality of the economy. Moreover, the family was seen as the primary institution for the generation of shared values—the basis of social order and consensus. Research in this area was therefore almost naturally directed towards internal relations within the family (e.g. the socialization process). A primary weakness was therefore apparent in the emphasis on the family as a normative institution, a materially divorced, yet complementary social department, from other social structures. In arguing for the all-around functionality of the modern nuclear family, there was a failure to consider the family's relation to the economy, particularly as regards its contribution to the reproduction of labour power, or to consider the consequences this had for the position of women in society, both in terms of their performance of domestic labour in the household and unequal participation in the social division of labour.

Recent feminist research has played a critical role in redressing the limitations of both traditional political economy and the conventional sociology of the family, developing a number of concepts and ideas which are of major significance. By the 1960s it was becoming increasingly apparent that functionalist accounts of the family were inadequate to comprehend the changing position of women in society, in particular the increasing participation of women in the economy, the persistence of domestic labour and the institutionalized inequalities experienced both in and outside the home. Feminist research turned towards a critical appropriation of political economy in order to highlight the 'hidden' connections between household structures, the position of women and the reproduction of capitalist social relations.[7] Thus the family in its internal processes and relations was increasingly seen as a constitutive moment in a social, economic and political totality. For one thing, the family was clearly an important consumption unit for commodities produced in the economy. As well, adults (usually women) confined to domestic labour in the household have come to constitute an important reserve army of labour, while unpaid domestic labour, although critically different in many respects from remunerated work in the economy, was nonetheless established as central to the reproduction of labour power itself. Finally, patriarchal relations were part of an elaborate and institutionally generated complex of hierarchical relations which went to the core of socially experienced power relations in society and reflected the structural separations experienced in the course of capitalist development. These discoveries have gone a long way towards approximating the net contribution of households to, as well as the costs imposed on domestic relations in, the social reproduction process.

However, while feminist theories of the family have succeeded in demonstrating the material contributions made by domestic labour to social reproduction, much less attention has been paid to the influence which economic rhythms and political decisions have had on the changing structure of the household. In other words, a full account of the position of women in contemporary capitalism must also situate the household at the intersections of the current economic crisis and state policy responses to it.

In an analogous fashion to functionalist treatments of the family, the state, as a contradictory element of social reproduction, has largely been ignored by conventional political sociology. Only with the displacement of pluralistic theories of political representation (which viewed the state as a more or less neutral arbitrator above social conflict) by class-based theories of the state has the maintenance of antagonistic social relations through state activity in the economic and social policy fields been posed as a serious research question.[8] Even here, however, attention has often remained glued to the political realm alone, with questions of political representation and autonomy receiving exclusive attention, albeit from a critical perspective; power elite studies are a case in point. While the question of class representation remains an important one, especially in modern democracies, the exercise of class power in the social reproduction process especially around social welfare, education, housing and health care cannot be overlooked.

The articulation of the state with household and economy represents different moments in the overall reconstitution of the wage-labour/capital relationship. Currently writers have focused on the role of the state in social investment *vis a vis* capital, and on the social control aspects of state policy with respect to populations made redundant by capital.[9] Less attention, however, has been given to the crucial role which state policy has assumed with respect to the reproduction of active labour forces through the development and extension of social or substitute wage programs. While a more recent factor in the evolution of capitalism, the subsidizing effects of social wages and their implications for capitalist development and household structures are topics long overdue for serious social scientific investigation. Clearly, however, a complete analysis of the welfare state also requires that the constraints and limitations placed upon state policies by economic and political forces beyond the control of the state be given due weight. Once again this poses the problem of clearly delineating the relations established under advanced capitalism between state, economy and households, and of indicating the scope of autonomous action for each institutional complex. This project, however, assumes a model of social reproduction around which the institutional elements of family, economy and state are arrayed. Such a representation can be arrived at most effectively by considering the reproduction process as made up of the several moments of productive, individual and collective consumption respectively.

Productive, Individual and Collective Consumption

Social reproduction is an outcome of the relationship or interplay between three major institutional realms: the productive consumption of capital by labour within the economy; the formation and maintenance of working class households through individual consumption; and the social interventions of the modern state which constitute collective or social consumption. These three basic institutional realms constitute the productive and reproductive moments of capitalist society, and if we are to grasp modern society as a totality, we must delineate the essential inter-connections between these spheres and describe the part they play in the reproduction of labour power as a commodity.

In the first instance, the production and reproduction of labour power is dialectically linked to the production and reproduction of capital. The essence of capitalism is the general production and accumulation of commodities on the basis of competition, markets and the exploitation of labour. What distinguishes capitalism from previous modes of production is not the production of an economic surplus *per se*, nor the appropriation of the surplus product of the direct producers by a ruling class, but rather the mode by which the surplus is generated by wage labour and its appropriation is in the value form.

In an industrial economy, the accumulation of capital is the result of its successive movement through the spheres of production and exchange. Initially money capital is transformed into constant capital (means of production, raw materials, etc.) and variable capital (labour power). At the point of production, the specific use-value of labour power, i.e. its ability to create more value than is used up in its own reproduction, is exploited by the purchaser of labour power, the capitalist. Assuming that the value of capital augmented in production is realized through exchange, the capitalist can, indeed must, return to the labour and commodity markets and replace the means of production used up, hence initiating a new production cycle. If the production process is repeated on the same scale as before, then the production and exchange cycle is said to constitute a system of *simple reproduction*; if realized surplus value is used to enhance the scale of subsequent cycles, then the system is one of *expanded reproduction*.[10] In this sense then, the capitalist economy consists of the productive consumption of capital by labour.

But capital, as such, is essentially a social relationship between groups since its production and accumulation is ultimately the outcome of the application of value-creating human labour power and the asymmetrical power relations between social classes which confront each other in a variety of markets and which facilitate the appropriations of surplus value. Generalized commodity production therefore presupposes the existence of two antithetical classes: on the one hand, a class which owns and controls the means of production and hence accumulation; and, on the other, a class of wage labourers who are divorced from the means of production and hence are forced to sell their capacity to work as the primary strategy of survival. In this sense, the production and accumulation of capital has its obverse in the production and reproduction of value-creating labour power. Without dependent wage workers being available in sufficient quantity at a certain price there can be no sustained extraction of surplus value. As Marx put it, the production and reproduction of capital therefore depends upon 'the production and reproduction of that means of production so indispensable to the capitalist: The labourer himself.' A part of capital, variable capital or the wage fund, must be set aside to provide means of subsistence for labour. The incessant *reproduction* of the labourer is therefore 'the *sine qua non* of capitalist production'. It follows therefore that 'the reproduction of the working class is and must ever be a necessary condition for the reproduction of capital'.[11]

Each mode of production has within it a distinctive mode for the reproduction of labour power—and in this regard capitalism is no exception. Indeed, under capitalism the social reproduction process is importantly and distinctively shaped by the special qualities of labour power itself. First, of all the commodities appearing in the marketplace, labour power is the only commodity that is inseparable from its human agency; since labour power is embodied in the capacities of the living person, its seller (the worker) must follow the buyer (the capitalist) into the sphere of production itself and there be organized, set to work, disciplined and controlled by the purchaser. In other words, the commodity labour power can never be fully alienated from its seller and, because of this, productive consumption is always of central concern to the labourer. Hence, unlike inanimate commodities (e.g. mechanical means of production) labour power actively resists its own consumption. Following directly from this trait is a second peculiarity which is expressed in the relative indeterminateness of the value of labour power. Thus, coinciding with the incomplete alienation of labour power from the subject is the social and historical element which enters into the constitution of its value. This means that the working class is reproduced at a socially and historically established standard of living; and consequently, it is possible for new needs to be incorporated (or indeed old ones eliminated) into reproduction that can lead to an increase (or fall) in the value of labour over time.

But for our purposes the most important and striking peculiarity of labour power is that, of all capitalist commodities, it is the only commodity that cannot itself be produced capitalistically i.e. on the basis of wage labour and the extraction of surplus value. Indeed, in this regard, the specific conditions of its production differ from that of most other commodities. There are no capitalist enterprises, no portion of total social capital, which are devoted to and specialize in the production of living labourers whose capacity to labour is then purchased as an input to the manufacture of other commodities. Labour power is unique in the sense that of all commodities under developed capitalism, its production and reproduction is antithetical to capitalist forms of organization and as such remains external to the sphere of surplus value production. This peculiarity determines the radical separation in modern capitalism of the sphere of the production of commodities from the sphere of the reproduction of labour power.[12]

This separation is itself fundamentally grounded in the distinction between productive and individual consumption. Now, both these acts of consumption are carried out by the proletariat, but in different social locations and with vastly different consequences. As we have already noted, in the production process the worker 'consumes' the means of production and converts them into commodities which have a higher value than the original capital advanced; this combination of means of production, raw materials and human labour is called *productive consumption*. On the other hand, there is the labourer's personal or *individual consumption* where the money paid for labour power is converted into the means of subsistence. This conversion of the wage into the necessities of life functions to reproduce the labourer and hence maintain 'fresh labour power at the disposal of capital for exploitation'.[13] In this respect, the individual consumption of workers may be said to reproduce labour power in a twofold sense: on the one hand, individual consumption transforms the value of labour power into means of subsistence which is necessary for the maintenance and reproduction of the labourer; on the other hand, since individual consumption essentially involves the continual 'annihilation of the necessaries of life,' it thereby secures the reproduction of the needy individual and hence the 'continued re-appearance of the workman in the labour market'.[14]

Following from the incomplete capitalization of reproduction, individual consumption of the wage is distinguished from productive consumption of capital in the labouring process in that individual consumption takes place external to and away from the point of production. While the reproduction of labour is *mediated* through the exchange of the capacity to labour for a wage, the *actual processes of reproduction* remain outside the value-producing economy. Indeed, as Marx noted, this sphere of individual consumption is precisely where the worker 'belongs to himself', where 'he performs his necessary vital functions outside production'. The capitalist can therefore, in effect, leave the reproduction of labour power to the workers' 'instinct for self-preservation and of procreation'.[15] Although an incomplete formulation, we can add that capital is therefore forced to rely on the working class undertaking something which cannot be included under commodity production proper, but which is nonetheless vital to it. The implications of this observation for the social organization of the working class was not really pursued by Marx, and indeed, it is only recently that this blind spot has received the rigorous theoretical attention it deserves.

Given these structural features of capitalism we find that the reproduction of labour power is externalized into a variety of historically specific non-capitalist institutions and agencies. Two primary institutional complexes are involved here, although it is possible to identify other more residual—or what we can call secondary—agencies which have at various points in the evolution of capitalist society and with varying degrees of effectiveness played an important role in the social reproduction process.

The first major institution is the household, the social locus of individual consumption where the worker is reproduced both on a day-to-day and generational basis. Individual consumption consists of the constant acquisition, transformation, consumption and hence annihilation of the necessities of life. It involves a series of activities including: (1) the purchase and consumption of goods and services i.e. the disposal of the wage on the necessities of life which appear in the commodity form; (2) the consumption of simple use-values and personal services produced on the basis of domestic labour within the household; and (3) the acquisition and maintenance of a private domestic sphere.[16] These relations of reproduction are usually, but not exclusively, organized around kin ties, are established through marriage and dissolved through death. Thus the *family* household appears as the primary institution of individual consumption and hence, in turn, is also the societal locus of generational reproduction through legitimate procreation, child bearing and initial socialization. Importantly, in a capitalist economy, this sphere appears to the worker as an island of self-determination in an otherwise very large ocean of externally-manifested hierarchical power and discipline relations. Hence, it is possible to observe throughout the history of capitalism both individual and collective strategies pursued by the working class which seek to extend and enlarge the parameters of self-determination and independence—for example, the struggle for higher wages and shorter working hours, home ownership, patterns of absenteeism, etc.

The separation of economy and household—of productive and individual consumption—coupled with the mediation of reproduction through labour markets establishes severe contradictions and tensions between these two locations of the proletariat. Certain features of these tensions are directly addressed in several contributions to this volume, and they inform the background to others. Thus, while accumulation in the economy is dependent upon the supply and regeneration of labour in households, the successful formation and maintenance of households is conversely dependent upon the capacity of the economy to generate employment opportunities and wages at levels which permit households to initiate and maintain the activities of individual consumption. Under capitalism, this is a condition of generalized uncertainty which may lead to a variety of crises in the relations between economy and household. Acquisition of the first form of proletarian subsistence, the wage, may be problematic because of unemployment, sickness or old age; wages accruing to households may not correspond to the subsistence needs of members; labour power may be consumed in production in such a way that calls into question the ability of workers to initiate the processes of self-managed reproduction. To the extent that these crises reflect structural dynamics within capitalism and not merely quirks in individual life-circumstances, then the reproduction process may break down and the renewal of labour power, particularly at the class level, may be called into question. At the very least, unattended structural crises in the reproduction process may induce severe economic as well as political problems. Sensitivity to the fractures, limitations and asymmetrical dependencies possible between economy and household bring us to the second major reproductive institution in contemporary society—the state and its social policies.

Reproduction at the collective or class level primarily, but again not exclusively, implicates public policies and state institutions. The articulation and implementation of social interventions by the state in the social reproduction process postdates capitalism and indeed the articulation of households, although increasingly state involvement is intimately tied up with the development and evolution of relations between household and economy. Within the history of capitalism these interventions were hesitant and limited at first, but they have expanded rapidly within the recent period and modern capitalist states are now often referred to as 'welfare states'.[17]

The central forms of state intervention pertinent to the analysis of the social reproduction process are several. First, there are industrial welfare policies directed at the point of production which regulate the capitalist consumption of labour power; included here is factory legislation which fixes maximum hours of work, promotes industrial safety and health standards and excludes certain categories of the population from certain branches of production. A second set of interventions sets parameters to the labour market; these interventions include the establishment of minimum wages, the exclusion of the young and old from selling their labour power through the formation of compulsory education and retirement policies, higher education and special training programs, and the pursuit of immigration policies which either promote or inhibit the influx of cheaper foreign labour—in short, interventions which effectively structure the boundaries of the active labour force.

A third set of interventions is directed to the point of reproduction. Two main types of intervention can be noted here. On the one hand, state intervention plays an important role in defining the position of women and children in society; procreation itself is to some extent regulated through the effects of abortion and contraception laws as well as inheritance laws, while the state claims to legitimate marriage and hence household formation. Additionally, the state regulates relations between family members through elaborate family property and child welfare laws. On the other hand, much state intervention—indeed that involving the greatest financial outlays—is designed to reproduce and maintain households through the provision of substitute wages and subsidized use-values. Included here are the transfer payments made under employment, medical, pension, disability and welfare programs; child or family allowances and other cash benefits; food stamps and other programs. It is this latter form of state intervention which has grown most rapidly; in general, this growth reflects the increasing contradiction between the imperatives of social production on the one hand and the limitations of privatized reproduction on the other.

Of course, the growth of the welfare state has not permanently resolved contradictions in the social reproduction process. For one thing, capitalist states primarily derive their income from tax revenues, and thus, like households, are dependent on the economy to generate resources. Moreover, political constraints on the state and its agents—indeed the penetration of capitalist interests at all levels of the state apparatus—restrict the state's autonomy, and hence its ability to act decisively to resolve contradictions in the reproductive process. The state, just like the household, must not be seen as an abstract and timeless category, but as an element of the social structure with a history that has been shaped by the forces of economic development. In an early essay, Marx captured this essentially derivative nature of the modern state:

> If the modern state wanted to abolish the impotence of its own administration, it would have to abolish the private life of today. But if it wanted to abolish private life, it would have to abolish itself, for it only exists in contradiction to private life.[18]

We have identified three major components in the production-reproduction system: *the economy*, which in its productive consumption of capital, generates employment and wages, the first form of proletarian subsistence; the *family-household*, the main institution for self-managed reproduction on the basis of individual consumption; and *the state*, the locus of collective consumption programs and policies directed towards securing the reproduction of labour at the collective or class level.

This simplified model can, and indeed must, be complicated by reference to a series of secondary or residual institutions which have played, and indeed to some degree continue to play, a part in the reproduction process. First, we can identify autonomous collective institutional forms at the level of the working class itself; these consist of self-help organizations such as friendly societies which are rooted within the culture and history of the working class itself. Second, there are direct ruling class interventions in the form of charitable, philanthropic and church organizations. And third, we can identify the provision by certain employers of a wide variety of services to their employees including subsidized housing, health and pension plans, educational, leisure and other programs as part of the labour contract—what some have called 'welfare capitalism'.[19] While these forms continue to be critical components in the reproduction process, it must be remarked that the imperatives of economic development and the rise of the welfare state (often on the basis of and at the expense of earlier non-state forms) have considerably reduced their significance. Indeed, many previously independent elements in the reproduction process have become thoroughly subsumed under the state.

Beyond a correlation between economic development and the expansion of social programs, it should also be noted that there is considerable national variation among the leading capitalist powers as to the number, nature, scope and means of financing state social policy interventions. There is also variation in the vitality and significance of the residual elements in the social reproduction process. Precise variations here have to be established through historical and comparative studies which, in turn, can then become important elements in the development of a more comprehensive theory of social reproduction and its relations to socio-economic development.[20] Bearing these provisos in mind, we can represent our model of the reproduction process in Figure 1.1. This figure represents the dominant relationships which are taken up by the contributions to this volume in their discussions of the social reproduction process.

The Contributions

This volume aims to extend and develop a structural understanding of the social reproduction process. The essays critically examine the relationships that have emerged between economic development, changes in household structure and the forms and function of state social interventions with the rise of industrial society. The contributors build on recent scholarship to establish the reproductive sector of society as a series of interconnected private (family) and public (state) institutions, and in doing so they develop an analysis of the relationship between the reproductive sector and the imperatives of the larger economy. In addition, aspects of the social reproduction process not adequately addressed in the current literature are investigated. Issues and topics are analyzed in theoretical and empirical terms that are sensitive to the importance of the historical dimension.

The essays have been arranged into four sections. Part I addresses aspects of the role family-household structures play in the social reproduction process. Readers will find, however, that the essays here bring

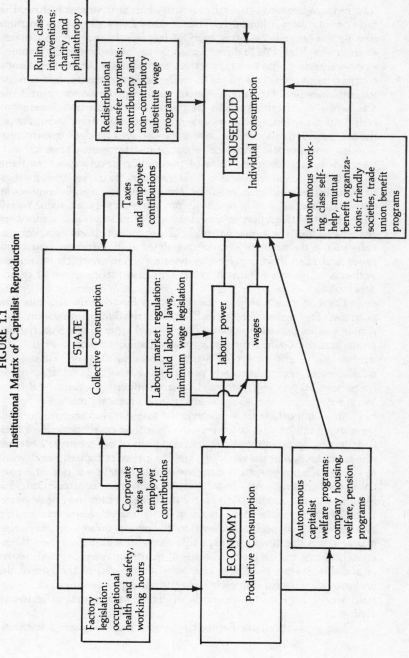

FIGURE 1.1
Institutional Matrix of Capitalist Reproduction

into range a broader series of concerns than is customarily found in the domestic labour literature. Thus, Seccombe, whose own contribution to the latter debate has been widely acknowledged, directs our attention in 'Marxism and Demography' to the demographic moment in capitalist development. He focuses our attention on the origins and comparative specificities of different fertility regimes as expressed in variant household forms over the course of capitalist development. As an essential part of this analysis, Seccombe extends the traditional mode of production concept to include the generational reproduction of human productive forces i.e. labour power, and he does this by considering the specific social or household arrangements which correspond to the dominant form of production at any given moment in an evolving capitalist society. This then permits the re-appropriation of the demographic as an essential element within an analysis of social change, a factor which up until now has largely eluded Marxist analysis. The integration of generational reproduction as a component element within the capitalist mode of production leads Seccombe to construct a dynamic model comprised of four different household types and corresponding fertility regimes, each of which is situated within a phase of capitalist development or specific regime of capital accumulation.

There is much that is suggestive in Seccombe's analysis. For example, the connections which remain relatively implicit in Seccombe's essay between working class household structures on the one hand, and dominant forms of capital accumulation on the other are made the specific object of study in Wayne's essay. Taking the equivalent of Seccombe's early proletarian household and drawing on household budget and income data from nineteenth century Britain, Wayne develops a model of the lifecycle of a typical proletarian household. In an important set of findings, he suggests that such households were in a position of income deficit over considerable periods of their functioning. In other words, under conditions of competitive capitalism 'the reproduction of the working class is a long run impossibility', while to complicate matters, such a regime of accumulation is not automatically forthcoming with social solutions to this contradiction. For Wayne, this set of conditions forms the material basis for the development of the welfare state, both in Britain and elsewhere, and its emergence as a specific element in the mode of reproduction that characterizes the developed capitalist economies. Both Wayne's theoretical findings and his innovative use of quantitative historical measures as social indicators should be of interest to analysts of the household, and provide a useful framework for future empirical studies of household size, budgets and standards of living in a variety of national settings.

The problem of mediating the relationship between a domestic sector of reproduction and a rapidly expanding capitalist economy is also the focal point of Eli Zaretsky's essay 'Rethinking the Welfare State'. Taking the first movements towards social welfare in the United States as his case, Zaretsky extends the findings of the two previous papers to argue that the state does not simply displace the household in a welfare function, but actively reconstructs the household as an economic and cultural artefact of capitalism. In turn, this restructuring of the family is premised upon the twin pillars of the family wage and the privatization of civil society, both outcomes of corporate capitalism. Ironically Zaretsky finds that the strengthening of the sexual division of labour that proceeded *pari passu* with corporate development was not the outcome of deliberate state policy, but rather was produced on the basis of autonomously converging trade union and feminist demands. These pressures functioned to reinforce cultural expectations with respect to the state, welfare and the family—influences which are still very much in evidence in contemporary American politics.

As the preceeding comments indicate, the state has been and remains a critical entity in the constitution and reconstitution of capitalist relations of production. In Part II some of the specific contributions which the modern state makes towards social reproduction *sui generis* are examined. The paper by Dickinson furthers the line of inquiry initiated by Seccombe and Wayne through a discussion of the evolution of state social welfare policy. Using a mix of theoretical and empirical observations, Dickinson argues that several structural crises affect working class reproduction and that these in turn parallel stages of capitalist development. As a corollary to this, state interventions progress through a series of regulatory, welfare and social security measures, eventuating in the introduction of elaborate 'substitute wage' programs to alleviate the insecurities of industrial life experienced by the working class in an increasingly economically articulated social formation. State social interventions are thereby established as specific responses to the contradictions induced in the reproduction process in the course of capitalist development.

The growth of social interventions by the state are not without important displacement effects of their own within the sphere of gender relations. Ursel's paper provides a stimulating analysis of the effects of state policy on the maintenance of gender dominance in society and depicts a transition from familial to social patriarchy within the growth of the welfare state. Defining patriarchy as the control of women in their reproductive and productive labour, Ursel examines the economy and the household as the principal social loci in and through which such dominance is exercised. By way of an in-depth analysis of state legislative responses to capitalist industrialization in Canada, she shows that as the basis of traditional familial patriarchy in the household economy was eroded, the state, through a series of labour, property and custody laws, was instrumental in asserting a new form of patriarchal dominance. The ensuing results—sexually segmented labour markets, the creation of the male 'breadwinner' role, and the maintenance of female dependency—serve as a caution to those who would equate, in any simple fashion, the socialization of reproduction with liberation.

A third paper in this section by Bandyopadhyay poses some critical questions for a political-economy of the state sector. What, for example, are the limits to state intervention into social reproduction? More specifically, what are the determinants of the policy-mix which any given state will actually employ to ensure the maintenance of social relationships and what factors account for cross-national and temporal variations amongst advanced capitalist states? Reworking some of the key concepts of the public finance literature and inserting them into a post-structuralist approach to the state, Bandyopadhyay provides some intriguing answers to these questions that will also be of interest to political sociologists and theorists of the state.

The common element to all of the studies in this volume is the centrality of labour force renewal in social reproduction. Under capitalism, this implies the maintenance of the labour forces in a commodity form, and hence ultimately the reproduction of the wage labour relation in society. This has two dimensions: the reproduction of individual producers and working class households, which is the main focus in Parts I and II; and the reproduction of the primary class relationships which defines capitalism. In Part III it is this latter theme which is pursued. State social policies are found not only to produce specific outcomes which support existing relations of superordination and subordination among social classes, but the very formation and operation of such policies are imbued with these relations.

This is documented in a novel fashion by the Mann, and the Fichtenbaum and Welty contributions. In her paper, Mann demonstrates by reference to the experience of the United States the operation of specific class interests in the formation and evolution of state social policies which impinge directly on women and their role in the generational reproduction of labour power. She carefully describes the evolution of abortion and day care policies, grounding this history in factors which have shaped the position of women in American society over the past century. In doing so she brings together the crucial categories of class and gender around the issue of reproductive rights. She concludes with an analysis of the dynamic factors in contemporary capitalism, especially the increase in female participation in the economy, which have favoured a fusion of class and gender politics in support of reproductive rights, a fusion which both she, and Zaretsky previously, have noted differs substantially from earlier political outcomes.

Fichtenbaum and Welty tackle a similar set of problems in their paper on 'The Norming of the Working Day'. Taking as their point of departure the inherent conflict between labour and capital under the capitalist mode of production, the authors demonstrate the critical significance of this conflict at the point of production in establishing parameters to exploitation and hence the establishment of conditions for the reproduction of labour power. Through a close textual reading of the relevant parts of *Capital*, they establish that the determination of a working day, the length of which permits the autonomous reproduction of labour, is an outcome of class struggle, the maturity of capital and the regulatory practices of the state. This analysis effectively serves to draw out the structural consequences from Marx's close examination of the factory acts in early British industrialization, particularly as regards the relationship between labour, capital and the state. Their discussion of the role played by issues such as the extent and quality of the working day within the history of strikes under capitalism thus effectively illustrates the crucial mediating activity of the state in moderating contradictions between capital and labour, production and reproduction.

It can no longer be assumed that social reproduction is carried out in a functional manner nor indeed that the reproduction of existing social relations of production and reproduction are socially functional. The final two essays in Part IV of this volume explore this theme in greater detail.

In an examination of private pension schemes, Stafford argues that funds which have been set aside in the form of deferred wages for social reproduction of the elderly now enter the circuit of accumulation and thus constitute important additional sources of surplus value that is appropriated from employees. Additionally, given the vast array of pension plans now in place, Stafford demonstrates how these have historically evolved and come to operate as a means of simultaneously stabilizing and fragmenting the work force and thus how they have become constituent elements in labour force control and segmentation structures. Both these effects provide important counter-tendencies to declining rates of profit and the shortage of capital in the core economies, but as Stafford notes, with aging labour forces such accumulation strategies are eventually likely to return to haunt corporate capital.

Such findings are generalized in Russell's paper which argues that state interventions into social reproduction are, in important respects, responsible for the current socio-economic crisis. This follows directly from the contradiction between market and extra-market forces that are internalized in the state around reproductive functions. This thesis is examined in relation to the major forms of state intervention—public goods provision and social security transfer payments—around which problems of disproportionality and fiscal crises have developed. Russell concludes by noting that unlike previous generalized crises, which were usually resolved through a deepening of the socialization of reproduction, such a scenario in the current context is unlikely.

The essays in this volume address important aspects of the social reproduction process from a variety of theoretical and empirical viewpoints. Our intention in bringing them together has been to stress the importance of moving beyond the fragmentary debates over domestic labour, the welfare state and political economy as currently exist in the social science literature, and to pose the question of social reproduction in terms of a sociological totality which encompasses the economic, familial and political structures of contemporary society. We trust that the essays which follow will serve a useful purpose in initiating such a discussion.

Notes and References

1. For an early discussion of the distinction between productive and individual consumption, see Karl Marx, *Grundrisse* (Penguin, Harmondsworth Middlesex, 1973), pp. 83-100. The externality of the reproduction of labour power is recognized in *Capital*, Volume I (Progress Publishers, Moscow, N.D.), pp. 356-7. See also *The German Ideology* where it is argued that reproduction, along with production and the generation of new needs, is one of the 'three moments which have existed simultaneously since the dawn of history . . . and which still assert themselves today.' Karl Marx and Frederick Engels, *Selected Works*, Volume I (Progress Publishers, Moscow, 1969), p. 31. Also, Engels in his *Origins of the Family, Private Property and the State* explicitly addressed questions of the transformation of the family and the position of women in society in relation to economic development, arguing that production and reproduction cannot be arbitrarily separated in a materialist analysis. He writes: 'According to the materialist conception, the determining factor in history is, in the last resort, the production and reproduction of immediate life. But this itself is of a two-fold character. On the one hand, the production of the means of subsistence, of food, clothing and shelter and the tools requisite therefore; on the other, the production of human beings themselves, the propagation of the species. The social institutions under which men of a definite historical epoch and of a definite country live are conditioned by both kinds of production: by the stage of development of labour, on the one hand, and of the family, on the other.' Marx and Engels, *Selected Works*, Volume 3 (Progress Publishers, Moscow, 1970), p. 191.
2. V.I. Lenin's *The Development of Capitalism in Russia* (1899), Rosa Luxemburg's *The Accumulation of Capital* (1913) and Rudolf Hilferding's *Das Finanzkapital* (1910) are classic examples of this theoretical concern.
3. For a critical review of the writings of the classical Marxists, including Marx, Engels, Lenin, Zetkin and Bebel, on the 'woman question', see Lise Vogel, *Marxism and the Oppression of Women* (Rutgers University Press,

New Brunswick, N.J., 1983).

4. Various writers here attempted to establish a link between the authoritarian family and the persistence of capitalism. For example, in the collective project of the Frankfurt School, *Studien Über Authoritäet und Familie* (1939), it was argued that 'as one of the most important educative forces, the family takes care of the reproduction of human characters . . . and to a great part endows these characters with the indispensable capacity for authoritarian behaviour of a specific kind on which the bourgeois order depends to a high degree.' Quoted in Frankfurt Institute for Social Research, *Aspects of Sociology* (Beacon Press, Boston, 1972), p. 145. The same reasoning is apparent in the work of Reich, especially 'What is Class Consciousness?', and *The Mass Psychology of Fascism,* where he writes: 'The interlacing of the socio-economic structure with the sexual structure of society and the structural reproduction of society takes place in the first four or five years and in the authoritarian family . . . Thus the state gains an enormous interest in the authoritarian family: it becomes the factory in which the state's structure and ideology are moulded.' (Souvenir Press, London, 1972), p. 30.

5. The recent publication of Rudolf Bahro, *The Alternative in Eastern Europe* (New Left Books, London, 1978) and Andre Gorz, *Farewell to the Working Class* (Pluto Press, London, 1982) are poignant reminders of this tension.

6. See especially Talcott Parsons, 'The Kinship System of the Contemporary United States', in *Essays in Sociological Theory* (Free Press, New York, 1965); and Neil Smelsner, *Social Change in the Industrial Revolution* (University of Chicago Press, Chicago, 1959). For a thorough survey of theoretical perspectives on the family, see David Morgan, *Social Theory and the Family* (Routledge and Kegan Paul, London, 1975).

7. Important early works in this area include Margaret Benston, 'The Political Economy of Women's Liberation', *Monthly Review* 21, pp. 13-27 and Juliet Mitchell, *Women's Estate* (Penguin, Baltimore, 1971). For exemplary recent work see A. Kuhn and A. Wolpe, *Feminism and Materialism* (Routledge and Kegan Paul, London, 1978), M. Luxton, *More Than a Labour of Love* (Women's Press, Toronto, 1980), and the series of essays edited by Bonnie Fox in *Hidden in the Household: Women's Domestic Labour Under Capitalism* (Women's Press, Toronto, 1980). For a survey of the literature, see Lise Vogel, 'Marxism and Socialist-Feminist Theory: A Decade of Debate', *Current Perspectives in Social Theory*, Volume 2 (1981), pp. 209-231.

8. Recent work on the capitalist state has been extensive. For a good summary and bibliography, see Bob Jessop, *The Capitalist State* (Martin Robertson, Oxford, 1982).

9. James O'Connor, *The Fiscal Crisis of the State* (St. Martin's Press, New York, 1973). See also F. Piven and R. Cloward, *Regulating the Poor: The Functions of Public Welfare* (Vintage, New York, 1972).

10. Marx, *Capital*, Volume 1, pp. 543-557.

11. Ibid., pp. 536-7.

12. On this point see Susan A. Mann and Emily Blumenfeld, 'Domestic Labour and the Reproduction of Labour Power', in ed. Fox, *Hidden in the Household.* See also A. Aumeeruddy, B. Lautier *et al.,* 'Labour Power and the State', *Capital and Class*, Volume 6, (1978).

13. Marx, *Capital*, Volume 1, pp. 536-7.

14. Ibid., p. 538.
15. Ibid., pp. 536-7.
16. The most systematic application of the categories of political economy to the analysis of the reproduction of labour power is in Wally Seccombe's 'Domestic Labour and the Working Class Household', in ed. Fox, *Hidden in the Household*.
17. Ian Gough's *The Political Economy of the Welfare State* (Macmillan, London, 1979) is pioneering work here.
18. Karl Marx, 'Critical Marginal Notes on the Article "The King of Prussia and Social Reform" ', in *Collected Works*, Volume 3 (International Publishers, New York, 1975), p. 198.
19. See, for example, R. Edwards, *Contested Terrain* (Basic Books, New York, 1979) and Stuart D. Brandes, *American Welfare Capitalism, 1880-1940* (University of Chicago Press, Chicago, 1976).
20. Recent work by Göran Therborn makes a promising start in this direction. See his 'Classes and States: Welfare State Developments, 1881-1981', *Studies in Political Economy* (14), 1984; and 'The Prospects of Labour and the Transformation of Advanced Capitalism', *New Left Review*, 145 (1984).

PART I

HOUSEHOLD, ECONOMY AND SOCIAL REPRODUCTION

2

MARXISM AND DEMOGRAPHY: HOUSEHOLD FORMS AND FERTILITY REGIMES IN THE WESTERN EUROPEAN TRANSITION

Wally Seccombe

The Great Evasion

The primary form of Marxism's traditional address to demography, dating back to Marx himself, has been through a virulent denunciation of its Malthusian versions. These polemics, however programmatically justified in countering largely reactionary Malthusian population *policies*, nevertheless have had an anaesthetic effect upon historical materialism, placing the demographic realm itself beyond the pale of legitimate scrutiny and investigation. In the process of dismissing Malthus and his successors, Marxists have abandoned the terrain to our enemies. And with the notable exception of some analysts of the Third World,[1] this abdication has been perpetuated within contemporary Marxism. Indeed there has been an unfortunate counterposition of the socio-economic to the demographic, as if these two dimensions of social relations were materially separable under capitalism or elsewhere, and as if the lines of causality ran, undialectically, only one way: from the socio-economic and political to the demographic.

Even the best of recent Marxist historiography continues this traditional dismissal. The work of Robert Brenner, for instance, which has attracted much attention for its rigorous and original approach to the transition between the feudal and capitalist modes of production, fails to recognize the specificity of demographic causes. Brenner launched an attack in *Past and Present* on the reigning neo-Malthusian orthodoxy of Postan, Ladurie, Habukkuk and others, concerning their interpretation of the growth and stagnation of late feudal formations in Western Europe. While the critique itself has many merits, Brenner

*This is a revised version of the article which originally appeared in *New Left Review* Number 137. Reprinted by kind permission of NLR.

displays a tendency to deny the explanatory power of demographic phenomena in asserting the primacy of class struggle dynamics. The core of his argument is the thesis that 'it is the structure of class relations, of class power, which will determine the manner and degree to which particular demographic changes will affect long-run trends in the distribution of income and economic growth, and not vice-versa'.[2]

A very subtle dislocation is revealed in this statement and persists throughout the article. Brenner turns a conflict over where to place the emphasis into an either/or counterposition. If he were merely insisting upon the *primacy* of class relations and the (diverse) outcomes of class struggles over demographic cyclical pressures in an overall model of feudal development, then that would be perfectly correct, particularly as it pertains to the transition to capitalism. But there is the final phrase, 'and not vice-versa', that effectively dismisses any incorporation or active feedback of demographic forces into his model of class relations and class struggle tendencies. In *counterposing* class relations to demographic pressures as the prime-mover of feudal economic growth and stagnation, Brenner 'over-corrects' his opponents to the extent of suppressing the autonomy of demography altogether. In this regard, it is worth quoting from Guy Bois's comment on Brenner's article in a subsequent issue of *Past and Present*:

> It is not enough to undertake a theoretical critique of the neo-Malthusian position, or to blame its proponents for under-estimating one or other level of analysis. To be convincing and decisive, the critique must attack the very kernel of Malthusian interpretation in order to separate with absolute precision the valid from the invalid elements. The whole strength of this model derives from the fact that is amply confirmed by detailed research: the importance of the demographic factor, the succession of long-term trends, the existence of ceilings of growth, and so on. By what strange perversion of Marxism is it possible to refuse to take such firm data into account on the absurd pretext that another theoretical construction rests upon it? . . . Postan or Le Roy Ladurie should not be criticized for giving too much importance to the demographic factor. They should on the contrary be criticized for stopping their process in midstream and for not integrating the demographic factor into the all embracing whole that is the socio-economic system.[3]

Bois's criticism here is, in my view, very much to the point. It could be extended far beyond Brenner's work to the entire legacy of classical Marxism.

The feminist challenge to Marxism—with which my own work

is concerned—also demands that this great evasion be squarely faced.[4] A central demand of the women's liberation movement is for women themselves to gain full control over their reproductive capacities, and intense political struggles continue to rage over this issue. As the slogan 'control of our bodies, control of our lives' suggests, women can never control their lives in a full sense until they gain control of their own biological capacities. We can state this proposition obversely: the social control of women is *centered* upon the control of their reproductive capacities in a vast range of societies. If this generalization is valid, then the conclusion seems to me inescapable: there are compelling feminist reasons for paying close attention to the demographic regulators of women's fertility and to their change over time. And yet, there has been surprisingly little attention paid by feminists to the field of demography. While feminist critics of 'malestream Marxism'[5] have sought to shift and supplement Marxism's traditional focus on 'production' with a decisive emphasis on 'reproduction', this has not generally been conceived in explicitly demographic terms. There has been a real breakthrough in the feminist study of mothering, together with speculative explorations of the immense implications of men's abstention from early childcare, yet little progress has been made on the closely related problem of forging a feminist analysis of the social regulation of fertility.[6]

Conversely (though much less surprising) demographers have largely ignored the burgeoning feminist scholarship of the past decade. Even a brief perusal of the principal English-language journals in the field *(Demography, Population Studies,* and *Population and Development Review)* will demonstrate that feminist perspectives and debates are rarely acknowledged, much less taken seriously, in their pages. One would never guess, reading these journals, that childbearing was a sex-specific and gender differentiated process.

Theories of Demographic Transition

In this article, I want to look at the demographic transition of the mid-eighteenth to early twentieth centuries in Western Europe, and particularly at the transformation of fertility patterns in families of the labouring classes which occurred in this period as the dominant mode of production was overthrown and replaced. I find in the works of a whole range of revisionist social historians and demographers—Lutz Berkner, Franklin Mendels, Rudolph Braun, Michael Haines, Hans Medick, David Levine, Charles Tilly, Louise Tilly and Joan Scott, to name only a few of the more prominent scholars—an emergent alternative to the dominant paradigm of the modernization school in explaining this transition.[7] Instead of 'industrialization and urbanization', these scholars place *proletarianization* at the heart of their analysis. They see this as an uneven, diverse, and protracted process, culminating finally in the formation of a mass urban factory proletariat, but beginning at least two centuries before in the precipitation of a mass of rural landless labourers. Transcending the limits of orthodox Marxist accounts, they perceive the process of proletarianization as a demographic revolution as well as a revolution in the prevailing social relations of production. Their studies have highlighted the intimate dialectical relation between these two dimensions of the proletariat's formation.

The modernization paradigm has run into considerable difficulties—now widely acknowledged—in light of the wealth of new local studies of the demographic transition in Western Europe. In essence, the demographic transition theory held that in traditional societies both fertility and mortality rates were 'natural' and high, tending to counterbalance one another in the long run so that the size of a community was checked at the limits of the means of subsistence available to it.[8] In the eighteenth century agricultural productivity rose, breaching this limit, and as living standards gradually improved, mortality rates declined. For over a century, however, fertility rates remained at their traditional levels or declined only slightly, still caught within the cultural constraints of the old order. The population boom of the late eighteenth and nineteenth centuries in Europe was thus attributable to a culturally induced lag between falling death and birth rates, which was greatest among the propertyless classes. Eventually in the late nineteenth century it was presumed that the processes of industrialization, urbanization and cultural modernization propelled the great mass of the population into a new environment, wherein they not only lived longer, but saw the economic rationale of implementing birth control in marriage and reducing overall family size, thus bringing fertility rates, once again, into line with mortality rates.

The main problem with this thesis is that it doesn't appear to have happened that way.[9] Fertility rates *rose* in many areas of the countryside in the period of early modernization and fell later in the late nineteenth and early twentieth centuries, with rural rates often declining as steeply as urban rates. Moreover, the early industrial workers usually had *higher* fertility rates and larger families than the 'premodern' peasants in Western European towns and villages. The fertility decline in France preceded industrialization, while in Belgium and Germany the opposite occurred. In urban England the decline came later, while in rural Normandy it was early and so on. So clearly, urbanization and industrialization do not correlate in any straightforward sense with the onset of the transition from relatively high fertility and mortality rates to relatively low modern rates.

The Revisionist Critique of Modernization Theory

As mentioned, in the past decade there has been a response to these difficulties by a revisionist school of social historians and demographers who appear to be heading (implicitly or explicitly as the case may be) in a critical Marxist direction. They remain dissatisfied with both the standard modernization thesis and the alternative orthodox Marxist account of the transition to industrial capitalism in Western Europe. I take their principal arguments against each to be, respectively, the following:

(1) The abatement of crisis mortality in the eighteenth century certainly made its own contribution to the decisive takeoff of population growth across Western Europe around 1750. But a rise in fertility rates, together with a shortening of the inter-generational reproduction span among proletarian and proto-industrial sectors of the labouring masses (still predominantly rural), was absolutely pivotal as well. The fertility factor is wrongly down-played by modernization theorists who want to see only a linear transition from 'high pre-industrial to low industrial fertility rates'. The *first* major breakout from the old peasant fertility regime on the land was predominantly upwards, well before its *eventual* decline a century or more later.

(2) The formation of the modern proletariat began long before the growth of the factory system in the First Industrial Revolution. While an initial proletarian mass was generated by the divorce of former peasants from the land, the *primary* source of the early industrial proletariat in Western Europe was rural proletarian and independent handicraft workers, not ex-peasants. It was the demographic growth of the landless rural poor (proletarian and proto-industrial—shading into one another in many cases) in the eighteenth century which established the indispensable labour supply precondition (a massive rural labour surplus) for rapid capitalist industrialization in the nineteenth century. While landholding agriculturalists fell rapidly as a percentage of the total labouring population in the eighteenth and early nineteenth centuries, their numbers did not diminish absolutely, and their offspring were not the primary source of first-generation factory workers. The old Marxist stereotype of peasants-into-proletarians is grossly oversimplified. This distortion flows from the failure to include the demographic dimension in the overall picture of the transition from late feudalism to early industrial capitalism.

I think that the revisionist consensus (I am forcing a consensus here which these historians themselves might eschew as premature) is substantially correct in these two contentions. I am also of the opinion that a Marxist attention to changes in the prevailing mode of production can nevertheless provide a relevant framework for interpreting the historical data which these scholars have developed. Considering that most Marxist historiography has tended to envision the transition from feudalism to capitalism in a rather schematic, linear and teleological fashion, largely ignoring its demographic dimensions[10], it is particularly significant that an important current of demographers should come to couch their explanations in broadly Marxist terms. Their empirical findings and interpretations offer an invaluable knowledge-base for more explicit and rigorous Marxist theorizations, centering on changes in the predominant mode of production through time.[11]

But before proceeding further, it is necessary to make two essential clarifications. First, I shall present a reworked version of the mode of production concept which integrates the production of labour power (as a productive force) *and* the social regulation of its daily and generational reproduction through household, family and kin relations. Secondly, it is important to recall briefly several valid tenets of the classical Marxist analysis of population dynamics.

Reworking the Mode of Production Concept

The problem of economism which has plagued historical materialism from Marx on has been widely recognized by Marxists of diverse persuasions in the past two decades. There is a broad consensus that the original sin of economism stems from an overemphasis on the economic dimension in conceptualizing modes of production and from a reduction of their political and ideological levels to mirror reflections or derivations of the economic base. While agreeing that the consequences of economism have indeed been pernicious for Marxism, I find the standard diagnosis of this ill to be misconstrued and, consequently, also the proposed antidote. In my view, the economist error has *not* stemmed from an exaggeration of the weight of the economic dimension (or more correctly, the socio-economic dimension), but instead from a false narrowing of the field of the socio-economic, and a failure to conceptualize adequately the *integration* of the socio-economic with politico-legal relations of state and the cultural formation of groups and classes.

In short, while others have scored the reduction of superstructures to infrastructures, I focus here on the arbitrary constriction of the infrastructure itself. The 'relative autonomy of superstructures' cannot possibly compensate for a reductive infrastructure which has been left intact and unchallenged. It is not as if the old blueprints for the first floor were fine but more work were merely required on the design of the house's upper storeys. If one misconceives the field of production, then one's theorization of a mode of production is bound to go awry.

In most Marxist literature, the field of production is reduced to the production of material goods; the productive forces to the instruments of labour; and the social relations of production to those relations found at the site of goods production. In this framework, the production of the species and its labour power simply does not appear. It is little wonder then, that feminists have criticized Marxists for elaborating the mode of production concept in a 'sex-blind' fashion.[12] For women's *first* production (whatever else they may produce in the way of material goods) has been consistently excluded from the conceptual field of Marxism's *central* theoretical category. The result of this displacement has been to assign the social organization of childbirth, infant-care and domestic socialization to the realm of Nature by default.

All human societies are necessarily involved in three interrelated productions which cannot be subsumed one to another: *(1)* the production of the means of production; *(2)* the production of the means of subsistence; and *(3)* the production of labour power on a daily and a generational basis. These three productions may be organized in a variety of ways. It is the task of concrete investigation in each case to identify their articulation in particular modes of production and in specific social formations. Moreover, whereas a mode of production is conventionally defined as a particular set of productive forces in combination with, and in (latent or manifest) contradiction to, a specific ensemble of relations of production; I am insisting that this *forces/relations* combination must be conceptualized for all *three* productions. If one takes labour power seriously as a productive force in *all* modes of production, the question of the specific relations within which it is produced and reproduced must be centrally addressed. And if we reject all naturalist complacency, then we must analyse in detail those historically specific social relations which regulate fertility—the infrastructure of the generational reproduction of labour power. The specific fertility regime of major classes, in other words, must figure as an integral component of the full theorization of the mode of production in question.

The problem of the generational replacement of labour-power is an absolutely critical one in two ways. First, all societies must establish an overall relation between the schedule of labour power's consumption in production and its demographic replacement through the medium of its small domestic groups. The way in which this relation is regulated (and upset) furnishes an important insight into the dynamics of the society as a whole. Secondly, the position of women in any society is closely bound up with the gender construct of *wife/motherhood*. How does a particular society deal socially with the biological fact that women bear children and lactate and men do not? Since this is a pre-eminently social question, it requires an historically specific explanation.

What then constitutes the social relations of labour-power's daily and generational reproduction? Here we are confronted with the question of the family. Definitions of 'the family' in the social sciences, reflecting ambiguities in colloquial usage, have oscillated between reference to kinship-at-large (relations by blood and marriage) and cohabiting kin (related persons living together 'under one roof'). The problem, widely recognized in the past decade, is one of multiple and shifting referents, with household and family often being used interchangeably. As a result of this critique, it is now common in family studies to uphold a *household/family* distinction. This settles one ambiguity, but a further one remains: 'family' still covers both the kin co-residence group and kinship filiation more broadly.

Household, Family and Kinship

I will therefore suggest a tripartite distinction between household, family and kinship, where the intermediate term—the family—is assigned the restricted meaning of the core kin group which is normally co-resident through various phases of the domestic cycle. It is recognized that *household/family/kin (h/f/k)* relations may organize more than the third production of labour-power outlined above. In many modes, they are integral to the production of the means of production and subsistence as well. But at the very least, we can state that *h/f/k* relations do organize the primary production of labour-power in all societies, though they may not do so exclusively; under capitalism, for example, the school system plays a major role. How then are the coordinates of a particular fertility regime set within the context of household, family and kin relations? I shall outline a simple four-step model conceived at the relatively abstract level of a mode of production, which then takes on additional complexity in the study of particular types of social formations in specific stages of their development.

The *first* step is for potentially reproductive couples to achieve a social status and an economic condition in which they are able to bear children—to get married and secure a minimally stable household space wherein childbearing may occur. (For the moment we leave aside 'illegitimate' fertility, usually unintended, and assume, for the vast majority of the population, the need to surpass these social and economic limits before partaking in childbearing. We include those conceptions—technically 'illegitimate'—where a couple marries upon discovery of pregnancy.[13]) At this initial level, we endeavour to specify the prevailing rules and conditions of marriage and household formation which are specific to a given mode of production and to a particular class' relation to the means of production and subsistence. These parameters demarcate a segment of the potentially reproductive population 'at risk'.

Within the population which is in a position to have children, we need to specify a *second* step: the particular balance of short and long-term costs and potential benefits which generate a basic incentive structure for having children. Once again, we can identify key variables: positive incentives such as the demand and utility of child labour as a potential contribution to the household, more than offsetting the additional upkeep costs of an extra member; the need, or the cultural desire, to perpetuate the family line beyond death through inheritance; the utility of children as a 'pension fund'—a form of old age security. On the other side, there are disincentives: the cost of bearing additional members and feeding them (spread out over the anticipated duration of their stay within the unit) and the hazards and hardships to mothers from further childbearing. (Whether this gender-specific disincentive is suppressed or is permitted room to operate will depend on the form and degree of patriarchal dominance within family households.) Furthermore, operating both for the unit as a whole and for women specifically, there are attractive alternative uses of their time and labour capacities which weigh against childbearing. Thus incentive structures may vary greatly both between and within particular modes of production.[14]

A *third* element then enters the picture: the cultural conditions shaping the relation of marital sex to procreation. Here we are looking at prevailing relations between spouses and at the institutions of a given community which have a strong impact on the conduct of marital sexual relations. The strongly patriarchal character of the European peasant family in the medieval and early modern periods for example, fortified by the Augustinian doctrine of the Church, made it virtually inconceivable for peasant women to deliberately practice any form of contraception in marriage. It was thus rare for women of this class and period to cease childbearing much before menopause, even when they had reached what might have been an ideal family size in economic terms.

Finally, a *fourth* step: the means available, given the will to do so, to limit and shape fertility according to the couple's or the wife's desires. Availability refers here to both the technical means of birth control at hand and the practical knowledge of their effective use, disseminated within the cultural constraints outlined in step three. Steps three and four vary within a range delimited by the mode of production according to its development over time and space. Moreover, we assume (given the ubiquity of the sex drive and heterosexual intercourse) that the total number of conceptions in a population will tend to exceed those desired within a given incentive structure, and this unintended surplus will be greater, the more imperfect are the means at hand. The opposite disparity between intention and result (where children are desired but cannot be produced or do not survive) also operates, but I estimate here—at least for the populations we are dealing with—that 'disappointments' are outnumbered by 'surprises'. A given fertility pattern then is taken to be 'rational' (i.e., reflecting a given incentive structure) within the economic and cultural constraints existing *except* for a small but variable excess which is the surplus product of unintended conception and deterred marriage, and which would be reduced if effective and safe birth control were readily available. (I reiterate, that 'availability' is not only a technical but also a cultural condition.)

Both the social relations of production and the productive forces at hand (in the expanded definition) enter into the fertility equation outlined here, and we must identify in each case their particular complementary or contradictory combination. This implies that the fertility dynamics of a given labouring class in a given mode of production cannot be read off as a single configuration of fertility forces, but rather should be conceived as a variable *range* within a set of limit-conditions. These limits are established by the relation of households to the basic means of production and subsistence, which structures the step one parameters within which a specific fertility regime develops. If these limits are breached, then the class relation itself is dissolved and some other mode of production has been entered.

Classical Marxism and 'Laws' of Population

In *Capital* Volume I, Marx writes: 'Every special historic mode of production has its own special laws of population. . . .'[15] This stands today as a bald assertion which subsequent generations of Marxists have never elaborated upon or sought in any sustained study to substantiate.[16] In a moment, I shall endeavour to mobilize it as a guiding hypothesis in making sense of the demographic transition of Western Europe, but first it is necessary to spell out several of its implications.

We should understand here by 'laws' of population what Marx means by laws in other contexts in his political economy: a set of persistent and long-run forces and tendencies which never operate purely or unimpeded in the real world, but which persist nonetheless as long as the mode of production is in place. We are not then speaking of 'a law' in the sense of a set of forces which guarantee a uniform outcome in diverse settings. We are speaking of a *characteristic interplay* of forces and relations of fertility and mortality which allows for developments *within* a given mode as well as entailing discontinuities in transitions from one mode to another. Moreover, it is important to note that Marx's assertion, quite consistent with his entire orientation to political economy, upholds the cardinal principle of *historical specificity* for each mode of production and each epoch in history, rejecting any natural or eternal law of human population growth or overpopulation. He makes this point explicitly while polemicizing with

Malthus. It is one that we shall want to uphold, as a first principle, in historical inquiry into particular population patterns.[17]

Applying the principle of historical specificity to household forms and fertility regimes, we generate the following methodological guideline: different modes of production will entail different $h/f/k$ configurations and fertility regimes. This does not mean that every element in the domestic ensemble is unique to a given mode, but only that the whole structure—the arrangement of elements—is historically unique: specific to a given mode and to social classes within the mode. This also means that the aggregate population result—the balance of fertility, migration and mortality—might be similar in societies where different modes of production dominate, but that the *way* this result was generated, would be markedly different in each case.

The principle of historical specificity as applied to population dynamics also entails a rejection of any demographic study which *abstracts* rates of fertility and mortality away from the specific social structure of the community which is being studied. As Marx writes in *Grundrisse:* 'Population is an abstraction if I leave out, for example, the classes of which it is composed . . . [population, in abstraction] is a chaotic conception of the whole.'[18] It remains a perfectly valid point and a telling indictment of a great deal of contemporary demography, which is still involved in just such abstraction, despite a growing awareness within the field of the problematic nature of macro-aggregation devoid of detailed historical and structural specification.

If we take Marx's assertion in *Capital* seriously that specific modes of production have their own characteristic population dynamics, it seems to me that we are committed to two corollary propositions in order to be consistent with the methodology of historical materialism: (1) The principal determinations of population dynamics are endogenous to each mode of production and we should seek to locate them there, in its inner-workings. (2) We should also postulate that population forces will periodically come into contradiction with themselves and with other elements of any given socio-economic system, and will tend to make their own contribution to the developmental propulsion of particular modes through time and space, and ultimately to their revolutionary transformation. I state this as an initial hypothesis consistent with the theoretical tenets of historical materialism, but it also appears to receive a compelling empirical confirmation in history. The two greatest revolutions of the productive forces in history are arguably the Agricultural Revolution (when nomandic foragers became sedentary and began to turn the soil, sow and reap) and the Industrial Revolution (when mass machinery replaced hand-powered tools as the dominant means of production). In both of these decisive and irreversible watersheds, it seems that sharp disruptions in earlier population patterns occurred in the gestation phase, immediately *prior* to

sweeping changes in the technology at hand. In both cases, the resulting rapid population growing apparently furnished its *own* accelerators
in the build-up of revolutionary momentum, effecting a transition from
one mode of population to another.[19]

Contours of the Demographic Revolution

In very broad terms, what were the outlines of the demographic
transition in Western Europe?[20] Until roughly 1750 (our perception gets
dimmer, of course, the farther back we look), the great peasant populations of Western Europe appear to have lived and laboured within
a homeostatic regime of demographic checks and balances, so that
population growth in the long run was very slight. (It took two
centuries for the population of Europe to return to the level which
had existed prior to the Black Death.) The term 'homeostatic' may well
be misleading for this was not any placid equilibrium, but a continuous
process of *equilibration*—of disruption, crisis and rectification—where
mortality crises periodically decimated the rural masses and, in their
wake, fertility rates increased in response to the eased availability of
arable land and earlier age at marriage. Nevertheless, the normal check
to population growth was not exerted through wars, epidemics and
famine, but rather through the control of fertility, primarily via the
delay and deterrence of marriage. In periods of non-crisis mortality,
when the land situation was generally tight, the average age of women
at first marriage rose (into the late twenties in most regions) and
checked fertility rates. In this characteristically Western European marriage pattern the average age of women at first marriage was around
26 years, at least 10 per cent of women never married, and only 2
per cent of children were born out of wedlock.[21] The delay and deterrence of marriage itself was thus the primary regulator of fertility in
the villages of Western Europe; effective birth control within marriage
was relatively weak or absent.

We shall return to look at this fertility regime more closely in a
moment. Here I merely want to emphasize that this was not a regime
of uncontrolled fertility. When demographers speak in sweeping terms
of a transition from 'natural and high fertility' to one of 'controlled
and low fertility', these loose descriptive labels mask the fact that: (a)
there was nothing particularly natural about 'natural fertility', and (b)
the early modern peasant fertility regime was *relatively low* compared
to the proletarian and proto-industrial regimes in the same period.

The Great Population Explosion

The growth rate of the population of Western Europe began to
accelerate around 1750, doubling by 1800. It was the *sustained* nature

of this boom, without offsetting cyclical contractions, which distinguished it from all previous growth spurts. In a century and a half the population of Europe almost *tripled*, swelling to 390 million by 1900 despite the exodus of some 40 million people—mostly to the Americas—in the largest inter-continental migration in history.

Historical demographers have long argued whether declining mortality or rising fertility furnished the driving force in this unprecedented vital revolution in Western Europe.[22] Swept up in the dynamic of polarized debate, most have plumped for the unilateral role of one factor, while minimizing or denying outright the contribution of the other. I have seen no compelling evidence or argument thus far presented to enter the lists for either camp. Certainly mortality crises declined on the European continent in the eighteenth century with a decrease in the ferocity and frequency of wars, famines and epidemics. (Mortality rates in normal non-crisis years, by contrast, did not decline much before the second half of the nineteenth century.) Local family-reconstitution studies also indicate, fairly consistently, that age-specific fertility rates rose among those swelling sectors of the rural landless who were engaged in cottage industry and year-round wage labour. So changes in *both* vital rates would appear to have contributed to the demographic revolution. How then do we weigh their respective effects and assess their interaction?

No real progress can be achieved in this regard until national aggregates for crude birth and death rates are broken down, and specific socio-economic *regions* of Western Europe are distinguished and compared, highlighting the demographic dynamics of the main (labouring) *classes* in each region.[23] In surveying the relevant literature, the following patterns seem to me to emerge for three distinct types of socio-economic regions of Western Europe: the great pre-industrial cities, the rural-agricultural zones, and the new industrial areas.

(1) The old pre-industrial commercial and administrative centres and capital cities of Europe had generally been net *consumers* of population throughout the medieval and early modern epochs, with mortality rates far higher than the surrounding countryside; urban influx checked overall population growth on the continent at least until the eighteenth century. Life expectancy improved slightly in the eighteenth century, tending by the end of the century to balance the reproductive equation, but the old urban centres did not become dynamic sources of indigenous population growth much before the second half of the nineteenth century, when a minimal infrastructure of running water, sewage and garbage disposal was finally established in the teeming slums of these cities, with dramatic improvements in the life expectancy of the labouring poor. Thus, before 1850, the main sources of population growth cannot be found in the great cities—their expansion was due almost entirely to in-migration.

(2) From the Middle Ages, the agricultural zones of the European countryside had been the primary source of population growth on the continent. Age-specific fertility rates among peasants, cottars and day labourers in agricultural villages do not appear to have risen much, if at all, from 1750 to 1850, and in some regions (e.g., parts of France) they definitely fell. The abatement of crisis mortality in the same period meant that a significantly higher proportion of married adults survived their reproductive years. The decline of mortality thus appears to be the primary factor in triggering the population boom in these regions among the agriculturally-based labouring classes.

(3) By far the fastest growing regions of Western Europe in the first century of the demographic transition were those rural areas where cottage industry mushroomed and new factory and mining towns sprang up. The primary contributor to the unprecedented population boom of these regions appears to have been a sustained rise in fertility rates.

The Proto-Industrial Rupture

The marital fertility rate of any population can be broken down into three age-specific averages: (a) women's age at first birth (starting); (b) intervals between births (spacing); and (c) age at last birth (stopping). The main difference between the fertility of the proletarianizing populace of the new industrial regions and the population of other regions appears to have been in this first factor. There was a decrease of two to three years in the average age at first marriage, a concomitant lowering of women's age at first birth, an increase in the number of births per completed marriage. The proportion of the population ever marrying also rose, as did the frequency of childbirth out of wedlock. These changes, in combination, increased the birth rate of women under 25 dramatically. As a result, the average generational turnover period was abbreviated, and the demographic expansion of one generation was compounded more rapidly by the next.

Average intervals between births also appear to have shortened slightly with proletarianization, but this compensation for increased infant and child mortality in the new industrial towns probably did no more than to offset the latter's rise. The average age of working-class women at last birth remained close to menopause and did not fall much before the last quarter of the nineteenth century. In short, it was changes in the age and frequency of marriage itself which played the pivotal role in inaugurating the new proletarian fertility regime.

While adult mortality improved somewhat among proletarian populations, infant and child mortality rates did not, remaining significantly higher than those in adjacent agricultural regions (at comparable levels of poverty) throughout the first century of the demographic transition. We cannot then plausibly attribute indigenous population growth in these regions to declining mortality rates; rising fertility appears to be much more significant.

Mass migration from agricultural to industrial regions was the other major factor in the population build-up of the latter. The growth of proto-industrial zones interrupted and detoured the old rural-urban migration pattern. The great cities ceased to absorb and to decimate the entire surplus of the countryside as they formerly had; new industrial regions became the primary catchment areas for the poor and unemployed of the agrarian areas. A very large proportion of this influx was of young adults of marriageable age, moving away from parental controls and the cultural constraints of village communities. This type of migration accentuated the differentiation of fertility patterns between regions, accelerating the shift to earlier and near-universal marriage in the new zones of nascent industrial capitalism.

Household Forms and Fertility Regimes

Let me now indicate, in a very stark and admittedly schematic fashion, how the expanded mode of production framework may be effectively mobilized in explaining the demographic transition for the main labouring classes in Western Europe. I shall do this by setting out four basic household types, each with a distinctive fertility regime.[24]

(1) A *peasant* household, dominant before the transition gets underway, which is still part of the feudal-seigneurial mode of production, now on its last legs. The primary mode of fertility regulation in the peasant village is the 'land-niche/late-marriage system' or what has been called the 'nuptiality valve'. This is not, overall, a secular growth regime.

(2) The *proto-industrial* household of domestic cottage industry, based on independent commodity production—a distinct, necessarily subordinate, but often widespread mode of production—which mushroomed across the countryside of Western Europe in the seventeenth and eighteenth centuries during the protracted transition to industrial capitalism.[25] The fertility regime operative here has been termed a 'demographic hothouse'—a system of *unmediated* short-run nuclear family labour demand, where the long-run intergenerational regulation of land inheritance has been overrun in the turn to non-agrarian commodity production. The proto-industrial household tends to give rise to large families, in good times and bad, contributing to impetuous population growth.

(3) The *early proletarian* family household, found primarily in rural areas or in new industrial towns, with most of its members not engaged in factory production (until late in the nineteenth century when we are passing into the phase of sharp fertility decline and out of this type). I shall follow Tilly and Scott here in terming this arrange-

ment 'the family wage economy', where the contribution of children's wages was indispensable to the unit's stable maintenance.[26] The fertility regime here was one of *mediated* short-run family labour demand (mediated, that is, by conditions in the labour market), and the overall trend is to fairly rapid population growth, but effected critically by the employment situation and real wage levels (for men, women and children—each distinctively), hence fluctuating upwards, depending upon these market conditions.

(4) The *mature proletarian* household, whose primary male breadwinners were mainly concentrated in fully capitalist industries—mines, mills and factories of intensive machinofacture; whose children were now overwhelmingly in school, at least until their teenage years; and whose married women were primarily confined to domestic labour (mostly wage conversion for family consumption, not domestic manufacture), especially through their childbearing years. This is a fertility regime of parity-dependent birth control in marriage, through stopping in the early thirties, where there are no longer economic incentives to have large families, based on children's prospective labour contributions to the family unit. Let us now consider each of these household types in turn.

Peasant Households

The households of the peasant village reproduced themselves from one generation to the next within a fairly closed system. They were involved, predominantly, in mixed subsistence farming for direct use and local barter, where surplus was sold to pay the rent, and not primarily to reap a profit. And while peasant families, through the male line, had effective possession of their means of agrarian production (above all the land), they were not yet completely free from seigneurial jurisdiction, traditional law and manorial custom. Their lands, particularly central arable parcels, were not freely and permanently alienable as commodities through market exchange; and local inheritance laws and customs still set the basic limits within which peasant househeads strategized inheritance options for devolving their patrimony. Peasant children reaching biological adulthood had to bide their time and wait for their elders to play their marital cards. Alternative livelihoods—sufficient to go off and from one's own household without parental approval—were few and far between; or at least far enough removed from the world of the peasant community to be unknown by, or intimidating to, village youth. In this situation, village endogamy (broadly defined to include neighbouring hamlets) prevailed, and most marriages had to await the availability of a land parcel (including livestock and farm implements) to be formalized and consummated.

Delayed marriage left a lot of young adults at loose ends for a limited span of years, and the peasant village regulated this residual population through the institution of domestic service, continually redistributing young adults en masse to the more productive holdings in the local area. As servants, they lived in the households of their social superiors and came directly under their control. This was an appendage of the patriarchal system and not an alternative to it. The limits of land availability, assigned marriage and inheritance customs, thus determined the pace of new household formation, and the vast majority of young adults preferred to wait to secure their own independent households rather than to marry and move in with parents (usually his).

Inheritance customs varied from one region to another, so it is difficult to generalize, but the actual forces in play varied somewhat less than the law. Peasant heads and seigneurs both agreed that it was desirable, above all, to keep the main land parcel—the major means of production—intact, avoiding its subdivision wherever possible. But weighing against the goal of land integrity was the keenly felt need to compensate non-heirs, especially to marry off daughters with dowries suitable to their station. It was therefore necessary to accumulate extra land, chattels or monetary wealth, above and beyond the basic holding, to compensate non-heirs and effectively exclude them from subsequent claim upon the patrimony. This is what I shall call a de facto inheritance system of *compensatory impartible* which tends to emerge 'between' the two pure forms of partible and impartible inheritance in conditions of seigneurial jurisdiction.

This then is a very rough sketch of the late feudal village of dependent peasant cultivators. Since marriage here was tied to the limited availability of arable land by virtue of patriarchal control and the relative absence of alternatives, and neo-locality was the norm, marriage was characteristically late and non-universal.[27] The primary mode of fertility regulation in these circumstances was at the first level outlined above: where marriage itself was blocked and delayed, and women, on average, bore no children for the first twelve to fourteen years of their fertile life-phase, until their mid or late twenties. This then was the nuptiality valve, eased or tightened in relation to the availability of land (or alternative employments—more and more prevalent in the eighteenth century).

The incentive equation within marriage (patriarchally biased by patrilineal concerns) initially weighed strongly in favour of having children to work on the farm, to inherit the holding (males preferably), and to care for parents in old age. But not too many children; since all those who were not in line to inherit the land constituted an eventual drain upon its chattel wealth, compelling the provision of dowries and other forms of pre-mortem inheritance. However, with the means of birth control being rudimentry and culturally discouraged or forbidden, it was difficult for couples to stop reproducing in their mid and late thirties, when they had reached what they might have regarded as an ideal family size. Birth spacing was easier to manage, and was in evidence in many areas; at the will of women—one assumes—insisting on abstinence, or through prolonged lactation and active nursing, much more than the sexual self-discipline of men.

Proto-Industrial Households

Proto-industrial households mushroomed in the eighteenth century in regions of the countryside of Western Europe where the soil was poor and subsistence farming had, by itself, become unviable.[28] Wherever an urban centre was within marketable distance and merchant capitalists were attentive to the possibilities of exploiting cheap domestically-based rural labour, then cottage industry sprang up, filling in the slack time of the year when the labour demands of agriculture were practically nil. This was a mixed livelihood, and the integration of subsistence farming and domestic handicraft production for supralocal markets was particularly tight. But, as time went on, the commodity production side of the household enterprise became increasingly dominant. We have, consequently, households dominated by the requisites of independent family production for the market—a new mode of production.

Not surprisingly, one finds an entirely different fertility regime. The imperative of land integrity has been weakened, since the household's livelihood was not primarily dependent on the land (and the size of the land parcel) anymore. Farming increasingly came to resemble extensive gardening, as smaller plots sufficed. The means of independent production were now mobile, as they became increasingly detached from the land, and a new household could be set up in business by a merchant and a loan. Patriarchal control over one's offspring was correspondingly weakened. The institutional constraints of the first level were thus dramatically eased, and age at first marriage dropped; moreover, the cost/incentive structure was tilted heavily in favour of childbearing since the labour supply was now strictly familial.[29] Servants and day-labourers were generally not prevalent as supplementary hands in these households. People were simply too poor to afford to pay wages; domestic service dried up when the age at marriage dropped, and parents could no longer control its timing and mate selection. The loss of parental control over marriage was not a disincentive to childbearing; the children of cottage handicraft workers tended to remain as productive members of their parents' households longer than peasant offspring, establishing their own households immediately, usually via marriage, when they did leave. Furthermore, the collapse of the dowry system and other forms of pre-mortem inheritance removed an additional disincentive to prolific childbearing for poor couples.

If children made the spinning wheels hum, they were also mouths to feed. Every time the merchants turned the screws of exploitation or market prices dipped, the only recourse of the family unit was to intensify its labour in commodity production. Increasingly, there was no turning back—land plots became smaller despite the marginality of the soil. More and more, non-food necessities were not available on the basis of local barter and had to be purchased in cash from distant towns. The need for year-round income rose. Intensified participation in small-scale commodity production, in long-run conditions of prohibitive competition from larger-scale capitalist workshops and factories, forced proto-industrial households up an economic blind-alley, in which their swelling numbers of children (consistent with an *extensive* mode of capitalist exploitation by merchants) went from being a salvation in boom years to an albatross in periods of market depression. This then was the economic and demographic double bind from which the prolific and rapidly swelling proto-industrial class could not ultimately escape. Increasingly, as the nineteenth century wore on and capitalist industrialization drove one cottage industry and region after another to the wall, this class spilled its children into the swelling ranks of an adjacent class—the proletariat—as its members lost effective possession of their means of production.

Early Proletarian Households

In the transition to capitalism in Western Europe, proletarianization (the formation of a mass of wage-dependent labourers divorced from the means of production) *preceded* industrialization (the generalization of the factory system and mass production by machinofacture) by a century or more. It would thus be wrong to think of a temporal sequence: 'from proto-industrialization to proletarianization'. In fact, both classes were swelling rapidly in the eighteenth century, both contributed to the demographic boom, and there was a great deal of traffic back and forth between them among the rural land-poor masses. This makes it very difficult to sort out the respective contributions of the two classes to the precipitous population expansion of that period, which obviously varied from one region to another. I emphasize, therefore, that what follows is more a line of reasoning than an empirically verified distinction between the demographic regimes of the two classes.

Unlike independent small producers, early proletarians had no property to transfer from one generation to the next, and therefore were completely removed from any effects of land inheritance patterns and even from the inheritance of trades from father to sons—except for a thin artisanal layer emerging from the guilds and early craft unions. The peak earning capacity of most proletarian adults—women as well as men—came early, in their twenties, and thus they tended to marry early. Households were not, for them, attached to an arable land parcel in any form and could be established quite readily by paying a money rent. (We should also note, in passing, that since marriage and stable household formation were now tied to regular wage employment, which was subject to the notorious insecurity of layoffs and business slumps, that the promise of marriage must often have been dashed, and this factor—mobile young men tramping around the countryside leaving women in the lurch—probably accounts for a good deal of the sharp rise in fertility out of wedlock which is closely associated with proletarianization in the century from 1750-1850.)

Proletarianization also entailed—at least for the first generation cohort who lost their place on the land—a certain loss of patriarchal authority of parents over their children, which was manifest in a greater capacity of young adults to court, to make their own mate selection, and to secure legal sanction for their marriages without awaiting parental approval. Without property inheritance as an infrastructure for parental mate selection and marriage timing, and with an increased capacity of young adults to secure their *own* wage income and accommodation, the institutional barriers to marriage and independent household formation were dramatically lowered.

Within marriage, making ends meet was extremely tough. Wages were low—primarily owing to a general glut of labour throughout this period—and the wage of the male breadwinner usually came nowhere close to covering the family's monetary needs in purchasing necessary consumer goods, except for the best-paid artisans. At the same time, married women who were childbearing were overwhelmingly knocked out of the labour market, since the advent of the capitalist mode of production's characteristic separation of household from place of employment *complicated* the combination of infant-nurture with extra-domestic employment for women. But this work, in combination with a husband's wage income (often irregular with long bouts of unemployment), was not enough to make ends meet, and the phase of early child-rearing, when children were not old enough to gain employment, was generally one of crushing poverty. The urgent goal was thus to make it over this hump and to be able to send the children out to work. The income of two or three youths, aged ten and over could constitute 40-60% of the household's total income. The incentive for childbearing was therefore strong, although mediated by the market and the chances of securing employment for children in the area where the family resided (within walking distance of the husband's workplace). The other inducement of this situation was to keep the teenage children at home, remitting their income, for as long as possible.

Proto-industrial and early proletarian families experienced a different linkage between the demand for labour-power and its internally generated supply, which affected the way each responded demographically to a prolonged slump in the market price of their respective commodities. While the labour-power which proto-industrial families required to meet a specific market demand was highly variable, and they were generally induced to *intensify* their total labour exertion in response to falling prices; proletarian families faced a labour market which often made it difficult in a recession to expand their total employment to offset falling wage rates. The substitutability of one family member's labour-power for another was sharply curtailed as labour power became a commodity which had to be set to work by an employer who was external and indifferent to the family's overall subsistence situation. For proletarians, then, the specific employment prospects *for children* were key in shifting the fertility incentive structure. Whereas proto-industrial families could always count on being able to set their children to work productively at a very young age, proletarian families could not.

Finally, it appears that the rate of infant mortality was higher for early proletarians than for other labouring classes throughout the late eighteenth and first half of the nineteenth centuries, as the slums of the new industrial towns were ecological disaster zones, with contaminated water supplies, open sewage, and so on. Epidemic disease took a frightful toll of infants and young children. If urban proletarians were not then poorer than the rural masses, they were nevertheless living in a much more lethal environment and their mortality rates were higher. There appears to have been a strong compensatory impulse in these circumstances to shorten birth spacing and reduce, as well, the average duration of breast-feeding, or to farm it out to a wetnurse; all of which contributed to a high fertility rate. The combination of high fertility and infant mortality thus made for an enormous squandering of women's labour-power, exhausting them and debilitating their health.

Industrial capitalism, in the moment of its triumphant breakthrough, here revealed its darker side. Private capitalists, under the whip of competition, displayed a ruinous indifference to the most elementary preconditions of the proletariat's life-reproduction, and above all, to women, forced to try to reconcile the antagonistic demands of the daily and generational cycles of labour-power. Without tracing, in detail, the entire causal chain, I want to suggest that there was an underlying, if mediated, connection between the dominant (absolute) mode of capital accumulation in this period of primitive accumulation, which consumed labour power *extensively* (prolonging the working day, utilizing child labour, and forcing women to rise from childbearing prematurely), and the dominant fertility regime of the proletariat—which produced future labour power 'extensively' as well, with an enforced assertion of quantity over quality as reflected in the character of the investment made in children.

Mature Proletarian Households

On a national level, fertility rates began a sustained descent in the last quarter of the nineteenth century, dropping from an annual average of 35 births per 1000 population in 1870 to 20 by 1930.[30] The relative simultaneity of the onset of this descent across Western Europe is a remarkable phenomenon, which has attracted a good deal of scholarly attention.[31] But this 'horizontal' synchronicity must not be permitted to obscure the 'vertical' *divergence* of fertility patterns between the main social classes in the first phase of the transition. Proletarian couples did not follow the lead of middle class spouses in the last two decades of the nineteenth century; their fertility remained high, while the birth rates of the urban propertied classes, led by professional strata, dropped sharply as average family size shrunk. This dramatic widening of the reproductive gap alarmed the upper classes, and triggered a wave of eugenicist agitation, replete with hysterical warnings as to the imminent genetic dissipation of the (superior) European races.

When the birth rates of working class couples did fall in the first third of the twentieth century, the changing domestic realities of proletarian subsistence evidently furnished more compelling arguments for avoiding conception and arresting further childbirth after two or three children had been successfully nurtured than the ideological tempest of their class superiors. The family wage economy, where children had provided indispensable financial support for their parents through a father's years of waning income, was now at an end. The traditional fertility regime no longer made any sense, economically or culturally. The most significant institutional change in this regard was undoubtedly the spread of universal schooling, with effective year-round attendance enforcement, bringing the era of extra-domestic child labour to a close. This fundamentally altered the cost/benefit equation for raising children.[32]

On the one hand, the prospective earning capacity of children living at home was drastically curtailed. Regular school attendance greatly reduced the time available for wage labour, and employers were legally forbidden to hire children to work during school hours. Furthermore, among children with some education (particularly boys), parents could no longer expect an automatic wage remission when they did eventually go out to work as adolescents. The erosion of the family wage economy deepened the fetishism of the wage form, which was increasingly seen to belong, by rights, to the worker who earned it.

This marked the beginning of a secular transition to the modern norm, where the acquisition of one's first full-time job is regularly associated with leaving home and living 'on one's own'.

On the other side of the ledger, per capita costs of raising children rose sharply with the advent of universal schooling. Above and beyond school taxes, fees, school books, and other obvious expenses, formal education exerted intense pressure on parents, often expressed through the demands of children themselves, for the provision of better clothing, hygene, nutrition and medical care. The rise of schooling not only altered the economics of child-raising, it also had a profound impact on the aspirations which working-class parents held for their children. 'A good education' was what working-class parents tried to bequeath to their kids to help them make their way in the world; and great sacrifices were made and justified with the consoling thought that, with an education, their children might at least be able to secure better jobs, and live in greater security, than they had.

As 'stopping'—the cessation of childbirth well before menopause—became a general norm for working-class women, it seems reasonable to infer that masses of working-class women must have been asserting their reproductive rights in an elementary sense. Information was disseminated and support extended in this endeavor through informal kin and friendship networks spreading out on a neighbourhood-by-neighbourhood basis. The regular practice of contraception does not appear to have been the primary means of inhibiting further childbirth within marriage for most working class women. Caps and diaphrams had become commonplace contraceptive devices among middle class women with some disposable income and access to family physicians; proletarian women, for the most part, resorted to more traditional means—coitus interruptus, abstention, and abortion when all else failed.[33] The success of such methods remained highly uncertain at an individual level, and the health hazards were potentially severe; yet their *aggregate* effect in curtailing fertility, particularly for women in their mid- to late thirties, was nonetheless considerable. Over the span of two generations fertility rates for married working-class women were cut almost in half.

The sharp decline in marital fertility constituted, in effect, a fundamental shift in the prevailing pattern of working-class investment in its future generation—from an enforced concern with quantity to one of quality. Once again, I want to relate this transformation in the replacement cycle of labour-power, to the dominant trends in labour-power's consumption in industry and in capital accumulation, which shifted in the same period from a regime of absolute to one of relative surplus-value extraction. In other words, both the capital accumulation and the labour-power reproduction cycles were converted from extensive to intensive modes of regeneration.

As capital shifted from an absolute to a relative mode of surplus-value extraction, major capitalists concentrated on intensifying the productive exertions of adult male workers (primary breadwinners) in the key industrial sectors. The employers relinquished, under considerable pressure, child labour and the twelve and then the ten-hour day. This shift to a higher male wage regime made it possible for a family of four to live on a trade-union wage. A single (male breadwinner) model of labour-power consumption and remuneration altered the larger socio-economic context within which proletarian couples were now keen to reduce family size by stopping conception once two of three children had been born. The unorganized labouring poor, sending their children to work at (or before) the legal school-leaving age, could not get by on fathers' wages, and were much more inclined to go on and bear four or more children. The wages of these offspring have continued to play a critical role in family maintenance for many poor and single-parent families down to the present day.

Conclusion

Since this article has been written in a frankly exploratory vein, it is appropriate to conclude with speculation. Is it not possible that the breakthrough to industrial capitalism in Western Europe (in contradistinction to other social formations with a comparable level of development) had at least something to do with the distinctive family form, marital pattern and fertility regime which prevailed among the rural masses in the early modern era?

I am not suggesting, as some have, that the dependent cultivators of England, for example, were really never peasants at all, but capitalist farmers living in modern atomized nuclear families as far back as the Middle Ages. Rather, it is the particular *discontinuity*—rupture and release—from the peasantry's traditional domestic arrangements which must be highlighted. The prevalent form of the Western European peasant family's reproduction cycle, where neolocality was combined with late and non-universal marriage, generated a very distinctive type of fertility control. Once this 'nuptiality valve' burst, with the spread of cottage industry organized by merchant capitalists, it unleashed a prolific capacity and employment-responsive form of household formation among the rural landless, which, in turn, supplied employers with a virtually inexhaustable reservoir of cheap, mobile and readily exploitable labour-power throughout the eighteenth and nineteenth centuries. The continuous regeneration of this reserve was instrumental in easing capital over the initial hump of primitive accumulation, based on extensive modes of capital accumulation and labour-power utilization.[34]

TABLE 2.1
Household Forms and Fertility Regimes

	Peasant	Proto-Industrial	Early Proletarian	Mature Proletarian
CONDITION OF HOUSEHOLD FORMATION	Inheritance of place on land; entry via marriage	Market or merchant-dependent; small plot & cottage	Family wage; rented dwelling space	Male breadwinner wage; rented dwelling space
ECONOMIC INCENTIVE FOR CHILDBEARING	Positive; but checked by complication of too many children	Positive; a direct return to child labour in family household	Positive; return to child employment mediated by labour market	Negative; costs of education and delayed entry into full-time wage work
MODE OF FERTILITY REGULATION	'Nuptiality valve'; delay and deterrence of marriage	Sporadic or absent	Slight, depending on women's external employment prospects	In-marriage 'stopping', via abstention and coitus interruptus
POPULATION DYNAMICS	Slow growth; equilibration, varying with availability of land	'Hothouse' growth, in good times or bad	Pulsating growth, in response to employment fortunes	Moderate growth, responsive to longer range economic fortunes and duration of childrens' education

This analysis, which emphasizes the demographic dimension of the early proletariat's growth from the ranks of the rural landless, need not be counterposed to the more traditional Marxist account of the peasantry's divorce from the land through enclosure, engrossment and competitive displacement. *Both* processes were indispensable to the proletariat's formation, though of course their relative importance and particular interaction varied greatly from one region to the next. Furthermore, nothing in this very general account supplants the need for specific and detailed analyses of uneven and combined developments in the various national formations of Western Europe. But it does perhaps suggest an ironic twist to E.P. Thompson's memorable dictum that the working class was present at its own making. For in the period of its formation the working class evidently 'made itself' in more ways than one.

Notes and References

1. See in particular: C. Meillassoux, *Maidens Meal and Money* (Cambridge University Press, Cambridge, 1980); M. Gimenez, 'Population and Capitalism', *Latin American Perspectives*, 4, 4, (1981), pp. 5-40; K.L. Michaelson (ed.), *And the Poor Get Children: Radical Perspectives on Population Dynamics*, (Monthly Review Press, New York, 1981); Sidney Coontz, emphasizing the role of labour demand, laid impressive groundwork for a Marxist integration of demography three decades ago in his *Population Theories and Economic Interpretation* (Routledge Kegan & Paul, London, 1957). His work was largely unheralded in the West at the time; it is now being accorded belated attention by radical demographers in search of some roots in the discipline.

2. 'Agrarian Class Structure and Economic Development in Pre-Industrial Europe', *Past and Present*, No. 70 (February 1976), p. 31. See also his 'The Origins of Capitalist Development: a Critique of Neo-Smithian Marxism', *NLR* 104 (July-August 1977).

3. 'Against the Neo-Malthusian Orthodoxy', *Past and Present*, No. 79 (May 1978), pp. 67-68. Bois is a Marxist whose own work, *La Crise de la Feodalisme* (Paris 1976), has drawn accolades even from Ladurie. He begins his commentary by praising Brenner's attack on 'the neo-Malthusian orthodoxy'.

4. My doctoral thesis, completed at the University of Toronto in 1982, sketches the daily and generational reproduction cycles of labour-power through household, family and kin relations in the slave, feudal and capitalist modes of production. Therein I advance a much fuller elaboration of a revised modes of production concept than I have been able to present below, including a consideration of the question of patriarchal domestic relations.

5. This is Mary O'Brien's neologism from *The Politics of Reproduction* (Routledge, London, 1981); I have been most fortunate to work with her

at the Ontario Institute for Studies in Education.

6. On mothering, cf. Nancy Chodorow, *The Reproduction of Mothering: Psychoanalysis and the Sociology of Gender* (University of California Press, Berkeley, 1978); Adrian Rich, *Of Woman Born*, (Norton, New York 1976); and Dorothy Dinnerstein, *The Mermaid and the Minotaur* (Harper Row, New York, 1976). For historical accounts of the public struggle over birth control, see Linda Gordon, *Woman's Body, Woman's Right: A Social History of Birth Control in America* (Viking, New York, 1976); and J. Reed, *From Private Vice to Public Virtue: The Birth Control Movement and American Society Since 1830* (Basic Books, New York 1978).

7. By way of introduction to a burgeoning scholarship, see: Lutz Berkner, 'The Use and Abuse of Census Data for the Historical Analysis of Family Structure', *Journal of Interdisciplinary History* (1975), pp. 721-38, and 'Inheritance, Land Tenure, and Peasant Family Structure: A German Regional Comparison', in J. Goody, J. Thirsk and E.P. Thompson (eds.), *Family and Inheritance: Rural Society in Western Europe, 1200-1800*, (Cambridge University Press, Cambridge, 1976); Lutz Berkner and Franklin Mendels, 'Inheritance Systems, Family Structure and Demographic Patterns in Western Europe, 1700-1900', in C. Tilly (ed.), *Historical Studies of Changing Fertility*, (Princeton University Press, Princeton, 1978); Rudolph Braun, 'Proto-industrialization and Demographic Changes in the Canton of Zurich', in Tilly, op. cit.; Michael Haines, *Fertility and Occupation: Population Patterns in Industrialization* (Academic Press, New York 1979); David Levine, *Family Formation in an Age of Nascent Capitalism*, (Academic Press, New York, 1977); Hans Medick, chapters 2 and 3 in *Industrialization Before Industrialization*, P. Kriedte, H. Medick and J. Schlumbohn (eds.), (University Press, Cambridge, 1981); Franklin Mendels, 'Proto-industrialization: The First Phase of the Industrialization Process', *Journal of Economic History* (1972), 32, pp. 241-61, and 'Social Mobility and Phase of Industrialization', *Journal of Interdisciplinary History* (1976), 7 (2), pp. 193-216; Charles Tilly, 'Introduction', in Tilly op. cit.; 'Demographic origins of the European Proletariat' in David Levine (ed.), *Proletariarization and Family Life* (Academic Press, 1984). Louise Tilly and Joan Scott, *Women, Work and Family*, (Holt, Rinehart, New York, 1978).

8. Natural fertility was first defined by the French demographer Louis Henry ['Some Data on Natural Fertility', *Eugenics Quarterly* (1961), 8, pp. 81-91] as the absence of deliberate birth control and family size limitation in marriage. The term is now in widespread use among demographers, although not without ambiguities. A population is held to be in a condition of natural fertility when, in the jargon of demographers, birth patterns show no evidence of being 'parity-dependent'. Married women, in other words, do not cease to bear children on the basis of the number of presently living children they have already borne; no 'target' of ideal family size is operative. If the fertility curve of a given cohort of women corresponds broadly to their natural fecundity curve, even through their late thirties and early forties, a regime of natural fertility is held to prevail. Customs and practices which affect birth-spacing, and hence fertility rates, but which are not parity dependent (such as breast-feeding norms and post-partum intercourse taboos), do not contravene a regime of natural fertility. The *natu-*

ral/controlled dichotomy tends to generate a simple bipolar model: pre-industrial peoples have 'natural and high' fertility, while industrialized populations exhibit 'controlled' birth patterns and register 'low' fertility rates. The simplistic nature of this dichotomy, so congenial to the modernization framework, is now ritually acknowledged by demographers and it is recognized that there are tremendous variations within each. A more elaborate and nuanced typology has yet to be established, which would take into account that *every* human fertility pattern is culturally bounded and socially regulated; no population on record has been found to approach a rate of natural breeding.

9. The other major problem with the demographic transition theory is that it is not a theory at all in a scientific sense, since it lacks any substantial explanatory elements. Instead, it is a descriptive model of sequential change in a set of 'factors' whose covariance, submitted to various measures of statistical significance, is somehow assumed to explain itself. The persistent substitution of description for explanation is a hallmark of the modernization paradigm with which the demographic transition theory is closely allied.

10. While Maurice Dobb's *Studies in the Development of Capitalism* (International Publishers, New York, 1963) certainly advanced well beyond crude schematism, his argument was nevertheless marred by the traditional Marxist counterposition of transformations in social relations of production to demographic changes (see p. 223 especially), arguing for the primacy of the former while downplaying the latter. He compounded the problem through an incautious acceptance of the then standard modernization consensus that 'the increase in population (from 1750-1850) is now known to have been due to a fall in the death-rate rather than a rise in the birth-rate' (p. 257). The subsequent debate in *Science & Society*, printed and expanded in *The Transition from Feudalism to Capitalism* (New Left Books, London, 1976), while ranging fruitfully far and wide, ignored the demographic coordinates of the transition to capitalism.

11. The opportunity to study with David Levine has contributed importantly to my thinking here, although he should not be implicated in any of the 'synthesis' essayed in the following pages.

12. See Heidi Hartman, 'The Unhappy Marriage of Marxism and Feminism: Towards a More Progressive Union', in L. Sargent (ed.), *Women and Revolution* (Pluto Press, London 1981).

13. The biological limit-condition of fecundity, of course, operates also, fluctuating over time and living conditions, but we treat this as a precondition to these social and economic constraints.

14. This incentive structure is established for reproductive couples at the level of the household as a pooling-sharing unit; this is the unit that assumes the costs of its dependent members, and stands to benefit from the eventual contribution of children. The specification of this incentive structure in no sense implies, as human-capital theorists do, that the interests of both partners are harmoniously aligned within the unitary household framework. Clearly the costs and potential benefits of children are not symmetrically borne; women's interests are regularly submerged—sacrificed 'for the sake of the family'. It is important to specify this interior alignment without losing sight of the unitary household framework. See

Nancy Folbre, 'Of Patriarchy Born: The Political Economy of Fertility Decisions', *Feminist Studies*, 9, 2 (1983), pp. 261-83.

15. Karl Marx, *Capital* Volume I (Progress Publishers, Moscow, 1954), p. 592.

16. John Caldwell has recently advanced a bold perspective which integrates the demographic dimension into a revised mode of production concept, see: 'Toward a Restatement of Transition Theory', *Population and Development Review* (1976), 2 (3-4), pp. 321-66; and 'A General Theory of Fertility: Conditions of High Stable Fertility and the Nature of De-stabilization', ibid (1978), 4 (4), pp. 553-77. His base/superstructure paradigm is sharply at odds with my concept of an expanded infrastructure and readers are urged to compare the two. (I shall not do so, having discovered Caldwell's work after this article was written.)

17. It is important to acknowledge, however, that Marx did not consistently uphold the principle of historical specificity with regard to population patterns in *Capital*, but often slipped back into the naturalist discourse which he criticized Malthus for. Cf. *Capital*, Volume I, pp. 537, 594 and 600.

18. Karl Marx, *Grundrisse* (Vintage, New York, 1973), p. 100.

19. On the Neolithic Revolution, see M.N. Cohen, *The Foods Crisis in Prehistory: Overpopulation and the Origins of Agriculture* (Yale University Press, New Haven, 1977).

20. I concentrate here exclusively on the mass labouring classes leaving the aristocracy and the bourgeoisie to one side. I do not assume that the labouring classes *followed* the ruling classes in altering their fertility patterns so much as they changed for their *own* socio-economic reasons.

21. Daniel Scott Smith, 'A Homeostatic Demographic Regime: Patterns in West European Family Reconstitution Studies', in R.D. Lee (ed.), *Population Patterns in the Past* (Academic Press, New York 1977).

22. In the past decade, the prevailing view has strongly favoured declining mortality as the prime factor, with the centre of controversy shifting to an explanation of this fall (i.e. improvements in medicine, climate, or living standards and nutrition). Wrigley and Schofield's *The Population History of England, 1541-1871* (Edward Arnold, London, 1981) will surely break up the mortality consensus, for England at least. They estimate that England's population boom in the eighteenth and early nineteenth centuries was largely due to rising fertility, with earlier and more universal marriage being the mediate cause (pp. 242-47).

23. Beyond local reconstitution studies, most historical demographers have accepted nation-states and their legal subdivisions as appropriate units of aggregation and analysis. The compilation of routinely generated statistics by government offices virutally compels the adoption of state-territorial units, at least as a first step. For most of the Western European states, viable demographic data exist from the mid-nineteenth century on. The Office of Population Research at Princeton University, under the direction of Ansley Coale, has sponsored an especially important set of studies on declining fertility rates in Europe, with different scholars adopting standard measures and common criteria in evaluating the demographic record of the various states. (See footnote 31.) National estimates for earlier periods have been developed by ingenious but still very problematic methods of aggregat-

ing and weighing local family reconstitution studies, with data generated in turn from a great variety of local sources, originally recorded by officers of church and state. Schofield and Wrigley's long-awaited *The Population History of England* is technically a *tour de force* which will undoubtedly stand for many years as a pre-eminent exemplar of quantitative reconstruction for the centuries prior to the inception of nationally uniform record-keeping. But larger conceptual problems persist, which no amount of technical sophistication and ingenuity can resolve. For the Princeton type of historical demography adopts national and provincial units of analysis *without* any sustained attempt to generate regional and class breakdowns on the basis of relevant socio-economic categories. The multi-class and mixed-region totals which are compiled, statistically manipulated and interpreted, inevitably mask structural variation along these lines. The result is an excessive preoccupation with national comparisons ('the French versus the English pattern'). Class and regional variations are generally treated as an afterthought in a lead and lag framework which is implicitly premised on a conservative cultural diffusionist assumption: lower classes and backward regions lag behind their superiors, but eventually follow them on the road to modernity and progress. It is to the credit of the revisionist social historians mentioned earlier that endogenously active class and regional dynamics have at least been highlighted in many local studies. International aggregations and synthetic interpretations based on regional and class axes have yet to be published in the English-language literature, although see Haines (op. cit.) for an international study based on job categories.

24. Within the space constraints of this article, I am dealing with immense and variegated classes as unitary social blocs, as if there were a single fertility regime for each class. Reality, of course, is more complicated, but such complexity need not defeat the conceptual framework outlined here. Consider the question of richer and poorer strata within the peasantry and the proletariat. Under the *ancien regime*, the richer strata of the peasantry, with more land and a greater need for family labour-power, tended to have larger families than small-holders, cottars and day labourers. If a change in the mode of production makes a significant difference then one would expect to find a very different pattern for the proletariat under capitalism; and, indeed, an opposite pattern prevails. Poorer couples, with an urgent stake in their children's prospective wages, tended to bear more offspring, while the better-paid strata of artisans, clerks and (later) office workers typically raised smaller families. Even patterned variations between strata within a class are class-specific phenomena and are best elucidated within a conception of social classes based in a given mode of production.

25. The term 'proto-industrial' was Mendel's coinage [see 'Proto-industrialization: The First Phase of the Industrialization Process', *Journal of Economic History* (1972), 32, pp. 241-66] and has since become a standard designation for cottage industry. I assume here that proto-industrial zones were organized predominantly on the basis of simple commodity production operating within an overarching formation dominated economically by merchant capital. As transitional forms, many areas of cottage industry bore relations of production that were already capitalist in a primitive sense.

in the eighteenth century.

26. See Tilly and Scott, *Women, Work and Family.*

27. J. Hajnal in a seminal article ['European Marriage Patterns in Perspective', in *Population in History: Essays in Historical Demography*, in D.V. Glass and D.E.C. Eversely (eds.), (Edward Arnold, London, 1965), pp. 101-43] first identified a distinctive Western European marital pattern characterized by late (23 years and over) and non-universal (90% or less) marriage. He detected such a pattern west of a line from Trieste to Leningrad as far back as the seventeenth century; to the east, marriage occurred somewhat earlier and was more universal. Subsequent research has tended to confirm Hajnal's findings, while bending his line of demarcation somewhat to include Estonia and Poland in the eastern region. As one would expect, different marriage patterns are bound up with divergent norms of household formation, co-residence and inter-generational wealth transfer. While in the West, neolocality prevailed and nuclear family households were the norm; in the East, patrilocality was customary in many regions and compound family forms of co-residence and co-operative production were commonplace.

It is unclear whether the Western European marriage pattern originated in the Middle Ages or was a product of later developments. It may well have been coincident with a distinctive manorial infrastructure comprised of the three-field strip system and nucleated village settlement, coupled with a strong tendency to local endogamy. Michael Mitterauer and Richard Sieder [*The European Family: Patriarchy to Partnership from the Middle Ages to the Present* (Basil Blackwell, Oxford, 1982)] posit that 'extensive changes in the agrarian structure brought about by the colonizing movement of the High Middle Ages were confined precisely to those areas in which the European marriage pattern and corresponding family forms developed'. (p. 38) The *East/West* difference in marital norms and family forms was probably related to the differentiation in prevailing modes of seigneurial exploitation, originating in the generalized crisis of the feudal order in the fourteenth century. While labour services on the lord's demesne tended to be commuted to product and money rents in the West, in Eastern Europe the corvée persisted. These divergent trends in the mode of exploitation appear to have fostered different patterns of land/labour-power equilibration. In the East, land tended to be redistributed around cyclical fluctuations in the size and dependency ratio of the co-resident family group; land integrity being safeguarded through the vertical extension of this group. In the West, land integrity was maintained through the delay and deterrence of marriage, and the labour-power of youth was redistributed between farmsteads through the institution of domestic service. See B. Ankarloo, *Journal of Family History*, 4, 2, (1979).

28. Note here how changes in the dominant mode of production profoundly alter settlement patterns and densities. Throughout the Middle Ages in the feudal-manorial zones of the European countryside, population built up on the best arable, and then extended out onto marginal lands in smaller and sparcer settlements. In the early modern era, as simple commodity production under the sponsorship of mercantile capitalism mushroomed in the countryside, population

tended to build up most heavily on the poorest arable, overflowing into the new industrial towns nearby. The population density pattern was thus completely inverted in the transition from feudalism to capitalism.

29. In the traditional villages, artisans tended to marry earlier than peasants, but not as early as their counterparts in open proto-industrial villages or new towns (Medick, op. cit., pp. 85-86). In this sense, they stood 'in between' the peasant and proto-industrial patterns being presented here. This is a simple illustration of the general principle that one should never isolate class relations from regional context in analysing household forms and fertility regimes. The prevailing mode of production operative in a region always conditions the dynamics of subsidiary modes and does not permit their full developmental logic to unfold.

30. France was the exception to this pattern: its national fertility rate was in decline for at least a century before the rest of Western Europe. There have been many attempts to account for France's precocity in this regard. My hunch is that it was due to the peculiar unevenness of the bourgeois revolution in France, which was uniquely advanced on the political and cultural fronts while being relatively backward in socio-economic terms. The French peasantry remained firmly ensconced on the land throughout the nineteenth century and the rate of proletarianization was relatively slow. As a result, the prolific capacity of the rural masses, damned up by the land-niche system of the *ancien regime*, was not unleased in the way that it was elsewhere, most notably in England. On the other hand, the French Revolution profoundly altered the culture and consciousness of the toiling masses, urban and rural, reaching deep into the peasantry. Cultural modernism and a particular form of secular rationalism took root in the French countryside almost a century before the advent of universal schooling. French peasants began to practice birth control in marriage on a widespread basis (with the tacit acquiescence of village priests) long before peasants or proletarians did elsewhere in either Protestant or Catholic countries. Since France's fertility began to decline earlier than the other countries of Western Europe, its transition to low fertility was a gradual and protracted process; however, it should be noted that fertility rates in France did fall considerably (22%) in the 1870-1900 period when rates in other nations were beginning their more rapid descent.

31. On the fertility decline, see the Princeton Group's studies (all published by Princeton University Press, Princeton, NJ): E. van de Walle, *The Female Population of France in the Nineteenth Century* (1974); J. Knodel, *The Decline of Fertility in Germany, 1871-1939*, (1974); R. Lesthaeghe, *The Decline of Belgian Fertility, 1800-1970*, (1978); M. Livi-Bacci, *A Century of Portuguese Fertility* (1971); and *A History of Italian Fertility*, (1977). Perhaps the best statistical overview of the fertility transition is Patrick Festy's La Fécondité des Pays Occidentaux de 1870 à 1970 (Presses Universitaires de France, 1979). The synchronicity of the decline can be usefully measured, as the

Princeton Group has done, by determining the date when fertility declines irreversibly by at least ten per cent. For countries of Western Europe, these dates have been estimated as follows: France ca. 1800, Belgium 1882, Switzerland 1885, Germany 1890, England and Wales 1892, Sweden 1892, Scotland 1894, Netherlands 1897, Denmark 1900, Norway 1904, Austria 1908, Finland 1910, Italy 1911, Spain 1918 and Ireland 1929.

32. 'Mass Education as a Determinant of the Timing of Fertility Decline', *Population and Development Review* (1980), 6, 2, pp. 225-55.

33. On the relative absence of mechanical contraceptive use among working class couples in the first phase of the transition, see A. McLaren, *Birth Control in Nineteenth Century England* (Croom Helm, London, 1978); and R.A. Soloway, *Birth Control and the Population Question in England, 1877-1930* (University of North Carolina Press, Chapel Hill, 1982). Knodel and van de Walle place the emphasis on cultural changes (never really explained) which makes birth control *conceivable* by masses of women for the first time around the turn of the century; see 'Lessons from the Past: Policy Implications of Historical Fertility Studies', *Population and Development Review* (1979), 5, 2, pp. 217-45. In Coale's words, fertility must 'come within the calculus of conscious choice' before a strong motivation to limit fertility can be personally realised and effectively acted upon (p. 239).

34. Third World formations today also furnish immense reservoirs of cheap and mobile labour power. Why then is indigenous capital accumulation of the extensive type not fostered there in the same fashion? To a limited extent it is, but the overriding drives of metropolitan capital erect (and selectively remove) barriers to rapid multifaceted industrialization in these countries. On the eve of the Industrial Revolution of course, Western Europe did not face such an imposing external force; its major states were already imperialist powers in their own right. Such is the privilege of going first.

3

THE FUNCTION OF SOCIAL WELFARE IN A CAPITALIST ECONOMY

Jack Wayne

Introduction

This paper seeks to ground state-sponsored social welfare in the logic of the capitalist economy. Many Marxists have investigated the role of the state in the reproduction of capitalism.[1] And some have looked at state-sponsored social welfare as a factor in this reproduction.[2] We shall extend the analysis here by demonstrating in a somewhat different way that social welfare is functional for capitalism and, more than that, by showing that without social welfare the reproduction of the working class is a long-run impossibility.

While social welfare is often understood to refer to the general well-being of a population,[3] in this paper we shall use the term in a more restricted sense, to denote state-regulated and state-administered supplements to or replacements for the wage. Our use of the term is thus limited to social assistance and social insurance schemes in which there is a transfer of value to members of the working class. Social welfare in this sense involves the provision of an income or commodities to individuals and families who experience a financial shortfall due to the operation of the market in labour power, due to the disadvantaged position of a worker in that market, or due to an unmanageable burden of household expense for the necessities of life.

The task of understanding social welfare can be approached both historically and logically. The historical task is the study of the emergence of social welfare, in its various forms, in specific national states.[4] The logical examination of social welfare, which is often undertaken in the context of specific studies of national histories of social welfare,[5] involves the elucidation of the function of social welfare within the political economy of capitalism. This paper will focus on the economic function of social welfare within capitalism. The object of the paper is to show that social welfare is, logically, a condition of existence of an economy in which labour power seeks to reproduce itself on the basis of the wage. That is, we shall demonstrate that within capitalism the working class cannot reproduce itself on the basis of the wage exclusively, and there is invariably produced a deficiency of wages when compared with costs of consumption for many working class families. Social welfare emerges as a way of bridging the gap between wages and these costs of consumption.

To be sure, the elucidation of the functions of social welfare does not explain its presence within capitalist economies. To say that something is a condition of existence of capitalism does not mean that it necessarily will emerge. If that were the case capitalism would be eternal.[6] The study of the logic of social welfare can, however, identify tendencies and countertendencies at work within capitalism, and advance our understanding of 'the natural laws of capitalist production'[7]. In the following pages we shall demonstrate that the operation of the market in labour power within capitalism cannot ensure the reproduction of it, and that exchange relations within capitalism generate contradictions in this sphere which must be resolved—if they are to be resolved at all—through intervention outside the wage relation.[8]

The paper is divided into three parts. In the first part we shall describe a model of a hypothetical capitalist economy in which labour power is paid at its value, and in which the reproduction of labour power takes place in households and is based exclusively on wages. In presenting the model we shall find that it does not work: if the reproduction of labour power is based on wages only, then the working class cannot reproduce itself.

In the second part of the paper we shall examine some aspects of the reproduction of capitalist enterprise, and argue that capital by itself cannot act to remedy the problem. We shall thus conclude that the reproduction of labour power must involve a transfer of value outside the wage, through a mechanism external to the firm. In the third part we shall argue that social welfare represents the only enduring solution to the crisis of working class reproduction.

The chief sources of our model of working class reproduction, beyond Marx, are observations made of family structures in nineteenth-century Britain where, almost uniquely in the history of capitalism, the working class did attempt to reproduce itself on the basis of wages alone.[9] Wage and consumption data for this model are largely taken from John Foster's *Class Struggle and the Industrial Revolution*.[10] The validity of the model is not limited to the region and time from which most of our illustrative material is drawn, however. If our reasoning is correct, the model should serve to demonstrate underlying tendencies within capitalism wherever it is found. Similarly, the wage and consumption tables, which have been constructed only to illustrate the model, are not drawn from the life-situations of specific families, nor do they necessarily correspond to the circumstances of any particular family. If our model is valid, however, characteristics of families in capitalist economies without widespread value transfers should approximate the distributions generated in our model.

Wages and Capital

The Contrast. The wage has two aspects. On the one hand, the wage is variable capital paid to the worker by the capitalist enterprise in exchange for labour power. On the other hand, the wage, in the hands of the worker, is a fund of consumption used to purchase the means of subsistence for the proletarian household. As variable capital the wage is committed as part of the cycle of the expanded reproduction of capital. As a fund of consumption it must support the family through the various stages of the reproductive cycle. The problem that occurs and recurs within capitalism is that the wage must fulfil very different purposes in each of these aspects. Thus, although the fund of consumption and variable capital are equivalent, they are at the same time functionally distinct.

Let us look first at the way in which the fund of consumption and variable capital are equivalent. Through the labour process the worker creates commodities. These commodities have value, the value in each case dependent upon the amount of labour time socially necessary for the production of them. In the process of reproduction of capital this value is apportioned into two magnitudes, the wages paid to the worker, and the surplus value appropriated by the capitalist. The surplus value appropriated by the capitalist is used to purchase raw materials, to replace worn out means of production, to provide the capitalist himself with a fund of consumption, and to underwrite the expanded reproduction of capitalism in many different ways. The paid value, the value created by the worker for which wages are advanced, becomes the worker's fund of consumption. The worker,

> . . . has, therefore, produced not only surplus-value . . . but he has also produced, before it flows back to him in the shape of wages, the fund out of which he himself is paid, the variable capital . . . What flows back to the worker in the shape of wages is a portion of the product that is continuously reproduced by him.[11]

The equivalence between variable capital on the one hand and the worker's fund of consumption on the other hand is three-fold. There is, first, mathematical identity: the magnitude of the one is identical with the magnitude of the other. Secondly, as variable capital and as the worker's fund of consumption the wage supports the reproduction of capitalism. In order for the capitalist to appropriate surplus value the worker must be sufficiently remunerated so that he/she, or a replacement, will appear the next day to renew the process.[12] If the wage paid is not sufficient for the worker to be maintained and hence be able to sell his/her labour power to the capitalist on successive days, production will not take place; unless the wage is large enough to support the maintenance and reproduction of labour power, the labourers, and the labour power they bear, will cease to exist. The existence of variable capital as a fund of consumption for the worker is thus a necessary condition for the reproduction of the capitalist mode of production.

Thirdly, as variable capital and as fund of consumption the wage enters into the circulation of money and commodities. Labourers, in order to maintain and reproduce themselves must, at a minimum, consume the necessaries of life. In order to do so they use the wage to buy commodities. It is in the purchase of commodities that workers actually obtain the share of the value created in production for which they are paid. As Marx puts it:

> The capitalist class is constantly giving to the labouring class order-notes, in the form of money, on a portion of the commodities produced by the latter and appropriated by the former. The labourers give these order-notes back just as constantly to the capitalist class, and in this way get their share of their own product ... Variable capital is therefore only a particular historical form of the fund for providing the necessaries of life, or the labour-fund which the labourer requires for the maintenance of himself and family, and which, whatever be the system of social production, he must himself produce and reproduce.[13]

These commodities are produced to a substantial degree by capitalist enterprise. The worker, by purchasing the commodities, not only obtains the share of value created, but also contributes to the capitalist's realization of surplus-value. In the purchase of commodities for wages the worker at once secures the necessaries of life, to renew and reproduce labour power, and contributes to the realization of value on the part of the capitalist. The worker's fund of consumption is, at the same time, a fund for both worker and capitalist to realize his or her respective share of value.

Thus the payment of the wage supports the expanded reproduction of capitalism through reproduction of the working class, while it contributes to the realization of value for both worker and capitalist through the process of circulation. It is after this transaction that the *contrast* between the wages taken home by the worker, and the variable capital while it was in the possession of the capitalist, begins to emerge.

The grounds of the contrast between the wage as a fund of consumption and the wage as variable capital are established by the contrasting bases of reproduction of the working class and the capitalist enterprise. The unit of working class reproduction in our model is assumed to be the family.[14] For our purposes it is useful to note that the family is at once a unit of biological and social reproduction, and a budgetary unit. The worker or workers from the proletarian family exchange labour power for wages. This wage is used to pay for subsistence needs. Once these subsistence needs are covered, the circuit of the wage as a fund of consumption is over. 'Within circulation,' Marx notes, 'if I exchange a commodity for money, buy a commodity for it and satisfy my need, then the act is at an end.' For the family, therefore, there is no production of wealth, no growing mass of machinery, raw materials, buildings, etc., and thus no accumulation of capital. In exchanging labour power for wages the worker seeks,

> . . . the satisfaction of his need. . . . What he obtains from
> the exchange is therefore not exchange value, not wealth, but
> a means of subsistence, objects for the preservation of his
> life, the satisfaction of his needs . . .[15]

On the side of capital, of course, the payment of the wage is one moment in the circuit of money and commodities. Variable capital, like other forms of capital, contributes to the expanded reproduction of capital, the accumulation of wealth by capitalist enterprise. Thus while the proletarian family is constituted only for a limited time-span related to the cycle of growth and decline of individual family members, the capitalist enterprise can sustain itself, if successful in the competition among capitals, beyond the individual working lives of its personnel, and beyond their life spans. The contrast between the proletarian family and the capitalist enterprise, therefore, is a contrast between two units connected by the payment and receipt of the wage. On the one hand, for the family, the receipt of the wage allows for consumption of wage-goods to restore and reproduce labour power. The family remains without property, cannot accumulate, and will inevitably decline and disappear. On the other hand, for capitalist enterprise, the payment of the wage enables it to accumulate if other circumstances are conducive. The wage allows the enterprise to maintain the dynamic in which surplus-value is appropriated, and reproduction of the enterprise takes place.

Let us look further into this question by examining the production of value in the proletarian family. For families that are fully proletarianized, this production of value occurs only in the production and reproduction of labour power which enters into the market in that commodity. We assume, with Marx, that in earning a wage the worker, on average, is paid the value of the labour power sold. But how is the value of that labour power determined?

'The value of labour-power is determined,' Marx wrote, 'as in the case of every other commodity, by the labour-time necessary for the production, and consequently also the reproduction, of this special article.[16] This labour-time is represented by the commodities consumed by the worker, the means of subsistence, and by the commodities consumed in the course of raising the next generation of labourers. '. . . The sum of the means of subsistence necessary for the production of labour-power must include the means necessary for the labourer's substitutes, i.e. his children, in order that this race of peculiar commodity-owners may perpetuate its appearance in the market.'[17]

On the basis of Marx's formulation, therefore, we may apportion the value of labour power into (1) the value of the commodities consumed in the course of maintaining the labour power, and (2) the value of the commodities consumed in the process of reproducing the labour power of the worker, the reproductive costs of labour power. It is necessary to include, in the determination of the value of labour power, the value of the commodities consumed by family members who do not themselves earn wages, yet are not members of the next generation of the bearers of labour power, that is, the non-working housewife, husband, or others who take a hand in labour within the family. This value is included because the activities of such persons genuinely enter into the maintenance and reproduction of labour power, and because the logic of the model becomes incomplete if there is a magnitude of value consumed in the household which is not reflected in the value of labour power. For purposes of this discussion it is necessary to assume only that a portion of the value consumed by non-waged family members in this category may be allocated to the maintenance costs of the present generation of workers, a portion of the reproductive costs of the next generation.[18]

For the working class, then, exchange value is produced only in the form of labour power and is realized in the consumption of commodities. But labour power, as with other commodities, may fetch a price that diverges from its value. If we assume that for the working class as a whole the total of the wages paid will exactly cover the total of the commodities consumed, this does not necessarily imply that any *specific* wage paid to any individual or group of family members will cover the consumption cost of some standard bundles of commodities. The value of labour power is established in the long run, by averaging out a great deal of variation in consumption. In a stratified and fluctuating labour market there is no guarantee that, in any particular act of purchase and sale of labour power, price and value will coincide.

The same variation obtains for the commodities which enter into consumption. The price of wage goods may rise above their values, leaving many workers in difficult circumstances. Or, conversely, the price of wage goods may fall below their values, allowing the family to increase its bundle of goods consumed. Even if we assume, therefore, some stable value of labour power and of wage goods, we cannot conclude that the wage will cover the commodities necessary for subsistence for any given family.

Further, the values themselves of labour power and wage goods may vary over time. In Marx's formulation,

> The value of the labouring-power is formed by two elements—the one merely physical, the other historical or social. Its *ultimate limit* is determined by the physical element, that is to say, to maintain and reproduce itself, to perpetuate its physical existence, the working class must receive the necessaries absolutely indispensible for living and multiplying. . . . Besides this mere physical element, the value of labour is in every country determined by a *traditional standard of life*. Is is not mere physical life, but the satisfaction of certain wants springing up from the social conditions in which people are placed and reared up.
> . . . This historical or social element, entering into the value of labour, may be expanded, or contracts, or altogether extinguished, so that nothing remains but the *physical limit*. . . . The *value of labour* itself is not a fixed but a variable magnitude.[19]

In this formulation the value of labour power is affected, first of all, by the value of the commodities which enter into consumption. If the values of those commodities fall, whether due to increased productivity in consumer goods industries, a cheapening of the price of food due to the opening of new lands for cultivation, or some other reason, the value of labour power will fall. But there remains the possibility that the value of labour power can be diminished by striking at the contemporary standard of consumption enjoyed by the working class, while the values of the goods which enter into consumption remain constant or even rise. In Marx's view the actual value of labour power 'always depends upon supply and demand',[20] i.e., on the state of the market in labour power. When there is a larger demand for labour power the price and value of labour power will rise; with a slackening of demand the value will fall. In the former case the workers can use the sellers' market to augment and enrich their standard of living. In the latter case capitalists can use the over-supply of labour power to drive down wages, diminish the value of labour power, and erode the traditional level of consumption.[21]

The problem that the family faces in attempting to live on the basis of wages is twofold. On the one hand the price of the labour power sold on the market may not cover consumption costs for the family, because the price may be below the value of the commodities consumed in that household, because the family may be forced to pay prices for commodities above their values, or because some combination of the two circumstances prevails. On the other hand, the value of labour power itself is always subject to change, predicated on the long-run movement of the supply and demand for labour power, in the context of 'the continuous struggle between capital and labour'.[22]

For the family attempting to earn enough to consume at what is socially understood to be an adequate standard of living, both sides of this problem are experienced in the same way, as a problem of securing enough income so that the family can continue to produce and reproduce itself and therefore produce and reproduce labour power. This struggle is, therefore, not a struggle *against* capitalism itself, but a struggle *within* capitalism to secure for the worker sufficient subsistence so that he or she, and his or her offspring, can take their places within capitalist production. It has usually been left to the workers themselves, for whom the insufficiency of the wage threatens their survival and reproduction, to pursue this struggle. As Marx noted:

> The maintenance and reproduction of the working-class is, as must ever be, a necessary condition to the reproduction of capital. But the capitalist may safely leave its fulfilment to the labourer's instincts of self-preservation and propogation.[23]

Once the contrast between the fund of consumption and variable capital has been established, it is possible to inquire separately about each. In the following section we shall examine the reproductive cycle of the family, and demonstrate the difficulties encountered by proletarian families in attempting to maintain and reproduce themselves on the basis of the wage system.

The Reproductive Cycle of the Family

By the term 'family' we refer to the conjugal unit of husband and wife, and any children co-resident with them.[24] This definition of family coincides with the sociologists' concept of a nuclear family. It is formed by marriage, and is dissolved by the children leaving home and by the death of one of the spouses.

This family experiences a number of stages in its reproductive cycle. There is no convergence in the literature as to how these stages might be characterized, but generally the boundaries of the stages are related to marriage, birth, the children leaving home, and the death of a spouse, which are understood to be biological and social turning points in the history of the family. For our purposes it is of interest that some of these events are related to budgetary turning points also, that is, are events which tip the balance between wages derived from the sale of labour power on the one hand and the costs of consumption on the other. We thus suggest a revised set of stages in the reproductive cycle of the family which reflects possible increments in income and increments in consumption for the proletarian family.

(1) **From marriage to birth of first child.** The timing and duration of this first stage in the reproductive cycle of the family is a direct function of the market in labour power, in our model. In all economies the household must have access to subsistence, but only for the proletarian family does this subsistence take the form of wages. In non-capitalist economies, where subsistence is related to access to agricultural land, or to ownership of a workshop or artisanal tools, marriage is contingent upon the inheritance of the land or to rights in land, to savings over a period of apprenticeship that allow for the purchase of tools, and other forms of gaining subsistence. Marriage is delayed until this possibility of subsistence is in hand, or it is renounced altogether by those who have no access to subsistence and are therefore condemned to vagabondage, emigration, military service, or domestic employment. Within the capitalist economy those with prospects of inheriting property are also likely to delay marriage until the time that this property yields an income for the family. For property-holders and property-users, therefore, the formation of families through marriage is related to property rights.

It is otherwise with proletarians. Their only form of 'property' is labour power, and the only source of subsistence is the wage. The earning of the wage is not connected with inheritance, but only with the biological and social maturity of the human organism to the point where sale of labour power on the market is possible. In an economy in which the youthful worker will be more readily taken by the firm because of his or her greater capacity for labour compared to older workers, and where skills are easily learned and experience counts for little, maximum wages are earned at a relatively young age. This means that marriage, once freed from a system of property rights, takes place at an earlier age than in economies in which peasant and artisanal production predominate, and is possible for almost all members of the class.[25]

Once the demographic shift is made to more frequent marriages and an earlier age at marriage, and the wage supplants property as the chief regulator of family formation, the market in labour power comes to be the important regulating mechanism. There appear to be two sides to this connection between the market in labour power and family formation. On the one hand, even in this market in which there are a great many uncertainties for the vendors, as is usually the case for the market in labour power, young workers have the best opportunities to secure employment.[26] On the other hand, *fluctuations* in the market in labour power can lead to fluctuation in family formation, as marriages must be delayed when the demand for labour power slackens,[27] but marriages are still undertaken earlier and more frequently than in a non-capitalist economy. The market in labour power comes to regulate marriage around a new set of norms, norms established by the dependence of the family on the wage, and the relative capacity of younger as opposed to older workers to secure wages.

Faced with declining wages and/or less certain wages in the future, the working-class newlyweds tend to experience a very short interval between marriage and the birth of the first child. Where children can, at an early age, contribute to the family's fund of consumption, through earning wages or assisting their parents in the production process, and where children can provide support in old age, it is likely to be considered advantageous for the conjugal unit to produce children whose capacity to labour will grow as their own strength is used up. Under these circumstances, children can be understood to be providing a form of security. For this reason this first stage in the reproductive cycle of the family may be brief, although it is the one in which the fund of consumption is greatest, relative to the number of consumers in the family. Whatever the duration of this stage, we assume that families will soon move into the next stage of the reproductive cycle.

(2) **From birth of first child to employment of a child.** The arrival of each infant in the proletarian family represents another consumer whose gainful employment is sometime in the future. Each birth thus places an additional burden on the family. The conjugal couple cannot, however, be certain that the first child born, or any child, will necessarily grow into a wage-earner or assistant to family wage-earners in the production process. With high infant mortality a great many births are necessary to ensure the future presence of a few children old enough to contribute to the family's fund of consumption. These conditions lead to high fertility in the proletarian family, and the limitation of fertility only when it appears certain that one or more children will be wage-earners.[28] The consequence of these considerations is that the proletarian family has a great many children in a short period of time, and finds itself in economic difficulty. The worker's wage may no longer cover the costs of consumption, and if time is to be spent nurturing dependent children, this creates the possibility that wives will withdraw from or limit their participation

in the market in labour power. With the arrival of the first child, and increasingly with the birth of subsequent children, the proletarian family faces difficulty in stretching the wage to purchase the necessaries of life.

(3) **From employment of a child to leaving home of last child.** Let us assume a mean age at marriage between 23 and 25 years of age for men, and the birth of a first child within the year after marriage. Children can earn substantial wages in their early teenage years, and reach their maximum earnings in the late teenage years. They can therefore add significantly to the family's fund of consumption by age 14, and add greatly to that fund by age 18. Ideally, this means that as the father in the household, who is usually the chief wage-earner, experiences a decline in earnings in his late thirties and early forties, there are employed children who help bridge the gap between the fund of consumption and the father's wage. The children can then contribute to the family's security, as anticipated.

As it turns out, however, it is unlikely that most families will realize this ideal state of affairs. First, as children enter employment, their consumption of food and clothing necessarily increases. Thus part of the increment in household income is used up in additional expenses that result directly from the wage-earning activity itself. Secondly, given that labour power is sold individually by the child, and the wage comes to him or her rather than to the family, there will be a tendency for children to limit their contributions to the family, and to retain a portion of the wage for private consumption outside the family.[29] Thirdly, and most important, as the child reaches the late teenage years he or she is reaching maximum earning capacity, and is likely to withdraw from the family altogether and establish a separate residence away from the financial demands made by the family.[30]

For the child this withdrawal from the family leads to the formation of a new conjugal unit within a few years. For the family it means that the first benefit anticipated from the next generation of wage-earners has failed to materialize. There is only a temporary expansion of the number of wage-earners the family is able to generate, and these wage-earners are able to limit their contributions to the family budget and to withdraw from the family altogether at an early date.

(4) **From leaving home of last child to death of a spouse.** This stage of the reproductive cycle of the family is likely to be brief, given prevailing mortality rates.[31] Yet old age can be regarded as another time of budgetary crisis in the family. While many older people are able to do useful labour, the sale of their labour power becomes problematic, because younger workers can do unskilled jobs more efficiently. For most older couples, therefore, the leaving home of the children marks the end of the family as a budgetary unit, and a time in which the

couple attaches itself to the family of one of the children of the marriage.

The Budgetary Crisis in the Proletarian Family

We have marked off the reproductive cycle of the family in terms of a number of budgetary turning points: marriage, birth, the maturing of children, and the leaving home of children. Except for marriage, each of these events marks some new turn in the problems faced by the family in trying to make the wage into an adequate fund of consumption. The birth of children adds consumers who are not to be wage-earners for a number of years and who, when they become wage-earners, are likely to limit their contributions to the family and eventually to withdraw altogether. Older couples, whose children have left home, do not recapture the budgetary surplus of the time when they were first married, because the sale of their labour power for wages is now problematic. In the absence of pensions, the security of older persons lies in attaching themselves to a child or children of the marriage. Indeed, for those who maintained a childless state this security would be lacking.

These budgetary turning points can be related to the questions of the price and value of labour power that we raised earlier. In the discussion of variable capital we saw that there were two sides to the problem of working class consumption in general: (1) the market-price of any family's labour power may be below the price of the commodities which enter into its consumption at any given standard of living; and (2) the price of labour power for the class as a whole can be pushed down, lowering the value of labour power and eroding the standard of living. Once we recognize that individual families have different balances between the prices of the labour power sold and the costs of consumption at different stages in the reproductive cycle, we can move the analysis one step further by suggesting that: (1) there are systematic variations of the balance between the price of labour power and the price of commodities which enter into consumption at different stages of the reproductive cycle of all families, so that the short-fall of wages is in most cases not random or accidental, but regularly produced by the cycle of human conjugality, birth, nurturance, and separation; (2) lowering the value of labour power will have different effects on families, depending on the stage of the reproductive cycle in which they find themselves. For families without children, lowering the value of labour power will not be as consequential as for those with a great many dependent children; in the latter case a fall in the value of labour power which has not been accompanied by a fall in the value of wage-goods may mean a reduction in consumption below the minimum necessary to sustain life.

Let us take up the first point, the problem of the changing balance between wages and consumption needs at different stages in the reproductive cycle. A simple, but somewhat lengthy, numerical example can be produced to show that because of the changing consumption costs in the family, a large proportion of all working class families will spend many years of the reproductive cycle earning wages which fall below the values of their specific labour powers. In order to produce this example, we will continue to assume that, *for the working class as a whole*, labour power is paid enough to cover the costs of consumption. Our example will show that the working class as a whole can earn wages equal to the costs of consumption, while individual families in substantial numbers regularly experience a short-fall of wages and become impoverished.

To begin we assume a constant average value and price of labour power and a constant average value and price of commodities. We also assume that there are no unusual expenses in the family, no unemployment, untimely deaths, and other misfortunes which reduce wages, eliminate them, or add burdensome expenses beyond subsistence costs. This means that no workers are underpaid, and that there are no extraordinary demands on the family budget which tax its capacity to cover the normal costs of consumption.

Our first task is to establish the average value of labour power in a competitive capitalist economy prior to the development of the welfare state. This value, which is equal to the average costs of consumption of all proletarians in the economy, can be derived by adding together the subsistence costs for major categories of expenditure. In Table 3.1 we have taken average weekly expenditures on food, clothing, rent, and fuel in mid-nineteenth century England to represent the average costs of consumption.[32] Table 3.1 reflects the different consumption costs of members at different age and sex categories of the population. Rent and fuel costs are based on households of five persons: one fifth of the average household costs are assigned to each family member, regardless of age.

It should be pointed out once again that the accuracy of the absolute level of thse costs is not of consequence for our argument, although these figures were drawn from standard sources on the nineteenth century. What is important is the fact that there are costs of consumption, that these vary among age and sex categories, and that they enter into the establishment of the average value of labour power.

Table 3.2 presents the age and sex distribution of the population of England and Wales for 1861. Taking the average costs of consumption for each of the age and sex categories of Table 3.1, and assigning them to the population of England and Wales, we can reckon that on

TABLE 3.1

Subsistence Costs in Old Pence per Week, by Age and Sex Categories,
Early Victorian Britain

Category	Food	Clothing	Rent	Fuel	Total
Adult Males 20-59	54d	8.0d	6d	3.6d	71.6d
Teenage Males 15-19	45.9	6.8	6	3.6	62.3
Adult Females 15-59	43.2	6.4	6	3.6	59.2
Children, Male and Female 5-14	27.0	4.0	6	3.6	40.6
Young Children Male and Female 0-4	18.0	2.7	6	3.6	30.3
Older Adults 60+	32.4	4.8	6	3.6	46.8

Source: John Foster, Class Struggle and the Industrial Revolution (Methuen, London, 1974).

average for every hundred people in the population the costs of consumption per week will average 5,332.1 old pence (d). This figure also represents the average value of labour power per hundred people; that is, in order to cover the subsistence costs of the population, wages must average 5,332d. per hundred people whose age and sex composition conforms to that of Table 3.2.

TABLE 3.2

Age and Sex Distribution, Population of England and Wales, 1861, in Per cent

	Sex	
Age	Male	Female
0-4	6.75%	6.71%
5-9	5.85	5.84
10-14	5.28	5.21
15-19	4.77	4.86
20-24	4.29	4.83
25-29	3.66	4.16
30-34	3.30	3.61
35-39	2.94	3.16
40-44	2.75	2.91
45-49	2.26	2.38
50-54	1.95	2.06
55-59	1.49	1.57
60+	3.43	3.98
	48.72%	51.28%

Source: Calculated from Samuel H. Preston, Nathan Keyfitz and Robert Schoen, *Causes of Death: Life Tables for National Populations* (Seminar Press, New York, 1972).

These calculations do not yield, as yet, an average value for individual labour power. We cannot divide the average value of labour power per hundred people by one hundred to give this average individual value, because many people, especially the very young and the very old, do not sell labour power. The average value of labour power must reflect this fact, and must take into account the further fact that the average value of labour power covers the cost of consumption of the worker and his family, the costs of maintaining and reproducing the family. In other words, the value of the labour power for all who work must cover the costs of all those who consume; in order for labour power to be paid at its value, wages must equal the costs of consumption of all who depend on those wages as a fund of consumption.

We must assess, therefore, the differential rates of participation in the labour forces of all those who work for wages, and the relative wages paid to each. For purposes of this demonstration we assume that all members of the population 5 years of age to 49 years of age are *potential* workers. We further assume that all men 15-49 years of age are actively selling labour power, half of the women 15-49 years of age work for wages, and that one-quarter of the children 5-14 years of age work also.[33] We follow Burnett, *A History of the Cost of Living*,[34] in estimating women's wages to be half those of men, on average, and children's wages to be one-quarter those of men. For our average hundred members of the population, as distributed in Table 3.2, men ages 15-49 will provide half the working population and through the sale of their labour power cover 75 per cent of the costs of consumption, women will provide 27.3 per cent of the labour-force and cover 20.4 per cent of the costs of consumption, and children will be 23.7 per cent of the labouring population and cover 4.9 per cent of the costs of consumption. (Figures for costs of consumption add up to more than 100 persons due to rounding errors). In terms of our numerical example we may now say that in order to cover the costs of consumption for the average population of 100 persons, reckoned at 5,332.1d., each man must bring home, on average, 121d. per week, each woman an average of 30.2d. per week, and each child 7.8d. per week.

People do not live, however, in units of 100 persons. We are assuming that this population lives in smaller, family units. Now that we know the average value of labour power for each category, and the average costs of subsistencies, we can put these together to see the average budgetary situation of different families of different compositions in different stages of the reproductive cycle. In Table 3.3 we have calculated the average costs of subsistence for families at different stages of the cycle, of different compositions, average value of labour power, and the surplus or deficit budgetary situation faced, on average, by different types of families. *The families presented in Table 3.3 are, of course, hypothetical.* We do not mean to imply that these families present all the age and sex combinations possible for family units, or that this table actually shows the range of families present in early Victorian England.

Table 3.3 shows that until the birth of the first child the conjugal couple with average income and average costs of consumption would show a small surplus of income over expenditure. The birth of the first child, however, would lead to a deficit on the average for the family and this deficit would increase with the birth of subsequent children. These figures are calculated on the basis of women continuing to work, and reflect the average of cases where that does take place,

TABLE 3.3

Average Subsistence Costs and Average Income in Old Pence per Week, by Reproductive Stage and Family Composition

Stage	Composition	Average Subsistence Costs	Average Income	Average Difference
1.	2 adults (male & female)	130.8	151.2	+ 20.4
2.	a) 2 adults, 1 young child	161.1	151.2	− 9.9
	b) 2 adults, 2 young children	191.1	151.2	− 40.2
	c) 2 adults, 3 young children	221.7	151.2	− 70.5
3.	a) 2 adults, 1 young child, 1 child	201.7	159.0	− 42.7
	b) 2 adults, 4 children	293.2	182.4	−110.8
	c) 2 adults, 6 children	374.4	198.0	−176.4
4.	2 older adults	93.0	0	− 93.8

and those where it does not.[35]

The maturing of a child or children to the point where they can sell their labour power alleviates this problem somewhat, but does not remove the deficit position of the family, because, on the average, children's wages do not cover their costs of consumption. For the older couples along the situation is extremely difficult. Although our not assigning an income to members of this category leads to an over-estimation of the degree to which families at this stage will live below subsistence, it still remains that the financial position of such couples is likely to be, on the whole, precarious.[36]

Give the subsistence costs detailed in Table 3.1, we are able to form a concrete notion of what it means to have costs of consumption below the average. Families in that circumstance would face the sharing of accommodation, and overcrowding, or residence in substandard dwellings whose rent was below the average, or both. They would also face a diet insufficient by mid-nineteenth century standards, inadequate clothing, and a lack of fuel for heating and cooking. These conditions would, of course, produce labour power easily used up, and incapable of a long period of intense work, posing problems for capitalist enterprise that we shall consider below. In this situation the hazards of human life among the working class present a great risk: unemployment, death of a wage earner, medical and funeral expenses, add a burden to families at the same time that many of these families are experiencing a systematic shortfall of wages. If we add to all of this the struggle to maintain the value of labour power, some appreciation of the structural problems of the working class in an exclusively market-based capitalist economy can be gained. The struggle over wages is a struggle for an increased fund of consumption, and is thus a struggle for family life at an adequate standard of subsistence.[37] This struggle is a struggle for a transfer of value, and the chief target of this struggle is the capitalist enterprise. Unfortunately, the widespread problems of maintaining a family at a level subsistence engenders a response among the proletariat that makes this struggle a difficult one, because it leads to increasing competition among workers for employment, holding wages at a low level and making organization difficult.

The Production of Labour Power

Given the logic of the reproductive cycle of the family, it will always be the case that a substantial number of proletarian families will live at a level below subsistence. In a sense, therefore, the economic struggle by the working class within capitalism can never be won, because a great many workers will always have a fund of consumption that is inadequate by the prevailing standards of their time and place. The only solution for the proletariat is to secure increased wages to the extent that those living at a level of subsistence below the average would at least be free from the day-to-day threat of death through starvation and disease. The mechanism for achieving this higher relative value of labour power is, of course, a collective struggle against capital. While individual labours, or even categories of labourers with some advantage on the market in labour power, may enjoy higher than average wages, this circumstance in itself does nothing to relieve the problem faced by the class as a whole.[38] The model we have advanced assumes a low average value of labour power. In the model a general rise in real wages is necessary to secure the maintenance and reproduction of the working class. As it turns out, the demographic response of the working class to its structural position is likely to work against the possibility of a rise in wages, and serve instead to create a tendency toward the lowering of them.

Taking first the reproductive cycles of the family in the economy we are modelling, we can find within its logic a constant tendency for the population to expand. Capitalist enterprise, as we have seen, seeks younger, more vigorous workers. Relatively high wages are reached early in life, and they are bound to diminish over time. As a result marriage and family formation takes place earlier in a capitalist economy than in a feudal economy. Moreover, looking forward to the time of the diminishing wage and unemployment, and understanding that children will be employable at an early age, the conjugal couple begins immediately after marriage to produce children. The mortality rates dictate the production of a great many childen in order to ensure the survival of a few who will be able to contribute to the family's fund of consumption and support parents in their old age. This dynamic leads to the constant increase of the proletariat, because it is more harmful to the family to underestimate the number of children necessary to have one or two reach maturity than it is to overestimate that number.

Once the problem of declining wages for the worker and security in later life for the conjugal couple lead to the production of many children, the supply of labour power begins to grow. Families with children cannot be supported at an average level of subsistence on the average wage paid in a competitive capitalist economy, as we have seen. Families are thus motivated to have women and children sell their labour power, even though this may lead to neglect of children's well-being. This increases the supply of labour power on the market, and further reinforces the tendency for capitalists to maintain wages at a low level. The demographic response of the working class thus works against the possibility of raising wages because of its effects on the economic mechanism of supply and demand. The intense competition for jobs also makes organization of the working class difficult in that hungry workers can easily be induced to take over the jobs of those on strike.

Considered by itself, then, independently of the cyclical dynamics of a capitalist economy, the logic of the reproductive cycle of the proletarian family leads to a tendency for the population to expand. With the expansion of the population comes an increase in the supply of labour power of even greater magnitude as more family members are motivated to seek work to augment the family's fund of consumption. Moreover, this labour power is conventionally paid at a lower rate than that of adult males, depreciating further the average value of the commodity. The production of labour power thus resembles the production of some other commodities produced by households within capitalist economies: as its price falls its supply increases, and it becomes increasingly difficult for producers to raise the price as the demographic dynamic intensifies competition among them. The result of this process is a crisis in the reproduction of the family.

Capitalism and Labour Power

We now must turn from the examination of the wage as a fund of consumption to an examination of its role as variable capital. We noted earlier that capitalists employ variable capital to buy a determinate quantity of labour power. In practice this means committing a variable capital of a certain magnitude to effect the hiring of a given number of labourers at a given rate of wages. The object for the capitalist is to maximize profits and to accelerate the further accumulation of capital which, at the level of the enterprise, involves an expansion of productive capacity. The employer therefore commits variable capital with a view to advancing these ends. We suggest above that the allocation of variable capital is not made in consideration of the consumption needs of the workers, but rather takes place in accordance with the requirements of the firm. We must now examine the expanded reproduction of capital in order to determine whether there is, within capitalism, any mechanism whereby the allocation of variable capital by the enterprise, and the amount of wages necessary for subsistence of the workers, are brought into equilibration.

There are, of course, circumstances under which capitalists would like to see workers enjoying a high standard of consumption. Producers of wage goods are fundamentally concerned with the purchasing power of the proletariat, which determines in part the ability of the enterprise to realize its products.[39] And all capitalists are concerned with the capacity of the workers to labour intensively for long periods of time, a capacity which can be linked in part to diet. But this concern for the level of consumption of the working class cannot be translated into higher wages paid by the individual enterprise without endangering the profitability and accumulation of that enterprise. Our argument is that the capitalist firm cannot resolve the contradiction between the wage as variable capital and the wage as a fund of consumption, even when capitalists are motivated to do so. In order for this difference to be bridged, capital would have to institute a system of differential wages so that wages would be paid according to the size of the family and its stage in the reproductive cycle, rather than according to the strength of the workers and the market in labour power. Or, there would have to be a general rise in wages in order to raise the level of consumption of the working class so that families with a fund of consumption below the average might yet enjoy a standard of living at an acceptable level.

The first possibility, that capitalists might pay higher wages to working men with families, does not require a lengthy discussion. There are, of course, differentials in wages paid within a capitalist economy. These differentials are linked to advantages in the market that some labourers are able to enjoy, because of demand for certain trades, the effectiveness of labour unions, regional scarcities in labour power, and other factors affecting the supply and demand for labour power. But there is no reason to suppose that extra-market factors, such as the size of the labourer's family, will enter into the determination of wage levels set in the purchase and sale of labour power. It may be the case that men with families will be understood to be more tractable or diligent employees, given the dependence of others on them for the earning of wages; but this circumstance will not lead the capitalist to pay such workers more and may, indeed, lead him or her to pay the worker less because such workers are less able to refuse an offer of employment, despite the fact that the wage bargain may be unfavourable. And if the principle of differential wages for employees with families were established by some third party, for example, the state or an association of capitalists concerned with the reproduction of the proletariat, the likely reaction on the part of individual capitalists would be to hire younger workers or those without families, to achieve the greatest possible reduction in the level of wages within the firm.[40]

The second possibility—that the crisis in the reproductive cycle of the family may be resolved by raising wages so that those with families, while enjoying a fund of consumption inadequate to provide the family with subsistence at an average level, might yet survive—requires a more extended discussion. Here we must consider the impact of the crisis of family reproduction on capitalist enterprise and on the capitalist economy.

On the one hand, the demographic cycle we have exposed does appear to have some utility for capitalist enterprise. The large number of unemployed put pressure on those in employment to work more intensively, and this serves to further reinforce the conditions that allow the capitalist to drive down wages.[41] And, as we have discussed, it is also the case that with families in a state of economic crisis the women and children who are motivated to work in order to provide the family with a fund of consumption are conventionally paid lower wages. As men accept lower wages for more work, and women and children enter the labour force, the price of labour power tends to decline, causing a rise in the mass of surplus value, which is, of course, beneficial to enterprise in the long run.

In the long run, however, the crisis of reproduction of the proletarian family is injurious to some sectors of capitalist enterprise. This can be understood if we think of the amount of labour power individual labourers can expend when undernourished, ill-housed and ill-clothed. The increasing population of labourers we have described is made up of 'generations of human beings stunted, short-lived, swiftly replacing each other, plucked so to say, before maturity'.[42] While the excess of population relative to jobs available serves to drive down wages, the conditions of this population makes the utility of its labour power problematic. The using of the labouring capacity of this population means that at any one time large numbers are not suitable for work, and that capitalists must consequently go to the countryside for new workers at some cost to themselves.[43] At the same time, and perhaps more important for the capitalist enterprise, this condition of the working class places limits on the expansion of profits and on accumulation. In the situation we have described, the mass of capital committed to any individual enterprise tends to be quite small. Variable capital is small, and takes the form of low wages paid to a relatively large number of workers. The value of constant capital, especially the machines used in production, also tends to be modest. There is a high *rate* of surplus value, however, and a high rate of profit. But accumulation is slow because the *mass* of surplus value generated in any one enterprise is small, and because there is in general little reason to achieve higher productivity through investment in more constant capital. Marx described the situation in the following terms:

> So far as it is based on a high rate of surplus-value, a high rate of profit is possible when the working day is very long, although labour is not highly productive. It is possible, because the wants of the labourers are very small, hence average wages very low, although labour itself is unproductive. The low wages will correspond to the labourers' lack of energy. Capital then accumulates slowly, in spite of the high rate of profit.[44]

In paying low wages, therefore, the capitalist commits himself to a system of production that place barriers to the expansion of the mass of profit available to him and to the amount of accumulation that might take place. In attempting to increase the rate of profit the capitalist has recourse to the increase of absolute surplus value by lengthening the working day or by increasing the intensity of work. But the lengthening of the working day faces diminishing returns: as the long working day unfolds the labourers' effectiveness diminishes, making the final hours of each shift inefficient and wasteful. Adding additional hours may add very little to production. Also the costs of supervision when an attempt is made to increase the intensity of work will be very high, given the natural lack of energy of ill-paid workers.[45]

Any attempt to increase profits and accumulation by attempting to increase relative surplus value through an increase in productivity is also problematic under these circumstances. With low wages there is little to be gained from replacing workers with machines. Despite the fact that profit and accumulation remain stagnant, although profits are high, capitalists are slow to undertake investment in constant capital that would raise productivity and reduce necessary labour-time. This system of production thus places barriers to the expansion of production, which can only take place by increasing the number of labourers set to work once the limits of the expansion of absolute surplus value are reached, that is, through extensive accumulation. And it also sets limits to the reproduction of labour power, as wages remain low or are driven down still further.[46]

It is also the case that labour power reproduced under these circumstances has limited use-value for any sectors of production which have invested more heavily in constant capital. With a conversion to machine production it is more costly to employ large numbers of stunted labourers than a small number capable of more intense work, because more constant capital, more machines, must be acquired to have a larger number of slower-working labourers producing the same quantity of commodities as a smaller number of workers labouring at a higher intensity.[47] As enterprises invest more and more in constant capital and as machines become more and more costly, it becomes even more important to have a smaller number of labourers of higher quality. Ironically, then, attempts to raise productivity run into a situation in which there are large numbers of labourers whose labouring capacity is limited and the reproductive costs of constant capital within the enterprise itself are likely to be high. Thus the quality of labour power itself sets barriers to the possibility of raising productivity.

In the economy we are discussing the expansion of profit and accumulation of the enterprise is limited to additive measures, that is, is restricted to increasing the capacity to make commodities by adding on new units of production at existing levels of productivity. Accumulation is slow, and small masses of variable and constant capital are committed by the enterprise. The restriction on variable capital leads to a low rate of wages. The low rate of wages produces a stunted proletariat, which in turn places barriers to raising either absolute or relative surplus value. While in theory capitalist enterprise might intervene to break this cycle by raising wages in order to help create a proletariat whose labour power is of high quality, the profit position makes this impossible; it is likely that by the time the labour power of higher quality appeared on the market, making investment in machines worthwhile, the enterprise itself would have suffered a severe reduction in profit, and its own reproduction would be threatened.

The crisis in the reproduction of the working class thus brings capitalism to the point where it is unable to solve it. Capitalists cannot increase wages without reducing profits and harming the competitive position of the enterprise. Even though a higher rate of wages serves to support the reproduction of labour power of higher quality which facilitates productivity increases and accelerates the rate of accumulation, capital is unlikely to raise wages on its own. Indeed, given the demographic response of workers to a low price for labour power, they are in general not likely to be in a position to force wage increases on capital.[48]

The equilibration between variable capital and family consumption costs is thus likely. The low rate of wages provides little motivation for capital to undertake the wholesale transformation of productive processes which ultimately would lead to an economy based on higher average wages but a lower production of variable capital employed in production. Thus a general intra-economic solution to the crisis somehow emerging from the logic of the expanded reproduction of capitalism cannot be envisioned.

The Solution To The Crisis

In our model of a capitalist economy the *sale* of labour power is social; it occurs within the nexus of the reproduction of capital. The *reproduction* of labour power is, however, private; it generally takes place outside the jurisdiction of capital, in families and households, and is separated from the circuit of capital. The use value of labour power is, of course, of interest to the capitalist but it is determined by processes and undertakings that occur behind 'closed doors'. The only point of intervention available to the capitalist is the wage. And the magnitude of the wage is, as we have seen, in this economy a product of economic factors which exist independently of the capitalist's interest in the production of labour power of higher quality. Capitalists raise and lower wages because of the operation in the market for labour power, which in turn can be influenced by the economic struggle of the working class. But there is no self-regulating mechanism within capitalism to establish wages at the level that will produce the optimum use value of labour power for capitalist production. Indeed the crisis in the reproduction of labour power can reach an apocalyptic stage, threatening capitalist production as a whole, while the individual enterprises remain helpless to redress the problem.

Two types of solutions to this crisis are possible. The first is an economic accident, the second lies outside of the exchange of labour power for wages. The economic accident is predicted on the fact that the non-equilibration of costs of consumption and variable capital can work in favour of the worker, and is based on the assumption that wages are less elastic than the prices of consumption goods.[49] We assume that when the prices of food and other wage goods fall, therefore, employers do not immediately lower wages, just as when prices rise workers must fight for wage rises which do not automatically occur. Under these circumstances a fall in the price of consumer goods will lead to a general rise of real wages, and a period of steady decline will lead to a continuing increase in real wages. A generation-long period of falling prices may lead to a rather substantial general rise in the value of labour power.[50]

This solution can be only temporary, however. It can always be reversed by a period of rising relative prices, and in any case leaves a substantial proportion of families at a level of consumption below the contemporary average, albeit at a level that represents some earlier average.

The second solution to the crisis of reproduction of the working class is enduring. It lies outside of the exchange of labour power for wages. The main lines of this solution lie in a transfer of value in the form of money or commodities to those families in the most critical stages of the reproductive cycle, or to those families without wages or whose wages are insufficient.

This second solution follows from the understanding that the crisis of working class reproduction is based on a *distributional* problem. The uneven distribution of wages on the one hand and consumption needs on the other means that some families have a surplus of income over subsistence costs, while other families experience a deficit. If there were some mechanism for redistributing wages among families to more closely cover consumption needs, then all families might be guaranteed survival. The second solution can be called into play by adopting an insurance scheme whereby unemployed workers receive some income, or a scheme where money raised through taxation is redistributed to those with larger families and hence larger consumption costs relative to income.[51]

The economic function of social welfare is, therefore, to act as a redistributive mechanism for money among working class families.

Social insurance legislation has, of course, been adopted in all industrial capitalist nations, and, as such, its introduction marks 'the basic institutional breakthrough of the modern welfare state'.[52] Through this mechanism the state gathers up and redistributes among the workers the contributions that they themselves have made, and thereby contributes to the solution of the crisis of working class reproduction. The redistribution of tax money through mothers' allowances and other forms of stipend completes the redistributive function of social welfare.

The history of the origins of these transfer payments, and the history of the discovery that taxes and premium levies from the working class could be used to support working class reproduction, lie outside the scope of this paper. We can say that insofar as these schemes are state-administered and stage-regulated they lead to state control over working class reproduction. The extent to which the state in contemporary industrial economies actually exercises this control is a question for further investigation, as are the contradictory outcomes of these interventions, some of which are addressed in other chapters in this volume.

Notes and References

1. For example, Suzanne de Brunhoff, *The State, Capital and Economic Policy* (Pluto Press, London, 1978); James O'Connor, *The Fiscal Crisis of the State* (St. Martin's Press, New York, 1973); and Michel Aglietta, *A Theory of Capitalist Regulation: The U.S. Experience* (NLB, London, 1979).
2. Representative discussions include Claus Offe, *Contradictions of the Welfare State* (Hutchinson, London, 1984); Ian Gough, *The Political Economy of the Welfare State* (Macmillan, London, 1979); and Jacques Donzelot, *The Policing of Families* (Pantheon, New York, 1979).
3. A discussion of the definitions of social welfare is found in Glenn Drover and Allan Moscovitch, 'Inequality and Social Welfare', in Allan Moscovitch and Glenn Drover (eds.), *Inequality: Essays on the Political Economy of Social Welfare* (University of Toronto Press, Toronto, 1981), p. 3.
4. Recent examples of work along this line are Derek Fraser, *The Evolution of the British Welfare State* (Macmillan, London, 1973); and Peter Flora and Arnold J. Heindenheimer (eds.), *The Development of Welfare States in Europe and America* (Transaction Books, New Brunswick, NJ, 1981).
5. As in Frances Fox Piven and Richard A. Cloward, *Regulating the Poor* (Vintage, New York, 1971). Piven and Cloward's study, subtitled 'The Functions of Social Welfare', relies heavily on historical evidence of the experience in the United States to elucidate these functions.
6. For an elaboration of this point, see Barry Hindess and Paul Q. Hirst, *Precapitalist Modes of Production* (Routledge and Kegan Paul, London, 1975), p. 19.
7. Karl Marx, *Capital*, Vol. I (Progress Publishers, Moscow, n.d.), p. 19.

8. This point is developed in Wolfgang Muller and Cristel Neususs, 'The "Welfare-State Illusion" and the Contradiction between Wage Labour and Capital', in John Holloway and Sol Picciotto (eds.), *State and Capital* (Edward Arnold, London, 1978).

9. The most useful sources are Michael Anderson, *Family Structures in Nineteenth Century Lancashire* (Cambridge University Press, Cambridge, 1971); Geoffrey Best, *Mid-Victorian Britain 1851-75* (Panther, Frogmore, 1973); John Burnett, *A History of the Cost of Living* (Penguin Books, Harmondsworth, Middlesex, 1969); S.G. and E.O. Checkland (eds.), *The Poor Law Report of 1834* (Penguin Books, Harmondsworth, Middlesex, 1974); E.J. Hobsbawm, *Industry and Empire* (Penguin Books, Harmondsworth, Middlesex, 1969); David Levine, *Family Formation in an Age of Nascent Capitalism* (Academic Press, New York, 1977); and Louise A. Tilley and Joan W. Scott, *Women, Work and Family* (Holt, Rinehart, New York, 1978).

10. John Foster, *Class Struggle and the Industrial Revolution* (Methuen, London, 1974).

11. Marx, *Capital*, I, p. 532.

12. '(Capital) . . . can spring to life only when the owner of the means of production and subsistence meets in the market with the free labourer selling his labour-power.' Marx, *Capital*, I, p. 167.

13. Marx, *Capital*, I, p. 533.

14. The family is not the only possible unit of working class reproduction, but it has tended to be the modal unit. Workers have lived in family units even when it was financially difficult to do so, and even when it was administratively difficult for workers to marry they have attempted to form 'free unions' with the stability of marriage. See Tilly and Scott, *Women, Work and Family*, p. 96-97.

15. Karl Marx, *Grundrisse* (Penguin Books, Harmondsworth, Middlesex, 1973), p. 283-284.

16. Marx, *Capital*, I, p. 167.

17. Ibid., p. 168.

18. c.f. Suzanne de Brunhoff, *The State, Capital and Economic Policy*, p. 13.

19. Karl Marx, *Wages, Price and Profit* (Progress Publishers, Moscow, 1947), p. 50-51.

20. Marx, *Wages*, p. 52.

21. It would be possible in the simple economy we are modelling here to have labour powers of different qualities with different values and different prices. It does not detract from the validity of our argument, however, to assume in the early stages of the discussion that all labour power is of average value and average quality, and to assume that quality is relatively low, that is, unskilled or semi-skilled. We shall later complicate the model by assuming that prices for labour power vary by age and sex.

22. Marx, *Wages*, p. 51.

23. Marx, *Capital*, I, p. 537.

24. For extended discussions of the definition of 'family' see, Lawrence Stone, *The Family, Sex and Marriage in England 1500-1800* (Harper Row, New York, 1979), Chapter 1; and Jean-Louis Flandrin, *Families in Former Times* (Cambridge University Press, Cambridge, 1979), Introduction.

25. Levine, *Family Formation*, p. 11.

26. As Levine points out in his study of proletarianized knitters in the early capitalist era, 'The propensity among framework knitters to marry earlier can be explained by the relatively few obstacles a young man had to overcome before reaching his prime earning capacity. Moreover, there was a significant likelihood that a stockinger's wife would also be employed, so that it was not as difficult for a young couple to establish a household.' Levine, *Family Formation*, p. 51. See also Anderson, *Family Structure*, p. 132.

27. Levine shows that when there was a depression in the framework knitting industry the age of marriage for men rose, but not to pre-capitalist levels. Levine, *Family Formation*, p. 63. See also Tilly and Scott *Women, Work and Family*.

28. Levine, *Family Formation*, p. 28. A slightly different strategy seems to have been adopted by Indian villagers whose children were destined for wage labour, as described by Mahmood Mamdani, *The Myth of Population Control* (Monthly Review, New York, 1972).

29. Anderson, *Family Structure*, p. 129.

30. Ibid., p. 128ff.

31. Anderson's data for 1851 indicate that by age 65 almost 65% of all women would be widows, and almost 50% of all men would be widowers. Foster's data show the proportion of old couples without children ranged from 2 to 18% of all families in the towns studied, a much smaller proportion in each town than in the previous state of the cycle. Anderson, *Family Structure*, p. 140; Foster, *Class Struggle*, p. 98.

32. Foster has used a variety of nineteenth century sources to arrive at these figures, although he relies most heavily on A. Bowley, *Livelihood and Poverty* (Bell, London, 1915). The figure for food is calculated on the basis of dietary habit for working class families at a subsistence level. The weighting of food and clothing expenditures for different family members follows Foster and Bowley exactly. Rent and fuel costs are averages assigned equally to all family members. These estimations leave out the major expenses which occur infrequently and for which budgeting is difficult: medical and burial expenses. The effect of these expenses when they occur, and the attempts of some workers to budget for them, are described in Maude Pember Reeves, *Round About a Pound a Week* (Virago, London, 1979).

33. These assumptions are based on Foster's figures for mother's and children's rates of employment in Northampton and Oldham, 1849-51. I have inflated the figures for female labour force participation to reflect the fact that non-mothers in the 15-49 year age group would be more likely to work outside the household.

34. John Burnett, *Cost of Living*.

35. These figures fit with the empirical experience of workers in the towns studied by Foster; his data show rates of poverty among the working class to vary between 78% and 89% of the families with young children.

36. Foster's empirical data are somewhat at variance with the outcome of our model, since some older people are actually able to secure an income and/or could depend on kin. In his study over 50% of the older couples lived at a level below subsistence.

37. See Bruce Curtis, 'Capital, the State and the Origins of the Working Class

Household', in Bonnie Fox (ed.), *Hidden in the Household: Women's Domestic Labour Under Capitalism* (Women's Press, Toronto, 1980).

38. A situation elaborated in E.J. Hobsbawm, *Labouring Men* (Weidenfield and Nicolson, London, 1968).

39. Marx, *Grundrisse*, p. 287; c.f. Michel Aglietta, *A Theory of Capitalist Regulation*, p. 181ff.

40. It is true that some capitalists, such as Lever in nineteenth century Britain, and Ford in the U.S. in the twentieth century have raised wages with a view to increasing the quality of labour power and turning workers into consumers. But such experiments have not been widely found in capitalism.

41. Marx, *Capital*, I, p. 595.

42. Ibid., p. 256.

43. Ibid., p. 254-5.

44. Karl Marx, *Capital*, Vol. III (Progress Publishers, Moscow, 1971), p. 245-6.

45. Geoffrey Kay, *The Economic Theory of the Working Class* (Macmillan, London, 1979), p. 47.

46. c.f. Marx, *Capital*, III, p. 247ff.

47. 'It is the absolute interest of every capitalist to press a given quantity of labour out of a smaller, rather than a greater number of labourers, if the cost is about the same,' because of this saving in constant capital. Marx, *Capital*, I, p. 595.

48. As Hobsbawm points out the skilled and organized workers may be able to secure wage rises, but this group is only a fraction of the working class. Hobsbawm, *Industry and Empire*, p. 160-61.

49. The source of this assumption is Foster's examination of wages, prices, and profits over time in the cotton industry. Foster, *Class Struggle*, p. 82-3.

50. This conjuncture actually did occur in the late nineteenth century in Britain.

51. The working class discovered long ago the virtues of redistribution of value through kin and friendship networks, friendly societies, and other mechanisms. See Anderson, *Family Structure*, p. 78-9 on the sharing of lodgings.

52. Flora And Heindenheimer, *Welfare States*, p. 50.

4

RETHINKING THE WELFARE STATE: DEPENDENCE, ECONOMIC INDIVIDUALISM AND THE FAMILY

Eli Zaretsky

Sociology and The Welfare State

Since the early nineteenth century sociologists have supplied much of the underlying rationale for the construction of the welfare state. The discipline of sociology arose in part by rejecting the individualism and rationalism embodied in classical political economy and political philosophy. The earliest sociological theories—for example, those of August Comte—reflect a romantic stress on the affective and moral ties that bind society together. Both Weber and Durkheim argued, against every variety of economic determinism, that economic transactions occurred within a moral and social, if not religious, context. When industralization and urbanism threatened to destroy the traditional moral structure of Western society, such figures as Lester Ward in America and Beatrice and Sidney Webb in England argued that an expansion of government was necessary to maintain the 'welfare function' traditionally provided by association and mutual aid. Even advocates of laissez-faire and opponents of the welfare state such as William Graham Sumner and William I. Thomas in America were mostly concerned that government might interfere with local, voluntary and group processes of self-help and mutual support. As Marcel Mauss wrote in *The Gift*,[1] 'we are returning to a group morality . . . The theme of the gift, of freedom and obligation in the gift, or generosity and self-interest in giving, reappear in our own society like the resurrection of a dominant motif long forgotten . . . I believe that we must become, in proportion as we would develop our wealth, something more than better financiers, accountants and administrators. The mere pursuit of individual ends is harmful to the ends and peace of the whole'.

The polemical stance which sociologists have adopted toward nineteenth-century political economy has tended to obscure an underlying continuity. A fundamental question, apparently never addressed within the discipline of sociology, concerns the relationship between group morality and 'social control' in the sociological sphere to competitive individualism and private property in the economic. Specifically, would not the disintegrative effects of capitalist market relations erode any program to strengthen ties of mutual obligation? This problem of social—not economic—privation motivates the following examination of the origins of the modern welfare state, and its relation to the family. How a society treats its helpless and dependent members is one of the best clues to its inner nature. For society, as for the individual, the capacity to give and receive aid is entwined with issues of trust, shame, ethical obligation and even with the capacity to embody and accept authority. Therefore, any elucidation of the relations between economic individualism and social interdependence should contribute to our understanding of modern society. I begin with an account of the general framework of thought within which the question has been posed.

Modern thinking concerning social welfare, aid to the indigent, the unemployed or the disabled is generally considered to have begun during the sixteenth century, for example in the writings of Juan Vives and other humanists. From the start its aim was to minimize, and if possible eliminate, the sphere of dependence. In contrast to the enormous charity and philanthropy in ancient and medieval society, and in the great world religions (sedakah, caritas), modern Western reform has sought to eliminate charity, rationalize philanthropy, and to whatever extent possible put in their place self-support. In this sense, the growth of the welfare state is a logical extension of the nation-state itself. Beginning in the sixteenth and seventeenth centuries, charity lost its religious meaning and society became the object of benevolence and enlightened planning. Republican ideals of virtue underlay this development: reformers sought an association of more or less equal, independent and mutually committed individuals (or individual families) as opposed to the older politics of lineage, estate and patrimonial dependence. As Morris Janowitz has pointed out, in the nineteenth century, the great liberal and laissez-faire theorists such as James Mill, Jeremy Bentham and John Stuart Mill supplied the rationale for social reform, including social welfare. A.V. Dicey in his influential lectures showed how government had freed the economic order i.e. the market from archaic and feudal restraints.[2] This served as a precedent for the idea that state laws and agencies could similarly transform archaic terms of charity into a social welfare system aimed at encouraging economic self-reliance rather than begging.

This argument, in turn, proved conformable with the growth of the modern 'nuclear' family with its own individualistic ideals. The reformers in nineteenth-century England and America who built the first state orphan asylums, mental hospitals, retreats and prisons took the well-ordered Victorian household as the model for their efforts. By the end of the century advocates of social welfare urged reforms—especially the abolition of child labour—aimed at eliminating 'paternal tyranny' in the working class family. Professional associations and state agencies, reformers argued, had now to perform a host of socially necessary tasks once performed by the family, such as care for emigrants or for the aged, or the vocational education of children.

In America, Jane Addams was probably the clearest and most influential early twentieth-century representative of the view that a growing sense of group morality and of individual independence and autonomy went together. In *Democracy and Social Ethics*, Addams argued the need to replace the sticky dependence of the 'family claim' with a 'social ethic' based upon individual responsibility to others.[3] In Europe Emile Durkheim argued that the growing interdependence of modern society enhanced individualism rather than undermining it.[4] William I. Thomas and Florian Znaniecki's *The Polish Peasant in Europe and America* warned social workers and reformers that state intervention invariably acted dissolvingly on group ties and urged the value of ethnic associations and other varieties of communal self-help in helping the immigrants to adapt to the individualistic world they had entered.[5] In *The Gift* (1925) Mauss similarly warned that modern welfare programs might take the individual, and not groups, as the 'social cell', and thereby undermine reciprocity, the social basis of individuality itself.[6]

The most systematic theory of the welfare state was produced by Talcott Parsons and his associates during and after World War Two. Parsons conceptualized a process of increasing 'differentiation' according to which the rise of specialized institutions left the family better adapted to its unique tasks, especially childrearing. Parsons explicitly portrayed 'professionals' as a new class, inexplicable in traditional Marxist terms, characterized by both individual autonomy and altruistic responsibilities. Adopting a 'systems' approach, Parsons and his followers argued that an increasingly 'differentiated' society would harmonize its different interests and needed no overall 'plan'. The concept of a 'transfer of functions' from individuals and private families to governmental institutions and professional services helped justify the enormous expansion of welfare services which occurred during the New Deal.[7]

The creation of mass programs of social welfare during the 1930s and 1940s intensified the interest of sociologists but no new macrosociological works were produced. T. H. Marshall, the British sociologist, in *Social Class and Citizenship* described the process by which political citizenship was extended and redefined to include the rights to receive social welfare or protection.[8] Richard Titmuss in Great Britain and Harold Wilensky in the United States tried to show, through comparative studies, that among industrialized nations the form of government was a secondary factor in determining the amount of welfare expenditures.[9] Instead, these varied with the size of the per capita gross national product, the length of time the welfare system existed and the size of the old-age population. Sociologists assumed that social welfare increased social equality and thereby strengthened political democracy, but by the 1960s it was shown that increased social welfare expenditures did not lead to any redistribution of income and that increases in social welfare were not reducing the demand for welfare, services and transfer payments but that, instead, these were steadily increasing.[10]

The first challenge to the sociological conventions concerning social welfare came from other disciplines. In 1971, David Rothman's *The Discovery of the Asylum* reframed the issue of social welfare to bring out its coercive aspects. Rothman's account of the first state institutions devoted to rehabilitating deviant and dependent individuals stressed their 'social control' aspect, which for Rothman meant their use by middle class Americans to 'control' lower class immigrants.[11] In spite of the great amount of research and rethinking which Rothman's work inspired, the concept of social control proved both vague and ahistorical. In particular, Rothman did not analyze the structure of nineteenth-century America to explain the roots of the then-new distinction between the 'normal' and 'deviant' individual or family. In the same year Frances Piven and Richard Cloward, two political scientists focussing on the 1930s and 1960s, argued in *Regulating the Poor* that public welfare expanded and contracted cyclically: 'expansive relief policies are designed to mute civil disorder, and restrictive ones to reinforce work norms.'[12] Like Rothman, Piven and Cloward viewed social welfare as an instrument wielded by the upper classes and the government against the poor; they did not account either for the fact that so much social welfare has been won *by* the lower classes, nor for the perhaps subtler coercive pressures that the welfare state placed upon those middle-class Americans who remained ostensibly within its norm.

More recently, three different lines of analysis have emerged, each containing elements that point toward a new synthesis. In France, Michael Foucault rejected the sovereignty theory of power according to which power is 'held' by a class, or by government, and wielded, 'at a distance'. Instead Foucault developed a kind of field theory of modern power relations involving an 'infinitely minute web of panoptic techniques.' Power for Foucault is not possessed, like property, but is immanent, non-subjective and relational; it functions like a piece of machinery which includes its objects. Its aspects include the 'distribution of bodies', 'hierarchical observation', 'normalizing judgement', examination, classification: the inner working of modern social science itself.[13] Foucault's account—which develops earlier insights of Nietzsche and Weber—redirects our attention to the microstructure of mutually constitutive relationships, equally comprising knowledge and power, which constitute the social structure of the welfare state. One work, directly influenced by Foucault, is Jacques Donzelot's *The Policing of Families* which shows how the dissolution of the traditional, patriarchal family in France was promulgated and followed by the emergence of a network of doctors, preachers, social scientists, government officials and mothers so that rule by the family became rule through the family.[14]

Independently, Christopher Lasch's two recent works established outlines of a related synthesis. In *Haven in a Heartless World* Lasch argued that the welfare state arose out of twentieth-century corporate capital's socialization and reorganization of the sphere of private or familial life (the 'second industrial revolution'). As opposed to Rothman and Piven and Cloward, Lasch described a society-wide transformation, and, rather than one directed at an underclass, like Foucault, focussed on the 'increasingly dense, opaque network of interpersonal relations so characteristic of advanced societies'.[15] Lasch's next work, *The Culture of Narcissism*, pointed to the disintegrative effects that this reorganization had on the character structure of all men, women and children. Rejecting criticisms of the welfare state in terms of failed economic promises or cultural and ethnic prejudice, Lasch argued that the expansion of the welfare state represented an assault on primary human ties themselves.[16] In both works, Lasch argued that modern social science rested upon utopian, perfectionist and behaviorist assumptions concerning human nature. In their place, Lasch used psychoanalysis to call attention to the instinctual roots of human individuality and creativity, the centrality of sexual love, parenthood and the family in the preservation and enhancement of these roots.

Finally, recent work by feminists such as Adrienne Rich, Barbara Ehrenreich, Dierdre English, Nancy Chodorow and others have revived an older feminist point—namely that the 'welfare functions' of modern society including health, education, welfare, etc., have traditionally been women's work and, to a great extent, remain so.[17] The asymmetry of the sexes, which begins with the mother-child relationship, sets in motion the psychology of human dependence and independence, the functioning of which in modern society is, from different points of view, both Lasch's and Foucault's primary concern.

Like Foucault, Donzelot, Lasch and the recent feminist works, my concern is with the psychosocial bases of the welfare state and its connections with the family. The second part of this essay is an account of the nature of dependence in traditional society and the relations between group relations of dependence and the couple. A third part describes the birth of modern thinking concerning social welfare and links it to the emergence of the modern ideal of the family. Part four examines the emergence of the welfare state in early twentieth-century America and seeks to show that the compromises involved in facing the questions of dependence in a modern industrial society were related to the limited capacity of the society to sustain and support sexually loving couples and marriages. Part five examines the political context that gave shape to the early welfare state and shows how the commitment to social welfare concealed a prior commitment to economic individualism in the form of the family wage. A conclusion summarizes the main points of essay.

Dependence and Inequality In Traditional Society

Marxism, sociology and psychoanalysis have all isolated different aspects of human interdependence: the social relations of production, the primordial ties of ethical obligation, and intimate object relations ultimately rooted in the mother/infant relationship. Of the three, however, psychoanalysis comes closest to identifying the problem of psychological dependence posed by an analysis of the welfare state.

In an important article, psychoanalyst Willard Gaylin described some of the biological and psychological limits of human independence. At one end of life, there is infancy, characterized by prolonged helplessness; at the other end, there is sickness, old age and death. 'All of us', Gaylin writes, 'inevitably spend our lives evolving from an initial to a final stage of dependence. If we are fortunate enough to achieve power and relative independence along the way, it is a transient and passing glory.'[18] This perspective directs attention to the fact that dependence, nurturance and mutual help are an inevitable part of any society, even one like our own ostensibly organized around individualism and independence. In addition, women, in their role as mothers, are the primary caretakers of those in need and, until recently, were themselves seen as the 'weaker' or more dependent sex. It is a tragic paradox that the bases of love, dependence and altruism in human life and the historical oppression of women have been found within the same matrix.

One clue to explaining this paradox lies in the relationship between nurturant care and sexuality ultimately arising from women's role in mothering. Freud believed that sexual desire arose, for both sexes, in the experience of being cared for but that social organization necessitated the repression of these original urges, wishes and desires. Adult sexuality, for Freud, involves a reawakening and transcendence of the passions of childhood as well as of the repressions against them. For the adult, this repression works through the superego, understood as the representative of the larger society, originally embodied in the parents, and operating as part of one's self. Sexual love always involves freedom from society (e.g., adultery), but never definance (with its implicit submission). In the long run the sexual couple needs to be able to return to the larger group from which it originally escaped. The group's acceptance of the genuine sexuality (i.e. experiences and feelings, not behaviours) of its members is a good mark of the capacity of a society to tolerate the individuality and freedom of its members. The fact that women as the primary caretakers are also the primary objects of love may be the reason why sexual repression in general—on which the social structure rests—has been primarily aimed at women, evidently on a world basis. Sexual repression is, of course, only one strand in women's oppression but it lends that oppression its special edge.[19]

My account of the origin of the welfare state follows Weber in distinguishing three periods in the West's sense of ethical obligation: 1) kinship and tribal relations, 2) Christian universalism and 3) economic individualism.[20] I add, however, that each period also changed the relations between the sexes. The shift from a tribally-based to a universalistic (i.e., Christian) ethic encouraged individual responsibility and a strengthening of the heterosexual couple but still as a subordinate part of the larger community. The gradual disengagement of the couple from the group made possible in the epoch of economic individualism encouraged some liberation of sexuality, especially female sexuality, but was accompanied by a heightened emphasis on domesticity and on women's role as mother: a process tending to continue the desexualization of marriage and the conformist submission of the couple to the group.

Until the rise of economic individualism, beginning in the sixteenth and seventeenth centuries, the idea that the individual, or private, nuclear family should be essentially responsible for supporting itself did not exist. Karl Polanyi writes that until the rise of a market system the individual was 'not threatened by starvation unless the community as a whole is in a like predicament ... The principle of freedom from want was equally acknowledged under almost every and any type of social organization up to about the beginning of sixteenth-century Europe, when the modern ideas on the poor put forth by the humanist Vives were argued before the Sorbonne.'[21] Similar principles characterize the 'moral economy' of peasants worldwide: subsistence conditions apparently necessitate a readiness to share.[22] A striking study of dependence in a non-Western setting is Octave Mannoni's study of colonial Madagascar. According to Mannoni, a Madagascaran native, receiving a favour from the French colonialist, expresses no gratitude but instead asks for further assistance or help. Gratitude presupposes equality. The Madagascaran, by contrast, seeks to re-establish his or her place in the network of dependencies which colonialism has disturbed.[23]

Medieval Christianity, writes Ernst Troeltsch, aimed at 'creating a haven of vital mutual aid within the pagan environment.' 'It is the aim of the Church to give parental care to the orphan, to be a husband to the widow, to help those who are ready for marriage to make a home, to give work to the unemployed, to show practical compassion to those who cannot work, to give shelter to the stranger, food to the hungry, drink to the thirsty, to see that the sick are visited, and that help is forthcoming for the prisoners.'[24] By the church was meant the community of all believers. Charity aimed at awakening the spirit of love in the donor as well as in the recipient, and thereby bound them together. According to Brian Tierney, the keystone of the medieval poor law was St. Ambrose's statement: 'no one may call his own what is common', in which 'common' meant 'to be shared in time of need.'[25] Within this ethical framework, the household with its 'family governor' or 'good lordship' was the primary institution responsible for maintaining charity and dependence—a large responsibility, given the still unmeasured extent of premodern poverty.

In colonial New England, the chief responsibility of the state was to see that family governors performed such responsibilities as care for the poor, the widowed, the disabled, education and training. If a family failed to perform these tasks the state might intervene; for example, the Massachusetts Assembly of 1745 ordered all children over the age of six who were still ignorant of the alphabet removed to another family. Similarly, in England until the middle of the seventeenth century, the insane were cared for almost wholly within private families.[26] The family, therefore, was, to a great extent, a 'public' institution. The beginnings of the modern welfare state, to which I now turn, was accompanied by the family becoming a 'private' unit, ostensibly subject to the unique desires of its members.

Prehistory of The Welfare State

In the sixteenth century the traditional Catholic ideals of charity came under attack from a variety of converging sources: merchants, Protestants, humanists and state officials among others. The common element in the diverse and far-flung state reforms of the era was the establishment of the distinction between the deserving, i.e. ill, crippled or aged, and the undeserving poor and the effort to put the latter to work. This was the subject of Vives' *De Subventiones pauperum* to which Polanyi refers. Venice, in 1528, for example, began an attempt to eliminate begging. This effort involved not only the forbidding of alms, but also new state responsibilities: to train and educate begging children, public works projects to put able beggars to work, taxation to finance these programs. Keith Thomas, in his explanation of the witchcraft trials, lays great stress on the breakdown of community charity; the 'witches' were poor elderly women beggars who were accused in part out of the guilt of those family heads then turning them away at the door. In England, much of the reform of charity took the form of strengthening large-scale private giving in the form of charitable trusts. These new donations were aimed at social reform—for example, the building of schools and foundling hospitals—and not at the achievement of piety in a personal relationship.

The English Poor Law of 1601, also adopted by the American colonies, made each parish or township responsible for its own poor, and created a system of governmental overseers and levies to accomplish this end. 'Nothing', wrote Keith Thomas, 'did more . . . to make the moral duties of the householder ambiguous.'[27]

The critique of traditional charity reflected the shift toward market-based, contractual relations and the accompanying decline in traditional ties. In the seventeenth century, Liebniz wrote of a shift from charity to justice as the fundamental principle governing social intercourse.[28] One motive, certainly, of the reform of charity was to transform the mental outlook of the poor so that, as Christopher Hill has put it, 'they no longer waited at the rich man's gate for charity, but went out to offer their services on the labour market'.[29] But the new emphasis on self-support and individual responsibility was associated with a growing sense of social obligation. Thus, cities, wrote Vives, had been founded 'for the increase of charity and human fellowship'. In other words, the emphasis on self-support and the sense of being able to reform and strengthen the social bond went together.

The attempt to reform the traditional modes of charity—i.e. to enforce a rationalized work ethic—was accompanied by the building of the first state institutions with responsibilities toward dependent groups: the poor, the orphaned, the mad, etc. These began at different points in different countries, generally as private institutions later taken over by the state. Foucault speaks of the 'great confinement' of the mad in the seventeenth century. In the United States it was not until the early 1820s that the famous reports of Josiah Quincey and John Yates led to the abolition of 'outdoor relief'—aid given the poor while they remained in their own or others' families—and the construction of the network of poorhouses in New York and Massachusetts. The first state mental hospital in America was built in Worcester, Massachusetts in 1835. The first orphan asylums were founded in the same period, and by 1850 had replaced apprenticeship as the main means of caring for orphaned children.[30]

The building of these institutions reflects the transition between a society organized around patriarchal families, with its accompanying obligations of mutual responsibility and the modern state based on the ideal of private, self-supporting families. The goal of these institutions was rehabilitation aimed at self-support. The thinking underlying them was that of economic individualism and utilitarianism. 'Moral treatment', the movement to reform psychiatric care, and the beginning of a scientifically-oriented psychotherapy, exemplifies the character of nineteenth-century reform. The purpose of moral treatment, wrote Francois Pinel in France, was to manipulate the mad person into recognizing his dependence on others. Once this was achieved he could take his place as a responsible citizen, independent and self-supporting once again.[31]

Rothman's notion of 'social control' misses the social basis of these institutions which was not so much the wish to impose the values of one class (native-born Americans) on others (immigrants, the poor) but rather to develop an internalized, family-centered morality in all classes. As Paul Faler showed in his study of Lynn, Massachusetts, the heightened nineteenth-century emphasis on discipline, order and industry was not only preached by the upper classes toward their workers but was a demand that the workers made upon themselves.[32] The new sense of individual responsibility was rooted in the structure of a market society whose advance, in the nineteenth century, destroyed the old forms of paternalistic and community responsibility, as well as establishing the new distinction between the normal (i.e. private, self-supporting) and abnormal.

In those famous passages in which he speaks of 'the tyranny of the majority' which 'acts upon the will as much as upon the actions', Tocqueville seems to have partly grasped that modern liberal capitalism had developed a new form of ideology, secular and personal in nature, rooted in the market structure of society.[33] In *Capital*, Tocqueville's near-contemporary, Marx, demonstrated how market relations in the sphere of exchange veil the enormously intensified interdependence brought about in the industrial capitalist sphere of production and give each person the illusion that he or she labours for him or herself alone. It was from this spurious sense of self-reliance that our Victorian forebears attacked all forms of 'undeserving' dependence. In an early nineteenth-century essay, 'Gifts', Ralph Waldo Emerson wrestled with the problems which giving to others posed for modern men and women. The theme of the essay is that a true gift is based on love: 'the flowing of the giver unto me, correspondent to my flowing unto him. When the waters are at level, then my goods pass to him, and his to me.' The predominance of capitalist private property renders every gift problematic. 'How can you give me this pot of oil or this flagon of wine when all your oil and wine is mine,' Emerson asks. Hence, he explains, the fitness of beautiful rather than useful objects as gifts. If a person is in need, Emerson writes, it is always necessary to supply his 'first wants . . . and to give all that is asked . . . necessity does everything well'. But 'it is a cold lifeless business when you go to the shops to buy me something which does not represent your life and talent, but a goldsmith's.' In any event, 'all beneficiaries hate all Timons [i.e. of Athens], not at all considering the value of the gift but looking back to the greater store it was taken from . . . For the expectation of gratitude [on the part of the giver] is mean, and is continually punished by the total insensibility of the obliged person. It is a great happiness to get off without injury and heart-burning from one who has had the ill-luck to be served by you. It is a very onerous business, this of being served, and the debtor naturally wishes to give you a slap.'[34]

The sociological basis of the liberal state, however, was not self-reliant individuals but private family units in which women had the primary responsibility for 'giving'. The new stress on economic independence and self-reliance was accompanied by a vastly heightened emphasis on the nurturant role of mothers and the special needs of children. The idea that infants needed a close and prolonged relationship with their own mothers only dates from the end of the eighteenth century; probably Rousseau was the pivotal figure influencing this development.[35] At the same time, the market structure of modern society rendered women's identification with altruism problematic for them, in important part for the reasons articulated by Emerson.

Nineteenth-century feminists responded with an effort to extend political economic individualism to married women. Thus the married women's property acts were the most important feminist reform in America in the first half of the nineteenth century. In ante-bellum America, there had been a general breakdown of a 'protective, regulative, paternalistic' conception of the law to one 'thought of as facilitative of individual desires'. Beginning in the 1840s, feminists challenged the patriarchal presumption of common law in which the wife's rights were subsumed by those of her husband and sought instead individual rights for married women, especially to trade and contract on the marketplace, to earn wages and to spend them.[36] The Civil War and Reconstruction supplied further precedents for the idea that government should intervene on behalf of individual rights. In the second half of the century there was a great upsurge in legislative and judicial action, often initiated by women and children against fathers but also reflecting the father's efforts to use the courts to uphold the waning of patriarchal authority. In an important decision, Judge Joseph Story tried to distinguish marriage as the 'basis of the whole fabric of civilized society' from other contracts which had a more voluntary character to them.[37] Similarly, in England, *The Times* argued that the Married Women's Property Act of 1882 would abolish 'the family in the old sense and break up society again into men and women'.[38] These Acts provided a victory for economic individualism but not for representative government, nor for the principle of equality between the sexes which was readdressed by late nineteenth-century feminists in terms of the sociology of their day.

By the late nineteenth century, women's preponderant reform activity was protectionist (or 'maternalist' as Lester Ward later called it). Even earlier, just as August Comte described the centrality of altruism in organizing society, so Catherine Beecher articulated the centrality of the home and the need to extend the principle of 'feminine' giving into other areas, especially teaching. Elizabeth Cady Stanton and Susan B. Anthony's *Revolution* was among the first journals in America to translate and publish Comte.[39] Feminists sponsored a number of reforms aimed at maximizing the importance of motherhood to society, for example, awarding child custody in the case of divorce to the mother rather than the father. Late nineteenth- and early twentieth-century feminists such as Jane Addams and Charlotte Gilman followed John Ruskin's utopian socialist distinction between 'wealth' (i.e. socially necessary labour such as mothering) and 'riches' (economic accumulation).[40] In *Herland* Gilman portrayed an all-female society whose central activities were childbearing and education in order to demonstrate that women's non-economic contribution to society was as essential as men's.[41] But in one regard economic individualism persisted: all feminists but a handful agreed that the wage should remain the economic basis of familial existence.

More than any single group, nineteenth-century feminist and women reformers shaped the thinking and politics concerning the family which informed the construction of the welfare state in the twentieth century. In moving from a political economic approach at the start of the century to a sociological approach by the end, feminists preserved the commitment to economic individualism which they hoped would be encouraged in the 'interdependent' world of the modern marketplace.

In conclusion, then, an examination of the origins of the welfare state brings out an essential point missed both by sociologists and historians. The rise of the state in modern history does not 'take over' responsibilities and functions from the family so much as it accompanies a shift from a patriarchal to a private, ostensibly non-political family unit. Rather than the state replacing the family, the modern nation-state and the modern family emerged together as the necessary complement of one another, each implying and presupposing the other. In order to see the connection between them, it is necessary to conceptualize the market economy as the crucial mediation first in securing the political rights of the private individual (or family unit) and later, as supplying the means by which interdependence and altruism was to be achieved. In this sense Marx wrote (against Hegel): 'The abstraction of the *state as such* was not born until the modern world because the abstraction of private life was not created until the modern times.'[42] What appears to Rothman and others as an expansion of governmental powers with the creation of the first state institutions, is better understood as the emergence of liberalism. The redefinition of the family in terms of private property established it as an 'autonomous' realm and was associated with a pushing back of government's power to intervene.

The Emergence of The Welfare State: 1890-1920

The 'welfare state' created in America at the beginning of the twentieth century had the authority to intervene generally into social and economic conditions, including those of the family, in order to 'promote the general welfare'. This change in the nature of the nation-state came about when the market-based or laissez-faire view of the relations of government to families came into question as a result of the harshness of industrialization, immigration and urbanization at the beginning of the twentieth century. These upheavals challenged the assumption that families could normally provide for their own members. The reforms of the Progressive Era created a host of new laws and agencies aimed at specific classes of dependents (for example, the children's bureau, the juvenile court, mother's pensions) as well as sponsoring a series of reforms aimed at shoring up the normal, self-supporting family (for example, workmen's compensation). In this sense, the Progressive Era reforms laid the basis for the global intervention of the New Deal, and post-New Deal eras. Nonetheless, while the expansion of government during the Progressive Era certainly modified laissez-faire thinking and practice concerning dependency, it did so in a way that preserved its essence: the goal of economic independence and the private family unit so that, in spite of the language of 'altruism' and 'interdependence' so prominent during the early years of our century, the reforms of the Progressive Era not only perpetuated but intensified the economic individualism their rhetoric condemned.

This paradox becomes plausible when we remember that the modification of market forces during the Progressive Era—for example, government regulation of business—took place in a context in which capitalism was expanding into new spheres of American life and in which working for a wage or salary was replacing, or had already replaced, the ownership of property as the basis of life. Just as the reformers of the early nineteenth century took productive property as the basis of the 'normal' and 'independent' family, so the reformers of the Progressive Era assumed a wage or salary would perform that function and fought for reforms predicted on this assumption.

General rationales for the welfare state during the Progressive Era stressed the possibilities for individual independence supposedly fostered by the 'interdependent' world of the large corporation. According to an almost universally held view, the spread of the market and, especially, the rise of industry, had destroyed the self-sufficiency of the old, petty bourgeois family, making it necessary to develop other institutions, particularly schools and neighborhood institutions, to perform tasks once performed by the family. This, in turn, would change the family leading, as Arthur Calhoun argued, to the 'waning of domestic monarchy' and the 'general democratization of society'.[43] The family would become smaller, more sociable, more democratic and cooperative, more personal and informal, less private and self-contained and would be based on the extension of individualism to include women and children. The function of government reforms was to protect these extended rights, particularly among the working classes where they were most threatened: the rights of women to motherhood, of children to childhood, of the family to a certain kind of environment.

The progressives believed that they were extending individual rights from the political to the social and economic spheres. John Dewey wrote, 'The crisis in liberalism . . . proceeds from the fact that after early liberalism had done its work, society faced a new problem, that of social organization.'[44] According to John Commons, the legal history of the early twentieth century had been marked by an 'enlargement of the idea of property . . . from that of ownership of tangible objects to that of ownership of one's labor; and the enlargement of liberty from personal liberty to economic liberty.'[45] In 1888, Carroll D. Wright, chief of the Massachusetts Bureau of the Statistics of Labor, used the term 'unemployment' for the first time in America. Wright's publications began the recognition that unemployment might be involuntary.[46] But in redefining one's livelihood as a social and political right, the most advanced progressives ignored the continued autonomy of market forces.

One of the clearest ways in which economic individualism was preserved in the form of social collectivism was the workmen's compensation system. Workmen's compensation was the only form of social insurance successfully enacted during the Progressive Era, and foreshadows the development of an enlarged 'social wage' during and after the New Deal. The nineteenth-century predecessors of workmen's compensation had been forms of mutual aid such as friendly societies, fraternal orders, unions, secret societies like the Masons, and, especially, immigrant organizations for whom insurance was often both inspiration and mainstay. These forms of insurance were themselves collective, either rooted directly in a community or, as in the case of funeral insurance, in the need to meet one's emotional and practical obligations to a community. These forms proved inadequate to both

workers and their employers with the development of large-scale corporations. The workers faced the erosion of sustaining communities,
while employers faced a welter of ersatz arrangements leading to many
lawsuits and unpredictable costs. Workmen's compensation legislation
tied insurance to the wage contract, as well as protecting the insurance
companies that served as private carriers. Its supporters argued that
it would replace 'paternalism' and ensure a 'democratic discipline' based
on the worker's individual foresight and initiative. As I. M. Rubinow
later argued for social security, it was made necessary by the decline
of the extended family and the 'increasing dependence of the majority
of mankind . . . upon a wage-contract for their means of existence'.
Although often portrayed as a victory for collective over individual
solutions, the history of workmen's compensation actually reveals the
reverse: the decline of community and the confirmation of individual
responsibility by the state.[47]

Behind the reforms of the Progressive Era was the desire to avoid
dependence. Just as Emerson articulated many of the problems which
nineteenth-century men and women felt in 'giving', so Jane Addams
rephrased these problems in the twentieth century context when the
individual's massive dependence on the state had become inevitable.
Addams began her great book, *Democracy and Social Ethics*, with a
story that defined the essential problem she faced at Hull House in
the 1890s. It is the parable of the rich and poor landlords. The rich
landlord 'collects with sternness . . . accepts no excuse, and will have
his own', while the good-natured landlord 'pities and spares his pover-
ty-pressed tenants'. The good-natured landlord receives 'the genuine
love and devotion' of many of his tenants while the rich landlord is
subjected to 'moments of irritation and of real bitterness'. But though
the rich landlord is unloved, he commands real admiration, while
toward the good-natured landlord there is a 'certain lack of respect.
In one sense he is a failure. Intermingled with the love his tenants bear
him, there is veiled but unmistakable contempt.'[48] The tale exemplifies
Addams' awareness of the difficulties in basing an ethical order on the
modern economic system. While an ethics based simply on economic
individualism lacked compassion, an ethics which overlooked economic
reality would be utopian and unrealistic. Quite plausibly, Addams'
tenants suspect that the good-natured landlord's actions are weak at
their root and hide unacknowledged motives, perhaps a fear of standing one's ground or an excessive need to be loved.

Addams was the heir to several generations of reformers who had
developed a parallel critique of traditional charity beginning in the early
nineteenth century, continuing in the 'scientific charity' movements of
the Civil War, Reconstruction and 'Gilded Age' periods, and culminating in the settlement house movements. The essential themes of
'scientific charity' were sounded by the Civil War Sanitary Com-

mission: paid experts rather than volunteers, strict administration, 'business principles', faith in social science. The Commission aimed at wrestling humanitarianism from the 'rising [predominantly female] tide of popular sympathy'. After the Civil War the movement gave rise to State Boards of Charity which sought to undercut the specific claims made by any group of dependents on behalf of society as a whole. The Charity Organization Societies formed during the depression of the 1870s stressed the dangers of any form of help. 'Next to alcohol', wrote one of its leaders, H.L. Wayland, in 1887, 'the most pernicious fluid is indiscriminate soup.' 'Let me have one cord of wood', wrote another, 'and I can ruin the best family in Boston.'[49] While Addams, and the generation of progressive reformers associated with her, rejected the laissez-faire presuppositions of these earlier currents in favour of government reform, they did not reject the critique of asking, giving and receiving among unequals. Like Addams, John Dewey in his *Ethics* attacked charity because it presupposed 'a superior and [an] inferior class'.[50] Finally, George Herbert Mead argued that giving was a primitive impulse whose ultimate basis was narcissistic and which worked to satisfy the giver. The impulse to give, Mead argued, should be replaced by social service and social work—'artificial island[s], as it were , in an ocean of primitive impulsiveness'.[51] By the early twentieth century the word 'charity' came into disfavour and has since come to be replaced by a series of uneasy euphemisms: aid, welfare, human resources.

In *Totem and Taboo*, Freud linked the issue of dependence to the problem of sexuality with the concept of taboo. The common quality which tabooed or forbidden persons or objects have, Freud wrote, is that of 'arousing forbidden desires in others and of awakening a conflict or ambivalence in them'. Thus kings are taboo because they arouse their subjects' envy and 'dead men, new-born babies and women menstruating or in labour stimulate desires by their special helplessness . . . The fact that a dead man is helpless is bound to act as an encouragement to the survivor to give free rein to his hostile passions, and that temptation must be countered by a prohibition.'[52] I am suggesting that the very act of compassion by which Americans, in the early twentieth century, extended their recognition of need, deprivation and suffering among their fellows was accompanied by an effort to rationalize and depersonalize the impulse to give, and subject the emotions—perhaps especially the hostile emotions—associated with altruism to rational, social control.

At the same time, something similar was occuring in the realm of the family. In a celebrated article, Carol Smith Rosenberg showed that early nineteenth century middle-class American women experienced their primary emotional relationships with other women and enjoyed largely formal relations with their husbands.[53] But the friendships and the marriages were predominantly nonsexual. By the early twentieth century a middle-class woman was faced with sexual opportunities with both sexes but, at least between men and women, the possibilities of greater intimacy and involvement also released strong currents of conflict and hostility. From the first, feminists recognized that the deepening of the sexual and emotional bonds between men and women necessitated movement toward genuine equality between the sexes. A significant feminist current rejected romantic love with its idealization of women. The romantic tradition, feminists argued, exaggerated sexual difference and over-valued emotionality. The idealization of women hid the fact of their suppression; the sexual passion men felt toward women often concealed a sadistic urge.[54] Without mentioning feminism, Max Weber argued similarly in 1915 that 'the brotherly ethic of salvation religion is in profound tension with the greatest irrational force of life: sexual love . . . the erotic relation must remain attached, in a certain sophisticated measure, to brutality.'[55] In place of mystery and ecstasy, feminists sought a love based on familiarity and cooperation between the sexes, gained through frequent contact with one another, in school, recreation, leisure and work. The feminist hope for a more cooperative society had, as a central goal, greater intimacy and even deeper love between the sexes.

Christopher Lasch has argued that the growth of the welfare state was an assault on the instinctual roots of human individuality. The Progressive Era was characterized by efforts to avoid conflict in every sphere: the rejection of Marxian socialism in politics, the rejection of punishment in favour of discretion and rehabilitation in law, 'balancing acts' and 'rules of reason' in government regulation, the emergence of the 'stewardship' concept of the Presidency, the beginnings of industrial psychology in the sphere of labour, even the search for a 'moral equivalent to war'. My argument is that the commitment to economic individualism worked, as all ideology works, to harmonize and smooth out contradictions which arose in the political sphere of social welfare and to assist the psychological tasks of denial and repression.[56] In the act of recognizing the significance of dependence, Americans denied that dependence was necessary and affirmed that the market could ultimately supply all human necessities. In the process they committed themselves to a way of life that sustained the repression they sought to lift.

The Family Wage: A Case Study In The Politics of The Welfare State

The American commitment to social welfare affirmed societal responsibility for dependent groups along with economic individualism. The aim of social legislation even in such areas as workmen's compensation and social security was to maximize self-reliance, i.e. dependence on the wage. Many Americans associate this aim with their hopes for a new stage in the evolution of the couple, one in which a 'living wage' assured men and women the security and personal freedom necessary for a good relationship. An examination of the politics surrounding the issue of the 'living' or 'family' wage shows how the commitment to wage labour changed the intended meaning of the early welfare state reforms.

The idea that wage labour would bring women independence was a staple of late nineteenth-century feminism. The particular contradiction addressed by the so-called social feminists of the Progressive era—such as Addams, Lillian Wald, Mary Beard, Suzanne LaFollette and, in my view, Charlotte Gilman—was that the spread of the market and the rise of the corporation, while they promised to free women from their dependent position within the family, also threatened to undermine the values of altruism and benevolence which had constituted women's sphere. For this first generation of college educated women, entering the labour force in the 1890s, the contradiction between the family and the market or, put psychologically, between dependence and autonomy, was particularly acute.[57] The social feminists therefore sought a politics that could combine wage labour, and even careers, especially for middle class women, with state protection of the family among the poor. Jane Addams expressed the characteristic synthesis of feminist and social reform ideas when she described government as 'enlarged housekeeping' and wrote:[58]

> From the beginning of tribal life women have been held responsible for the health of the community, a function which is now represented by the health department; from the days of the cave dwellers, so far as their home was clean and wholesome, it was due to their efforts, which are now represented by the bureau of tenement house inspection . . . Most of the departments in a modern city can be traced to woman's traditional activity, but in spite of this, so soon as these old affairs were turned over to the care of the city, they slipped from women's hands.

While the contribution of social feminism to progessive reform was vast and diverse, there is little question but that the protection and extension of the working class family was a central part of it, both in intention and in result. The reforms of the Progressive Era, which the late nineteenth-century women's movement anticipated and which social feminists played a leading role in securing and implementing, include reforms aimed at protecting the place of mothers within the family, especially protective legislation for women, laws aimed at protecting the special character of childhood, such as the attempt to abolish child labour, the extension of the school day and the school year, and the raising of the age of sexual consent and marriage and laws aimed at eliminating the sexual double standard and at reforming the ethical basis of the family, such as the attempts to outlaw prostitution or to encourage censorship, for example of the new movie industry. Perhaps more important than any specific reform was the high value late nineteenth- and early twentieth-century feminists asserted for motherhood in general, and not only in its middle-class or Victorian form. Taken in combination with developments in psychology, this new esteem may well have provided the crucial spark of respect for the working class family that distinguished the reforms of the Progressive Era from those of the nineteenth century. Social workers and reformers of the Progressive Era adopted the then-new principle that needy children were better off in their homes than in institutions, a principle integral to a whole series of Progessive Era innovations—the Mother's Pension movement, new encouragement for daily care, foster care and probation, and the juvenile court reforms, among others.[59]

The social feminists believed that the growth of government services assisting the family would produce both a more cooperative society, as well as one advanced toward women's equality. The failure of these hopes can be perhaps best understood when the social feminist program is considered alongside American labour's apparently unrelated activity during the same period. The Progressive Era was the time in which the labour movement—which had included labour parties, cooperatives, fraternal and reform associations in the late nineteenth century—was being reduced, as David Montgomery has written, to a collection of trade unions. Like feminists, the ideologues of the emerging trade union movement stressed the independence and self-reliance of the working class family. Samuel Gompers' famous definition of the goals of modern trade unionism—'More, more and more'—is rarely quoted in full. He went on to say 'We shall want more and more . . . Then I think you will find your eleemosynary occupations will be gone.' And in another speech: 'What the Working men want is less charity and more rights.' The central concern of the AFL in the 1890s and the early twentieth century was to gain control of the supply of labour in particular crafts. Craft control would enable union members—mostly male—to maintain leverage over wages and hours, and to sustain unions at a time when the market value of many older skills was being eroded in the face of the early twentieth century corporate counter-offensive against unions. A central form of trade union political activity therefore supported any legislation that promised to lessen the effects of what was called 'cheap labour'. This included protective legislation for women, the abolition of child labour, immigration restriction, the control of the apprenticeship system and the eight-hour day. Where the trade union movement resisted government intervention was in the wage labour relationship itself. Gompers expected that collective bargaining and the workings of the labour market itself would provide the necessities of life.[60]

In retrospect, we can see that the politics of feminism converged with those of the labour movement of the same period. Unlike feminists, the labour movement had no 'program' for the family, any more than feminists had a 'program' for the economy. In both cases, however, it was the element left unexamined—the wage basis of familial existence—that proved critical and that established a generally unremarked basis of agreement between the politics of working-class men and those of middle-class women. Protective legislation is the best example. Supported from different motives by labour and by the women's movement, it had the same implications for both: a sex-stratified work-force which assumed that the task of primary breadwinner belonged to the man, although women would work marginally, especially before marriage. At a time when it required everyone within a household to support a family, the goal of a single wage for a single breadwinner was extremely desirable. At a time when most of a woman's adult life span corresponded to the years of pregnancy and childbearing, most women shared this goal. Support for the 'family wage', as it was called, may in part have reflected the fact that immigrant families still tended to be embedded in ties of kinship, ethnicity and community so that the costs to women of the modern sexual division of labour were not anticipated.[61]

The strength of the family, including the couple's ability to sustain their love, depends on the strength of the community. Two people in love need to be able to withdraw from group life and create a world of personal meaning of their own, but they equally need to be able to return. The attempt in early twentieth-century America to encourage freedom and autonomy in the realm of personal life while eroding and undermining the ties of interdependence which hold communities together was bound to fail.

Conclusion

As many scholars have observed, the organization of modern family life around wage labour conformed to the needs of an ascendent capitalist class and a new imperialist state that proclaimed children its most important national resource.[62] But state policy toward the family was not dictated by a capitalist conspiracy. Rather, it was the outcome of a series of single issue reform movements, each one of which was 'realistic' enough and 'pragmatic' enough to take the rise of corporate capitalism for granted and to seek to attain specific goals, even the worthiest ones such as the abolition of child labour, within those confines. A common historical process shaped the acquiescence of feminists in the domination of capital at the workplace and the acquiescence of labour in the domination of men within the home.

Far from the state 'invading' or 'replacing' the family, a certain kind of alienated public life and a certain kind of alienated private life have expanded together. The form in which the welfare state expanded was public; the content was private. The vast growth of government spending that marked the New Deal and post-New Deal era far from eliminating the strength of market forces in our society may well have strengthened them.[63] The social reformers of the early twentieth century were right to stress that healthy families, which includes not only economic security by sexual love, would depend on a healthy civic life; but their inability to face directly the competitiveness and privatization inevitably bred by large-scale corporate capitalism, taken along with their acceptance of the idea that women have special capacities for the maintenance of human ties, has left the collectivity they sponsored hollow and serialized, and increasingly leaves families the same.

To conclude I will summarize my major points. First, rather than viewing the state as slowing encroaching upon, or supplementing or replacing the family, the modern state and the private family should be viewed as arising more or less together and in a definite relationship to one another. Missing from the previous accounts is the role of the economy, first the market, and then the corporation, in shaping both state and family, and in mediating between the two. Second, the assumption underlying government responsibility for social welfare and for the care of dependents from the beginning has been that normally families would support themselves without government assistance and that most forms of dependency would be met privately by women within the home. It is not so much that the stress on social control is wrong but it is drastically incomplete. Third, the sociological approach to understanding society in terms of a moral order, or consensus among subjectively acting individuals neglects the *social* privation—the continued destruction of group ties—bred by economic individualism. Finally, the inability of social feminists and of feminist-influenced social reformers to face these facts—their tendency to take refuge in such euphemisms as 'interdependence'—severely compromised the steps they took toward the enhancement of collective life, on one hand, and toward genuine equality, reconciliation, and even love, between men and women, on the other. These were the two goals which, rightly I think, they took to be inextricable.

Notes and References

1. Marcel Mauss, *The Gift* (Norton, New York, 1967), pp. 66, 75. For supporting documentation for the arguments advanced in this essay see Eli Zaretsky, 'Progressive thought on the Impact of Industrialization on the Family and Its Relation to the Emergence of the Welfare State, 1890-1920' (Ph.D. dissertation, University of Maryland, 1979); and his 'The Place of the Family in the Origin of the Welfare State' in Barrie Thorne (ed.), *ReThinking the Family* (Longmans, New York, 1982).

2. Morris Janowitz, *Social Control of the Welfare State* (Elsevier, New York, 1976); A. V. Dicey, *Lectures on the Relation between Law and Public Opinion in England During the Nineteenth Century* (Macmillan, London, 1930).

3. Jane Addams, *Democracy and Social Ethics* (Macmillan, New York, 1901).

4. Emile Durkheim, *De la division du travail social* (Alcan, Paris, 1902).

5. William I. Thomas and Florian Znaniecki, *The Polish Peasant in Europe and America* (University of Chicago Press, Chicago, 1918); and (Badger Press, Boston, 1920), Vol. 1, pp. 197, 509. See abridgement of all five volumes, edited by Eli Zaretsky (University of Illinois Press, Urbana, Illinois, 1984); and Oscar Handlin, *The Uprooted: The Epic Story of the Great Migrations that Made the American People* (Little Brown, Boston, 1951).

6. Mauss, *The Gift*, p. 66.

7. Talcott Parsons, Robert F. Bales, et al., *Family Socialization and Interaction Process* (Free Press, Glencoe, Illinois, 1955); and Neil Smelser, *Social Change in the Industrial Revolution* (University of Chicago Press, Chicago, 1965).

8. T. H. Marshall, *Social Class and Citizenship* (University of Cambridge Press, Cambridge, 1970).

9. Richard Titmuss, *Essays on 'The Welfare State'* (Allen Unwin, London, 1958); Harold L. Wilensky, *The Welfare State and Equality: Structural and Ideological Roots of Public Expenditures* (University of California Press, Berkeley, California, 1975).

10. Janowitz, *Social Control*, p. 7.

11. David Rothman, *The Discovery of the Asylum: Social Order and Disorder in the New Republic* (Little Brown, Boston, 1971). See also Michael Katz, 'Origin of the Institutional State', *Marxist Perspectives*, Vol. 1, No. 4 (Winter 1978).

12. Frances Fox Piven and Richard A. Cloward, *Regulating the Poor: The Functions of Public Welfare* (Vintage, New York, 1971), p. xiii.

13. Michael Foucault, *Discipline and Punish* (Pantheon, New York, 1977), pp. 224 and *passim*.

14. Jacques Donzelot, *The Policing of Families* (Pantheon, New York, 1979).

15. Christopher Lasch, *Haven in a Heartless World* (Basic Books, New York, 1977), p. xvi.

16. Christopher Lasch, *The Culture of Narcissism* (Norton, New York, 1979).

17. Adrienne Rich, *Of Woman Born* (Norton, New York, 1977); Barbara Ehrenreich and Dierdre English, *For Her Own Good: 150 Years of the Experts' Advice to Women* (Doubleday Anchor, Garden City, New York, 1978), see especially chapters 5,6, and 7; Nancy Chodorow, *The Reproduction of Mothering* (University of California Press, Berkeley, California,

1978); Heidi Hartmann, 'Capitalism, Patriarchy and Job Segregation of Sex' in Zillah Eisenstein (ed.), *Capitalist Patriarchy and the Case for Socialist Feminism* (Monthly Review Press, New York, 1979).

18. Willard Gaylin, 'In the Beginning: Helpless and Dependent', in Willard Gaylin et al. (eds.), *Doing Good: The Limits of Benevolence* (Pantheon, New York, 1978).

19. Otto Kernberg, 'The Couple and the Group', in *External World, Internal Reality* (Jason Aronson, New York, 1979).

20. Benjamin Nelson, *The Idea of Usury* (Princeton University Press, Princeton, New Jersey, 1949).

21. Karl Polanyi, *The Great Transformation* (Beacon Press, Boston, 1944, 1957), pp. 163-64. Also see Hace Sorel Tishler, *Self-Reliance and Social Security 1870-1917* (Kennikat, Port Washington, New York, 1971), pp. 4-5.

22. James C. Scott, *The Moral Economy of the Peasantry: Rebellion and Subsistence in Southeast Asia* (Yale University Press, New Haven, Connecticut, 1976).

23. Octave Mannoni, *Prospero and Caliban* (Praeger, New York, 1966).

24. Ernst Troeltsch, *The Social Teaching of the Christian Churches* (Macmillan, New York, 1931, and 1949), pp. 134, 166.

25. Brian Tierney, *Medieval Poor Law* (University of California Press, Berkeley, California, 1968).

26. Edmund Morgan, *The Puritan Family* (Harper & Row, New York, 1966), pp. 142-43; Rothman, *Discovery of the Asylum*, chapter 1; Willystine Goodsell, *A History of the Family as a Social and Educational Institution* (Macmillan, New York, 1915), p. 335, quotes from Plymouth Laws: 'No single person be suffered to live by himself or in any family but such as the selection of the town shall approve of . . .'; Robert Bremner (ed.), *Children and Youth in America: A Documentary History, Vol. I, 1600-1865* (Harvard University Press, Cambridge, Massachusetts, 1970), pp. 103-104; and Bernard Bailyn, *Forming of American Society* (University of North Carolina Press, Chapel Hill, 1960), p. 17.

27. Keith Thomas, *Religion and the Decline of Magic* (Scribner's, New York, 1971).

28. Patrick Riley, *The Political Writings of Liebniz* (Cambridge University Press, Cambridge, Massachusetts, 1972).

29. Christopher Hill, 'The Puritans and the Poor', *Past and Present*, Vol. 2 (1952), p. 36.

30. Rothman, *The Discovery of the Asylum*.

31. Marcel Gauchet and Gladys Swain, *La pratique de l'esprit humain* (Gallimard, Paris, 1980), Norman Dain, *Concepts of Insanity in the United States, 1789-1865* (Rutgers University Press, New Brunswick, New Jersey, 1964), p. 110; Rothman, *Discovery of the Asylum*, pp. 65, 243-44; and Henri Ellenberger, *The Discovery of the Unconscious: The History and Evolution of Dynamic Psychiatry* (Basic Books, New York, 1970), p. 197. On ante-bellum environmentalism, see Winthrop Jordan, *White Over Black: American Attitudes Toward the Negro 1550-1812* (Norton, New York, 1968, 1977), pp. 308-10.

32. Paul Faler, 'Cultural Aspects of the Industrial Revolution: Lynn, Massachu-

setts Shoemakers and Industrial Morality, 1826-1860', *Labor History*, Vol. 15 (Summer 1974), pp. 381-91.

33. Alexis De Tocqueville, *Democracy in America*, (Vintage, New York, 1954), Vol. 2, p. 203.

34. Ralph Waldo Emerson, 'Gifts', *Collected Essays* (Random House, New York, 1964).

35. Elisabeth Badinter, *Mother Love* (Macmillan, New York, 1980).

36. Morton J. Horwitz, *The Transformation of American Law 1780-1860* (Harvard University Press, Cambridge, Massachusetts, 1977), p. 253; Norman Basch, 'Invisible Women: The Legal Fiction of Marital Unity in Nineteenth Century America', *Feminist Studies*, Vol. 5, No. 2 (Summer, 1979); and Jacobus tenBroek, 'California's Dual System of Family Law: Its Origin, Development and Present Status', *Stanford Law Review*, Vol 16, No. 2 (March 1964), p. 297n. In this volume, see the essay by Ursel, 'The State and the Maintenance of Patriarchy'.

37. William O'Neill, *Divorce in the Progressive Era* (Yale University Press, New Haven, Connecticut, 1967); Morton Keller, *Affairs of State: Public Life in Late Nineteenth Century America* (Harvard University Press, Cambridge, Massachusetts, 1977), pp. 461-72.

38. *Times Literary Supplement*, 6 April, 1984.

39. William Leach, *True Love and Perfect Union: The Feminist Reform of Sex and Society* (Basic Books, New York, 1980), p. 148.

40. Jill Conway, 'Stereotypes of Feminity in a Theory of Sexual Evolution', in Martha Vicinus (ed.), *Suffer and Be Still: Women in the Victorian Age* (Indiana University Press, Bloomington, Indiana, 1972), pp. 140-54.

41. Charlotte Gilman, *Herland* (Pantheon, New York, 1971).

42. Karl Marx, 'Critique of Hegel's Doctrine of the State', in *Early Writings* (Vintage Books, New York, 1974), p. 90.

43. W. Arthur Calhoun, *A Social History of the American Family*, Vol. 3 (Barnes and Nobel, New York, 1960), pp. 157-58.

44. John Dewey, *Reconstruction in Philosophy* (University of Chicago Press, Chicago, 1935).

45. John Commons, *The Legal Foundations of Capitalism* (Macmillan, New York, 1924), p. 153.

46. James Leiby, *Carroll Wright and Labor Reform: The Origin of Labor Statistics* (Harvard University Press, Cambridge, Massachusetts, 1960).

47. Roy Lubove, *The Struggle for Social Security, 1900-1935.* (Harvard University Press, Cambridge, Massachusetts, 1968), pp. 4, 52, 82, 115, 314-15; and James Leiby *A History of Social Welfare and Social Work in the United States* (Columbia University Press, New York, 1968), pp. 191-216.

48. Addams, *Democracy*, pp. 24-25.

49. Josephine Shaw Lowell, *Public Relief and Private Charity* (Putnam, New York, 1884), p. 66; Marion E. Gettleman, 'Charity and Social Classes in the United States, 1874-1900', *American Journal of Economics and Sociology*, Vol. 22 (April 1963), pp. 313-30 and Vol. 22 (July 1963), pp. 417-26; and George Frederickson, *The Inner Civil War: Northern Intellectuals and the Crisis of the Union* (Harper & Row, New York, 1965), pp. 98-112.

50. John Dewey, *Outlines of a Critical Theory of Ethics* (Hillary House, New York, 1957); and Merle Curti, *Social Ideas of American Educators* (Scribner's, New York, 1935), p. 523.

51. George Herbert Mead, 'Philanthropy from the Point of View of Ethics', in Ellsworth Faris, Fern Laune, and Arthur J. Todd (eds.), *Intelligent Philanthropy* (University of Chicago, Chicago, 1930), pp. 133-48; George Herbert Mead, 'The Psychology of Punitive Justice', *American Journal of Sociology*, Vol. 23, No. 5, (March 1918); and T. V. Smith, 'George Herbert Mead the Philosophy of Philanthropy', *Social Service Review* (March 1932).

52. Sigmund Freud, *Totem and Taboo* (Norton, New York, 1950), pp. 32, 33, 61.

53. Caroll Smith-Rosenberg, 'The Female World of Love and Ritual', *Signs*, Vol. I, No. 1 (1975).

54. Leach, *True Love and Perfect Union, passim.*

55. Max Weber, 'Religious Rejections of the World and Their Directions', in Hans Gerth and C. Wright Mills (eds.), *From Max Weber* (Oxford University Press, New York, 1958), p. 348.

56. Louis Althusser, 'Ideology and Ideological State Apparatuses', in *Lenin and Philosophy* (Monthly Review Press, New York, 1972).

57. Leslie Woodcock Tentler, *Wage-Earning Women: Industrial Work and Family Life in the United States, 1900-1930* (Oxford University Press, New York, 1979).

58. Jane Addams, *New Ideals of Peace* (Macmillan, New York, 1907), p. 202.

59. Ruth True, *The Neglected Girl* (Survey Associates, New York, 1914), p. 48; David J. Pivar, *Purity Crusade: Sexual Morality and Social Control, 1868-1900* (Greenwood Press, Westport, Connecticut, 1973), pp. 104-05, 139-46; Mark Leff, 'Consensus for Reform: The Mothers' Pension Movement in the Progressive Era', *Social Service Review*, Vol. 47, No. 3 (September 1973); Carl Kelsey, 'The Juvenile Court of Chicago and Its Work', *Annuals of the American Academy of Political and Social Science*, Vol. 17 (March 1901); and Charlotte Perkins Gilman, *Women and Economics* (Harper & Row, New York, 1898 and 1966).

60. Samuel Gompers, 'Organized Labor's Attitude Toward Child Labor', *Annals of the American Academy of Political and Social Science*, Vol. 27 (1906), p. 339; Irwin Yellowitz, *Industrialization and the American Labor Movement, 1850-1900* (Kennikat Press, Port Washington, New York, 1977), p. 104. Gompers is quoted in Tishler, *Self-Reliance*, pp. 64-65; and in Heidi Hartmann, 'Capitalism, Patriarchy and Job Segregation by Sex'.

61. W. Jett Lauck, *The New Industrial Revolution and Wages* (Funk & Wagnalls, New York, 1929), p. 19; J. Noble Stockett, *Arbitral Determination of Railway Wages* (Houghton Mifflin, Boston, 1918), chapter 3; Herbert Feis, *Principles of Wage Settlement* (Wilson, New York, 1924); Bureau of Applied Economics, *Standards of Living: A Compilation of Budgetary Studies* (Bureau of Applied Economics, Washington, D.C., 1920), pp. 96-101; and Robert Bremner, *From the Depths: The Discovery of Poverty in the United States* (New York University Press, New York, 1956), pp. 230-243.

62. For an English version of this argument see Anna Davin, 'Imperialism and Motherhood', *History Workshop*, No. 5, p. 49 (1978).

63. I do not here take up the question of whether the New Deal marked a fundamental departure from the tendencies I have described.

PART II

THE STATE AND SOCIAL REPRODUCTION

5

FROM POOR LAW TO SOCIAL INSURANCE: THE PERIODIZATION OF STATE INTERVENTION IN THE REPRODUCTION PROCESS

James Dickinson

Introduction

In recent years many writers have pointed to the centrality of the state in the reproduction of capitalism as an economic and political system. Others, more interested in social policy developments, have addressed the role of the state in the reproduction of capitalism's most important commodity, labour power.[1] The combined effect of much of this work has been to overcome the rather narrow conceptualization of the state as the institutional locus of legitimate violence in society and to encourage the treatment of the economic and social policies pursued by modern states as constitutive elements in capitalist social relations themselves. Building on such previous work, this chapter investigates aspects of the social reproduction process and develops an explanation of the increasing levels of state intervention, particularly as regards an important feature of practically all the advanced capitalist societies—the expansion of state intervention into the realm of industrial welfare and the transformation of a limited form of social welfare provision into a more elaborate and universal form of social security. Basically, the chapter aims to provide a framework for the periodization of social policy in terms of the underlying dynamics of the capitalist economies.[2]

Existing attempts to develop a structural history of capitalist social policy are generally limited. One typical approach has been to periodize social policy in terms of significant 'turning points'; usually, however, these turning points are somewhat arbitrary as, for example, where the account is organized around pre-war/post-war designations; or are formalistic, as where turning points in social policy are identified in terms of movement from a limited to a universal form of coverage.[3] As a result, the established 'periods' or 'stages' in the history of social policy advanced in these accounts are of limited value precisely because they do not root the changes in the underlying development of the economy.

A more sociological approach has stressed a necessary relationship between industrialization and the expansion of welfare; here the emergence of the welfare state is seen as part of a larger process of social differentiation, with the state gradually incorporating functions which were previously embodied in other social institutions such as the family.[4] However, these functionalist accounts tend to establish teleologically the inevitability of social welfare by reference to objective system needs. While close to some varieties of Marxist theorizing, the functionalist approach generally ignores the role of dynamic factors such as the class struggle in social change, and, being more interested in explaining the convergence between industrial societies with respect to social welfare provisions, is usually less able to account for national variation in such matters.

Explicitly Marxist accounts of the welfare state have been developed, but again the question of periodization has not been resolved satisfactorily. Gough, for instance, draws a sharp distinction between the nature and scope of state interventions in competitive and monopoly stages of capitalism. But he devotes relatively little space to investigating the relationship between capitalist development *per se* and social policy, only noting briefly that proletarianization, technological change, the division of labour and urbanization have implications for the extension of state involvement in specific areas.[5]

Piven and Cloward have, however, developed a theory of the relationship between welfare policies and development. The main argument advanced in their influential book, *Regulating the Poor*,[6] is that social welfare systems are largely related to the effects of the business cycle on labour markets. On the one hand, when employment levels are high, restrictive welfare is used to discipline those who are marginal to the work world; on the other hand, when unemployment rises, welfare becomes less restrictive as attempts are made to control the unemployed and restore social order. In this account, Piven and Cloward down-play the significance of the more liberal social security/social insurance systems, arguing that such schemes—at least within the American experience—have not been unconditional in terms of providing access to benefits, exclude some low-wage, low-skill occupations and provide such low benefits that 'social insurance programs are not fully free of the taint of being a form of relief.' Indeed, from their point of view, social welfare policy in capitalist society is generally repressive and responds to the need for different forms of social control:

> The historical pattern is clearly not one of progressive liberalization; it is rather a record of periodically expanding and

contracting relief rolls as the system performs its two main functions: maintaining civil order and enforcing work.[7]

They are perhaps too quick to dismiss the significance of social insurance and fail to see this as a revolution in social policy; they concentrate on those marginal elements of the work-force and urban population who are not generally covered by such schemes, and who by definition therefore, because they stand on the boundary of the labour markets, alternatively need 'disciplining' or 'mollifying' depending on the general level of economic activity.

Basically, Piven and Cloward's social control thesis fails to periodize social welfare policy in relation to structural stages of economic development. Because they understand social welfare developments as simply a matter of expansion-contraction of welfare rolls they are unable to distinguish any real turning points in social policy where new modes of relief are instituted in relation to the maturation of a capitalist labour market and the appearance of new stages in the production and accumulation process. Welfare policy is therefore understood cyclically, rather than in terms of 'periods' or 'stages.'[8]

What is still needed then is a theory of how the development of social policy is linked to the political economy of capitalism. Such a theory presupposes more than a simple correlation, as is found in the developmentalist literature, between economic growth and expenditures on social programs. Rather, it can best be generated by looking at the structure of the reproduction process and the interrelation of family, economy and state at different stages of economic development.

The central argument of this chapter is twofold: first, that the social and economic organization of capitalist society generates a series of crises in the sphere of reproduction which constantly threatens the effective renewal of labour power on a daily and generational basis; and second, that the changing nature and extent of state social intervention—indeed, the rise of the welfare state itself—is a systematic response to these crises. The analysis proceeds by identifying three structural crises affecting the autonomous reproduction of labour in households. These crises derive from: (1) the tendency of capital to over-exploit labour, consuming it at the point of production at a faster rate than it can be reconstituted in the domestic sphere; (2) the contradiction between the value of labour power and the demographic and life cycle characteristics of households such that wages accruing to certain households may fall short of the socially defined subsistence needs of household members despite the payment of labour at value for the economy as a whole; and (3) the failure to valorize labour power due to the operation of impersonal factors such as work-related accidents and illnesses, unemployment, sickness and old age. Each crisis can be conceived of as characteristic of, but by no means limited to, a particular stage in the development of capitalism and the evolution of the wage labour-capital relation. Thus, the first crisis is typical of early industrialization and absolute surplus value production; the second is charateristic of an era of competitive capitalism with minimal social wage provisions by the state; and the third crisis is characteristic of a mature, fully articulated capitalist economy based upon relative surplus value production.[9]

Moreover, these crises are not isolated incidents effecting only a few households at any particular time. Rather their significance is that as structural outcomes of the relation between the economy and households at particular stages in the evolution of the capitalist mode of production, they make the establishment and maintenance of households—the primary institution for the reproduction of labour power—an enduring problem. Thus, the crises discussed here not only represent the generalized uncertainties facing the working class at different stages of economic development but also express the fundamental contradictions between the productive and reproductive moments of capitalist society.

Various responses or strategies for the management and containment of these crises are identified and discussed. Some strategies represent theoretical possibilities only; others have an empirical referent in the social history of capitalism. On the one hand, there are those responses which do not directly involve the state in the articulation of a social policy; these include such possibilities as employers becoming more humane in their treatment of labour, the self-managed redistribution of resources among the working class, spontaneous limitations on family size and so on. Indeed, the social history of capitalism records the relative importance of these strategies in managing structural crises in the reproduction process. However, it is argued here that autonomous responses either by labour or capital embody fundamental limitations which ultimately call forth some form of state intervention. Indeed, the effective reproduction of labour power under capitalism, especially at the collective or class level, appears to require that the state articulate and implement a social policy which transcends the contradictions that affect reproduction and the limitations which capitalism places on alternative solutions. Further, as capitalist social formations mature, the state is increasingly implicated in the organization and structuring of the social reproduction process.

State social interventions can be periodized in relation to stages in the capitalist process of economic development. State intervention in response to the problems engendered by absolute surplus value production initially takes the form of regulation of the point of production through factory legislation, industrial welfare and the institutional maintenance of labour market boundaries. As capitalism matures, however, state intervention is extended to include regulation of the point of reproduction and the development of an appropriate social welfare policy designed to secure the maintenance and reproduction of dependent households. In this respect two distinct types and corresponding periods of social welfare policy are distinguished. First, there is the organization of transfers of wealth in society on an inter-class basis as occurred under the old and new poor laws in England, the United States and Canada; this type of social welfare is characteristic of competitive capitalism and indeed in many ways bears the imprint of an earlier age. Second, there is the intra-class organization of transfers on the basis of contributory social insurance programs. This modern system of social security is more characteristic of relative surplus value production and hence a later stage of capitalist development. Indeed, as capitalism matures, new crises emerge to affect the reproduction of labour, contradictions and limitations appear in the old system of relief and pressure builds for a 'revolution' in social policy whereby welfare is replaced by social security and social wage programs. In this regard then, both the crises and strategies considered here not only form distinct analytical possibilities, but also, in an important sense, constitute an historical progression corresponding to stages in the evolution of the capitalist mode of production.

Central to this argument is the recognition that, on the one hand, the uncertainties facing the proletariat under conditions of mature capitalism are best dealt with and modified by social insurance; and, on the other, that the political aspirations of the working class are checked by this reform of social policy. Social insurance has played a decisive role in securing the reproduction of capitalist social relations and its introduction may go some way toward explaining why the working class has, with some very important exceptions, failed to live up to Marx's expectations concerning its revolutionary potential—despite the maturing of the capitalist economy largely along those lines predicted by Marx.

A word of caution is in order before we proceed. What follows is largely a theoretical account which does not do justice to the rich and diverse social history of capitalism. Our model of capitalist economic development is drawn from Marx's *Capital* and thus closely reflects the British path of development; similarly, historical material, where introduced, is drawn primarily from the British experience. Despite these limitations, we believe our theory of state intervention is not without value for comprehending the patterns of social policy intervention elsewhere. Indeed, the purpose of this chapter is not to write a history of social policy, but rather to sketch out a framework which may be useful for understanding, organizing, and even criticizing, that history.

The Over-exploitation of Labour

The first type of crisis which may appear in the reproductive sphere results from the tendency of capitalist production to exploit labour. Employers demand that their labour force work for such long hours, for such low wages and under such appalling conditions that the reproduction of the worker in the long and short run cannot be assured despite the actual valorization of labour power. Over-exploitation prevents workers from effectively constituting themselves in households and thus limits the ability of the working class to secure its own autonomous reproduction external to the world of production.

This crisis is typically associated with the ascendancy of absolute surplus value production, a period when capitalists sought to extend the working day, employ the very cheapest categories of labour and economize on all expenses related to the safe operation of plant and machinery as the primary mode of enhancing profits. Under extreme circumstances, over-exploitation can lead to the consumption of labour power in production at a faster rate than it can be regenerated external to production. In this sense, over-exploitation can be seen as characteristic of unregulated capitalist industrialization and was, for example, widespread in Britain during the early decades of the nineteenth century prior to legislation restricting the employment of young persons and limiting the length of the working day.[10]

It is important to note that the crisis of over-exploitation is generated by the logic of capitalist production itself, and is not a function of the capriciousness of individual capitalists nor simply a consequence of cultural factors. This is particularly evident if we consider the contradictions involved in establishing a 'normal' working day—a working day which permits the reproduction of the worker at some socially and historically established standard of living—under conditions of early, unregulated capitalism. As Marx noted in his discussion of factory legislation, there was a tendency for capitalists to transgress both the moral and physical bounds of the normal working day and to lengthen it as much as possible; this was despite the fact that the sustained expanded reproduction of capital was dependent upon the establishment of such a normal working day.[11] However, while it would appear to be in the interest of capital in general to operate within the limits of a normal working day (since over-exploitation shortened the productive life of workers and thus required their replacement at a faster rate than would otherwise be the case) this consideration was not necessarily a determining factor in establishing the level of exploitation. As Marx wrote:

> . . . It is not the normal maintenance of the labour-power which is to determine the limits of the working day; it is the greatest possible daily expenditure of labour-power, no

matter how diseased, compulsory or painful it may be, which is to determine the limits of the 'labourers' period of repose. Capital cares nothing for the length of life of labour-power. All that concerns it is simply and solely the maximum of labour-power that can be rendered fluent in a working day.[12]

The profitability of nascent capitalism depended upon a radical extension of the working day because of the general inefficiencies and low level of productivity of labour, and the widescale introduction of machinery was to have a similar effect. The higher fixed capital costs associated with the mechanization of production, and consequent falling profit rates, could be offset to some degree by making existing labour work longer hours. Indeed, as Marx noted: 'The ever-mounting need to increase fixed capital in modern industry . . . was one of the main reasons prompting profit-mad capitalists to lengthen the working day.'[13] As a result, long hours and shift-work were an almost natural corollary of industrialization. Indeed, in Britain, as elsewhere, the working day was extended to 14, 16, even 18, hours.[14] A new, more demanding, industrial rhythm of work was beginning to be established, a work routine which appears to have been considerably more oppressive than that which prevailed under earlier cottage industry and predominantly agricultural production.[15]

Moreover, the extension of the technical division of labour and the introduction of machinery not only tended to lengthen the work day but also had the effect of deskilling work and depressing wages. On the one hand, as had been observed by classical political economy,[16] the productivity of labour could be dramatically increased by simply extending the technical division of labour at the point of production; with each production process broken down into its many constituent parts, the capitalist was now free to assign cheap, unskilled labour to perform the majority of simple tasks involved in the production of a commodity and employ the more expensive, skilled labour only for those few remaining tasks which still required a degree of skill. This was, of course, in direct contrast to the previous mode of production where the skilled artisan or craftsman performed all steps in the production process irrespective of the degree of skill required. As Charles Babbage put it, a basic principle of capitalist manufacture was:

That the master manufacturer, by dividing the work to be executed into different processes, each requiring different degree of skill or of force, can purchase exactly that precise quantity of both which is necessary for each process; whereas, if the whole work were executed by one workman, that person must possess sufficient skill to perform the most difficult, and sufficient strength to execute the most laborious, of the operations into which the art is divided.[17]

A consequence of the deskilling of labour was to radically extend competition within the labour market thus depressing wages. As Marx wrote:

> As the *division of labour* increases, labour is *simplified*. The special skill of the worker becomes worthless ... His labour becomes a labour that anyone can perform. Hence, competitors crowd upon him on all sides ... The more simple and easily learned the labour is, the lower the cost of production needed to master it, the lower do wages sink.[18]

Moreover, the adoption of machinery merely enhanced this competition in the labour market:

> Machinery brings about the same results on a much greater scale, by replacing skilled workers by unskilled, men by women, adults by children.[19]

The dynamics of capital accumulation and its effect on labour markets set in motion a vicious spiral. As specialization and mechanization increased the demand for cheap unskilled labour, so more women and children were drawn into factory employment. From the employers' point of view, mechanization had reduced the importance of physical strength and skill in the production process such that women and children could be employed on a grand scale; on the other hand, from the labourers' point of view, the entry of additional family members into the economy was necessary to supplement the increasingly meager wages of men. As Marx put it: 'The labour of women and children was the first thing sought for by capitalists who used machinery.'[20] Again, this influx of women and children extended competition in the labour market and acted to further depress wages.

A characteristic feature of early capitalism was therefore that most family members were forced into wage work. Men were often hired only if accompanied by a child. Indeed, for a period child labour practically formed the basis of the factory system in England, with certain kinds of work, especially in textiles, being done exclusively by children.[21] Moreover, women were extensively employed in mining, textiles, dressmaking and a variety of manufacturing trades.[22] This situation has been described as the 'family wage economy': no single breadwinner was able to command a wage sufficient to maintain a household and meet the subsistence needs of its members, hence forcing additional family members into the labour market.[23]

There is evidence that the long hours worked by children and the early age at which they could be employed resulted in significant problems for long- and short-term reproduction. The incidence of respiratory disease increased due to the high temperature and humidity which prevailed in many factories. In fact, a whole generation or more was physically deformed by factory labour with 'the long hours of standing and bending producing the characteristic weak legs and arched back of the former child operatives'.[24] Again, infant mortality rates were higher in areas where mothers worked away from home for long hours.[25]

The impact of early industrialization on the standard of living of the working class is a much debated topic. At least in the short run, it appears that households under the family wage economy were compromised in their reproductive functions and that there was a negative impact on the standard of living. There were many indicators of this breakdown. Housing conditions deteriorated in both city and countryside.[26] Food consumption declined in England and elsewhere.[27] Mortality rates in Britain, after an apparent decline up until the beginning of the nineteenth century, rose once again until the 1840s, especially among working men between the ages of 30 and 60.[28] Some factory employment was so hazardous that heavy drinkers tended to live longer than their abstemious colleagues simply because they were absent from work more frequently.[29] Indeed, as one contemporary observer noted, the current generation (of English workers in the 1830s) 'had a lower degree of vitality than their predecessors'.[30] Not least, the subjective basis in the working class of ideological hegemony appeared to be breaking down, if not entirely absent.[31]

Absolute surplus value production is therefore associated with increased competition in the labour market, low wages and the excessive exploitation of the worker at the point of production. This in turn had consequences for the reproduction of labour power: because of the employment of most family members at low wages under extremely dehabilitating work conditions, adequately functioning households were difficult to maintain. Thus the initial mode in which capital consumed labour power made the long term reproduction of the working class problematic.

Given a structural tendency in early capitalist development towards over-exploitation, how can the effects be mitigated? In other words, how does the reproduction of labour power occur under conditions of absolute surplus value?

One possible strategy, at least from the employers' point of view, is to secure a steady flow of adult labour from outside the industrial economy to replace the labour consumed so rapidly in production, thus alleviating the need to organize working class reproduction under capital or state auspices. This flow can take two forms: (a) intra-societal migration where labour moves from the countryside to the city within the parameters of a national economy; and (b) inter-societal migration where labour moves from the underdeveloped and peripheral regions and countries of the world to the centres of economic growth. The former case would be typified by the enclosure movement in England which legally dispossessed the rural population of the means of production, or the clearing of the highlands of Scotland which achieved the same end by the use of military force. The latter case would be typified by the massive inter-societal migration from Central, Eastern and Southern Europe to North America during the late nineteenth and early twentieth centuries.[32] Basically, the large-scale migration of labour at least temporarily obviates the need for the state to step in and develop a social policy that will effectively check overexploitation and establish conditions for the reproduction of households.

However, this strategy *via* migration has certain limitations. First, it implies the generation of a constant stock of fresh labour power which is external to the capitalist sector of production and which can be persuaded or coerced to migrate to the industrial centres. Second, the existence of such a surplus population is an historical phenomenon contingent upon the uneven development of capital, and extensive social differentiation within the countryside either at home or abroad. Migration has therefore certain absolute limits related to the development of capital on a world-wide basis. Furthermore, a constant influx of immigrants from a variety of cultures compromises the state's ideological function of forging an homogeneous and relatively culturally undifferentiated population. Migration, since it is a *contingent* phenomenon, lying outside the parameters of synchronic reproduction, does not really solve long-term problems of reproduction.[33]

A second response depends upon the victims of over-exploitation organizing to limit competition in the labour market, pressing for a reduction in the length of the workday and for a wage that is sufficient to maintain a stable household. Indeed, Marx was convinced that workers had to 'put their heads together, and, as a class, compel the passing of a law, an all-powerful social barrier that shall prevent the very workers from selling . . . themselves and their families into slavery and death'.[34] However, a major limitation in class struggle acting as a variable in the transition to 'welfare' capitalism is that whilst individual capitalists might be compelled by industrial action to reduce exploitation, there was no guarantee that organized workers could alone secure this reduction at the level of the economy as a whole or on an enterprise by enterprise basis. For one thing, the constant generation of an industrial reserve army in the process of capitalist development would in all likelihood undermine attempts to achieve the complete unionization of the labour force, which itself would be a precondition if workers were to force a national reduction in exploitation.

A third possibility consists of state intervention at the point of production to check and regulate the way in which capital consume labour power through the promotion of industrial welfare. This, it is suggested, became the predominant mode by which over-exploitation was checked. Initially intervention took the form of factory legislation which gradually limited the hours of work for women and children, excluded them entirely from certain branches of production and regulated the layout of machinery etc.; later legislation established maximum hours of work and minimum rates of pay for adult males as well.[35]

In its regulation of the point of production, the state not only checks exploitation by establishing institutional boundaries to the labour market, but also helps fashion conditions for the establishment and reproduction of households; by excluding categories of workers, particularly women, from production, the state facilitated the creation of the role of full-time domestic worker. To the extent that legislation forced women out of the labour market, they were more able to undertake childrearing and those essential but non-valorized domestic tasks which are required for the smooth maintenance and reproduction of the productive worker.[36]

The way in which the crisis of over-exploitation was contained historically appears to have been through a combination of class struggle and state intervention. Under pressure from below, the state stepped in to establish parameters to the permissible level of exploitation for all capitalists. Indeed, it was only when the capitalist class realized that regulations and restrictions would affect all employers equally, thus giving no one capitalist a competitive advantage, that opposition to factory legislation from these quarters was finally overcome. To be effective then, the state had to universalize legislation on particular abuses in order to treat all capitalists equally.

In this regard an important distinction must be made between two levels of the existence of capital. On the one hand, there is the level of *capital in general* which can be understood as the average or general conditions of production which appear as the consequence of the competitive interactions of the many individual capitalists; it is at this level of economic activity that the tendential laws of capitalist production and circulation operate. On the other hand, there is the level of the *individual capitalist* (the 'firm' or enterprise) whose subjective actions go into establishing the general conditions of production, and who, in turn, is required to operate within the objective constraints set by these general conditions.[37] The interests or requirements of capital in general, i.e. the demands of the system as a whole, are qualitatively different from those of any one capitalist or indeed fraction of capital. For example, the individual capitalist will be concerned to reproduce as cheaply as possible that portion of the labour force he employs, but will not necessarily be concerned about the reproduction of the working class as a collectivity, thus giving rise to the general crisis of reproduction for the system as a whole dicussed above.

It is worth noting that the state is implicated both in the 'creation' of the crisis of over-exploitation and in the strategic responses to that crisis. On the one hand, state policy was an integral aspect of the process of proletarianization and primitive accumulation, and hence important in breaking down traditional restraints on the level of exploitation. As Marx noted, labour statutes from the middle of the fourteenth to the end of the seventeenth century had as their purpose the extension of the working day.[38] Clearly immigration—whether it is encouraged or restricted—is a state policy, and when the state pursues open immigration policies allowing the flow of adult labour into the national economy, it does in part actively reproduce the conditions for continued over-exploitation; in these instances the state thus buttresses absolute surplus value production. On the other hand, where successful, pressure from the working class for the reform of labour conditions does result in specific state policies to reduce exploitation.

In its enactment of factory legislation, the state represents the interest of capital in general and thus moves to overcome an in-built limitation within an economy composed of many capitals with respect to the reproduction of labour power. Factory legislation is thus the first mode of state intervention into the reproduction process and corresponds to absolute surplus value production under early capitalism.

The Value of Labour Power and the Demographic Composition of Households

A second type of crisis in the reproduction process can be identified; this is grounded in the contradiction between the value of labour power as a commodity and the demographic composition of family-households. In this instance, the wages accruing to many individual households, once established, may not correspond to the consumption needs of those households despite the fact that total wages paid to the working class may equal the costs of reproduction of that class; thus a significant portion of working class households may not be reproduced despite the rewarding of labour at value.

Now the value of labour power itself is determined the same way it is for all other commodities: by the amount of labour-time necessary for the production, and consequently also the reproduction, of this special commodity. In this sense, the value of labour power is equal to that mass of commodities necessary for the maintenance of the labourer; this total must therefore also include the value of training or education, as well as the means necessary to ensure generational reproduction i.e. the cost of raising future substitutes. At the level of the economy as a whole, total wages paid to the working class (variable capital) constitutes a consumption fund equivalent to the value of all commodities needed to ensure the reproduction of the working class at a socially and historically established standard of living.

The price paid to labour power may diverge from the value of labour power in two ways. On the one hand, especially under conditions prevalent during early capitalism, the total wages paid to the working class may fall below the value of labour power due to excessive competition in the labour market. As such, workers will generally experience a fundamental decline in their standard of living and, if this payment below value continues for any prolonged period, then workers may be consumed in production at a faster rate than they can be reconstituted in reproduction. Such discrepancies between the value and price of labour can only be sustained for any length of time in the absence of state intervention where there is a ready supply of labour available to be injected into the capitalist labour market. On the other hand, to say that wages are equal to the costs of existence and reproduction of the working class does not mean that all workers will necessarily receive a money wage that actually meets the subsistence costs of the particular household to which they belong. As Marx pointed out, the concept of the value of labour power being equivalent to wages 'does not hold good for the *single individual* but for the *species*. Individual workers, millions of workers, do not get enough to be able to exist and reproduce themselves; *but the wages of the whole working class* level down, within their fluctuations, to this minimum.'[39]

Thus, since wages are always paid to the *individual*, the price of labour may diverge from the subsistence needs of the household of which the individual wage earner is a member; this discrepancy may occur on a substantial scale even if it is assumed that labour power is being rewarded at value at the level of the economy as a whole. Indeed, this relationship between working-class household subsistence cost structures (rather than low wages or unemployment *per se*) and the experience of poverty had been discovered by Rowntree in his classic book, *Poverty: A Study in Town Life*. Here Rowntree established that poverty was associated with particular points in the family life cycle such that the 'the life of the labourer is marked by five alternating periods of want and comparative plenty'; these periods of want and plenty reflected different ratios of breadwinners to dependents, especially the exclusion of the young and old from the labour market at the beginning and end of the life cycle.[40]

In his article in this volume, Wayne has further analyzed this lack of congruence between wages and the subsistence needs of households in the era of competitive capitalism by examining the relationship that might be supposed to exist between the various stages in the life cycle of the proletarian household and the likelihood of budgetary surplus or deficit. Of all modes of production, capitalism favours early family formation. This is because, on the one hand, the sale of labour power, rather than access to land, is the essential precondition to gaining the means of subsistence; and, on the other hand, because wage rates are likely to be higher for the youthful workers in an as-yet low technology economy where strength and vigor are still prime labour market assets. Thus, at least in the initial period following its formation, the working class household is likely to be in a budgetary surplus prior to the arrival of the first child. That is to say, the individual wage accruing to the household is likely to exceed the value of reproduction of household members.

However, the addition of successive dependent children is likely to reduce the budgetary surplus of the household unit because as consumption needs increase, wages may not necessarily rise accordingly. Indeed, household wages may even decline because of the advancing age and decreasing energy of the worker, or the withdrawal of women from the labour market to bear and raise children since, given the separation of industry from the home, it becomes more difficult to combine paid work and domestic work.[41] Moreover, at a time when public health was underdeveloped, this progression of the family household life cycle into a period of budgetary crisis is likely to be exacerbated by the high fertility rates needed to ensure the survival of at least some offspring into maturity.[42] Finally, when the additional family members gained by procreation are themselves bringing in a wage while remaining at home, then the original household may experience a brief return to budgetary surplus prior to that point when the last child leaves home and the original founding members sink into the poverty of old age and labour market obsolescence. Following Rowntree, these stages in the life cycle of the proletarian household can be illustrated by means of the diagram in Figure 5.1.

This discussion of the life cycle of the proletarian household allows the identification of a significant but somewhat neglected contradiction of capitalism: even assuming that labour power is rewarded at value, i.e. that total wages paid to the working class are equal to the total subsistence or reproduction costs of variable capital, some portion of working class households may experience severe budgetary crises due to their particular demographic composition (ratio of breadwinners to dependents) and the particular stage they are at within the household's natural life-cycle; however, other working-class households, because of their own peculiar compositional character, may be in a surplus budgetary position, with income substantially exceeding consumption needs.[43]

This contradiction ultimately rests upon the fact that labour power is compelled to seek its reproduction in privatized family households. Since households vary in their income levels and subsistence costs, the

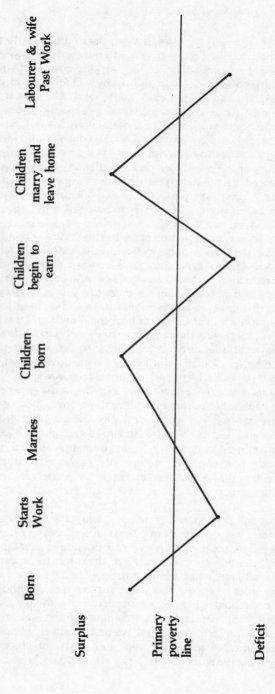

FIGURE 5.1

Poverty and The Family Life Cycle

Sources: S. Rowntree *Poverty: A Study in Town Life* (1910) and Phillip Abrams, *Work, Urbanism and Inequality* (Weidenfeld and Nicolson, London, 1978) p. 9.

total wage paid to the working class becomes distributed in such a way among these households that a significant number are not in fact reproduced, and the reproduction of the working class as a whole is thus made problematic. Indeed, in the absence of a uniform demographic composition to working-class households which secures income equal to subsistence costs, some transfers of wealth must occur in order to secure the reproduction of those households in deficit, and hence the proletariat as a collectivity. This particular crisis classically appears during a competitive stage of capitalist development when the proletarianization of the population and articulation of labour markets are much advanced, yet the state is restricted in its organization of social wage programs. A good example would be mid-Victorian Britain where laissez-faire extended not only to the economic realm but also to the social policy field as well.[44].

There are several possible outcomes to this contradiction. Again these range from the theoretically possible to the historically relevant. One scenario would be a general increase in wage rates sufficient to ensure the reproduction of those households whose unfavourable ratio of wage earners to dependents pushes them towards budgetary crisis and deficit. In this case, all wages would have to be raised in order to secure the reproduction of the larger household units and this would have the effect of increasing the prosperity of those households already in surplus. However, it is difficult to imagine under what conditions the working class, particularly during the competitive period, could actually struggle for and achieve such a general raise in wages. Wayne's analysis suggests that a quite substantial increase in the general wage rate would be necessary in order to achieve the reproduction of deficit households, an increase that would probably eliminate the profits of most industries and lead to the rapid demise of capitalism. Moreover, it must be remembered that wage rates are ultimately limited by conditions in production (e.g. the productivity of labour) rather than conditions which prevail outside production in the household, and thus depend in an important way on the investment priorities of the capitalist class.

A second solution to the problem could take the form of a limitation in family size since, in one sense, the crisis is a function of too many dependent children. However, a reduction in average family size is dependent upon two factors. First, there has to be decline in the infant mortality rate which obviates the need to have large numbers of children in order to ensure that some survive into adulthood; the limitation of household size is also dependent upon the development and spread of reliable contraception techniques to the working class. In Britain's case, both factors seem to have been relatively late developments and their impact was not apparent until the twentieth century.[45] Second, underlying the reduction in family size and a decline of fertility is the changing incentive structure for families to have children. Here again state policy is important; with the extension of factory legislation to include child labour laws and the rise of compulsory schooling, children gradually became dependents for a longer period of time, and hence increasingly costly since they were unable to contribute to the family budget. The decline of the multiple-income household and the rise of the single-breadwinner family towards the end of the nineteenth century reflects the changing relationship between internal household incentive structures and external forces in the labour market and economy.[46]

The third and most significant response to the contradiction between the reproduction of individual working class households and the reproduction of the working class as a whole is by effecting a series of transfers between those households which are in surplus and those households which are in deficit.

There are two possible ways to organize such redistribution. On the one hand, redistribution can be organized on an *inter-class* basis with transfers occurring between classes in society; or on the other, it may proceed on an *intra-class* basis with transfers being effected between and within the working class itself. Let us discuss each of these in turn. Inter-class redistribution involves taxing the propertied classes in some way so as to provide funds for supplementing the income of working class households. The typical forms of inter-class redistribution found during early capitalism were largely inherited from the past; in most countries these comprised a combination of poor law, philanthropy and charity.

Basically the poor law was an attempt to provide social welfare to the dependent worker along quasi-feudalistic, patriarchal lines. For example, under the Old Poor Law in England (1600-1834), individuals had the right to relief from public funds in the parish of their birth. Each parish in turn was empowered to levy a tax, the poor rate, on the propertied classes and distribute the funds so accumulated to the needy. Under the Old Poor Law, such relief was provided in an 'outdoor' form i.e. as a cash payment, wage supplement, or directly, in kind. However, under the New Poor Law (1834-1910) welfare relief was organized under much more repressive lines: support was to be given to the supplicant only on demonstrating destitution and on the condition of entering a special institution, the workhouse. Indoor relief by and large replaced outdoor relief.[47]

As the primary mode of redistributional social welfare under competitive capitalism in Britain both the Old and the New Poor Laws had definite limitations. For one thing the upper classes strenuously objected to supporting those in difficulties, especially as the number needing support grew with the development of capitalist social relations. Whilst some employers had taken the chance to exploit the Old Poor Law by offering low wages knowing that they would be supplemented by the parish, on the whole capitalists objected to the system since they felt the liberal features of outdoor relief not only limited the mobility of labour but also failed to inculcate the necessary degree of fear so as to discipline the working class for wage work.

In the long run, the New Poor Law proved to be an equally limited and inappropriate basis for redistributional welfare—and this became more evident as capitalism developed. First, the New Poor Law still organized welfare on the basis of inter-class transfers. Again, by offering an extremely individualistic approach to the problem of poverty and welfare, the New Poor Law was unable to deal with the structural generation of poverty or loss of income under advanced capitalism. Moreover, its repressive, stigmatizing qualities made the New Poor Law an anathema to the working class and engendered considerable hostility towards the government and local power structures which administered it.

The New Poor Law was supplemented by the activities of charitable and philanthropic agencies. However, since charitable aid took the same 'outdoor' form of relief as the Old Poor Law, the continued independence of the working class household from the discipline of the market was a problem, and charity eventually gave way to philanthropy. Philanthropy differed from charity in that its administration involved direct intervention by some agency in the lives of what were now 'clients'. Accordingly, poverty was held to be a consequence of the way in which the wage itself was disposed of within the household, and a result of its waste on such undesirable commodities as liquor, rather than any objective shortcoming of the economy. Numerous organizations and agencies such as the Salvation Army and the Charity Organization Society sprang up during the nineteenth century whose expressed aim was to conquer poverty by moralism and the 'disciplining' of the worker by the 'officials' of philanthropy.

However, as a solution to the redistributional contradiction noted above, charity and philanthropy, like the Poor Law, have certain limits. For one thing, philanthropic interventions were very unpopular with the working class which saw such invasions of privacy and limitations on self-determination as an adjunct of repressive state social welfare. For another, these supplementary forms of relief advanced individualist, subjectivist solutions to what were basically structural distortions and inequalities in society. Finally, no amount of moralism or improved budget management could make up for an absolute shortfall of domestic resources.

Redistribution may also proceed on an *intra-class* basis. In this case, transfers are effected within the working class itself and can take the form of redistributions over time for each household (e.g. savings) or redistributions between layers of the working class (e.g. unemployment insurance). Such redistribution can theoretically be managed either by the working class itself or by some other entity such as the state. In our view, self-managed redistribution carried out by autonomous working-class organizations, despite the significance of such schemes in the social history of capitalism, embodied fundamental economic and political limitations which led eventually to the replacement of such schemes and their incorporation into state-organized and controlled system of transfers. These limitations are discussed in the next section. For now let us note that self-managed intra-class redistribution would require the development of autonomous, legitimate working class institutions which could establish the various regulations and principles on which distribution is to take place, as well as effectively enforce the redistributional decisions thus made. Such a comprehensive redistributional and sanctioning machinery would in effect constitute the self-government of the working class. For example, for self-administered intra-class redistribution of income to occur, trade unions and other working class organizations would have to have powers, both ideal and real, at least equal to, if not far beyond, those claimed by the national state itself. Such developments would inevitably compromise the wage labour/capital relationship by significantly disrupting the labour market. In any case, it is difficult to imagine that a self-governing working class would reproduce labour in a way that was compatible with a system of capitalist accumulation. For these reasons, the redistribution of wealth by the working class is an unlikely outcome and, indeed, is historically unknown. Thus, self-managed intra-class redistribution tends to be a political as well as an economic impossibility under capitalism.[48] These observations, of course, do not mean that such redistributions were not vigorously demanded on occasion by the working class.

The above discussion suggests that to the extent that intra-class redistribution becomes the primary mode by which the working class is reproduced on a class level, such redistribution tends to be organized and controlled by the state. The second mode of state intervention into the social reproduction process consists, therefore, of regulation of the point of reproduction through state-organized transfers of wealth. Initially, under conditions of competitive capitalism, this intervention took the form of inter-class transfers based upon a limited and repressive system of social welfare. However, the limited extent of transfers under the poor law and the relative weakness of autonomous redistributive mechanisms within working class culture resulted in a low standard of living for significant sections of the working class, an inability to moderate the insecurities of industrial life, and consequently, the experience of poverty as the almost natural reward for wage labour. It was not until a later stage of economic development that these limitations were to some degree overcome through social wage measures such as social security and child allowances. Indeed, as the economic system matured, additional contradictions appeared in the reproduction process which eventually precipitated a revolution in social policy wherein the state began to organize intra-class redistribution of wealth on the basis of social insurance.

The Failure to Valorize Labour Power

In addition to over-exploitation and contradictions with respect to the distribution of the total wage, a third structural crisis which threatens the reproduction of the working class can be identified. This threat derives from the maintenance of the private household domicile being dependent upon securing regular employment and a regular wage. That is to say, without the valorization of labour power in the first place, households cannot be supported at all and hence labour power cannot be reproduced as a commodity. The successful sale of labour power is thus the primary step in initiating reproduction. As Seccombe has put it:

> . . . The wage *must* be the first form of proletarian subsistence. Without it, the second form (consumer goods) cannot be obtained, and the third form (the household) established through previous labour, will soon fall into jeopardy.[49]

While the failure to valorize labour power is possible under all stages of capitalist development, the increasing economic articulation of society under advanced capitalism is likely to accentuate problems as regards the acquisition of the first form of subsistence, the wage, by the proletariat. Indeed, as capitalism matures the insecurities facing the working class become more threatening, with the loss of income possible from an increasing variety of impersonal causes. First, the economic articulation of capitalism entails the ever-increasing proletarianization of the population: as the social relations of capitalist production mature, greater numbers of the workforce are deprived of all income-producing property other than labour power and are concentrated together in urban areas. With the decline of petty production, especially in agriculture, the modern worker finally loses contact with the countryside and hence the ability to retreat to the rural sector to obtain subsistence during economically-depressed times in the city. Certainly, in most major capitalist countries, the capitalization of agriculture effectively precludes any possible return to rural subsistence for the urban proletariat. Thorough-going proletarianization means, therefore, the final demise of the rural safety value to the absence of a wage for the industrial worker.[50] This development also has an international dimension which finds expression in the closure of agrarian frontiers in the settler-colonial states which, in turn, greatly reduced the possibilities of petty bourgeois emigration in the post-1914 world economy.

Second, the increasing dependency of the proletarian household upon the wage is compounded by the intensification of the labour process which accompanies the development of capitalism. This intensification is, as noted earlier, a constant feature of capital accumulation and related to the increasing organic composition of capital. It is therefore a particular feature of relative surplus value production. For the worker, intensification poses the threat of loss of income due to accidents at the work-place and, in addition, places a premium on continual good health and strength. Intensification also holds out the promise of the premature exhaustion and death of the worker, and hence the loss of household income due to death or incapacitation of the breadwinner. Mature capitalist societies tend to develop mechanisms to offset the effects of the general intensification of production upon the working class. Most important in this regard is the extension of factory legislation and development of workmen's compensation.[51]

Another obstacle to the valorization of labour power is that in old age, workers are likely to experience loss of income due to labour market obsolescence. Survival into old age is likely to be associated with a reduction of income leading to the phenomenon, so common in late Victorian society for example, of the 'aged poor'. Under capitalism old age itself is likely to be a prime cause of increased poverty.[52]

Perhaps the most important consequence of the articulation of capitalism as far as potential interruptions in the valorization of labour power is the integration of various economic cycles to form a unified and singular business cycle which affects activity in all branches of production. Indeed, the fundamentally *cyclical* character of capitalist production has been regarded by many as the hallmark of capitalist development. Marx, for example, argued that while there is a constant tendency under capitalism for the revolutionizing of the means of production, such transformation of the basic technical infrastructure only occur periodically; upswings and downswings in economic activity are organized around this periodic replacement of the means of production, constituting the classical business cycle that gives capital accumulation its uneven character.[53] To the extent that the cycles in each major branch of production became synchronized, new forms of economic crisis and insecurity emerge. For the working class these primarily take the form of structural and cyclical unemployment which are the most important causes of loss of income to households in a mature capitalist economy.[54]

In pre-capitalist and early capitalist society, wage workers could to a degree move between branches of production as a solution to seasonal or other fluctuations in the demand for labour; for example, agricultural workers could supplement income during the slack winter months by engaging in cottage industry; or if one branch of industry was depressed, then it was possible to switch to another where demand was high. Flows of labour between agriculture and industry and between branches of industry were possible because the activities in various sectors of the economy were as yet imperfectly integrated, reflecting the lack of mobility of capital and the absence of an average rate of profit to dictate the flow of capital.

The vulnerability of households as regards reproduction therefore increases with the articulation of capitalist social relations. In particular, dependent households divorced from opportunities for petty commodity production face increased insecurities in industrial life. Loss of income may be caused in a variety of ways: illness, death of breadwinner, accidents at work, old age and unemployment. The regulation of these insecurities of industrial life therefore primarily involves the provision of a *substitute wage*. As noted above, there are two basic ways substitute wages can be organized: either autonomous working class organizations develop mechanisms for the intra-class redistribution of resources; or the state can act as the prime agency for the organization of alternative sources of income. Before turning to a discussion of state-managed reproduction on the basis of social insurance, let us briefly indicate the inherent weakness of the autonomous working class regulation with respect to the provision of substitute wages on a scale commensurate with the crisis of valorization.

A possible strategy that can be pursued by the working class in the absence of a wage is to attempt to regulate the uncertainties of industrial life through the development of organizations such as friendly societies, burial societies, trustee savings banks and a host of other self-help mechanisms rooted within the culture of the class itself. Thrift now, as it were, could provide income later. Indeed, throughout its history, a portion of the working class has, because of its ability to command wages above subsistence costs, been able to participate in various voluntary insurance schemes for protection against loss of income or other unexpected expenses; some privileged strata were even able to insure themselves against unemployment as well as the more usual sickness, burial and death of breadwinner risks.

In effect these voluntary schemes of self-insurance constitute transfers, not between strata of the working class, but rather *within* the temporal life cycle of particular households; thus *individual* workers may set aside money to alleviate and regulate their *own* anticipated insecurities lying in the future.

The extent and effectiveness of working class institutions of thrift and self-help is by no means clear. According to the historian Supple, membership in friendly societies in Britain grew rapidly during the nineteenth century, with about half of all adult males belonging to a society by 1850; burial societies and commercial assurance attracted some 1.6 million subscribers, and by 1850, 570 trustee saving banks had attracted over a million depositors.[55] However, it is not obvious from Supple's account how these benefits and services were distributed among the working class or how effective they were in meeting real life hardships. The extent of poverty would suggest that the efficacy of self-help was considerably less than membership figures would indicate. Indeed, Hobsbawm presents an altogether grimmer picture with only the labour aristocracy—some 15 per cent of the workforce—able to secure wages high enough to moderate the risks of industrial life and organize their own social security.[56]

In any case, it does appear that intra-class redistribution on the basis of voluntary self-insurance proved to be historically and structurally limited. First, self-help organizations tended to limit protection and redistribution to a relatively privileged section of the working class; benefits paid out by insurance schemes which required regular contributions were only available to those who were in a position to make such contributions—and certainly this did not include the entire working class. Second, many friendly societies took special care to exclude bad risks i.e. precisely those elements of the population in greatest need of protection against the insecurities of industrial life. Third, only some trades were sufficiently organized into unions capable of providing unemployment insurance and other benefits; and, at least in Britain, when engaged in strikes, these unions tended to suspend all sickness, unemployment and pension benefits.[57] Finally, being voluntary, such autonomous schemes lacked the organizational capacities to achieve redistribution and regulation on a class-wide basis; they were simply not structured to effect transfers between the well-off and poorer sections of the working class on a large enough scale to resolve the typical crises of reproduction apparent under mature capitalism. Indeed, in Britain it would require government compulsion to force these societies to admit the bulk of the working class to their schemes, thus universalizing the self-insurance principle.[58]

Regulation of the insecurities facing the working class under advanced capitalism is therefore more effectively secured through the organization and provision of substitute wages by the state. However, the provision of adequate substitute wages on the basis of the poor law was largely impossible; the previous limited inter-class system of transfer payments was replaced by a more comprehensive, universal and flexible system of intra-class transfers which could supply alternative forms of income to households that failed to valorize labour power. An effective vehicle to achieve this on a scale commensurate with the needs of the working class appears to be through the organization, by the state, of a series of compulsory social insurance programs designed to regulate the insecurities of the proletarian condition.

Quite simply, social insurance proved to be a most effective way of integrating the reproduction of the working class with the ups and downs of capitalism. This was the great discovery of reformers like Beveridge.[59] First, social insurance, since it is compulsory, forces workers to make provision for those future uncertainties for which they might otherwise avoid planning; moreover, under social insurance, claimants have the right to relief independent of their moral state since what is effected is really compulsory *self*-insurance, not charity. Second, social insurance establishes reproduction on the basis of *intra*-class transfer payments and absolves the propertied classes from paying a tax to ensure reproduction of the lower levels of the working class as had been the case under the poor law. Thus, under modern systems of social security, reproduction of the working class is achieved by forcing transfers of wealth between sections of the working class; this amounts to the self-financing of reproduction by the working class itself. A critical question then became the mode of financing for these programs. From the state's point of view it was desirable that they be established on a contributory as opposed to a non-contributory basis, while the more radical section of the working class demanded that they be funded out of general taxation.[60] Thus, state insurance, when established on a contributory basis, does not disturb basic property relations in society and, indeed, can be seen as a regressive form of redistribution in that it reduces the significance of inter-class transfers.

Third, social insurance is an ideal mechanism by which to secure the reproduction of labour through a variety of individually and collectively experienced risks and insecurities. Most importantly it can effectively reproduce labour through cyclical forms of unemployment; thus social insurance reproduces a floating reserve army of labour and prevents the decay or dispersal of labour power during temporary interruptions of employment generated by the business cycle. Fourth, social insurance is flexible; it can be used to relieve a large or small number of claimants and, since it is uninterested in the subjective makeup of these claimants, saves the state considerable policing and enforcing costs.[61] In brief, the main virtue of social insurance is that it socializes the risks and uncertainties experienced by the working class and places the main burden of class reproduction upon the distribution of income within that class itself.

Finally, while social reformers tended to promote social insurance in terms of the systemic effects listed above, what attracted politicians to such schemes was that they thought such schemes admirable vehicles to enhance the political incorporation of the working class into capitalist society. This is true for Bismarck in Germany, Churchill and Lloyd George in England, and politicians in the United States and Canada. Indeed, it is significant that social insurance schemes were generally introduced into western capitalist societies under conditions of intensifying class conflict—and often had with the explicit aim of undercutting working class militancy and the consequences of labour's increasing political representation by independent working class rather than bourgeois political parties.[62]

Social insurance effectively undermined the autonomous character of working class self-help organizations and, by incorporating these organizations into state-administered schemes, served to link the working class to the state. Although in Britain the introduction of state social insurance was originally envisaged as taking place on the basis of friendly societies, in reality, working-class input either in the form of control over the various administering bodies or the accumulated funds was extremely limited, and here the introduction of social insurance was to lead to a progressive decline in the vitality of working class organizations, not their revival. As a result, the working class was increasingly forced to look towards the state for its well-being since the state was now an important contributor to the income maintenance of many households. This has had the effect of taking pressure off employers, for no longer was the wage obtained from the exchange of labour with productive capital to be the *exclusive* source of working class subsistence funds.

Moreover, in its capacity of securing the long-run reproduction of the working class as a collectivity, the state endeavored to reproduce the working class not simply as a unity but rather as a *fragmented* unity. From the beginning, social insurance had important consequences in this regard and acted to establish inequalities in benefits and contributions, thus enhancing the internal stratification of the working class. Divisions were initially established between those workers to be included under the compulsory schemes and those who were excluded; many of the provisions served to duplicate the old distinction between the deserving and undeserving sections of the working class. In sum, the universalization of the state was tempered by the practical division of the working class into distinct benefit categories; the moralism of the nineteenth century was thus replaced by structured inequalities established on the basis of objective categories and regulations. The creation and management of these divisions among the working class have become the fine art of government in the modern era, a prime function of social policy and hence an integral feature of the welfare state.

Conclusion

The above discussion has demonstrated that capitalism is reproduced in part through the capacity of the state to develop strategies of intervention which check the effects of the crises between economy and household, crises which it has been argued are structural outcomes of capitalist development; in this sense the state social interventions described above make an essential contribution towards the reproduction of the working class. Moreover, the pattern and mode of these interventions broadly parallel changes in the accumulation process. Thus, in early capitalist development where accumulation is based upon the mode of absolute surplus value production, the state initially intervenes at the point of production to regulate the capitalist consumption of labour power. As accumulation proceeds under mature capitalism more on the basis of relative surplus value production, then new crises appear in the reproduction process and the state increasingly intervenes at the point of reproduction through the articulation of a social welfare policy whose primary function is to provide substitute wages and other forms of income for dependent households.

One of the most important factors operating to secure the reproduction of capitalist society has been the transformation of social welfare policy and institutions from an old deterrent-based system of poor law relief prevalent during the nineteenth century in Britain (and elsewhere) into the modern system of social insurance or social security which now generally prevails. The principles and practices guiding social policy have indeed undergone a fundamental change over the past century in all the leading capitalist countries such that it is possible to distinguish radically different approaches in social welfare policy between the period of early competitive capitalism and the later period of monopoly capital. This chapter has suggested that the rise and evolution of social insurance to regulate the uncertainties of industrial life and to redistribute the total wages paid to the working class serves to distinguish the new from the old, and, as such, the institution of social insurance represents a revolution in social policy in both economic and political terms. Social insurance has played a decisive role in securing the reproduction of capitalist social relations of production.

It is useful to conclude by drawing out some of the major differences between the old system of relief—the deterrent-style poor law—and the newer system of social security primarily based on social insurance. A distinction between these two forms has been made in terms of a *residual* concept of social security where a minimal, temporary type of service is offered at the discretion of the granting agency, and an *institutional* concept of welfare that provides relief in a nonstigmatizing fashion to those who experienced the impersonally caused insecurities of urban industrial life.[63]

These two approaches to the administration of welfare differ in several important respects. On the one hand, the old system was primarily intended to deal with the lower level or marginal elements of the workforce; the criterion for benefits was usually compelling need and coupled with punishment for moral failing. The basis of legitimacy lay in a kind of *laissez-faire* individualism which tended, however, to be moderated by economic and political realities into a sort of paternalism. The goal of such a deterrent poor law was primarily the disciplining of individuals for wage work and was thus appropriate for an early capitalist era.

On the other hand, modern systems of social security address broad categories of wage and salaried workers. On the whole, individuals acquire rights to benefits which in turn, because of their compulsory inclusion in schemes, are paid out irrespective of the individual's actual needs or moral character. As Churchill succinctly put it when advocating the advantages of social insurance: 'You qualify, we pay.'[64] In contrast to the paternalism of the earlier systems, the legitimacy of modern social security thus rests on either the notion of *contract* i.e. contributions paid in or work performed is sufficient to establish right to benefits; or *status* i.e. the condition of being a propertyless wage worker or a citizen *in itself* gives the right of access to social security. Again, in contrast to the particularistic goals of deterrent poor law, it is possible to detect a more universalistic goal for modern systems in the sense that they are designed to secure the reproduction of entire or core elements of the working class through the uncertainties of industrial life rather than the control or disciplining of marginal elements. We can summarize the major differences between the two systems of social welfare in Table 5.1.

While our discussion of state policy has largely been theoretical, such transformations as we have outlined cannot be seen as taking

TABLE 5.1

Two Systems of Social Welfare

	Deterrent Poor Law	Social Security based on Social Insurance
Criteria for benefits	Compelling need coupled with punishment for moral failing	Right established by contributions or status
Extent of population coverage	Particularistic; limited to lower level, marginal elements of workforce	Universal; extended to cover broad categories of wage/salary workers
Inclusion	Voluntary; last resort	Compulsory contributions; right to benefits irrespective of need
Basis of legitimacy	Individualism moderated by economic/political realities; paternalism	(a) Contract: contributions, work performed establish rights to benefits (b) Status: condition of wage labour or citizenship establishes right to benefits
Goal	Discipline and moral revival of individuals; social control; definition of parameters of workforce	Non-stigmatized reproduction of core elements of workforce through the management of long- and short-run insecurities of industrial life
Accumulation Regime	Competitive capitalism	Mature, fully articulated capitalism

place in a social and political vacuum; they are not simple 'mechanical' responses by the state to the 'logical deficiences' of capitalism as a social system. While it is true that the advanced capitalist countries have all by and large adopted social insurance as the primary strategy to regulate the insecurities of industrial life, there is of course considerable national variation here especially as regards the historical timetable of reform, the range of programs in place and the mode of financing and internal organization of such programs. Thus, for instance, Germany under Bismarck was the first industrial society to develop the social insurance principle to any great extent despite the fact that it was considerably less developed economically at the time than Britain. Similarly, not all the advanced countries have the same programs in place; thus even today the United States lacks child allowances and a national medical insurance system.[65] What accounts for this complexity? While it has not been the intention of this chapter to write a history of state intervention, it is possible to point to the following variables which 'moderate' the impact of the 'structural' factors outlined above. Very broadly these include: differences in political culture and institutions particularly as they effect the nature of the state itself and its perceived role in society; the legacy of the previous pre-capitalist mode of welfare and the degree to which patriarchal relations persist or a thorough-going *laissez-faire* philosophy prevails; and differences in the strength, character and organization of the working class.[66] Of these factors, perhaps the latter is most important; it is pressure from below that stirs the state to intervene and moderate the reproduction process. A complete account of state social intervention must combine these logical and historical factors.

Social policy interventions of the state are part of the reproduction process in capitalist society and the state itself is a constituent element in the reproduction of capitalist social relations. But state intervention does not resolve once and for all the contradictions in reproduction. Rather, the state and its programs have become the locus of new crises and tensions, some of which are investigated in other chapters of this volume.

Notes and References

I would like to thank Wally Seccombe for his very useful comments on an earlier draft of this chapter.

1. Recent literature on the state is enormous. On economic and political aspects see: Ernest Mandel, *Late Capitalism* (NLB, London, 1975) especially chapter 15; Suzanne de Brunhoff, *The State, Capital and Economic Policy* (Pluto, London, 1978); Ralph Miliband, *State in Capitalist Society* (Weidenfeld and Nicolson, London, 1969); and his *Capitalist Democracy*

in Britain (Oxford University Press, New York, 1982); Nicos Poulantzas, *Political Power and Social Classes* (NLB, London, 1973); John Holloway and Sol Picciotto (eds.), *State and Capital* (Edward Arnold, London, 1978). On social policy aspects see: Ian Gough, *The Political Economy of the Welfare State* (Macmillan, London, 1979); and his 'Theories of the Welfare State: A Critique', *International Journal of Health Sciences*, Volume 8, 1, (1978); James O'Connor, *Fiscal Crisis of the State* (St. Martin's Press, New York, 1973); A. Aumeeruddy, B. Lautier *et al.*, 'Labour Power and the State,' *Capital and Class*, Volume 6 (1978); Ramesh Mishra, *Society and Social Policy* (Macmillan, London, 1977); and Claus Offe, *Contradictions of the Welfare State* (MIT Press, Cambridge, Mass., 1984).

2. Social policy refers to a very broad range of state interventions including social welfare and social security programs, public health and housing, education and factory and labour legislation; it can be extended to include the development and operation of social control institutions such as prisons and asylums. For definitions of social policy see John Goldthorpe, 'The Development of Social Policy in England 1800-1914', *Transactions of the Fifth World Congress of Sociology*, Volume IV (1964); and T. H. Marshall, *Social Policy* (Hutchinson, London, 1975). In this chapter we restrict ourselves to a discussion of social *welfare* (maintenance of individuals and households on basis of inter-class transfers of wealth; social *security* (substitute wages provided through intra-class transfers usually organized on a compulsory social insurance basis); and *industrial* welfare (restrictions and regulations affecting the labour market and employers' utilization of labour).

3. A formalistic periodization is given by T. H. Marshall in his *Class, Citizenship and Social Development* (Anchor Books, New York, 1965). Most conventional histories of social policy use arbitrary divisions. See also John Carrier and Ian Kendall, 'The Development of Welfare States', *Journal of Social Policy*, 6, 3 (1977), pp. 273-78.

4. H. Wilensky and C. Lebeaux, *Industrial Society and Social Welfare* (Free Press, New York, 1965). See also Neil Smelsner, *Social Change in the Industrial Revolution* (University of Chicago Press, Chicago, 1959). For a critique of the functionalist approach see Carrier and Kendall 'Development of Welfare States;' and Gough, *Political Economy of Welfare State*, pp. 7-9.

5. Gough, *Political Economy of Welfare State*, pp. 32-38.

6. Frances Piven and Richard Cloward, *Regulating the Poor: The Functions of Public Welfare* (Random House, New York, 1971).

7. Ibid., p. xv.

8. Piven and Cloward's later book, *The New Class War* (Pantheon, New York, 1982) argues that the New Deal reforms represent a fundamental change in subsistence rights and makes a much more forceful case for the periodization of social policy in relation to the development of labour markets.

9. For distinction between absolute and relative surplus value see Karl Marx, *Capital* Volume 1 (Progress Publishers, Moscow, n.d.), pp. 276-77. See also Geoffrey Kay, *The Economic Theory of the Working Class* (Macmillan, London, 1979), pp. 44-53.

10. This should not be taken as meaning that the crisis of over-exploitation is restricted to some historical period dominated by 'dark satanic mills.' Certain sectors of the advanced capitalist economies, especially the lower levels of the secondary labour market still employ 'sweated' (very often illegal) labour. Also a central feature of Third World industrialization is employment at very low wages, the extensive use of female labour and very high industrial accident rates.

11. Marx, *Capital*, Volume 1, Chapter X for a discussion of the working day under capitalism. See also Fichtenbaum and Welty in this volume for a close textual analysis of this chapter of *Capital*.

12. Ibid., pp. 252-253.

13. Karl Marx, *Capital*, Volume III (Progress Publishers, Moscow, 1971), p. 77. David Ricardo in later editions of his *Principles of Political Economy and Taxation* came to the conclusion that the adoption of machinery was in fact detrimental to the working class because it decreases the fund 'upon which the labouring class mainly depend' such that it 'renders the population redundant, and deteriorates the condition of the labourer.' (Penguin Books, Harmondsworth, Middlesex, 1971), p. 380. John Stuart Mill also noted that 'It is questionable if all the mechanical inventions yet made have lightened the day's toil of any human being.' *Principles of Political Economy* (Penguin Books, Harmondsworth, Middlesex, 1970), p. 116. There is thus general agreement on this point between all forms of political economy.

14. Jurgen Kuczynski, *Labour Conditions in Great Britain* (International Publishers, New York, 1946), p. 46. See also Marx, *Capital*, Volume I, pp. 226-281 for data on the length of the working day in various branches of British industry during the first part of the nineteenth century. For Canada see, Gregory Kealey (ed.), *Royal Commission on Relations of Labor and Capital: Canada Investigates Industrialism* (University of Toronto Press, Toronto, 1973).

15. Whilst Engels' characterization of pre-industrial England as a time when 'workers vegetated throughout a passably comfortable existence. . . . They did not need to overwork (and) had leisure for healthful work in garden or field. . . . Their children grew up in the fresh country air, and if they could help their parents at work, it was only occasionally; while of eight or twelve hours work for them there was no question' may be something of an exaggeration [Frederick Engels, 'The Conditions of the Working Class in England,' in Karl Marx and Frederick Engels, *On Britain* (Progress Publishers, Moscow, 1953), p. 36] it is nonetheless true that patterns of work and exploitation were considerably different prior to the rise of industry. As Benedix has written: 'For the peasant, work varied with the season, involving long hours during the summer months and short hours during the winter. Moreover, many peasants were also occupied in the putting-out system . . . and the routine of their work entailed unwitting adaption to a variety of tasks and to an irregularity of performance which were incompatible with the specialization and machine-driven regularity of factory work.' Under cottage industry there was an 'alternation between frenzied work and frenzied recreation.' R. Bendix, *Work and Authority in Industry* (University of California Press, Berkeley, 1974), p. 38.

16. Adam Smith, *Wealth of Nations*, Edited by Edwin Cannan (Modern Li-

brary, New York, 1937), Chapter 1, 'On the Division of Labour', especially pp. 7-8.

17. Charles Babbage quoted in Harry Braverman, *Labour and Monopoly Capital* (Monthly Review Press, New York, 1974), pp. 79-80.

18. Karl Marx, 'Wage Labour and Capital' (1849), in Karl Marx and Frederick Engels, *Selected Works*, Volume I (Progress Publishers, Moscow, 1969), p. 171.

19. Marx, 'Wage Labour and Capital,' p. 171.

20. Marx, *Capital*, Volume 1, p. 372.

21. Kuczynski, *Labour Conditions in Great Britain*, p. 45. Prime Minister Pitt around the turn of the century proposed that children should start work at the age of five.

22. For a discussion of women workers in the nineteenth century, see Wanda Neff, *Victorian Working Women* (AMS Press, New York, 1966); Ivy Pinchbeck, *Women Workers and the Industrial Revolution* (Cass, London, 1969); and Louise A. Tilly and Joan W. Scott, *Women, Work and Family* (Holt, Rinehart and Winston, New York, 1978).

23. See Tilly and Scott, *Women, Work and Family*, chapter 6. The authors note that during early industry the insufficiency of the husbands' wages accounted for much of married women working, but when children were available and the opportunity present for them to work, wives tended not to work. p. 133. This characterization of early industralism as a family wage economy made up of multiple income households has to be distinguished from the movement pressing for a *family wage* i.e. a single income sufficient to maintain a household.

24. Derek Fraser, *The Evolution of the British Welfare State* (Macmillan, London, 1973), p. 12.

25. Tilly and Scott, *Women, Work and Family*, p. 132.

26. See Engels' accounts of urban conditions in London, Glasgow and elsewhere in his 'The Condition of the Working-Class in England,' in *On Britain*, pp. 56-109. See also Fraser, *The Evolution of the British Welfare State*, pp. 51-55. Most urban developments lacked drainage, sewers and water supply—essential services for the prevention of disease. For a description of rural housing conditions see William Cobbett, *Rural Rides*, Volume I (Reeves and Turner, London, 1893), p. 21.

27. For data on Britain see E. J. Hobsbawm, 'The British Standard of Living 1790-1850,' in *Labouring Men* (Weidenfeld and Nicholson, London, 1968), pp. 83-87, where it is noted that not only did *per capita* consumption of meat, cereals, sugar and milk decline, but that most consumer goods were heavily adulterated. For the European Continent see C. Lis and H. Soly, 'Food Consumption in Antwerp between 1807 and 1859: Contribution to the Standard of Living Debate,' *Economic History Review*, Volume XXX, 3 (1977), pp. 460-485 where it is concluded that 'the average *per capita* diet in Antwerp declined drastically, both quantitatively and qualitatively, in the first half of the nineteenth century.'

28. Hobsbawm, *Labouring Men*, p. 72.

29. Engels, 'Condition of the Working Class in England,' in *On Britain* p. 237, quotes a doctor in Sheffield to the effect that 'the hardest drinkers among the grinders are the longest lived among them, because they are the longest

and oftenest absent from their work.' Indeed, the mechanization of a trade was likely to have deleterious consequences for the operatives; thus whilst grinder's disease was virtually unknown in Sheffield prior to the introduction of steam power, by 1850 50% of grinders in their thirties, 79% of those in their forties and 100% of those over fifty were reported to be suffering from this terrible affliction. E. J. Hobsbawm, *The Age of Revolution* (Mentor Books, New York, 1962), pp. 238-248.

30. Quoted in Hobsbawm, *Labouring Men*, p. 75. See also Marx, *Capital*, Volume I, p. 235 where one medical practitioner is quoted as noting that 'each successive generation of potters is more dwarfed and less robust than the preceeding one.'

31. The failure to reproduce an appropriate normative structure in children who worked is graphically illustrated by material Marx quotes from the Children's Employment Commission of 1866; here various young operatives are reported as describing the devil 'as a good person,' and a king as 'him that all the money and gold.' See the material drawn from the Children's Employment Commission in Marx, *Capital*, Volume I, p. 247.

32. On capitalist development and migration, see Michael J. Piore, *Birds of Passage: Migrant Labor and Industrial Societies* (Cambridge University Press, Cambridge, 1979); Alejandro Portes, 'Migration and Underdevelopment,' *Politics and Society*, 8, No. 1 (1978), 1-48; Alejandro Portes and John Walton, *Labor, Class, and the International System* (Academic Press, New York, 1981); and A. Redford, *Labour Migration in England, 1800-1850*, (A.M. Kelley, New York, 1968).

33. This does not mean to say that labour migration is no longer an important feature of capitalism; migrant labour, legal or otherwise, is often significant in agriculture, menial services and competitive sector firms in the advanced capitalist societies. For a full discussion of current patterns of labour migration in Europe see Stephen Castes and Godula Kosack, *Immigrants Workers and Class Structure in Western Europe* (Oxford University Press, Oxford, 1973); and Elizabeth McLean Petras, 'The Global Labor Market in the Modern World Economy,' in Mary M. Kritz, Charles B. Keely and Silvano M. Tomasi (eds.) *Global Trends in Migration: Theory and Research on International Population Movements* (Center for Migration Studies, New York, 1981), 44-63.

34. Marx, *Capital*, Volume I, p. 285.

35. For a brief review of factory legislation see Fraser, *The Evolution of the British Welfare State*, pp. 15-27. The regulation of child labour by the state (which violated the principles of *laissez-faire*) was apparently overcome by the argument that since the relationship between child labourer and employer was not freely entered into, then children were entitled to public protection. The legal restriction on factory work for women was also accompanied by numerous efforts to 'educate' women into the domestic arts. See Ward and Neff, *Victorian Working Women*, pp. 76-85.

36. For a discussion of domestic labour in the family wage or multiple income household economy, see Tilly and Scott, *Women, Work and Family*, p. 136-139. Apparently reformers noted that married women's work away from home 'diminished their own domestic abilities' and 'deprived their daughters of the "education" a housewife required.' For a discussion of

the role of working class struggle and organizations in pressing for a 'family wage' i.e. the single-breadwinner family and the exclusion of women from production, see Jane Humphries, 'Class Struggle and the Persistence of the Working-class Family,' *Cambridge Journal of Economics*, Volume 1, 3 (1977), pp. 241-258.

37. Elmar Altvater, 'Some Problems of State Intervention,' in Holloway and Picciotto (eds.), *State and Capital*, pp. 40-43.

38. Marx, *Capital*, Volume 1, pp. 257-8.

39. Marx, 'Wage Labour and Capital', p. 159.

40. Seebohm Rowntree, *Poverty: A Study in Town Life* (Macmillan, London, 1902), pp. 136-7.

41. Wally Seccombe, 'Domestic Labour and the Working Class Household,' in Bonnie Fox (ed.) *Hidden in the Household* (Women's Press, Toronto, 1980), p. 80.

42. Tilly and Scott, *Women, Work and Family*, p. 99, note that high rates of infant mortality tended to keep fertility high. It is also important to note that, with the rise of industry, *childhood* mortality rates were very high; and that *class* differences in mortality rates began to appear. See Susan Klepp, 'Childhood Mortality and Class in Philadelphia 1720-1830,' paper presented to The Society for Eighteenth Century Studies, Huntington Library, San Marion, California, February 1984.

43. Rowntree found that 'largeness of family' accounted for 22.16% of those in 'primary poverty.' See *Poverty: A Study*, p. 121.

44. Foster presents evidence for mid-Victorian England that incomes of a majority of working families were below subsistence costs as defined by the Poor Law authorities; and that all working families experienced deprivation at certain stages in their development, especially old age or before young children could work. See John Foster, *Class Struggle and the Industrial Revolution* (Methuen, London, 1974), pp. 95-97.

45. Fertility rates peaked in Britain at 35 births per thousand between 1862-1878 and then began to decline after 1879, reaching about 25 per thousand in the early 1920s. By the 1930s it had dropped sharply to under 20. Tilly and Scott, *Women, Work and Family*, pp. 90-91. In mid-Victorian England, 72% of families had four or more children whereas by 1925 this proportion had shrunk to 20%. See David C. Marsh, *The Changing Social Structure of England and Wales* (Routledge and Kegan Paul, London, 1965), pp. 41-43.

46. Various reformers advocated the forced sterilization of the poor and the breakup of families in order to limit working-class procreation. For example, at the turn of the twentieth century, the eugenics movement argued that marriage should only be permitted when the couple could show that their 'progenitors have been entirely, or largely, free from nervous prostration . . . hysteria . . . epilepsy' as well as 'alcoholism, pauperism, criminality, prostitution and insanity.' Quoted in Anna Davin, 'Imperialism and Motherhood,' *History Workshop Journal*, 5 (1978), p. 20.

47. For a discussion of the poor laws in Britain see, Maurice Bruce, *The Coming of the Welfare State* (Butsford, London, 1968); and Karl de Schweinitz, *England's Road to Social Security* (Perpetua, New York, 1975). For the United States see, Walter Trattner, *From Poor Law to Welfare State* (Free

Press, New York, 1979). For Canada see, R. Splane, *Social Welfare in Ontario 1791-1893* (University of Toronto Press, Toronto, 1965); E. Wallace, 'The Origin of the Social Welfare State in Canada 1867-1900' *Canadian Journal of Economics and Political Science*, 16 (1950).

48. This, of course, does not mean that the working class did not attempt to take over the institutions of social welfare, or advocate reforms which would have instituted self-managed reproduction. For example, in Poplar, London socialist councillors, through control of the Board of Guardians, tried to provide relief on more liberal grounds than had previously been the case. See Miliband, *Capitalist Democracy*, p. 138.

49. Seccombe, 'Domestic Labour and the Working Class Household,' in *Hidden in the Household*, p. 55.

50. This aspect of proletarianization was very advanced in Britain. By 1850 a substantial proportion of the population was urbanized; by the Great War only 8% of the labour force was engaged in agriculture. See E. J. Hobsbawm, *Industry and Empire* (Penguin Books, Harmondsworth, Middlesex, 1969), pp. 157-159.

51. For a discussion of the intensification of labour under the Second Industrial Revolution see David Landes, *The Unbound Prometheus* (Cambridge University Press, Cambridge, 1969), pp. 265. On factory legislation and workmen's compensation see Elie Halevy, *Imperialism and the Rise of Labour* (Barnes and Noble, New York, 1961); and Bentley Gilbert, *The Evolution of National Insurance in Britain* (Michael Joseph, London, 1966).

52. For a discussion of old age, poverty and the pension movement in Britain see Bruce, *The Coming of the Welfare State*, pp. 173-181; Halevy, *Imperialism and the Rise of Labour*, pp. 232-236.

53. For a discussion of Marx's theory of the industrial cycle, see Ernest Mandel, *Late Capitalism*, Chapter 4. See also Joseph Schumpeter, *Business Cycles*, Volume I (McGraw-Hill, New York, 1939), for a thorough discussion of the cyclical character of capitalist production and accumulation.

54. Economists generally distinguish between various types of unemployment. First, there is *frictional unemployment* which occurs when workers must move from one job to another whenever demand moves from one product to another; in a fully articulated capitalist economy, this form of unemployment does not account for the majority of those out of work. More important is *seasonal* unemployment which results from the seasonal character of demand or production. Third, there is *structural* unemployment which results from changes in the structure of industry and technology and demands that workers learn new skills, change industries, move to new areas, etc. Finally, there is *cyclical* unemployment which results from the depression phase of the business cycle. Structural and cyclical forms of unemployment are the most prevalent forms under developed capitalism, the former reflecting longer cycles of investment in new technologies and the latter the fluctuations of the shorter business cycle. See E. K. Hunt and Howard J. Sherman, *Economics* (Harper Row, New York, 1972), pp. 318-319, 322, 589. The discovery of structural and impersonal causes of unemployment (and hence poverty) was a long drawn-out process. See Jose Harris, *Unemployment and Politics* (Oxford University Press, Oxford, 1972); Gilbert, *Evolution of National Insurance in Britain*, passim; E. P.

Hennock, 'Poverty and Social Theory in Britain,' *Social History*, I (1976) for a discussion of Booth's work; and William Beveridge, *Unemployment: A Problem of Industry* (Longmans, Green and Co., London, 1931).

55. Barry Supple, 'Legislation and Virtue: An Essay on Working Class Self-Help and the State in the Early Nineteenth Century' in Neil McKendrick (ed.), *Historical Perspectives* (Europa, London, 1974), pp. 214-221. One problem with using friendly society membership figures to indicate the proportion of the working class covered by such schemes is that often one worker belonged to several clubs. See Rowntree's discussion of friendly societies, *Poverty: A Study*, pp. 355-361.

56. Hobsbawm, *Industry and Empire*, p. 155.

57. Halevy, *Imperialism and the Rise of Labour*, p. 215.

58. Friendly societies expressed fears that Lloyd George's plans to introduce pensions and health insurance would 'kill voluntary organizations like ours.' Originally, Lloyd George intended to make these democratic and non-profit organizations the central vehicle for universalizing social insurance, but this was severely compromised by concessions to private economic interests. See Gilbert, *Evolution of National Insurance*, p. 294 and passim.

59. Beveridge's work was critical in presenting the principle of social insurance as the most efficient solution to the problem of unemployment and the limitations of the poor law.

60. For disputes over contributory and non-contributory proposals in the British labour movement, see A. Marwick, 'The Labour Party and the Welfare State 1900-1947,' in H. R. Winkler (ed.), *Twentieth Century Britain* (New Viewpoints, New York, 1976), pp. 175-6.

61. As Churchill put it when promoting unemployment insurance: 'Our concern is with the evil, not with the causes, with the fact of unemployment, not with the character of the unemployed.' Quoted in Gilbert, *The Evolution of National Insurance*, p. 272.

62. As Bismarck put it when speaking on the social insurance question in 1884: 'Give the working-man the right to work as long as he is healthy; assure him care when he is sick; assure him maintenance when he is old. . . . If the state will show a little more Christian solicitude for the working man, then I believe the (Social Democrats) will sound their bird call in vain, and that the thronging to them will cease as soon as the workingmen see that the government and legislative bodies are earnestly concerned for their welfare.' Quoted in W. H. Dawson, *Bismarck and State Socialism* (Swan Sonnenschein, London, 1890), p. 34. Churchill echoed similar sentiments: 'I feel that the system of insurance . . . is going to be an absolutely inseparable element in our social life. . . . It must lead to the stability and order of the general structure.' Quoted in Miliband, *Capitalist Democracy*, p. 3. For the Canadian case see, Carl Cuneo, 'State Mediation of Class Contradictions in Canadian Unemployment Insurance, 1930-1935,' *Studies in Political Economy*, 3 (1980), pp. 37-67. The Marsh Report in Canada argued that 'The genius of social insurance is that it enlists the direct support of the classes most likely to benefit and enlists equally the participation and controlling influence of the state.' Quoted in Bob Russell, 'The Politics of Labour-Force Reproduction: Funding Canada's Social Wage, 1917-1946' in *Studies in Political Economy*, 14 (1984), p. 73.

63. Donald Guest, *The Emergence of Social Security in Canada* (University of British Columbia Press, Vancouver, 1980), pp. 1-2; and Gaston V. Rimlinger, *Welfare Policy and Industrialization in Europe, America and Russia* (John Wiley, New York, 1971), pp. 3-6.
64. Churchill quoted in Harris, *Unemployment and Politics*, p. 313.
65. See Mishra, *Society and Social Policy*, p. 93 for national variations in terms of social welfare coverage.
66. For a comparative analysis of economic, political and social factors in the introduction of social insurance in Germany and Britain see my Ph.D. dissertation, 'Regulating the Insecurities of Industrial Life,' University of Toronto, 1982; and Rimlinger, *Welfare Policy and Industrialization*, passim.

6

THE STATE AND THE MAINTENANCE OF PATRIARCHY: A CASE STUDY OF FAMILY, LABOUR AND WELFARE LEGISLATION IN CANADA

Jane Ursel

This chapter is part of a larger study[1] of the relationship between the family and the state in Canada which seeks to explain the persistence and dynamic of patriarchy in contemporary capitalist societies. In order to analyze the connection between capitalism and patriarchy this chapter explores the relationships between production and reproduction as it is revealed in the intersection of family, labour and welfare law. The selection of a legislative focus for the analysis of patriarchy is the outgrowth of a theoretical perspective which identifies the state as the critical mediator in the co-ordination of productive and reproductive relations in contemporary industrial society.

I define reproduction quite specifically as the production of human life which involves three processes: procreation, socialization and daily maintenance. My definition of patriarchy, on the other hand, is more general and refers to a system or set of social relations which operates to control reproduction through the control of women both in their reproductive and productive labour. Given this general definition, however, it is critical to the analysis of patriarchy that the operation of such systems be specified, as the achievement of this general goal—controlling reproduction—is accomplished through different means in different historical periods. In the debates over the utility of the concept of patriarchy, feminists have identified the need for such specificity, and, by and large, have concurred that it is contingent upon a more specific theorizing of reproduction. It is necessary to begin, therefore, by outlining in general terms the modes of reproduction that have existed historically and the forms of patriarchy that have supported them.[2] Two forms, familial and social patriarchy, are identified with class society, and as such, are of special interest to this analysis. In order to understand the generalized transition from familial to social patriarchy, which is described in greater detail in the following section, a case study has been selected for special scrutiny. In it, I examine the crucial role that the Canadian state played in a period of early industrialization (1884-1913) in restructuring crucial components of the reproduction process. A detailed analysis of state intervention into the domains of factory legislation, child welfare law and property law demonstrates both the continuing existence of patriarchy as a regulator of reproduction in industrial capitalism and its change from a familial to social form.

Theorizing Reproduction

Feminist theory has been developed over the past decade in an attempt to write women and reproduction into historical and contemporary analyses of society. Among socialist feminists various theoretical strategies have been pursued, all of which revolve around the central question of clarifying the nature of the relationship between production and reproduction. As socialists, there is an acceptance of the Marxian concepts of base, superstructure and determination. As feminists, however, there is debate over where reproduction fits into this scheme; does it fit into the base or superstructure, and is it determined or codeterminative? While there is a general consensus that orthodox Marxist analysis has rendered reproduction opaque there is little consensus as to the theoretical causes of this problem or the theoretical solutions.[3]

I suggest that the single-base model of society found in Marxism, which locates production as base and relegates reproduction to some indeterminant location—variously conceptualized as a response to or a 'moment' of production—is the heart of the problem. Despite caveats to the contrary, the single-base model has led to a linear understanding of production determining reproduction 'in the final analysis'. Thus, when the 'real' dynamic of society is seen to lie in production, attention is diverted from the dynamic of reproduction. The solution to this theoretical conundrum is to redefine base and reconceptualize determination. For instance, it is possible to argue that reproduction is an essential component of the base, not because it is grafted on to production, but because of the fundamental material reality that humans must reproduce as well as produce in order to sustain themselves and society. Thus production and reproduction are distinct but interdependent modes of organization. This concept implies divergence from traditional theory not only in the location of reproduction but also in the understanding of determination.

Within this model of society which sees production and reproduction as interdependent modes of organization there are two strategies for theorizing reproduction. The first strategy attempts a parallel analysis of reproduction with production. The goal of this theorizing is to specify a dynamic, a set of contradictory relations and a dialectic within each of the modes of production and reproduction and then to discuss the intersection between the modes. An example of this strategy is the work of O'Brien[4] which concentrates on specifying the dialectic of reproduction but is somewhat vague about the intersection between the two modes.

The second strategy, which will be pursued here, puts greater emphasis upon the co-determinative character of the two modes and suggests that the dialectic is best understood as intermodal rather than a set of parallel, separate dynamics within each mode. While both production and reproduction have a dynamic of their own as each organizes different aspects of human labour, the existence of contradictions and the dialectic of any given social system lies precisely in the interaction of the two modes. This strategy not only requires a detailed theorizing of reproduction but also a serious reconsideration of the dynamics of production, which, within Marxist orthodoxy, is seen as self-contained.

In order to understand the interaction between production and reproduction the components and the dynamic of the two spheres must be clearly specified. While Marx provides a clear analysis of production it is also necessary to build upon the work of Levi Strauss, Rubin[5] and Meillassoux[6] to specify the components and the dynamic of reproduction. In locating the components of relations of reproduction Rubin begins with Levi-Strauss' provocative observation that 'the sexual division of labour is nothing else than a device to institute a reciprocal state of dependency between the sexes'.[7] From this perspective sexual divisions of labour are not seen as some concession by production to biological differences but rather a conscious structuring of production relations in the interests of the social organization of reproduction. As well as suggesting the concept of co-determination this statement implies that heterosexuality, the most fundamental prerequisite of procreation, has to be institutionalized. Based upon Levi-Strauss' deductions, Rubin identifies three critical components of reproduction which operate at the most general level: the sexual division of labour, gender, and the structural enforcement/re-enforcement of heterosexuality.

The feature which we are concerned with, the dynamic of reproduction, is the process by which a system maintains balance within reproductive relations as well as between production and reproduction. Meillassoux provides concepts for analyzing this dynamic. He argues that all societies must maintain a balance between the productive and unproductive members in the community. This balance is achieved by regulating procreation rates so that each generation of productive adults produces and supports a sufficient number of children so as to ensure a future labour supply as adults age and become less productive. This balance is in turn predicated upon a balance within the sphere of reproduction itself. The nature of any specific reproduction dynamic is governed by the operation of the sex-gender system with its rules of marriage, sexual taboos and practices, infanticide, etc., which operates to vary, sometimes dramatically, fertility rates within a set demographic unit characterized by a given productive capacity.

From this dynamic the intersection between the modes of production and reproduction can be located as an exchange of resources: labour resources, the product of reproductive relations, are exchanged for subsistence resources, the product of productive relations. Variation in resource allocation flows can alter the demographic composition which in turn can alter the productive capacity through changing current and future labour supplies. This approach effectively replaces the Marxian model in which production is said to determine reproduction with a more sophisticated model of codetermination. Any given economy or productive capacity (if we take that as our arbitrary starting point) is itself determined by the existing demographic composition (labour supply) of the community, which in turn is a product of prior interactions between the productive and reproductive modes. Conceived in this way, the relation between production and reproduction is cyclical or dialectical rather than linear or parallel.

At this abstract level it is possible to conceive of the organization of reproduction involving specific allocations of labour on the basis of age and sex and some restrictions of male and female sexual behaviour which does not, at least in theory, necessitate the subordination of women. However, the emergence of patriarchy as a means of organizing reproduction alters both the components and dynamic of the sex-gender system as outlined above. In addition to the sexual division of labour, gender and compulsory heterosexuality, female subordination now becomes a fundamental component of the system. The essential condition for the subordination of women within any patriarchal system is *control of women's access to the means of their livelihood*. By making women's access to subsistence contingent on entry into particular reproduction relations or by restricting their ability to be self-sufficient, women's labour, both productive and reproductive, becomes subject to comprehensive control. This control is the essence of patriarchy, its universal function and effect. The means of achieving control, however, varies according to the political and economic structure of the social system in question. Therefore, the next step is to outline major structural features of different societies which share the organization and operation of patriarchy.

In order to specify the different types of patriarchy which increase our understanding of the interaction between production and reproduction, the concept of modes of reproduction must be introduced. Three distinctive modes of organizing reproduction can be enumerated.

These are (a) *communal patriarchy*, which corresponds with pre-class, kin-based social systems; (b) *family patriarchy*, which corresponds with class-structured social systems characterized by decentralized processes of production; and (c) *social patriarchy*, which corresponds to advanced wage labour systems. This chapter will identify and distinguish the latter two modes as it is the transition from familial patriarchy to social patriarchy which is the object of our analysis. Moreover, it is within these two modes of reproduction that the state emerges as an important mediator between production and reproduction.

Specifying Patriarchy

In pre-class societies people produce to meet the needs of the reproductive kin-based group, whereas, in class societies reproduction is regulated to meet the needs of production. In pre-class societies it was in the direct material interest of the individual and the kin group to reproduce. In class societies the material advantage of reproduction, i.e. the productive potential of labour power produced, increasingly accrues to those who control production rather than those who produce and reproduce. Thus in class societies the logic of the relationship between production and reproduction is reversed and the two spheres become separated in the process.[8]

A consequence of this separation between production and reproduction is the emergence of a real distinction between the social (economic and political sphere) and the familial (reproductive sphere). The necessity of controlling the reproduction process and making it responsive to class interests results in a division of patriarchy's operation into two spheres, the social and familial. Familial patriarchy is the hierarchical sexual organization for the reproduction of sex-gender identities and relations as it exists in the family; in contrast, social patriarchy is the societal organization of sex-gender relations through rules and laws concerning marriage, property, inheritance, and child custody.

Both familial and social patriarchal structures operate in class societies. While social and familial forms of patriarchy are complementary, under differing material conditions one aspect will emerge as the critical locus of power and authority over women with the other form playing a secondary or facilitative role. In a familial patriarchal mode, power and authority over women is decentralized, operates at the household level and is based upon the patriarchs exclusive control of women's access to necessary (survival) resources. Within this system social patriarchal rules are facilitative, empowering the patriarch with such control through marriage, property and inheritance laws. In the social patriarchal mode, the power and authority to control women's access to resources is increasingly vested in the state through the promulgation of labour, welfare and family law. Within this mode, familial patriarchy is essential in providing the structural unit for reproduction in the nuclear family, but is secondary as the source of power over women.

Class societies are marked by two fundamental imperatives, the short-term extraction of surplus in the interests of the dominant class, and the long-term reproduction of the labour supply which is in the interest of the system as a whole. An important role of the state in class societies is to ensure a balanced allocation of labour and non-labour resources between the two spheres of production and reproduction so that the system is maintained both in the long and short term. In brief, the state is the guarantor of the rules of class and the rules of patriarchy and must insure that one system does not disrupt the other.[9] In petty commodity production systems this process is facilitated by the structural interpenetration of production and reproduction which requires a minimum of state intervention. In capitalist production systems, however, the structural separation of production and reproduction tends toward contradictions in the satisfaction of the short and long term requirements of the system which necessitates much more direct state intervention and regulation.

Patriarchy is important because the state cannot (inspite of some ill-fated attempts)[10] legislate procreation. It must instead set up a system via family, property and marriage laws which will serve to translate social and economic requirements into compelling household imperatives. The characteristic feature of familial patriarchy is its pronatalist dynamic. This results from the nature of the interaction between class and patriarchy which creates a determinant relation between productivity and procreation at the household level. The dynamic of familial patriarchy can be characterized as follows. The family is the productive unit and the patriarch is the head of this unit. The family has a vested interest in increasing its productivity because this will improve its standard of living. However, the class system insures that the head of household has *limited* control over resources necessary to increase production. Certain resources (e.g. land) are out of the hands of the patriarch and are controlled by the dominant class. Technological innovation in peasant societies is also limited. The only resource controlled by the patriarch which can enhance productivity is labour power. In labour-intensive peasant societies, therefore, more children may well translate into greater production. Hence, there is a logical relation between production and procreation at the household level. Thus, in societies in which the family is the basic unit of production, the dynamic of familial patriarchy tends toward the maximization of procreation.[11]

Historically, the balance between production and reproduction within the familial mode of production was achieved through a finely co-ordinated system of centralized and decentralized authority. While control of production necessitated the vesting of authority over land in the hands of the dominant class, the control of reproduction required a decentralized system of authority in which the household patriarch exercised direct control. These dual levels of authority were structurally complementary because of the amenability of the resource (land) to privatization in conjunction with the decentralized nature of the productive process. The authority and interest of the patriarch did not compete with those of the dominant class precisely because the material conditions of his household authority (access to land) were based upon submission to class authority. This symbiotic relationship between class and patriarchy was possible as long as the production process was decentralized and the family operated as a productive unit.

Familial patriarchy remained a viable system of control throughout the transition from the feudal mode of production up until the early commercial stages of capitalism. This was a result of the decentralized nature of production which maintained the family's function as a productive unit for the bulk of the population. Although a class of propertyless wage labourers evolved during this period, the definitive disassociation of family formation from control of productive resources did not emerge until the massive proletarianization of the population effected by the rise of industrial capitalism.

Industrial capitalism centralized the process of production and its successful expansion was dependent upon the predominance of the wage labour system. An important change was that wages now replaced access to productive property as the economic basis of the family. Gradually, the household lost all productive resources other than the labour power embodied in each member. This transformation seriously undercut the material basis of the patriarchal family for control of productive resources was the basis of the patriarch's own authority. The husband/father's ability to control the labour power of family members was lost to those who now controlled access to productive resources i.e. employers. Furthermore, the husband/father's ability to reap rewards from the control of family labour power was diminished because gains from productivity increases were appropriated by employers who left workers with a wage that was seldom sufficient to cover their own maintenance costs. Lastly, the husband/-father's interest in controlling the labour power of family members could, and often did, come into conflict with employers who were interested in unfettered access to the cheapest labour possible. Thus the male worker not only failed to reap the benefit of his wife's and children's labour but also confronted women and children in the workplace as direct competition and hence a serious threat to his own wages and job security. In short, under the centralization of production, industrial capitalism upset the delicate balance between centralized and decentralized authority which had permitted a complementary co-existence between class and patriarchy in earlier types of society. Class interests under capitalism were now structurally incompatible with patriarchal interests.

The wage labour system is individual and contractual in nature, with the value of labour power responding to market forces rather than to reproductive requirements, for example, size of family or number of dependents of workers. Therein lies the flexibility, economy and efficiency of the wage labour system compared to previous productive relations. Indeed, it is precisely these characteristics which make the capitalist system so unresponsive to the reproduction needs of the population that also makes it so effective as a system of extracting surplus. The operation of this system is, therefore, non-negotiable in terms of the interests of the dominant class. However, the operation of the wage labour system in an unmediated form threatens to absorb all existent labour and capital for its own expansion, bleeding resources from and hence impoverishing the reproductive sphere. The early stages of industrialization revealed this potential and caused considerable alarm especially over the conditions of female and child labour, declining standards of living, high infant mortality rates and abortion.

The dynamic of the wage labour system to maximize the extraction of surplus requires the unrelenting commodification of labour which ignores the long-term needs of the social system to maintain and reproduce the population. Under capitalism, however, the existence of the population is dependent upon an adequate allocation of resources to the reproductive unit. The state, charged with preserving the system as a whole, is faced with a major challenge in attempting to mediate the now fundamentally contradictory spheres of production and reproduction. It is under these conditions that social patriarchy emerges as a new regulatory role for the state.

The material basis of patriarchy has always been male control of resources essential to the maintenance of the family. What distinguishes social from familial patriarchy is the increasing centralization of control, with access to resources dominated by the employer on the one hand and the state on the other. The individual patriarch is no longer the central force in the maintenance of control over reproduction. The employer's interest in the maintenance of patriarchy is a distant second to interest in the extraction of surplus; when the two conflict it is a foregone conclusion that the interests of surplus extraction predominate. Thus the state stands alone as the only entity which has both an interest in preserving patriarchy and the material resources to do so.

With the destruction of the decentralized base of patriarchal authority in household production, and the subsequent deregulation of reproductive relations, the state was increasingly pressured to assume many of the supportive and regulative functions previously confined to the family. Consequently, there was a shift in the locus of power from familial to social patriarchy. As some of the patriarchal relations of the family were undermined by social and economic developments, the state, through the system of social patriarchy, attempted to reinforce familial patriarchy. Hence the peculiar paradox of our time: the liberalization of family law, the emergence of women's and children's rights, while appearing as the end of patriarchy, are, in fact, a manifestation of the growth of social patriarchy.

While the problem of balancing production and reproduction is inherent in their incompatible structures and hence ongoing, changing material conditions produce different manifestations of the problems necessitating different strategies of intervention. The following review of legislation in Canada chronicles the state's response to the earliest manifestations of imbalance between the two spheres. A problem, variously described in the Victorian rhetoric of the early reformers as 'the woman problem', 'race suicide' or 'child saving', was that of the disorganization of reproductive relations occasioned by the lack of fit between the old patriarchal order and the new economic system.

The Family and the State in Canada 1884-1913

In 1884 Ontario passed a Factories Act; this has been long recognized as an historic moment in industrial relations in Canada since these acts became the model for most early labour legislation in the English-speaking provinces. This chapter argues that it was also an historic moment in reproductive relations. With the exception of some earlier legislation in the area of the family, 1884 marks the onset of a flurry of legislative activity in the areas of labour, family and welfare law which, when examined as a whole, reveals a remarkable pattern of state intervention into the process of reproduction.

Increasing state intervention in the 1880s was in response to growing evidence in the larger cities of serious disruptions in reproductive relations. The first victims of the disjuncture between the old patriarchal order and the new economic system were women and children. They worked under the worst conditions for the lowest wages, roamed the streets as 'urchins' and prostitutes and filled the houses of refuge and public charitable institutions.[12] Under increasing pressure and demands for reform the state introduced a number of statutes designed to effect a better fit between the demands of work and family life. Because the state showed no inclination to fundamentally restructure production to better meet the needs of reproduction, the legislative activity of the state is best understood as an attempt to reduce the extreme consequences of imbalance i.e. to ameliorate the most troublesome symptoms of the structural contradiction. In this period, however, the disjuncture was so extreme that state intervention necessitated a reformation of the wage labour system and a transformation of patriarchy.

State intervention involved three processes. First, state-commissioned inquiries served to translate broad-based demands into specific recommendations upon which the state could act; second, there was the passage of specific legislation; and third, regulatory agencies were developed to enforce the provisions of legislation. The latter element is clearly as critical as the legislation itself. Although the reform of the wage labour system and the transformation of patriarchy are structurally and historically interconnected, these processes are manifested in different inquiries, legislation and agencies. Therefore, this analysis of state activity begins by examining how the wage labour system was reformed by labour laws which increasingly limited the use of child and female labour in the productive sphere. Then changes and developments in family and welfare legislation are examined. It is argued that both of these processes were critical in realigning the patriarchal order with the new economic system. The analysis follows the same trajectory as actual state intervention i.e., inquiries, legislation and regulatory agencies.

Reproduction and the Reformation of the Wage Labour System

According to Pentland[13] the state in Canada has a long history of mediation in the labour process which significantly predates industrialization or the Factory Acts. Prior to 1884 state interventions in the labour process were primarily designed to repress and police labour in the interests of employers. Commenting on state intervention in the early nineteenth century Pentland writes:

> "Labour relations" in the period when canals and railways were built meant troops and mounted police to "overawe" the labourers, governments spies to learn their intentions, and priests paid by the government and stationed among the labourers to teach them meekness. Here was a full program of intervention, immediately on behalf of contractors, basically to promote economy for the state by encouraging contractors to make low bids in the expectation that low wages could be paid, and then enforcing the low wages.[14]

An examination of labour legislation before 1884 indicates that there were only a few labour statutes in Canada such as the Master and Servant Act and the Apprentices and Minors Act which contained any clauses protecting workers' interests or rights. While these laws provided some protection for workers, the absence of any system of enforcement or regulation suggests minimal commitment by the state to the protective intentions of these acts. Indeed, until 1872 the criminal code of Canada treated unions as criminal combinations in restraint of trade (unregistered unions were criminal until 1889). The General Railway Act (1868) set fines of $400 or five year jail terms for strikers, and the Militia Act (1868) provided troops to local governments to police labour.

In the 1880s, however, a change in the character of state mediation began to emerge. Canadian historians[15] point out that the late-nineteenth and early-twentieth century was a period of growing labour organization and resistance. One indication that this was putting pressure on the state as well as employers is the number of federal royal commissions dealing with labour disputes throughout this period. Under such pressure the state could no longer politically afford the public role of employers' henchman and it became increasingly necessary to make some concessions to labour. As a result the promulgation of labour legislation accelerated dramatically after 1884. While the amount of legislation marks a substantial break with the past the most important difference lay in the content of the legislation which for the first time set out to regulate conditions of work and employment (e.g. Factory and Mines Act of 1884 and 1890) as well as to provide some legal recourse to workers abused by the system (e.g. Wages Act and Workmen's Compensation Act of 1886).

This new mediating role of the state, deriving from its mandate to balance production and reproduction, is best understood as an attempt to modify two of the most troublesome aspects of the wage labour system: first, the relentless drive towards the commodification of labour, and second, the indiscriminate consumption of labour power regardless of age or sex. These tendencies not only provoked great resistance on the part of labour but were also particularly problematic in their effect on reproductive relations. As discussed in the previous section, the commodification of labour is merely the process whereby employers disassociate their short-term surplus extraction interests from their long-term interests in reproducing the labour force. The result was wage levels set so low that they barely ensured the daily maintenance of the workers themselves, much less their generational reproduction. As well, no compensation beyond the actual labour time worked was available. Thus the Workmen's Compensation Act of 1886, limited as it was, involved an important restriction on the commodification process by extending the obligation of the employer to the worker beyond the actual labour time paid for by providing compensation to workers injured under certain circumstances. This legislation is a good example of the intricate balancing act involved in the state's mediation of productive and reproductive pressures by playing off employer-employee interests. On the one hand, the act was a major piece of protective legislation which guaranteed the right of workers and their families to make claims upon their employers in case of accidents in the work place; on the other hand, the act also served to protect employers by institutionalizing a limited degree of liability.

The Factory, Shops and Mines Acts of 1884, 1888 and 1890 respectively are examples of attempts to modify the second aspect of the dynamic of the wage labour system, the indiscriminate consumption of labour power. The increasing scale of female and child employment in industry raised a dual specter: on the one hand, the exhaustion and/or abuse of female workers implied the depletion of society reproducers; on the other the exhaustion and/or abuse of child labour implied the depletion of future labour resources. The more benevolent sections of these acts therefore served to limit the use of labour and to improve the health and safety conditions under which such labour worked.

A second unintended effect of the system's indiscriminate use of labour was that there was no assurance that the employment of women would respect certain patriarchal imperatives, i.e. the maintenance of women's subordinate status relative to men. Patriarchal tradition and perhaps the physical conditions of work during the early industrial period resulted in a clear sexual division in the labour force with women concentrated in light industry and men concentrated in heavy industry. However, with the advent of machino-facture there was no mechanism within the wage labour system itself which would insure the perpetuation of such a division. Employers in their short-sighted pursuit of profit could well extend the use of cheap female labour to other, previously male, occupations. If the pursuit of profit was a stronger motive than the perpetuation of patriarchy this could seriously disrupt the sexual segmentation of the labour force. Since the appeal of the wage labour system lay precisely in its ability to facilitate the short-term extraction of surplus, regardless of reproductive considerations (including a disregard for patriarchal traditions that do not directly enhance the surplus extraction process) then it is not unreasonable to assume that the unmediated dynamic of the wage labour system could have a leveling effect. Not only would the extensive integration of women in the labour force threaten the patriarchal premise of female subordination and conflict with the long term process of generational reproduction, but it would also erode women's special appeal to employers as a cheap reserve army of labour. Women's status as a reserve army is dependent upon their marginalization, and if they became an integral part of the labour force this particular characteristic would be lost. Thus an important aspect of labour legislation is the role it plays in perpetuating the sexual division of labour, maintaining women's role as primarily reproductive and reinforcing patriarchal structures by effectively restricting women's productive role.

While we have postulated two separate but related thrusts in the pattern of state mediation—containment of the commodification dynamic and reinforcement of the sexual division of labour—it is the second aspect which is most often neglected in histories of state intervention. Although limiting the commodification dynamic undoubtedly has important implications for reproduction, reinforcing the sexual divisions of labour is more important for determining the form patriarchal relations of reproduction take and, therefore, is more revealing of the relation between state and family. In the seventeen years between Canadian confederation and 1884 there were thirty-one royal commissions in Canada, only one of which—an inquiry into labour laws in Massachusetts—dealt with the concerns of labour. However, the growth of the labour reform movement in the 1880s exerted increasing pressure on the federal and provincial governments of central Canada. Although bills to regulate factories were introduced in nearly every session of the federal parliament during the 1880s, no legislation was enacted.[16] The Macdonald government resisted legislation on the grounds of constitutional jurisdiction but did initiate a series of investigations in an attempt to placate labour reformers. Indeed, between 1884 and 1913 there were no less than twenty one federal royal commissions concerned with labour and industrial disputes. Ontario, the most industrialized province, followed suit; there was a royal commission in 1910 on the questions of workmen's compensation, and three special committee reports, one concerning female labour in 1900, one concerning child labour in 1907 and a report on underground work in Ontario mines in 1912.

Two consistent themes emerged from the federal and provincial inquiries. First, there was a growing conviction that the state had to play an active mediating role in employer-employee relations. Secondly, there was a strong assumption that female labour was different from male labour and therefore that it had to be subject to special protections and restrictions. The commissioners' vision of the role of the state is illustrated in the routine recommendations that the state regulate hours and conditions of work through the initiation and enforcement of factory acts. Recognizing of the importance of expanding the state's role in this area, the Royal Commission of Labour and Capital of 1889 (Labour Commission) advocated the institution of a Labour Bureau, which would monitor labour conditions across Canada. An act establishing the Labour Bureau was passed in 1890 although it did not become operative until 1900. It is interesting to note that although the Labour Commission was divided according to its members' class sympathies, there was a general consensus on two points: the need to expand the mediating role of the state and the need to regulate and restrict the role of women in the work-place.

Inquiries which addressed the issue of female labour had several features in common. First, it was argued that adult women workers be separated from adult male workers and that they be included with children in recommendations on hours and conditions of work; secondly, special attention was paid to the impact of employment on women's health; and finally, there was a unique concern with the impact of employment on the morals of female labour.

The Commissioners' special concern for women's health reflects the common assumption during this period (actively fostered by the medical profession) that women's reproductive capacity made them vulnerable physically and that, if women were to be employed, then the work environment must take this into consideration. As the Labour Commission noted: 'Medical testimony proves conclusively that girls, when approaching womanhood cannot be employed at severe or long-continued work without a serious danger to their health, and the evil effects may follow them throughout their lives.'[17] Thus 'girls' unlike 'boys' were perceived to become more vulnerable with age rather than less. The report of the commissioners on the dispute between Bell Telephone and their operators contained some unusual recommendations which can only be understood in terms of reproductive considerations. In addition to the usual issues of hours of work, age at employment and conciliation, they recommended the appointment of a commission of medical experts, regular health examinations and better seats for this largely female labour force.

The concern for morals tended to focus on two issues—the intermingling of the sexes on the job and the importance of separate sanitary facilities. While it was recognized that sex-segregated work places would be impractical, recommendations stressed the importance of minimizing and controlling contact between the sexes on the shop floor. To this end the Labour Commission recommended the employment of female factory inspectors and shop floor supervisors:

> 'Female inspectors should visit factories in which females are employed, in order that inquiries may be made which men cannot properly make of women. Where considerable numbers of women and children are employed their immediate supervision should where it is possible, be entrusted to women.'[18]

The issue of washroom facilities came to be seen as an important measure of the moral tone of the workplace as the following observation reveals:

> 'It has been sufficiently demonstrated that in some factories closets are used indiscriminately by the operatives of both

sexes, and where the employer is thus careless of the moral feelings of his operatives it should be the duty of the State to interfere and see that the properties of life are strictly observed.'[19]

This sort of approach to the question of female labour suggests that the very first steps taken by the state to mediate between women and the productive process not only reflected a nineteeth century patriarchal image of womanhood but also, through its recommendations, served to insure that this model with its procreative assumptions would not be abandoned in the face of a major economic transformation. These underlying reproductive considerations are also evident in the legislation which institutionalized the special status of women workers recommended by the commissions.

The manifest concern of the early factory legislation, as stated by the legislators, was the improvement of the conditions of labour. Beneath this manifest goal, however, particularly in the case of female labour, there was a more fundamental and determinant concern—the balancing of the productive-reproductive needs of society. Labour legislation directly addressed the intersection of production and reproduction through laws which determined the special conditions of female and child labour, and distinguished it from the conditions of male labour. It is possible to assess the extent to which these laws spoke to the presumed interests of women as reproducers, the self-expressed interests of women as workers and the existing sexual segmentation of the labour market as a means of illustrating the latent goals and concerns guiding state intervention.

Table 6.1 presents a summary of the labour legislation in Ontario between 1884 and 1913 which applied exclusively to women and children. Included here are the Factory, Shops and Mining Acts which initiated legal distinctions between male and female/child labour. These three acts are important because they institutionalized the patriarchal conventions from which these distinctions were derived and set parameters for subsequent legislation which expanded upon and perpetuated such conventions. Also, the acts encompassed a broad range of occupational fields, covering all of the manufacturing and mechanical sector (Factory Acts), much of the commercial sector (Shops Act), and an important part of the primary sector (Mining Operations Act). Finally, throughout the period under discussion, these three laws were subject to frequent amendments and consolidations which served to introduce more distinctions between male and female/child labour. It is important to note that these amendments were cumulative. Indeed, by 1912 these three acts contained twenty three major distinguishing clauses which enumerated and entrenched the legal distinctions between male and female labour.

TABLE 6.1

Ontario Legislation: Changes in the Regulation of Female and Child Wage Labour, 1884-1913

Year	Legislation	Exclusions	Restrictions	Protections
Prior to 1884		None	None	None
1884	Factories Act	Boys under 12, girls under 14 cannot be employed in factories	Boys 12-14, girls 14-18 need parental approval for employment in factories	Women cannot clean machinery with moving parts during machine operation
			Children & women may work no more than 10 hrs/day or 60 hrs/week	Children & women must have 1 hr/day for meals
1888	Shops Act		Boys under 14 & girls under 16 may work no more than 74 hrs/week; 12 hrs/day; 14 hrs/Saturday	Women must be provided with seats or chairs
1889	Factories Act		Women and children no more than 36 days of overtime per year	

TABLE 6.1

Ontario Legislation: Changes in the Regulation of Female and Child Wage Labour, 1884-1913

Year	Legislation	Exclusions	Restrictions	Protections
1890	Mines Act	All women, boys less than 15 cannot be employed in mines	Males between 15 & 17 cannot be below ground more than 8 hrs/day, 48 hrs/week	
			Males under 20 cannot be in charge of transportation machinery in mine, under 16 if machinery is animal drive	
1895	Factories Act	Government may exclude boys under 16, girls under 18 from dangerous or unwholesome employment		
1897	Shops Act	Children under 10 cannot be employed in shops	Children & women cannot be employed before 7 A.M. or after 6 P.M.	
		Women and children employed full-time in factories cannot be employed in shops		

Year	Act		
	Mines Act		Males between 15 & 17 cannot be employed underground on Sundays
1908	Shops	Children 12 & under cannot be employed in shops	
	Factories Act		Youth category of males between 14 & 16 introduced. All restrictions and protections for women & children apply to youths
	Mines Act	Exclusions of women and girls waived for mica trimming operations	
1912	Mines Act	Boys less than 14 cannot be employed in mines. Girls & women can be employed as stenographers and bookkeepers in mining companies	Males less than 17 cannot be employed underground Males less than 18 cannot be in charge of hoisting apparatus in mines

A number of social historians have observed that this legislation had more to do with women as reproducers than with women as wage workers.[20] As the architects of this legislation, the reformers and commissioners clearly had a one-dimensional definition of womanhood, i.e. woman as mother. In this sense, the legislation can be understood as a form of legal recognition of the value of women's reproductive role since it protected women as active or potential reproducers from being totally consumed in the production process. The legislation introduced limitations on the hours women could work, the places in which they could work and the quality of the work environment. One consequence of this preoccupation with women's procreative potential was that many issues regarded by labour as secondary were elevated to a level of central importance precisely because of their supposed effect on women's health and morals. These often were the work environment clauses which provided for separate lunch rooms, regular breaks, seats for women in shops, separate lavatory facilities, etc. Such measures highlighted the protective, benevolent character of the acts, and were included in the factory inspectors' reports of improvements in the safety, health and sanitary conditions for female labour.

The legislation appears to have been fairly responsive to the presumed needs of women as reproducers, even if it was not working women themselves who defined these needs. In fact, there is some evidence that working women did not share the patriarchal model of womanhood incorporated into the legislation. Given the general anti-natalist dynamic of the wage labour system, the legislators' option was to circumscribe women's productive role in deference to the requirements of reproduction. However, the increasing demand for birth control and abortion and the declining birth rate suggest that women had another accommodation in mind. Furthermore, on the occasions when women workers' demands have been recorded their concerns as workers for better wages, better hours and unionization were not much different than those of men.[21]

Analysis of the impact of this legislation on women as workers cannot help but note the number of workers excluded. The omissions in the legislation are as telling as the acts themselves. The single largest category of employed women, domestics, were excluded from any protective legislation.[22] Similarly, women working in their homes doing piece work or women working in small establishments were also exempt, since the factory acts initially applied only to places employing twenty persons or more. It appears that the closer work and the working environment approximated women's traditional place in society the less appropriate legislators felt the need for state regulation and intervention, regardless of how exploitative the conditions of labour were.

The most significant ommission, however, was the legislation's failure to address the most compelling problem for women workers—the wage disparity between men and women. While it is true that the issue of wage scales did not enter into any legislation during this period, it is important to note that in making the case that women were a special category of labour subject to special concerns and in need of special protection, a rationale existed for intervention into pay inequality. Of all the 'special needs' of women workers the wage discrepancy was clearly the most fundamental.

Evidence available from the Ontario Bureau of Industries and the *Labour Gazette* indicate that throughout the period of industrialization it was nearly impossible for a female factory worker to make a living wage. The wage and cost of living figures for female factory workers in 1889 clearly illustrates this problem. Table 6.2 shows that female workers without dependents made a tiny surplus over subsistence costs. However, for female workers with dependents Table 6.2 shows that wages fell significantly short of necessary expenses. A report in the *Labour Gazette* twenty

TABLE 6.2

Earnings and Budget Position of Female Workers in Ontario, 1889

	Women over 16 Years of age Without Dependents	Women over 16 Years of age With Dependents
Average number of dependents	0	2.10
Average number of hours/week worked	54.03	58.20
Average number of days/year worked	259.33	265.43
Average wages/year from occupation	$216.71	$246.37
Extra earnings aside from regular occupation	0	$ 23.05
Earnings of dependents	0	$ 16.48
Total earnings/year	$216.71	$285.90
Total cost of living/year	$214.28	$300.13
Surplus/Deficit (−)	$ 2.43	$−14.23

Sources: Annual Report of the Bureau of Industries for the Province of Ontario, pt. 4, 1889, *Ontario Sessional Papers*, Vol. 22 pt. 7 pps., 43, 49. L. Rotenberg, 'The Wayward Worker: Toronto's Prostitute at the Turn of the Century' in *Women at Work in Ontario 1850-1930* (Women's Press, Toronto, 1974).

four years later indicates that the situation of women workers had still not substantially changed. Professor C.M. Derrick of McGill University reported in the *Gazette* that the average wage of female factory workers in Canada for 1913 was $261/year or $5/week; the living wage at that time was considered to be $390/year or $7.50/week.[23]

Further evidence of the extent and serious consequences of low wages for female workers was provided by the Social Survey Commission which was established in 1913 to investigate the problem of prostitution in Toronto. The Commission argued that women's inability to make a living wage was a major factor in contributing to prostitution and recommended the passage of a minimum wage law. Despite the fact that female factory workers were among the most protected workers under the legislation of the time this protection did nothing to alleviate the primary economic problem they faced. By 1914 one third of employed women were working in factories in Ontario yet their ability to earn a living wage was no better than before the passing of the Factory Acts.[24]

So far we have considered what the legislation did and did not do for women as workers and women as reproducers. But what was the impact of reform on the sexual segmentation of the labour force? This raises a number of questions. First, was legislation really necessary given a rather clear segmentation of the labour force at the time of its passage? Secondly, was it merely a symbolic piece of legislation honoring or perhaps unconsciously reflecting the dominant patriarchal ideology of the times? In order to address these questions and to suggest that there was intent and effect involved, it is necessary to consider briefly some legal implications followed by some economic observations.

The first legislation which distinguished between male and female labour marked an historic transition; the norms and traditions upon which the sexual segmentation of the workplace was based became codified within legal structures. As legal historians point out, the transition from informal norms to a formalized legal code reflects a societal recognition of the fundamental importance of the norms and the consequent necessity to insure their enforcement through state power. Implied in this transition is the suspicion (on the part of the legislators or the populace as a whole) that the norms themselves are no longer sufficient to the task and require substantive institutional reinforcement. Furthermore, the commitment to enforcement through the development of the factory inspectorate suggests an active rather than passive commitment by the state to the sexual segmentation of the labour force.

Because of the sexual segmentation of the labour force prior to the passage of labour legislation we do not have a simple before and after measure of its effect. Within the parameters of the period, however, there are some indications of its short term impact. The creation of legal distinctions between male and female labour created economic and political disincentives for employers tempted to extend the use of cheap female labour into traditionally 'male' occupations.

The special conditions attached to the employment of women, children and youths meant that the most economic use of such labour occurred in areas of industry where they were already highly concentrated. The introduction of women into factories traditionally employing men would mean capitalists would have to establish special hours for women workers, special facilities and special rules—all of which would add up to extra expense and extra surveillance from factory inspectors. The introduction of women into heavy industry during World War One suggests that this resulted in improvement of working conditions, as well as a dramatic increase in the number of factory inspectors.[25] The early labour legislation created some real economic disincentives for employers considering the integration of women in non-traditional areas of work. Furthermore, the legal recognition of women as a different category of labour provided political and ideological support for organized labour which resisted employers' attempts to introduce women into traditional 'male' occupations. However, while these political and economic effects reduced the benefits to be gained by employing women in 'male' occupations, the benefits to employers of female labour in 'female' occupations were not seriously disrupted.

One indication of the seriousness with which the Canadian state pursued its new mediating role is revealed in the establishment of government agencies/bureaucracies which, in the case of labour, had two functions. First, labour bureaus both at the federal and provincial levels operated as ongoing commissions of inquiry compiling labour statistics as well as reports from labour representatives on current issues of concern or controversy. Second, the factory inspectorate, at the provincial level, monitored employers' compliance with state regulations, informing employers of violations and fining or prosecuting offenders when necessary.

A brief examination of the institution of these agencies suggests that the state was reluctant to assume its new policing role as in most cases there was a significant time lag between the passage of legislation and the establishing of such bureaucracies. At the federal level there was a ten year lag between the passage of legislation establishing a labour bureau in 1890 and its actual operation in 1900. In Ontario a labour bureau was established in the Department of Agriculture in 1882 but did not begin operating as such until 1900 when it was relocated in the Department of Public Works. The Ontario factory acts passed in 1884 called for the inspection of factories; however, the first inspector was not hired until 1887 and in 1890 there were only three inspectors for the whole province. These numbers increased only gradually; in 1895 the first female inspector was hired and in 1904 a second woman was added. By 1909 there were nine inspectors including two women for the province. Once hired, however, the factory inspectors in Ontario were diligent and from 1888 the Ontario sessional papers contain detailed annual reports on factory conditions throughout the province.

The factory inspector's reports are a good indicator of the philosophy and practice of government intervention in the sphere of production. Here the Ontario reports reflected and amplified the same patriarchal assumptions and concerns as articulated earlier by the commissioners and legislators. The rationale for protective legislation and the necessity for enforcement was eloquently expressed by one factory inspector in the report for 1905:

> When I tell you that today we have in this province, women working in the foundaries, machine shops, and breweries, some of the weaker sex, and not a few of their champions will be surprised. I do not mention this as meaning to say that labour for women and children is degrading, but rather to show ample reason why they should be protected . . . the effect of propagation by the present race and the degeneration of future generations.[26]

The activities and recommendations for the inspectors were circumscribed by a complex set of factors in addition to the imperatives of the patriarchal perspective. Among the critical determinants of the ways in which they conducted their work was their general perception of the role of the factory inspector, as well as the very real limits to their authority established by the legislation itself and the economic realities of industry at the time.

The inspectors' perception of their role, reflected the dominant reform philosophy of the time which maintained that government regulation was designed to protect employers who wanted to initiate reform as much as it was to protect workers. As one inspector put it: 'factory laws are for the mutual benefit and protection of both manufacturing and labouring classes'[27]. The aspiration to serve both employer and employee limited the inspectors to peripheral issues, most frequently to those which concerned the working conditions of women and children. Concern with the health and morals of the working woman translated into detailed reports on lunch room facilities, seats for women, communal drinking pails and above all, the provision of separate, modest and clean lavatories.

The inspectors preoccupation with peripheral issues was reinforced, if not determined, by the limitations imposed on them by the legislation. The labour laws did not interfere in the central nexus of employer-employee relations—the wage. The legislation not only ignored the issue of exploitative wage rates in the case of female and child labour but also failed to deal with well-documented abuses of the wage system; for example, the legislation did not address the manipulation of apprenticeship/training periods or excessive fines for errors or lateness which frequently left women and children with reduced wages by the end of the week. Even when the legislation permitted and the inspectors rose above the peripheral issues, the limits to their authority made it clear they were no match for the industrialists when a serious conflict of interest occurred. For example, in the 1908 inspectors report there was a lengthy discussion of the employment of children in mica factories in the Ottawa area which involved violating the existing labour law. The inspector reported that when he confronted the employers with these violations, they stated that if attempts were made to enforce the law, the industry would simply relocate to Quebec where restrictions were not so severe, or establish a putting-out system. Indeed when pressed to comply with the law, the employers carried out their threat to relocate with impunity.

Imbued with the enthusiasm and paternalism of the reform era but restricted by the letter of the law, emphasis on the 'motherhood issues' (health and morals) became an attractive and effective outlet compensating inspectors for the structural limitations on their real ability to improve the conditions for working women. As Roberts and Klein remark, the celebratory tone of the inspectors' reports suggest, '. . . once separate lavatories are defined as central indices of progress, each new firm which complied was a victory in the inspector's eyes.'[28]

The final stage of state activity, the development of regulatory agencies, is consistent in process and perspective with the preceding stages. All levels of intervention are characterized by a sustained, if somewhat reluctant, extension of the state's mediation role and an increased commitment to a specific pattern of protecting women as reproducers.

The lack of fit between the new industrial capitalist system and the older familial patriarchal form precipitated not only reforms of the wage labour system but also a transformation in the form of patriarchy. The transition from familial to a social patriarchy can be broken down into three component processes: first, the erosion of the patriarch's legal authority over women and children, coupled with a shift in the focus of family legislation from father/husband's rights to father/husband's responsibilities; second, the assumption of that authority by the state; and third, the provision of resources to subsidize the familial unit of reproduction. This transition process can be traced in two other areas of state activity—family and welfare law.

The analysis of family law concentrates on two specific aspects of the legislation, laws determining the disposition of children and laws determining the disposition of property within a marriage and upon its dissolution. Corresponding to this the discussion of welfare legislation focuses on two features: the extension of state authority over the care and disposition of children, and the growth of welfare resources to meet the needs of certain dependency categories. We begin by discussing the transformation of patriarchy within family law since this both precedes and provokes developments in welfare law.

State, Family Law and Patriarchy

During much of the nineteenth century in Canada there was no clearly defined category of family law; in fact, the category of family law is itself quite recent, dating from the mid-twentieth century. As a result, early laws regulating family relations were embedded in a variety of property laws, devolution of estate statutes, illegitimacy and guardianship acts. This results in a number of differences in the development of family legislation relative to the other legislation under review in this chapter. First, during this period no inquiries or commissions specifically addressed family relations. Secondly, no regulatory agencies were established to enforce the legislation. The existing court system continued to deal with cases concerning disposition of property or children in an adversary rather than regulatory manner. Finally, family law, unlike labour or welfare legislation, was marked by a high degree of legislative activity prior to 1884. Table 6.3 summarizes the changes in family law which reduced patriarchal authority over family property, guardianship and maintenace.

The first step in the erosion of the patriarch's legal authority over women was the Married Women's Property Act of 1872. Prior to this act marital property law was based on the common law concept of 'legal unity' whereby women's married identity was submerged in that of her husband's. Thus all property upon marriage belonged to the husband. The Married Women's Property Act preceded industrialization in most provinces of Canada, whereas, in European countries reform in this area was more a consequence of industrialization. The old Canadian laws, derived from British common law, reflected the primacy of the interests of the family of origin[29], and functioned to preserve and consolidate aristocratic land-holdings and wealth. Thus in Europe the industrial revolution and the development of a class of commercial and industrial entrepreneurs was a necessary precondition for challenging those interests and bringing about reform.

In Canada, as in the United States and Australia, the absence of aristocratic class interests and the lack of substantive economic gains to most classes of men, reduced opposition to the reform of family law. At the same time, the pressures for change were more tangible. First, with the rapid transition of a frontier society into an industrial society, few in the economic system benefited from the old laws.[30] Second, there were growing pressures on the state to orchestrate this transition, as the numbers of destitute dependents increased greatly in the migrations from old country to new, rural to urban, job to job. The disruptions to family structure caused by social change resulted in an overwhelming proportion of women and children constituting the destitute.[31] Consequently, the reform in women's property rights was not only consistent with the long term trend, introduced by the wage labour system, towards the individual contract, but also promised some reduction of or relief to the growing number of homeless and destitute generated as a result of the tensions between the new economic order and the old patriarchal laws.

The Married Women's Property Act (MWPA) and subsequent amendments gradually extended to married women the same property rights as enjoyed by single women, thus abrogating the common law concept of 'legal unity'. A consequence of the Act was the elimination of the common law practice of curtesy, included in a number of property laws, which had ensured a husband's claim on his wife's property. The complement of curtesy was the dower law which ensured a wife's claim to a portion of the husband's property if he died intestate and which prohibited a husband from willing all his property away from his wife. Interestingly enough, the dower law was not abolished with the introduction of the MWPA. Thus curtesy, which reflected a patriarchal right, was abolished while dower which reflected a patriarchal responsibility was maintained through specific Dower Acts.

In keeping with this new emphasis on male familial responsibility, legislation was introduced which made husbands liable for support of wives and children in cases of desertion or separation. However, such acts as the MWPA and its various amendments, while significantly reordering the balance between rights and responsibilities, contained some unambiguously patriarchal clauses, the adultery clause being the most significant. Under this clause, a woman lost all right to sue for an order for protection, to maintenance by her husband or to claim her children, if she was found at any time to have committed adultery without her husband's collusion. Thus, regardless of how brutal the husband, how long the separation or desertion, or how legitimate her claim to her children, all would be lost if the woman did not maintain a chaste existence. Since marriage laws essentially contracted a women's sexuality to her husband, regardless of the dramatic changes in property rights for married women, this fundamental premise of patriarchy was left untouched. Given the general inaccessibility of divorce at this time,[32] a husband in effect maintained a lifetime ownership of his wife's sexuality, and this feature was preserved in the new property laws. Thus, although a husband may have lost access to his wife's sexuality through legal separation, he never lost control in law over that aspect of the woman's reproductive capacity.

The general erosion of the patriarch's legal supremacy in property law was repeated in the area of child custody. Under British common law children belonged solely to the father who was the only family member endowed with legal personhood. Thus women had no legal claim to their children within a marriage in cases of separation, desertion or divorce. Even in widow-hood, if the husband chose to will custody to an adult other than the mother, the mother had no legally recognized recourse. Indeed, the first legal recognition of a mother's claim to her children appeared in Ontario in 1859; and through the Infants Act and the MWPA the right of the mother's claim to custody and guardianship was extended in law.

Although the changes listed in Table 6.3 are dramatic, it is important to note that throughout the nineteenth century fathers were assumed to be the rightful custodian and mothers' custody rights were granted under particular circumstances, i.e. the 'tender years' concept, cruelty or desertion. Thus while this era witnessed the establishment of equity of property rights within the marriage there was no concept of equity of parental rights. Furthermore, all custody rights extended to mothers were subject to the same adultery clause which limited the rights of married women in property law—a clause which never applied to men.

As men's rights over their children were being eroded their responsibilities however were being extended. This pattern is particularly clear in the Illegitimacy Acts of the period. In Upper Canada prior to 1859 a father of an illegitimate child could be ordered to pay restitution to the mother's guardians on the assumption of loss of service during time of pregnancy, birth, etc. In 1859 the act was amended significantly changing the legal basis of restitution from one of lost services to one of responsibility for one's progeny. The entrenchment of a mother's right to sue for support simultaneously served to recognize the mother as a legal person in her own right rather than as a ward, and to legislate a father's economic responsibility regardless of marital state.

The crises in familial patriarchy brought on by the wage labour system was a product of the loss of control by the male household head over the resources necessary to sustain his family. This translated into a declining ability of men in general to support their dependents and a consequent decline in their authority. The end product of this development was the transformation of married men's status from that of *patriarch* to *breadwinner*. This transition should make clear that the 'bottom line' of patriarchy is *not* male privilege *per se* but control of reproduction through control of women. The above legislation suggests that traditional male privileges were dispensed with when they got in the way of controlling reproduction.[33] The reforms in family law were necessary for such a transition and reveal a consistent goal—to maintain and enforce, where necessary, the privatization of the costs of reproduction. This was accomplished by legislating male responsibility and by removing legal encumbrances which had prevented women from assuming the responsibility in the absence of a functioning breadwinner. Table 6.3 presents a summary of the four major pieces of legislation which reordered the rights and responsibilities of husbands and wives in the area of property, guardianship and maintenance. The overall pattern which emerges is, as predicted, an extension of women's rights and an extension of men's responsibilities.

Family law reform was a necessary but not sufficient step toward accommodating patriarchy to the new economic order. The declining ability of men to support their dependents, the declining benefits to men for assuming such responsibilities and the limited earning power of women meant that there were many cases in which the norm of privatizing reproductive costs could not be enforced. Thus a necessary corollary of the revisions in family law was the development of welfare legislation which attempted to fill the gap created by declining male authority and a growing number of destitute dependents.

Child Welfare and the State

In response to the resource and authority crises of the family, state welfare intervention in Canada was characterized by increasing levels of authority over the family and an increase in resources to certain categories of dependents. In order to illustrate the process by which state authority supercedes familial patriarchy in the regulation of reproduction an examination of the extension of state authority over the care and disposition of children is provided below.

Typically, analyses of state welfare activity have focused on the provision of resources to families and have emphasized the apparently benevolent character of such intervention. The question of what transformations in authority structures this has entailed has been under-theorized and under-analyzed. However, our analysis suggests that the assumptions of greater authority over the family by the state is an integral and critical feature in the transformation to social patriarchy.

The model presented here suggests that the control of reproduction is achieved by making access to necessary resources conditional on submission to particular reproductive policies. Although control of women is a consistent and universal feature of this process, the mechan-

TABLE 6.3

Ontario Family Legislation: Reductions in Patriarchal Authority Over Family Property, Guardianship and Maintenance, 1855-1888

Year	Legislation	Property	Guardianship of Children	Maintenance
Prior to 1855		Dower right Curtesy		
1855	Custody of Infants Act		Mothers, married, separately domiciled may petition court for guardianship of child less than 12 years old	Father may be sued for the maintenance of his children in mother's custody
1859	Support of Illegitimate Children Act			Woman may sue father of illegitimate child for financial support
1872	Married Women's Property Act (MWPA)	Married Women have rights to ownership of property, wages and inheritance, just as if unmarried		

Year	Act			
		Curtesy revoked		
1873	Amendment to MWPA	Married women can convey real estate with Husband's consent		
1877	Amendment to MWPA	Married women may get an order of protection to secure children's earnings		
1887	Infants Act (formerly Custody of Infants)		Mother may petition for guardianship of child older than 12	
			Mother can appoint guardians for her children *via* wills	
1888	Amendment to MWPA	Married women can convey real estate without husband's consent if husband is insane, imprisoned or separated		
1888	Maintenance of Deserted Wives Act			Husband must support wife living apart for just cause

ism of control can vary dramatically from one society to the next, with men as a class having authority over women as a class (communal patriarchy), or individual males having authority over individual females (familial patriarchy), or finally the state having control over the reproductive unit (social patriarchy).

The rapid substitution of state authority for the waning authority of the familial patriarch suggests a continued commitment by the state to the control of reproduction. While the transformation of such control was most blatant in the revision of the criminal code in 1892 in which birth control was criminalized and penalties for abortion increased (S.C. 1892 C.29), the operation of the regulatory clauses in welfare law also provides an indication of the subtle and pervasive character of this control.[34] The following discussion of the extension of state authority over children enumerates conditions of family life meriting dramatic intervention (state custody) and gives a good indication of the model of family life that the state was committed to supporting and enforcing. This model, when considered in conjunction with the limitations imposed by labour and family law, suggests a clear and conscious commitment to patriarchy by the state, albeit in a revised and modernized form.

Commissions and Inquiries Into Social Welfare

The extension of state welfare intervention involved inquiries, legislation and regulatory agencies. While there were no specific 'welfare commissions' during this period, many boards of inquiries especially those dealing with labour, crime and health, made reference to and occasionally recommended welfare programs or policies.

These inquiries on the whole questioned the prevailing assumption that parents had the best interests of their children at heart and suggested that parents' ideas of the child's best interest could be seriously at odds with that of the state. In the past the only explicit indications of the state's interest in protection of children were the laws prohibiting infanticide or severe physical abuse. What commissioners and reformers alike came to advocate was the necessity for a series of laws to make more explicit the conditions for child well-being. Child welfare legislation was to be not merely a list of crimes to be punished, but rather, a series of positive conditions to be required as judged by the health, education and behaviour of the child and the legal, economic and moral condition of the parents. This reordering of familial authority between parents and the state led to the emergence of a new concept of 'children's rights'. Indeed, J.J. Kelso, the long-time social reformer (who was the first Superintendent of Neglected Children in Ontario) began his first report in 1894 with a quotation from Bernardo:

Are parental rights to be regarded as sacred when parental duties have not been neglected but outraged, and when the parents have done all in their power to make the life of the child while with them bitter and degraded! Has a child no rights? Are all the rights parental?[35]

Splane's analysis of social welfare in Ontario identifies the 1890 Royal Commission on the Prison and Reformatory System as the most important inquiry advancing public knowledge and official action in respect to child welfare. As he points out, the terms of reference of the commission were sufficiently broad to cover much of the contemporary field of social welfare. 'Child welfare, was in fact, directly involved in each of the first three of the seven matters referred to the commission for investigation: Those relating to the causes of crime, the improvement of the industrial schools and the rescue of destitute children from criminal careers.'[36]

In discussing the causes of crime the Commissioners gave foremost attention to the importance of family life and expressed great concern over '. . . the want of proper parental control; the lack of good home training and the baneful influence of bad homes, largely due to culpable neglect and indifference of parents and the evil effects of drunkenness.'[37] Their concern with bad home environments and bad upbringing led to a series of recommendations that promoted increased state regulation of child rearing and outlined a series of steps to that end.

The recommendations made by the Commission advocated a much more active role for the state in the regulation of domestic life. The recommendations were particularly important because by and large they were implemented by 1913, thus suggesting a high degree of responsiveness on the part of the state. Included in the report was the recommendation that 'an association . . . be formed having local boards in every important center of the Province who shall take upon themselves the important but delicate duty of looking after and caring for these (improperly cared for) children.'[38] This was realized the same year with the founding of the Children's Aid Society. Furthermore, the Commissioners recommended that the province defray 'the actual expenses incurred' by the proposed voluntary association. Along the same lines, they made a strong recommendation in favour of expanding the number of industrial schools and suggested they be included under the provisions of the Charity Aid Act, thus qualifying the schools for much more extensive state support. Also emphasized was the importance of school attendance and measures were recommended for its 'vigorous enforcement'. As preventive measures the Commissioners recommended municipal curfews, and supervised municipal playgrounds and gymnasia. Finally, in the area of corrections, they recommended the separate detention and trial of children. This issue was a central concern to prison reformers and was eventually realized in the Juvenile Delinquency Act of 1908.

While no other inquiry seems to have been as wide-ranging in its approach to and recommendations for child welfare as the 1890 Commission, subsequent inquiries stressed the continued necessity for state intervention. The Special Report on Immigrant Children in 1898 prepared by the Superintendent of Neglected Children applauded the Child Immigrant Act but advocated further regulation and monitoring of immigrant children.[39] The Special Committee appointed to report on the Condition of the Feeble-Minded called for greater government attention to separating out and institutionalizing the 'feeble minded', reflecting in this proposal a popular eugenic concern of the time with preventing the deterioration of the 'white race.' Finally, the Special Committee on Infant Mortality and the Royal Commission on Milk (both in 1909) called for greater government initiative and activity in insuring the physical and social welfare of children.

Helen MacMurchy, who was the director of the inquiry into infant mortality, identified a number of social factors contributing to the problem of infant deaths. Women's employment was seen as particularly troublesome to the well-being of young children. In response to this problem MacMurchy suggested, but did not formally recommend, several possible solutions. First, recognizing the link between women's employment and the low wages of men she stressed the importance of a family wage: '. . . Any man who does useful and necessary work . . . should be paid enough to allow him to marry and support a family.' Addressing the situation where women were forced, through economic need, to return to work immediately after the birth of a child, MacMurchy stated: 'It should not be allowed to happen. The mother should have a pension, if necessary, to take care of the family.'[40] As a general measure to improve the quality of child care she recommended a state-sponsored education campaign including health and nutrition pamphlets and visits to mothers and families by employees of the Public Health Department.

Despite differences in terms of reference, the child welfare inquiries shared with the labour inquiries of the period a consensus on the necessity of increasing government intervention and regulation. The commissioners' and reformers' conviction that many people could not or would not be good parents paved the way for the state and its regulatory agencies to assume increasing authority and control over women and children in the family and to justify increasing intervention on the grounds that the state was the best, and most impartial judge of a child's well-being. However, these inquiries differed from the labour boards in that their recommendations for intervention were implemented much more promptly through the enactment of necessary

legislation and the creation of necessary agencies, indicating the importance the state put on regulating family life at the point of reproduction.
Prior to 1844 Canadian welfare law consisted of two statutes, the
Apprentices and Minors Act and the Charity Aid Act. Both of these
acts contained provisions for the care and support for the destitute.
The Apprentices and Minors Act provided for the indenture of children who were orphaned or abandoned. The Charity Aid Acts established provincial support for hospitals and institutes for the destitute
which with the Ontario Charity Act established a formula for funding.

1887 marks the onset of systematic state welfare activity in Ontario. The most important pieces of legislation were the Industrial
Schools Act, the Infants Protection Act (later known as the Maternity
Boarding Homes Act), the Child Protection Act and the Child Immigration Act. These four statutes formed the legislative framework for the
child welfare system. The goals of the new legislation were threefold:
the extension of support to public welfare institutions, increased government regulation of public welfare institutions and the increased
regulation of children's environment and behaviour both within public
institutions and in private families.

The extensive legislation of the period reveals an expansion of
government intervention in and regulation of family life by increasing
state authority over the disposition of children.[41] Such indicators of
increasing state authority over children include the specification of
conditions for catchment of children (including familial status, acts of
children and acts of parents), the proliferation of agents of state
authority and the growth of institutions or agencies for the disposition
of children.

The amendment to the Industrial Schools Act in Ontario in 1887
marked the onset of increased legislative activity to extend state
authority over children. The amendment removed industrial schools
from the authority of school boards and empowered charitable institutions to develop and supervise such schools. Board members of charitable institutions took on their new responsibility with enthusiasm and
the first industrial school was opened in Toronto in 1887. With the
establishment of such institutions provisions of the act which permitted
state apprehension of children under certain conditions were now
enforceable. These conditions were very important because they are
the precursors to all later welfare clauses which provided for apprehension of children. Among the conditions for apprehension of a
child under fourteen years were any:

(1) Who is found begging or receiving alms, or being in any
street or public place for the purpose of begging or receiving
alms;

(2) Who is found wandering, and not having any home or

settled place of abode or proper guardianship or not having any lawful occupation or business, or visible means of subsistence;

(3) Who is found destitute, either being an orphan or having a surviving parent who is undergoing penal servitude or imprisonment;

(4) Whose parent, step-parent or guardian represents to the police magistrate that he is unable to control the child, and that he desires the child to be sent to an industrial school under this Act;

(5) Who, by reason of the neglect, drunkenness or other vices of parents, is suffered to be growing up without salutary parental control and education, or in circumstances exposing him to lead an idle and dissolute life.[42]

In the same year as the amendment to the Industrial Schools Act, an Act for the Protection of Infant Children was passed which provided for state regulation of maternity boarding houses, usually private homes which took in destitute pregnant women. This act is particularly important because it reflected the first attempt by the state to regulate adoption procedures. The 1897 amendment to the act required that the Children's Aid Society supervise and determine the adoption of all children under one year of age from private maternity homes. A 1912 amendment extended Children's Aid Society's authority over adoption by including all children under the age of three born in these homes. Although a specific adoption law did not appear until 1922, the state was, through this and other acts, slowly expanding its authority over adoption procedures.

The 1888 Child Protection Act provided for state apprehension and custody of children under sixteen years of age who were judged ill-treated, neglected or delinquent and promises were made for the prosecution of parents found guilty of neglect or abuse. In 1893 an amendment appointed a superintendent of neglected children under the direct employ of the provincial government. This amendment also empowered the Children's Aid Society, as the major regulatory agency, to inspect homes, apprehend children and place them in institutions or foster homes. Interestingly enough, neither this act nor the Industrial Schools Act, which were the major legislative devices for removing children from the custody of their parents at the time, undermined the tendency toward the privatization of the costs of reproduction. Indeed, both acts contained clauses permitting the state to sue parents for support of their children while in government institutions. Thus, although parents lost legal rights to their children, they were still held responsible for the maintenance costs of those children.

In 1897 the Child Immigration Act was finally passed after years of controversy among social reformers as to the impact of immigrant children upon Canadian society.[43] While these children had initially been welcomed as an inexpensive source of labour, growing concern about the quality of a child's environment, the purity of the 'race' and the increasing demands on public welfare funds led to a more critical view of child immigrants. Some commentators argued that they were of 'inferior stock' and filled the jails and poor houses, leading true Canadian children astray. Other critics pointed out that the conditions to which these children were subject in Canada were often neglectful or abusive. These concerns, in conjunction with organized labour's objection to the importing of cheap child labour, led the government to tighten control over the children who were being admitted to Canada and to carefully monitor their activities during the first few years in the country.

The acts and amendments mentioned above provided the legal apparatus for extending state control over children. The acts were cumulative, adding more conditions for the apprehension of children, more agents to apprehend and supervise them and more institutions into which the state channeled their wards. A quick before and after comparison makes the point quite clearly.

Prior to 1884 *one* law, The Apprentices and Minors Act, under *one* condition, a child without legal guardian, empowered *three* agents, Charitable Institutions, Mayors or Magistrates, to provide for such children in *one* way, apprenticeship. By the end of the period under study, legislation had led to a proliferation of conditions under which the state could assume wardship, an expansion of institutions and programs for the disposition of such wards and the growth of regulatory agents to supervise and regulate public and private institutions of child care. As of 1913 the welfare statutes legislated twelve different conditions for state custody (in addition to the original condition of a child without a legal guardian). These conditions could be established by the activity of parents or children. Parents found to have engaged in immoral conduct, neglect, or commitment of a child to a welfare institution could lose custody of their children. Children found to be in a condition of vagrancy or to have engaged in petty crime or begging could be made wards of the state. At the same time the number of regulatory agents or agencies empowered to apprehend children and/or regulate their institutions increased from the original three—mayors, magistrates and charitable societies—to eight different government or charitable agencies. Finally, the number of agencies or institutions for the disposition of state wards similarly increased from the one provision of apprenticeship to seven different provisions ranging from institutionalization in an industrial school, to adoption or to deportation in the case of immigrant children.

In summary, welfare legislation affecting the disposition of children reveals two main points. The acts during the period 1887-1913 were clearly more regulative than supportive; the usual solution to a 'bad' home environment was removal of the child and, frequently, prosecution of the parent. Also, it became increasingly evident that in order to enforce such legislation a comprehensive regulatory network had to be developed. The Children's Aid Society (CAS) assumed that responsibility and acquired a unique status as a quasi-state agency, empowered and financed by the state yet operating as a private agency run by its own board.

The use of a private agency to meet welfare needs was not unusual considering that most welfare agencies such as orphanages and refuges were in this era run by private boards and largely funded by private contributions. What was unusual about the CAS was that it was empowered to legally enforce aspects of welfare law, specifically the apprehension of children. Further, unlike many other agencies incorporated into the state, the CAS retained its private status and experienced minimal government regulation. With the decentralized CAS organization reporting to the superintendent of neglected children, the government could now launch its new policy of monitoring childcare, not only in public institutions but also in private homes.

The expansion of Children's Aid Societies was rapid in comparison to the growth of the state inspectors of public institutions. Between July 1893 and December 1895 the superintendent of neglected children in Ontario helped no less than twenty nine Societies to organize. As the number of Societies expanded the number of children coming under their care also increased. By 1897, the CAS in Ontario was placing 200 children or more a year. The numbers increased steadily and annual placement rose from 500 to 600 between 1910 and 1913. More important perhaps than the numbers were the type of children coming under the care of the CAS. From the earliest records it is clear that the majority of children were not orphans or abandoned but were apprehended by CAS from undesirable homes. A sample of wards' backgrounds in 1902 revealed that out of 200 only 63 had been abandoned or orphaned, while on the other hand 112 had been apprehended because of 'immoral homes, pauperism, lack of control;' the remainder had been apprehended because of parental neglect, abuse or drunkenness.⁴⁴ More detailed reports in 1912 and 1913 revealed that over 70 per cent of CAS wards were apprehended from undesirable homes with cruelty or neglect accounting for only 9 per cent of the apprehensions in 1913 and 20 per cent in 1912.

The shift from parental rights to parental responsibilities evidenced in family legislation was more rigorously enforced in the welfare legislation. While family law limited itself to enforcing parent's economic responsibility to children, the CAS—through various clauses in the Child Protection Act—took on the task of enforcing the parents' moral responsibility. The superintendent of neglected children's 1911 report contained an important paper entitled 'Parental Responsibility' written by C. S. Pedley of the Woodstock CAS. Pedley began with the assertion that 'Parental affection is an instinct, . . . but parental responsibility is something different.'⁴⁵ Because even some affectionate and well-meaning parents may fail in their responsibility, it was the task of the CAS to correct the situation; as Pedley put it: 'in the very act of taking their children from them we do something to bring their responsibility home to them.' While he spoke of the advantage of returning children to their parents on probation Pedley also emphasized that there were some cases where this should not be done: '. . . if the natural parents are too far below average, so that the State steps in and takes charge of the children, it is not a question of interference, and an invasion of parental right—it is just the resumption of a trust out of the hands of trustees who have failed to make good.'⁴⁶

The Superintendent's report in 1913 indicates of just how frequently parents were found to be 'too far below the average.' While 72 per cent of their wards that year were apprehended from undesirable homes only 17 per cent were returned to their parents on probation. From the beginning, officers of the CAS proved to be vigorous and enthusiastic moral entrepreneurs. There is, however, evidence of resistance to these 'child-saving' program. The continued efforts by parents to regain custody of their children is indicated by an amendment to the Child Protection Act two years after the CAS has been empowered to apprehend children. This amendment made it a criminal offence for a parent, or indeed any person, to induce a child to run away from an institution or home to which they had been committed under the Child Protection Act.

While controversy has surrounded the CAS from the beginning, there is no doubt that its work, philosophy and unique relation to the state epitomized, perhaps as no other single organization did, the great transformation in authority which characterized this period. CAS policies reflected a remarkable integration of the two imperatives of social patriarchy: maintaining the privatization of reproductive costs on the one hand and increasing the authority of the state over the family on the other. Its policy of deinstitutionalization, its aggressive interpretation of the breadwinners' responsibility, its commitment to keeping mothers in the home—all under the increasing scrutiny of the state—seemed the perfect blue-print for social patriarchy. Even its organizational structure anticipates the great transition from private philanthropy to the rise of public health and welfare bureaucracies and the professionalization of social work in the twentieth century. In the end, Children's Aid Societies had changed from a diverse group of 'child savers' to a powerful regulatory agency and were well on the way to greater integration in the state welfare bureaucracy.

Conclusion

The primary manifestation of the contradiction between production and reproduction during early industrialization in Canada is a disorganization of reproductive relations and the establishment of a central role for the state in reorganizing and stabilizing those relations. The resolution of this contradiction involved a reorganization of the wage labour system and a transformation of patriarchy. Evidence of the reorganization of the wage labour system comes from the early labour laws, particularly the legislation which distinguished between male and female labour. This legislation was both supportive and regulatory in terms of reproduction. Its supportive thrust is revealed in the discriminatory clauses which protected reproducers (women) and future labour (children) from being completely exhausted in the production process. These same clauses also regulated the character of reproductive relations in that legislation reinforced the distinction between male and female labour and thus operated to preserve and solidify the existing sexual segmentation of the labour market. The outcome of this was, in most cases, to maintain women in an economically dependent position compared to men, and hence to preserve the fundamental component of patriarchy—female subordination.

While the state intervened in the production process to accommodate certain patriarchal necessities it was at the same time involved in restructuring patriarchy to fit it with the new economic system. Through substantive reforms in family law the state dismantled the old patriarchal system and transformed patriarchs into breadwinners. This transition accorded greater legal rights to women and more economic responsibilities to men. While some have seen this as the beginning of the end of patriarchy it is better understood as a *restructuring* of patriarchy. Expanded legal rights of wives and mothers were contingent upon observance of the ubiquitous adultery clause which insured that women's sexuality continued to be subject to male authority. Coupled with the labour laws which made women dependent upon male support, female subordination in an emerging industrial economy was reinforced. The increased responsibilities of the patriarch-turned-breadwinner were necessary, in light of the sexual division of labour, to insure the continued responsibility of private families for the costs of their reproduction. Finally, the expansion of welfare legislation completed the restructuring process by recasting the authority and resource gaps created by the transformation of patriarchy. In doing so the state progressively extended its control over the family, maintained the principle of privatization of reproductive costs and provided a back-up system when family support systems broke down completely.

Having developed the legislative framework of restructuring and preserving patriarchy on a much more precarious economic base than in the past, subsequent manifestations of the production-reproduction contradiction have tended to be the form of a resource allocation problem. Given the combined effects of the social reforms to reduce the number of breadwinners per family, and the demographic changes, subsequent periods of capitalist development are characterized by increasing costs of reproduction without a similar increase in allocation of resources for reproduction. In later periods government in Canada and elsewhere were increasingly called upon to alleviate what appears at the household level as a cost of living crises for the family. Prophetically, the last federal inquiry to be called in 1913 was the Commission to Investigate the Increase in the Cost of Living in Canada.

Notes and References

1. This chapter is based on my Ph.D. dissertation which examines state activity through an analysis of labour, welfare and family law from 1884 to 1968 in Canada. In the original manuscript a comparative analysis of Ontario and Manitoba legislation is presented. For the purposes of this Chapter I have limited my discussion to trends in Canada generally and used legislation in Ontario as the illustrative case. This seems an appropriate choice because during the time period examined Ontario was the initiating province in all three areas of legislation for English Canada.

2. For a detailed discussion of my theoretical approach and its implications for analysis of patriarchy, see *Contemporary Crisis*, Vol. 8 (July 1984), pp. 265-292.

3. For a more detailed presentation of socialist-feminist theorizing, see A. Kuhn and A. Wolpe, *Feminism and Materialism* (Routledge and Kegan Paul, London, 1975).

4. Mary O'Brien, *The Politics of Reproduction* (Routledge and Kegan Paul, London 1981).

5. G. Rubin, 'The Traffic in Women: Notes on the "Political Economy" of Sex' edited by Rayna Reiter, *Toward an Anthropology of Women* (Monthly Review Press, New York, 1975).

6. C. Meillassoux, *Maidens, Meal and Money* (Cambridge University Press, New York, 1981).

7. C. Levi-Strauss, 'The Family', in H. Shapiro (ed.), *Man, Culture and Society* (Oxford University Press, London 1971), p. 348.

8. For an excellent discussion of the changing dynamic between production and reproduction during the transition to class-structured societies see Muller, 'The Formation of the State and the Oppression of Women,' *Review of Radical Political Economics*, Vol. 9.

9. My conceptualization of the state's mediating role replaces the 'autonomy' of the state concept. Evidence of state policies violating short-term economic interests of the dominant class are explicable in terms of the structural necessity of balancing production and reproduction.

10. During the feudal period the state attempted to exact special taxes on bachelors in order to promote marriage and procreation. See G. Homans, *English Villagers of the Thirteenth Century* (Norton, New York, 1975). More recent examples of pro-natalist legislation include the criminalization of abortion and/or the use of birth control. See L. Gordon, *Woman's Body, Woman's Right* (Penguin Books, New York, 1976).

11. Potential problems resulting from 'over'-reproduction are managed through laws determining access to land. Inheritance laws, like primogeniture, insured that an increasing population density would not interrupt surplus extraction by disinheriting excess family members. Most effective perhaps were marriage customs in Ireland during the nineteenth century which required that a man have title to land before marriage. This drastically delayed the age of marriage, hence lowering birth rates.

12. Between 1884 and 1912, women and children continuously accounted for 80 per cent or more of the institutionalized destitute in Ontario. See Inspector of Charitable Institutions, *Annual Reports*, Ontario Sessional Papers, 1884-1912.

13. C. Pentland, *Labour and Capital in Canada* (Lorimer, Toronto, 1981).

14. Ibid., p. 190.

15. Ibid., See also B. Palmer, *A Culture in Conflict* (McGill-Queen's University Press, Montreal, 1979); and G. Kealey, *Toronto Workers Respond to Industrial Capitalism* (University of Toronto Press, Toronto, 1980).

16. G. Kealey (ed.), *Canada Investigates Industrialism* (University of Toronto Press, Toronto, 1973) IX.

17. Ibid., p. 22.

18. Ibid., p. 14.

19. Ibid., p. 46.

20. A. Klein and W. Roberts 'Besieged Innocence: The "Problem" and Problems of Working Women, Toronto, 1896-1914', in *Women at Work* edited by J. Actor, P. Goldsmith and B. Shepard (Canadian Women's Educational Press, Toronto, 1974).

21. Ibid.

22. G. Leslie, 'Domestic Service in Canada, 1880-1920' in *Women at Work*.

23. *Labour Gazette*, Vol. 13, No. 12, p. 1373.

24. Report of the Royal Commission on Unemployment, 1914, p. 59.

25. C. Ramkhalawonsingh, 'Women During the Great War' in *Women at Work*.

26. *Report of Factory Inspectors in Ontario*, Sessional Papers, 1905, Vol. 37, p. 21.

27. *Report of Factory Inspectors in Ontario*, Sessional Papers, 1908, Vol. 49, p. 58.

28. Klein and Roberts, 'Besieged Innocence' in *Women at Work*, p. 225.

29. M. Glendon, *The New Family and the New Property* (Butterworths, Toronto, 1981), p. 15.

30. Ibid.

31. R. Splane, *Social Welfare in Ontario 1791-1893* (University of Toronto Press, Toronto, 1965).
32. The average number of divorce decrees granted in Canada was very low, ranging from three in 1871-75 to eleven in 1890-1900. See Dominion of Canada, *Canada Yearbook* (King's Printer, Ottawa, 1912) p. 825.
33. C. Lasch and J. Donzelot equate patriarchy with male privilege and, on the basis of this, falsely conclude that the growth of the welfare state and the reforms in family law indicate that patriarchy is dead. See C. Lasch, *Haven in a Heartless World* (Basic Books, New York, 1975) and J. Donzelot, *The Policing of Families* (Basic Books, New York, 1979).
34. For an extended analysis of the state and abortion policy, see the chapter by Mann in this volume.
35. *Report of the Superintendent of Neglected Children*, Ontario Sessional Papers: 1894 #47, p. 13.
36. Splane, *Social Welfare in Ontario*, p. 268.
37. *Report of the Royal Commission on the Prison and Reformatory System*, Ontario Sessional Papers, 1891, No. 18, p. 5.
38. Ibid., p. 18.
39. *Special Report on Immigrant Children*, Ontario Sessional Papers, 1898, No. 60, p. 17.
40. *Report of the Special Committee on Infant Mortality*, Ontario Sessional Papers, 1910, No. 9, p. 8.
41. By disposition of children I refer to conditions in which children become wards of the state with parental loss of custody and control of their children. Thus I am not including educational institutions which play an imporant role with parents in the socializing process, but include only those situations in which the parents role is usurped altogether.
42. *Statutes of Ontario 1874*, C. 29, Sec. 4, p. 219.
43. N. Sutherland, *Children in English Canadian Society* (University of Toronto Press, Toronto, 1976), p. 33.
44. *Report of the Superintendent of Neglected Children*, Ontario Sessional Papers 1902.
45. Ibid., 1911, p. 101.
46. Ibid., 1911, pp. 101-102.

7

THEORETICAL APPROACHES TO THE STATE AND SOCIAL REPRODUCTION

Pradeep Bandyopadhyay

Introduction

The state in capitalist societies has been the object of wide-ranging Marxist discussion over the past couple of decades. The scattered writings of Marx, Engels, Lenin and Gramsci on the state have been scrutinized and attempts have been made to take stock, identifying the diversity of claims and, where possible, systematize and unify the various strands.[1] It is generally recognized that a coherent and theoretically complete account of the state consonant with Marxist political economy is not as yet readily available. There have been two controversial initiating impulses in this effort: the early claims, systematically developed in the sixties, regarding a new phase of capitalism i.e. the theory of state-monopoly capitalism (SMC); and the debate around the contrasting seminal works of Miliband and Poulantzas with its methodological and substantive theoretical dimensions. The latter source of analysis, in particular, has spawned a number of studies of *personnel inter-locks* between state institutions and capitalist organizations on the one hand, and studies of the *ideological and social functions* of the state as aspects of its 'relative autonomy' on the other hand.[2] It is not the object of this paper to provide a critical review of this work: such a study is already available written from a particular viewpoint.[3]

The concept of social reproduction is being considered in the general and comprehensive sense of the maintenance of the structural identity of a social formation through time. The identity of a social formation depends upon a complex of social relations and associated beliefs including the social organization of production and distribution, specific modalities for the experience of power and political participation, and sets of interdependent background assumptions in forming and justifying the activities of the agents involved in these relations. A particular complex structuring of social relations and the recurrent activities it engenders can be distinguished from other distinct complex structures of social relations, thus enabling the identification of, and discrimination between, different social formations. The activities of the state, through its agents, affects the identity of the social formation of which it is a part in various purposive and unintended ways. It is the purpose of this chapter to examine this role of the state in attempting to reproduce the identity of the structured complex of social relations of which it is a part. We do not presuppose that in this role the state is necessarily or wholly successful. Quite the contrary is historically evident since we do observe the passage from one kind of social formation to other kinds, and also the passage from one kind of state, as indicated by its social composition and activities, to other kinds. The sources of such transitions in, and transformations of, social formations cannot be wholly localized in the state and are not the object of this paper. The role of the state in social reproduction in this general and comprehensive sense does involve particular activities directed at reproducing *specific* relations and elements in the whole complex of social relations. In capitalist social formations a major specific relation is that between capitalists and workers. Increasingly we observe activities of the state directed at this social relation: the reproduction of labour power as wage-labour in capitalist social relations of production and distribution. The complex social processes directed at the social reproduction of labour power and the role of the state in all this will only be incidentally addressed, as it is the main object of other papers in this volume. The aim here is to focus more narrowly on the theoretical analysis of the role and necessity of the state in a capitalist social order as regards the social reproduction of that order and to analyze the problems and incapacities that may ensue in that process.

In order to accomplish this we will examine not only some of the Marxist contribution but also the powerful ideas expressed, in a limited form, by ostensibly non-Marxist sources such as the work of economists and political scientists concerned with public goods, collective action and 'external effects'.[4] It is the claim of this chapter that a primary source of the inadequacies of much Marxist work on the state is its neglect of issues in the analysis of collective action and the role of positive externalities in the social reproduction of capitalist societies; and, conversely, that the inadequacies of the latter work arise from the disregard for, and absence of, an analysis of the forms of exploitation, class relations and the effective control over the 'productive forces' that characterize capitalist societies and which affect the constitution of relevant, strategically oriented agents. In short, the failure of the orthodox economists and public choice theorists stems from the error of positing only individuals and a single collective (represented by the 'general interest', 'aggregate social welfare' etc.) and ignoring the antagonistic and asymmetric reciprocities constituted by the social relations of production and the various collectivities this engenders. The failure of much of the Marxist work is to rightly identify a set of structurally related, hierarchically ordered classes but ignore the fact that classes are sets of individual agents who seek both individual and collective benefits and who face certain problems in achieving collective action. That is to say that members of various social classes are agents whose actions are strategically interdependent both within and between classes in the pursuit of both individual and collective ends. Both these types of analysis have tended to ignore the *cumulative, emergent effects* of strategic decision-making by various individual and collective agents which are often unintended, unanticipated and counter-productive. It is these latter that constitute one set of what Marxists term the 'contradictions' of capitalist social dynamics.[5]

The argument of this chapter is developed in three stages. First, there is a discussion of the contrasting assumptions, problem formulations and results of the traditional Marxist and individualist economic theories, leading to the presentation in outline of a strategic interactionist Marxian framework. Second, we elaborate a concept of the socialization of social action explaining the growing importance of the state as the agency through which collective benefits can be realized, which in turn leads to the decline of voluntary contractarian solutions. Finally, a third section analyses the modalities through which the state influences and seeks to regulate social reproduction with varying, and possibly contradictory, emergent effects. The main conclusion is that in capitalist social formations the activities of the state will have contradictory components, unintended contradictory effects on social reproduction, and will not necessarily be cumulative in a linear manner. This is not to suggest that the state should or could withdraw from its involvement in social reproduction, for the growth of that involvement is a function of the growing social inter-dependence and the consequent socialization of social action which requires the production of positive public externalities through the state apparatus. The basic argument could be further strengthened, in some aspects, through an analysis of results in social choice theory and strategic manipulation of voting but that would unduly expand the scope of this chapter.[6]

Global Equilibrium and Social Reproduction: Alternative Principles

What is proposed is not a balanced synthesis based on mutual correction by symmetrically and inversely inadequate theories, for that is not the relation in which the two distinct approaches stand. The faults of the orthodox economists' approach are fundamental and incorrigible without a shift in primary assumptions and mode of analysis. The theory of 'public goods' ultimately fails to provide a theory of the state because there are few, if any, pure public goods and, in any case, the actual activities of the state in market economies go well beyond the provision of any identifiable pure public goods. Pure public goods (or services) are goods that exhibit non-excludability in their consumption and enjoyment, i.e. members of the relevant public cannot be excluded from their benefits. They cannot be distributed through the market mechanism of individual payment for individually appropriated quantities. They are also, in the purest case, non-divisible; that is, their production cannot be quantitatively graduated in accordance with the number of consumers: their quantitative level of production is either unique or a set of discrete steps. The usual real world examples are national defence, maintenance of clean air, etc. Most publicly provided goods and services are in fact 'mixed goods' in that the level of provision can vary, in principle market provision is possible, and the relevant public is not necessarily co-extensive with the total population under the jurisdiction of a single state. The problems of the degree of 'public-ness' and asymmetries of benefit and evaluation plagues conceptual clarity in this domain. The actual range of state produced non-market public goods and services far exceeds what is admissible under neo-classical economic theory which treats the category as a residual beyond market possibilities.[7] These aspects of the state's activities are, in such an approach, liable to be dismissed as an aberration, an indication of the failure of the state to be 'rational'.

The state as correction for 'market failure', in the presence of external effects, natural (i.e. irreducible) monopolies and increasing returns to scale, is also insufficient because that can, at best, identify a *normative* role for the state as the *global social optimizer;* this, however, involves a utopian perspective, both from the viewpoint of the feasibility of the necessary computations and because it postulates evaluative judgments that are not naturally held universally. This entire analysis suffers from the self-imposed limitation of postulating a global equilibrium, i.e. a state of affairs where no agent has any reason to act differently since the result obtained cannot be improved upon. Such a perspective either assumes away uncertainty or seeks to incorporate uncertainty and incomplete information by means of elaborate normative proposals for rationality. But in either case the account ignores a central and inescapable feature of the real-world dynamic process: that all social actions operate in irreversible time and cannot be reversed to recover the *status quo ante*, and that there almost always are unforeseen composition effects which differentially affect the individuals involved, many or all of whom may find the overall outcomes individually sub-optimal. In a temporal sequence many agents will alter their strategies in order to seek their most preferred individual outcomes. From the viewpoint of global *collectively optimal* results, some or all individuals may have to be constrained from seeking their most preferred outcome from an individualist perspective. By starting the analysis from a postulated initial situation of equally independent individuals freely seeking their individually preferred outcomes, the analysis is trapped between the Scylla of being purely normative with such weak normative assumptions as to purchase assent at the cost of relevance, and the Charybdis of being historically and empirically false when used in explaining actual historical development.[8]

The economists' approach cannot incorporate the sociological insights on the *asymmetries* arising from the social relations of production without abandoning its primary model of social relations as no more than resource constrained contractual exchange between independent agents with independent, exogenously given preferences. That is, it is not *theoretically extensible* to cover the hierarchically ordered asymmetries in social relations and, consequently, to recognize the limited scope of the logic of market exchange given the absence of a universal, primary preference for global collective optimization on the part of social agents. The state, in this framework, can be no more than a supplementary, alternative means for the realization of individual optima when these are unobtainable through market exchange or voluntary contractual relations. Ironically, the pursuit of such individualist maximization analysis based on the market model has led, in the fields of political competition and bureaucratic behaviour, to a successful demystification of the widespread ideological belief that the state (and its agents) serve the 'public interest' or realize the 'general good'.[9] Nevertheless in spite of failure, this kind of work has left us with the recognition that any satisfactory theory of the state must provide an adequate account of human agency and choice; and that the state itself is *not* a monolithic or single agent, but a concatenation (more or less coordinated) of interdependent agents whose decisions may have consequences unanticipated by them. This outcome of the individualist, maximizing-agent model of interaction makes it clear that the ideas and tools used by the analysis is not necessarily and irremediably tied to a liberal ideology. Indeed, many of the results serve to undermine such an ideology. Much of this work can be prised out of the defective sociology with which it is associated and can be used fruitfully to extend Marxist accounts.

When one turns to the analyses (from sociologists, political scientists and dissident economists) which do not take market relations in general, and Pareto-optimality in particular,[10] as paradigmatic, one mainly encounters a type of traditional functionalist analysis in which 'system-maintenance' or 'social reproduction' is viewed as the positive outcome from the vantage point of which the activities of the state can be explained either as purposive measures intended to realize the outcome, or as mediating structural effects which maintain (reproduce) certain invariant structural properties of the social formation. These accounts, whether in the purposive-voluntaristic versions or in the structuralist-systemic versions assume that the main function of the state is to produce (or reproduce) a structured social order and to argue from the results to the 'causes'. There are three complex difficulties with such accounts: one, the well-known logical difficulties of relating functional explanations to causal explanations;[11] two, the exclusion of unanticipated or unintended negative emergent effects, i.e. the exclusion of the possibility that the outcome of state activities is not only 'social reproduction' of order but also of social disorder, and that the process of 'reproduction' may itself generate new disorders; and three, the problem of *selection* from functionally equivalent sets of activities or institutions, i.e. why the state has acted in a particular way when a number of alternative activities would realize the function of social reproduction. Why, for instance, does the intervention of the state take the form of direct production in some cases, regulation in others, subsidies for voluntary organizations in some cases, legal repression in others, and withdrawal from activities or impositions in still other cases? Similarly, these approaches tend to ignore the functional alternatives to state intervention. They are inadequate not only on questions relating to *how* a state intervened but also on the question of *whether* the state had to intervene to satisfy a need as against some other way of satisfying that need.

It may be observed that the concept of 'social reproduction' in such works with an explicitly functionalist assumption, has an analytical status comparable to 'equilibrium' in the individualist optimization studies. Both functionalist 'social reproduction' and 'equilibrium' describe end-states which play a significant part in justifying, or accounting for, the claims made for the role of the state in capitalist social formations. However, the concept of 'social reproduction' can be relevant with no *presumption that a collective optimum* (not to mention the attendant problems of definition and measurement) *is realized*. What is reproduced is a complex structure of relations, many of which are asymmetric, which preserves a certain identity along with its conflicts, inequalities and sub-optimal features. This allows theorists of social reproduction, when free of functionalist preconceptions, to develop an endogenously dynamic analysis of historical processes in which *strategic behaviour* is endemic, where the sub-optimal outcomes of one reproduction period set the inter-dependent conditions for the next round of antagonistic, cooperative or mixed-motive actions on the part of various agents, be they independent individuals or organized collectives or coalitions. The historical social process here is not a seamless web of inter-personal relations between *equivalent* individuals but one of ordered or nested, asymmetries differentiating the agents in terms of various effective resources and the range of alternative options available.

Marxist theorists argue for the definite primacy of the social relations of production which, when exploitative, usually exhibit con-comitant relations of domination, subordination and control.[12] Individuals who are inter-related by the social relations of production (which are themselves qualitatively distinguishable into separate sets) are distributed into identifiable social classes asymmetrically related to each other. These class relations, with a characteristic structure, provide the identity relations for social reproduction, i.e. they are the invariant properties of a social formation allowing the identification of social *reproduction* as historical process. Two related issues must immediately be recognized: one, not all individuals in a society necessarily and definitely have a locus in the structure of production relations, nor is it necessary that those who *are* so located have a *unique* locus, many may be variously related to different others in the total nexus of production relations; two, the ordered asymmetries of production relations are not the only asymmetric social relations in which individuals are involved. Non-Marxist theorists (who are not necessarily anti-Marxist) have, on the basis of both the above points, questioned the primacy accorded the social relations of production.[13] They have claimed that asymmetric relations (of domination or inequality of rights and powers) involving language, gender, ethnic identity, occupation etc., do act as distributive principles placing individuals in different classes. They are not necessarily causally less important in under-standing social processes than the classes based on production relations. Marxists have counter-argued that the predominance of the social relations of production is indicated by the *relative invariance* of these relations observed in the historical course of social reproduction (including the reproduction of the 'contradictions' these relations engender) whilst the other relations do show greater variability and change through state activities or collective and individual actions, within limits set by the production relations. Further, some have tried to show that hierarchical or subordination relations involving characteristics such as gender or ethnicity have a smaller causal efficacy in accounting for certain results such as income or asset inequality, and that their causal role is itself dependent upon the structures of class relations.[14]

Class structures are subject to transformation, through processes of revolutionary social re-construction, when the productive forces have altered, both as regards their *level* of development and the extent of their *socialization*, to the point where a prevalent set of production relations are no longer effectively able to efficiently use the productive forces (or develop them further) for gains in the level of satisfaction of currently specified needs and wants in the subordinate population. The structural transformation, if there is one, is the result of various strategies of collective action on the part of the contending social classes, and the new relations of production may be viewed as a collective benefit for one or more of the formerly subordinate classes or collectively organized fractions of them.

This summary statement of the basic Marxist theoretical claim is a particular one, not necessarily universally shared amongst Marxists. However, without arguing for its merits here, it will inform the subsequent analysis.[15] It has a number of properties that will be important. First, it takes as relevant and valid the *analytical* distinction between 'base' and 'superstructure'. The base consists of the productive forces and their forms of utilization in given sets of production relations, i.e. it is a structure of relations of effective control or use of resources, the elements of which are productive forces and human agents; the superstructure consists of those social institutions that are both required by and controlled by the base with both requirement and control exhibited in the course of historical social reproduction. The state, in its institutional aspects, is part of the super-structure, and thus both required and constrained by the base or 'economic structure' of the social formation.[16]

Secondly, the base or 'economic structure', which determines the social classes and their relations (without any presumption regarding the 'class consciousness' or otherwise of the individual members of the various social classes) is itself subject to historical reproduction and, under certain conditions, transformation through the agency of cumulative individual or collective actions. This is accomplished through two processes: first, the development (with various consequent changes in the extent of socialization) of the productive forces. This conditions production possibilities in general (and consequently leisure-time possibilities) for given levels of wants and needs. It is brought about either through various agents' intentional rational actions within the established relations of production, or in part, as unintended effects of other activities (e.g. the pursuit of knowledge, seeking competitive advantage, the growth of reproductive fertility, etc.). This process increasingly engenders, given a set of production relations, difficulties for the effective utilization of the changing productive forces in terms of the interests of the subordinate social classes. This latter claim is warranted by the logical independence of production relations and productive forces and the contingent possibility that a given set of production relations is not appropriate for the efficient utilization of changing levels and types of productive forces.[17]

Second, the difficulties and incapacities arising from productive development will find expression in conflicting strategic actions and contradictory demands on the part of various agents directed at maintaining or altering prevalent social relations. Some of these strategic actions will be collective actions by variously organized collectives pursuing different and often contradictory collective benefits, including specific class interests, directed at the state. The state, in its various institutional forms, will be the focus of class-struggles, expressed through varying levels of organization, to which its responses will also be strategic, aimed at realizing the most orderly social reproduction possible. The objective of orderly social reproduction may be inferred from the fact that the state is itself able to act only through the agency of individuals or groups of individuals occupying the (at least partially) ordered positions of its institutional apparatus, and that the maintenance of the ability to act of these agents (whatever their personal objectives) depends crucially on orderly social reproduction including the social reproduction of their relational powers.

Whether the social relations of production will be transformed or not will depend on the strategic resources and options available to the contending social classes and the courses of action chosen. What these resources and options are will depend on the prevalent 'economic structure' and the extent to which the contending classes are organized for collective action, which in turn will depend on strategic choices made by individuals in response to the interactional environment in which they find themselves. The state, or more precisely, its variously empowered agents, is located in this field of rolling strategic actions, in which it is itself a strategic agent. But, in so far as the state *is* a single collective agent, in a capitalist social formation, it does not have effective control over the productive forces and their utilization and is dependent on tax-receipts, and consequently on the continuation of organized production, as the major source of resources.[18] The social class in effective control over the productive resources, and *a fortiori* any resource large sub-groups within this class (e.g. large or multi-national firms) will be advantaged in its strategic interaction with the state. This will effectively place limits on the activities of the state, constraining it to adopt policies that maintain the invariance of the class relations, whatever the effects of its policies on some individual members of the different classes. The types of state intervention and the institutional forms through which these are conducted do not, therefore, have a wholly autonomous character but are forms more or less adequate to particular strategic tasks. The interrelations between the 'public' and 'private' social activities imply that particular institutional forms of the state are not instrumentally adequate for and extensible to realize any and all strategic objectives. It is in this sense that given institutional forms of the state are 'best' suited to realize the reproduction of particular social structures.[19]

The third aspect of our strategic interactionist Marxian approach is that whilst it is possible to present the base and super-structure relation in terms of a diachronic functionalist theory,[20] there is no necessity to do so. For the distinction between the two categories and their asymmetric relation can be viewed, as in this account, as a distinction between levels of control in a hierarchical, multi-level system with the base being the level that imposes the most fundamental invariance requirements. These invariance conditions are not functional imperatives of an organic system, but the primary strategic interests of specifiable agents with resources such that they have available strategies in the pursuit of their interests which dominate, over wide ranges of possible circumstances, the strategies available to other agents in the pursuit of their different or contrary interests. The invariant features of a structure of social relations are those that are recurrently reproduced as the outcome of strategic interaction. In other words there is no presumption about 'structuralism' or 'structural imperatives' in this account, and no presumption that social reproduction implies structural stasis, but rather that it involves the dialectical unity of invariance and change such that in certain specifiable circumstances the strategic achievement of the invariance of given production relations may no longer be successful.[21] This explicitly recognizes individual decision-making in generally asymmetric and inter-dependent interactional contexts as that which provides *traction* to human history, whilst also recognizing that class relations are primary in that the relations of production condition the strategic resources, and consequently the options, available to various agents in the pursuit of various objectives. The group which effectively controls the production possibilities of a social formation can effectively dominate the strategies of other agents because even when products are not in themselves the objectives sought by others they are necessary inputs or 'intermediate goods' for the realization of other objectives.

It follows from the arguments above that the state is not the locus of all collective power in a capitalist social formation. It is not even, at any given time, the locus of all authority or legitimate power because whenever the effective control over productive or other resources is legitimated through legally sanctioned property rights, authority over these resources is vested in those with such rights. The state and its agents and institutional forms cannot be treated as standing *apart* from the rest of the social formation. It is, even when integrated to the point where its agents act like a single agent, a constrained and controllable agent limited by the powers available to other agents, primarily those in control of the conditions of production. There is then no reason to assume either that a given state apparatus is *necessarily* unified or that it *necessarily* crystallizes, distills or focuses all the class contradictions or conflicts of a social formation. In class-structured social formations it cannot even occupy the position of a cybernetic control centre for it is embedded in the strategic relations, not independent of them. It is not merely a processing centre for information regarding conditions or demands.

In this respect, many recent attempts to view the state as the *regulatory mechanism* for the reproduction of social formations experiencing changing states of disequilibrium are misleading in so far as they neglect two things: first, the *specific* strategic objectives of various agents of the state (not invariably reducible to the objectives of particular social classes or sub-groups of them, nor assimilable to 'public choices' representing the aggregation of the separately identifiable 'choices' of any well-defined and stable public); and, second, the unintended, and possibly negative or counter-productive collective effects of the state's activities. The extent to which it can be a *successful* regulatory mechanism is a historically contingent matter in part dependent upon the uncertainties and information inadequacies to which it is subjected, even apart from the limitations imposed by the activities of other powerful agents in the social formation.[22] The state is itself subject to changing states as it is both an instrument of collective action on the part of various other collectives in a social formation, and a more or less unified strategic agent itself. It is a historically changing and changeable institutional embodiment of changing relations between the 'collective' and 'individual' dimensions of social interaction. The *scope* of its activites will grow or diminish and the *forms* of its interventions will alter with changes in what may be termed the *extent of socialization of social actions* as mediated through the asymmetric strategic interaction noted above.

Socialization of Social Action and the Role of the State in Collective Action

The concept of 'socialization of social actions' is being proposed as the partial analogue within Marxist theory of the economists' concept of 'external effects' or 'externalities'. Whilst their denotations, in part, overlap their connotations are different owing to the great differences in the respective theories in which the concepts are embedded. The concept also bears an obvious analogy, within Marxist theory, with the concept of the socialization of the productive forces. The latter, imprecise as it is in Marxist theory, refers to the relation between the various kinds and quantities of productive forces as regards the extent of their inter-dependence in use, and consequently has implications for the adequacy or inadequacy of given sets of property relations to efficiently and effectively use them. The growing socialization of some of the productive forces is one source of the growing 'lumpiness' of capital requirements; of the need for certain quantities and kinds of workers to be concentrated in a given production process; of the forward and backward linkages between various firms, branches of production and sectors of the economy such that stoppages or slow-downs in one firm, branch or sector affects the utilization of the productive forces in the others. The extension of socialization of the productive forces, Marx claimed, comes into 'contradiction' with the property-relations of capitalism and the autonomous and independent decision-making in market economies in the sense that the productive forces are increasingly inefficiently used from a collectively social view-point, necessitating changes in property relations and the introduction of collectively planned utilization of the productive forces.

By a partial analogy, the extent of socialization of social actions refers, on the one hand, to the extent to which the realization of the objectives of individuals (whether these relate to collective or individual benefits) requires collective or conjoint action on the part of many; and, on the other hand, the extent to which particular social actions or, interactions have effects on various sets of individuals not directly a party to those social actions or interactions. The latter embraces all that economists designate by external effects including all emergent effects, whilst the former refers to the extent to which particular individual objectives are unattainable through individualist strategies but require collective or joint strategies. In summary, it is an index of the extent of inter-dependence and 'mutual interference', irrespective of intentions, that prevails in a given social formation. The standard literature usually studies collective action as a problem in the provision of collective goods, but the socialization of social action refers us *also* to situations where collective strategies are the only viable ones even for the provision of separable individual benefits, i.e. it is about the characteristics of successful strategies rather than about the characteristics (collective or individual) of the benefit con-ferred. It indicates the collective or public implications of actions, and its growth implies a decline in the degree of privatization of our social actions.

The relevance of this growing socialization of the forms of social action to the analysis of the role of the state in capitalist social forma-tions comes from two directions. On the one hand, the failure or unviability of individualist strategies consequent upon the growing inter-dependence and interference amongst social agents leads to collec-tive strategies for state provision of benefits; and on the other, the production (or, as we shall see, the non-production) of certain external effects may choke the process of social reproduction unless these external effects (or their absence) is remedied through some form of enforceable collective action. Whilst in theory it has been argued that such collective action is possible on a voluntary contractual basis, there are good reasons for mistrusting that theory, and as historical fact it can be observed that the state *has* been subjected to growing demands for regulation, suppression or provision as the case may be. The fact that it is possible to conceive of contractual, market-type remedies is important in one respect though, viz. it shows that there is no absolute and irreversible necessity for the state's activities, and depending on the circumstances the state may cease to act in certain ways and withdraw its activities, leaving the problems to contractual, market or other social solutions. Since the state is itself dependent on the reproduction of the conditions of production and productive activities, the dominant social class may successfully 'roll-back' the state's activities or alter the forms which it takes, in order to further its own objectives even if the consequence is a worsening of collective social welfare. The agents of the state, it has been argued, cannot be presumed necessarily to have the maximization of collective welfare as their primary objective.

Economists who have analyzed the role of external effects and the provision of collective goods or benefits in a market economy have usually started from a recognition that the competitive market economy cannot by itself reach an equilibrium state that is Pareto-efficient as regards the allocation of resources in the presence of negative or positive external effects, or in the provision of public goods. They have stumbled upon the state as they reached the limits of market exchange as a mechanism for the realization of certain specific concepts of efficiency and optimality. They have, therefore, looked at the implications of various external effects *after they have effectively been produced*, even when working (as is usually the case) with models which describe hypothetical states of affairs. They have not investigated the *positive external effects* which are either *underproduced or not produced in capitalist market economies* but which, when produced, increase capital accumulation, profitability, growth, innovation, mobility of labour and capital, consumption levels, etc. The approach to this kind of issue, in the traditional literature is in terms of *pure* public goods, with the underprovision of the latter often being treated as a 'produced' *negative* external effect. Yet it is surely intuitively possible, when considering a capitalist market economy in which capitalists are in competition with each other, to conceive of *capitalist* public goods (in the sense of public goods *for* capitalists) which will be underproduced or not produced by single (or collectively unorganized) capitalists for fear of providing a positive externality to competitive rivals. If we do think counter-factually in this manner it is possible to identify a class of positive external effects which provide positive benefits to capitalists but which are not necessarily positive externalities in an equivalent manner to non-capitalists, i.e. a class of collective goods whose benefits (or use-value in Marxist terminology) are restricted to a particular social class or, when more-widely beneficial, confer benefits *asymmetrically* to the various social classes. Such exclusively or primarily capitalist public goods will pose a problem of non-provision or under-provision if left to individual capitalist effort. This is because of the well-known 'free-rider' problem. Since a collective benefit is non-exclusive, it is enjoyed by all members of the relevant collective irrespective of whether they have shared in the cost of its provision. This implies that the net benefit enjoyed by a member is greater if sharing or bearing costs can be avoided.

Following Mancur Olson's now classic distinction between 'privileged groups' and 'latent groups' it can be argued that capitalists, as an unorganized collectivity, often find themselves in a 'latent' state with regard to certain general facilitating conditions of production, e.g. means of transportation, urban infrastructure or a local labour market.[23] As a latent-group, no one amongst them will find it rational to wholly bear the cost of providing the general service from which other, competing capitalists may derive benefit, possibly a greater benefit than that enjoyed by the one bearing the cost of provision. The preference for the 'free-rider' status on the part of *all* members, and the fear of others being 'free-riders' and thus gaining advantage, will lead to non-provision of the collective benefit on a purely voluntary basis at least in so far as the capitalists are in a competitive relation. The implication of such non-provision may be negative not only for the capitalists but also for those workers who will not be employed or who will receive lower wages in the absence of the positive externalities for the capitalists. It has been shown that such situations, where the logic of 'free-riding' defeats the realization of a collective benefit, share the logical structure of the prisoners dilemma game, i.e. there is available a dominant strategy of defection which leads to a collectively sub-optimal outcome. The outcome is sub-optimal not only in the weak, modern sense of Pareto-optimality (at least one person's situation can be improved without worsening any one else's situation) but also in the more robust sense of Pareto's own original usage (*everyone* involved can be made better-off) in connection with social utility.[24] In the language of game-theory, this is a non-zero sum game where the cooperative course of action is welfare-superior to the defection strategy, but the latter is the individually rational course of action both from the viewpoint of minimizing possible losses and maximizing possible gains.

In such situations not only are capitalists mutually involved in a prisoners' dilemma, but many *workers* will have an interest in the capitalists securing their collectively optimal position for that will lead to greater employment and, through collective bargaining, higher wages. Capital accumulation, in its employment or income augmenting effects is *not* a zero-sum game between all workers and all capitalists—although the struggle over the real wage rate under *given* conditions of production and employment is.

Whilst it is again possible in theory for some capitalists to form an exclusive 'club' to mutually share the cost of providing some kinds of positive externalities to themselves, this is not possible where basic characteristics of a 'free-market' are at stake, e.g. where the free mobility of capital and labour is adversely affected. In our terminology, these are positive externalities that cannot be exclusively privatized because of the high socialization of the activities involved—not to mention the transaction costs, information asymmetries and the opportunity-costs of constant vigilance and contract enforcement. The cost-effective alternative is to have a specialized institution for enforced cost-sharing, viz, the state, provide the collective benefit (a positive externality from the view-point of individual capitalists) through public expenditures drawing on taxes. This has the added advantage of allowing capitalists the possibility of reducing their own share of the costs through the *shifting of taxes* on to others. At any rate proportionality between benefits received and share of the costs is difficult to establish and monitor. In these circumstances there is a convergence of interests between sub-groups of capitalists and agents of the state to increase public provision through public expenditure. Where the real incidence of the taxes is not transparent this kind of state provision of externalities through public expenditure will receive the support of sub-groups of workers as well if employment opportunities and/or real wages are expected to rise.

In designating such public expenditures as positive public externalities (for some relevant public) we are both limiting and extending the usual denotations of the concept of external effect. *Public* externalities are more limited in that their reference includes only externalities resulting from *state activities* (at whatever level of the institutional structure of the state), and positive public *externalities* are more extended in reference in that it includes not only the effects which are *not taken into account* in maximizing some objective function by an agent, in this case the state, but also includes deliberate and *calculated benefits provided to other agents as an external benefit without the objective of maximizing returns* to the state, i.e. benefits provided without regard to the profitability of the action, in the usual sense, to the state. The state is engaged in these activities to varying degrees of coherence for a complex set of reasons on the part of its various agents, including maintenance of office on the part of the government, career development and employment stability on the part of public employees, extension of the scope and power of their activities on the part of bureaucratic directors, maintaining social support or a particular notion of a just social order, etc. To some extent these partial objectives converge on the general objective of orderly social reproduction of the given social formation, but they may, in some circumstances, diverge, especially the interests of electoral success dependent politicians and stable-career dependent bureaucrats.

The main point is that the state neither has the objective of maximizing profits, nor any other analogous single objective. It is a partially coherent collective agent in the historical process of social reproduction incapable, at least in class-structured social formations, of optimizing any global objective function. However, in capitalist social formations it is a *non-capitalist* agent *not* itself governed by the maximization (or optimization) of profitability, although strategically constrained to assist that objective on the part of capitalists or particular subgroups of them.

In this context it is worth noting that the expression 'the capitalist state' which is current in some Marxist circles is both misleading and unnecessary. It is misleading because it suggests that the objectives pursued and the behavioural and environmental constraints faced by the agents of the state are identical or similar to those of capitalists. This is clearly not the case as even a cursory examination of public expenditures will show. The state does not seek profits and the problems of the structure, volume and collection of taxes is quite distinct from the problems of investment, technical choice, wage-rates and commodity sales facing capitalists. It is unnecessary because the intention behind such a designation, viz, that the state in a capitalist social formation is subject to capitalist class control, can be argued on strategic grounds without suggesting any necessary institutional integration (whether through personnel interlocks or otherwise) between the capitalist class and the various agents of the state.[25] Indeed, it will not be in the interests of the capitalist class as a whole, given the competitive (and therefore strategic) relation in which they stand to each other, to have some capitalists in a personnel inter-lock with the state unless the relevant persons are delegates of the class as a whole selected by some acceptable collective choice rule. Otherwise, particular capitalists will be advantaged to the detriment of others and collective class interests will no longer be assured. Of course, if in the course of historical capitalist dynamics, through concentration and centralization of capitals, the capitalist class is itself internally stratified to the point where systematic divergences in the profit-rate occur (and, therefore, all capitals are no longer equivalent in proportion to volume), it is possible for the dominant fraction of the class to seek to place its own agents as agents of the state. But in that case we must designate the state a monopoly-capital state or a finance-capital state, if the relevant fraction is collectively organized to act as a single individual. Precisely this issue is one major theme of the theory of state-monopoly capitalism, but in that analysis one can no more escape the question of how competing capitalists can organize for collective action than we can the question of how individual workers, differentiated by income, occupation, branch and firm can collectively organize for *class* action.[26]

The beneficial, and indeed necessary, role of the state for capitalist development through the production of public externalities was identified by Marx as regards spatial mobility and locational issues, i.e. as regards transportation and urban hierarchies and infrastructure. Marx was equally aware that such public externalities were *not* pure public goods equivalently beneficial to all citizens, but class-related public goods primarily aiding capitalist accumulation and imposing on geographical space a structure in accordance with the general law of capitalist accumulation, viz, promotion of concentration and centralization of capital, and the polarized locational distribution of the productive forces including the induced mobility of labour.[27]

The Modalities of State Involvement in Social Reproduction

The scope of all state produced public externalities (for capitalists or other collectivities) has greatly increased since Marx's days in three directions differentiated by the collectives involved as beneficiaries. Broadly, we may classify the beneficiaries of state-produced positive externalities in capitalist social formations into three categories: (1) capitalists (or a dominant segment of them), (2) non-capitalists, variously differentiated into separable collectives, and (3) the whole population of the social formation subject to a single state. In the first category, the range of relevant positive public externalities for the capitalist class as a whole has expanded beyond transportation facilities and urban infrastructure to include capitalist production related growth in knowledge and technology (i.e. research and development), state production of certain qualities in the general labour-force (such as functional literacy and some widely used industrial skills), and state production of intermediate goods which are likely to develop into natural monopolies for whatever reason. In the second category, the public externalities produced by the state have been further specialized so as to be relevant to particular groups other than capitalists as a class or the entirety of the population, i.e. the state is now providing collective benefits to well-defined *target* collectives: certain sub-groups of the population (which may or may not be identical to sub-groups of social classes). In some cases, the latter could be targeted to single firms and be beneficial asymmetrically only to the capitalists and workers organized in that firm. It would be a mistake to regard all state activities as universalistic, and therefore providing *collective* benefits, or avoiding *collective* ills for more or less well-defined and numerically extended collectives. In the third category, are certain public externalities that are state provided, to varying degrees, in all social formations with a state, viz. internal order, defence against external attack, enforcement of contracts, etc. These are included in the economists' notion of pure public goods and it is generally agreed that they are minimally necessary functions of a state.

The difference between the first two directions of growth in the role of the state lies in their beneficiaries: the dominant social class as a whole or other categories of the population. The first set of activities mainly address what Marx termed the *general conditions of capitalist production*. These are the facilitating conditions which were difficult or impossible for particular firms to privatize or internalize so as to exclude other capitalists from tapping the positive external effects, and their provision is consequently plagued by the 'free-rider' problem and would lead to mutual frustration and sub-optimal levels of capital accumulation and activity. These come closest to the traditional concept of public goods, even though the relevant public may be only the capitalist class. They generally arise in connection with *discontinuities* in investment or allocational decisions where step increments are involved rather than marginal calculations, and where *interdependencies* between sets of decisions, made by decision-makers with independent property, is high. Consequently, they become barriers to the *restructuring*, as against steady, balanced expansion, of productive capital or production conditions. Spatial restructuring of capital or labour, inter-sectoral or inter-branch redeployment of capital, and stepwise or threshold changes of technological level are prime examples. Because of this, the state provision of the externalities involved is not going to be a *linear* function of time showing a steady expansion in the state's role. On the contrary, the state's activities in this regard will exhibit historical discontinuities showing rapid expansion of public expenditure and production during re-structuring periods of capital accumulation followed by a withdrawal and a shift of activity during periods of steady capital expansion. There will, of course, be resistance to withdrawal on the part of some of the state's employees and some bureaus engaged in the production of these positive externalities owing to the subdivisional structure of the state apparatus itself. But support will come, for retreat by the state, from those capitalists seeking investment opportunities for money-capital (in the main, finance capitalists and conglomerates) as regards those state activities which can be produced and marketed as commodities (i.e. those public externalities which are not pure public goods and for which a solvent private demand is apparent). The capitalist class as a whole, and aggregate capital accumulation, will not benefit from the re-commodification of those state produced positive externalities which are likely to be (owing to production conditions with increasing returns to scale or whatever) natural monopolies able to charge monopoly prices and restrict output. The invariance condition of expanded capitalist social reproduction implies that the state's withdrawal in order to assist re-commodification will be more likely in those areas where withdrawal leads to the expansion of consumer markets for final consumption goods but does not affect general capitalist production conditions.

It is for this reason premature to speak of irreversible growth of public expenditure or the necessary growth of *collective consumption* for it is precisely in the components of collective consumption (state produced positive consumption externalities for households) that re-commodification for capitalist expansion can occur. Nevertheless, during periods of re-structuration (especially spatial or technological restructuration) qualititative characteristics of the labour-force such as adequate supply, skill-level, locational commitment, work-regularity, etc., become *aspects of the production conditions* of capitalists uncertain over whether the commodity-form provision of the implied housing, technical training, health maintenance and transportation will be initially and simultaneously available. It is in these circumstances that state provision of these labour-force conditions is a necessary positive externality for expanded capitalist social reproduction. But when the threshold jumps have been made, relatively stable and favourable labour-market conditions obtained, and the *productive* circulation of money-capital is slowing, capitalists will favour a withdrawal of the state and recommodification or re-marketization of those goods and services.[28] Strategically, they will be successful if the state's expenditure and activities are deficit financed, tax-receipts are stagnant or falling, and capital accumulation is negative or low.

The second set of state activities has to do with positive externalities, not for the capitalist class as a whole, but for various target groups of different size and kind. Here, the external benefits conferred by the state may or may not be directly in the form of *collective* goods, for the benefit may take the form of a once only transfer of resources to a *particular* firm. In general, however, transfers of resources operated by the state are targeted to *categories* of the population and thus are a collective benefit to those eligible. With regard to this second set of positive externalities the state has a wider range of instruments: grants (in the form of non-contributory transfer payments, lump-sum money allocations, tax exemptions, transfers of credit-worth through guaranteeing loans); non-capitalist financing (support through no-interest or low-interest loans); administration of financially autonomous contributory insurance schemes (pensions, unemployment benefits); budget financed direct provision of certain services to target groups (education, nationalized health, care of the handicapped); and state purchases of materials and services from capitalist or self-employed producers (government purchases and public contracts). This last can be effectively used for directing capitalist development but the externality produced is directed at individuals rather than collectives. These allow the state to respond to a wide variety of collectives or individuals demanding services or benefits, and permits flexibility of response since few of the target groups are numerically so large, or so well organized for collective action, or so well-endowed with strategic resources, as to pose any significant strategic threat to the state on a shift of policy. To this extent, this type of public externality allows greater scope for alternative mixtures of targeted expenditures, which can be a function of putting together coalitions of the electorate with the objective of winning elections in electorally competitive political systems for access to state power, or undertaken to minimize activities disruptive of a given form of social order. The first set of state-produced externalities for capitalist producers is more directly related to the invariance conditions for social reproduction of the capitalist social formation and therefore more vigilantly defended against erosion by the dominant social class who are able to enlist the support of at least some segments of the subordinate classes since, in the absence of the organization of an alternative viable system of production, the decline in output that may ensue from the violation of the invariance conditions of a capitalist economy will leave almost everyone, including most workers, worse off.

It is possible, however, that a sub-group of capitalists, sufficiently differentiated from the rest of the class in terms of function and power in the economy, may become the object of this second set of state activities. Two such bases of internal differentiation of the capitalist class, which may lead to partly overlapping but not necessarily identical memberships, may be noted. One is the growth of a *monopoly sector* owing to the dynamic and cumulative processes of concentration and centralization of capital which segments the capitalist class into a small number of industrial and financial groups on the one hand, and a large number of non-monopoly capitalists subject to the constraints of both intra-sectoral competition and unequal exchange (through monopoly or monopsony power) with the monopoly sector.[29] The growth of large financial-industrial groups in the form of giant conglomerates or multi-national corporations allows capital to internalize the costs of capital mobility, frees it from competitive pricing of a wide-range of inputs thus allowing administrative pricing of internally-traded products so as to reduce the volume of taxes, and allows forms of oligopolistic competition over market shares and product innovation with equilibrium prices higher than perfectly competitive prices through tacit collusion. The major role of product innovation in oligopolistic competition forces monopoly capital to invest in research and development and disproportionately benefit from positive public externalities in that domain. Together their volume of capital, market share, and employment share in several branches of production far exceeds the volumes under the control of the far more numerous non-monopoly capitalists. The branches of production dominated by monopoly capital can be shown, usually, to be the dominant branches of production in terms of the inter-branch input-output relations in the economy as a whole, i.e. they can seriously constrain or assist the overall growth of the economy.[30] In these circumstances, monopoly capital can strategically force the substitution of its own growth and profitability, in place of that of the capitalist class as a whole, as the invariance conditions for social reproduction. This implies that the asymmetries of class-relations will be overlaid with the asymmetries of unequal exchange and power within the capitalist class. But for this to happen one must ascertain the structure of inter-monopoly competition and the extent to which the various monopoly capitals are organized for collective action to secure collective benefits. Nevertheless, it is possible that some of the targeted instruments of the state's provision of positive public externalities are directed at aiding the growth, profitability and technical restructuring of monopoly capital as a whole or particular financial-industrial groups.

The *second* basis of internal differentiation of the capitalist class relates not to the asymmetries of exchange and strategic power or the systematic differentiation of profit rates, but to differences of constraints and consequently of behaviour between sub-groups of capitalists. Given the substantial increase in the volume of inter-national economic relations under relatively free-trade conditions, some economists have differentiated the roles (for the state of the economy as a whole) of those capitals subjected to competition from the exterior (the externally constrained sector) and those capitals relatively free from foreign competition (the sheltered sector.)[31] The implication is that the state's activities directed at expanded social reproduction of the 'economic structure' should be differentially formulated for the two sectors. The positive public externalities to be effective cannot be directed at the capitalist class as a whole but must be differentiated. Others have argued that from the viewpoint of orderly social reproduction minimizing the conjunction of inflation and recession, the relevant primary differentiation of capitals is that between the capital goods sector and the other sectors, with the state's policies directed at producing public externalities, of the appropriate kind, for the former.[32] Whatever the analytical validity of these latter theories, they basically address the first set of public externalities, i.e. those which produce *capitalist* public goods, with benefits to others only to the extent that capitalist success in growth and efficiency is a non-zero sum game between capitalists and others. But the distinction relating to the strategic dominance of monopoly capital does have, if valid in the relevant ways, a wider set of implications for the structure of antagonisms in a capitalist social formation and the role of the state in social reproduction. If both the first two types of positive public externalities are predominantly directed at maintaining the *expanded* reproduction of monopoly capital, the distinction itself collapses and the range of strategic options available to the state is reduced, with the bulk of public expenditure *irreducibly* required for monopolist reproduction.

It has earlier been argued that some of the first set of public externalities do not necessarily have to grow in a linear manner, but may involve state withdrawal to allow recommodification of public services or collective consumption benefits. This has taken place, particularly within many capitalist countries such as the U.K. and France. This means that the major causes of the observed linear expansion of total *public expenditures* in capitalist social formations since World War Two have to be sought either in the second set of public externalities or have their source in an ever-rising need for capitalist public goods to reproduce capitalist production conditions, thus involving the state in a direct and permanent role in the production process. This is indeed the claim of the theory of state-monopoly capitalism. The growth of the various components of public expenditure do not arise from a single source and the historical patterns of growth of disaggregated components of public expenditure are not identical.[33] This is the reason for distinguishing public externalities for the capitalist class, where the volume and range of state expenditure may vary with the discontinuities in capital accumulation and opportunities for the expansion of capitalist commodity production, from those public externalities which can be targeted to social categories that are not necessarily capitalist. The latter, in so far as they are not capitalist-oriented public externalities, may pose obstacles to the expansion of capital (whether monopoly or not) and as such be the object of a triangular strategic struggle involving capitalists, targeted beneficiaries and the agents of the state.

In electoral political systems with competing political parties, the parties and politicians will become the objects of strategic influence and exchange relations trading electoral support, with or without side payments, for particular policies with regard to such targeted public expenditures directed at the social sectors. The expansion of the state into the non-capitalist provision of various potentially marketable services which are not public externalities for capitalist production restricts the domain of capitalist expansion and accumulation. Exclusion of certain sectors of production from the market (and its associated form of efficiency under capitalist competition) restricts the inter-sectoral mobility of capital, as capital in various other sectors is over-accumulated, and faces declining or negative profit rates. Some capital, especially monopoly capital, will under these (and some other) circumstances be mobile out of the country into other economies in multinational corporate, holding company or portfolio forms, but much of nationally located capital will seek recommodification of these sectors. Success in this regard will confer a collective benefit on the whole capitalist class. Appeal to ostensibly competitive market efficiency as against the 'inefficiency' of tax-based public provision (or budgetized provision) will be an ideological strategic option in the electoral arena. In so far as these second-type targeted public expenditures are not class-related but targeted at weakly organized or unorganized minorities, their volume will fluctuate with the success or failure of competing 'political entrepreneurs' in putting together various coalitions in the electorate. These elections and party mediated struggles over this type of public expenditure is of interest to capitalists even if they are not bearing the relevant tax burden (i.e. even if these expenditures are covered though non-capitalist intra-class transfers of costs and benefits) when opening up new sectors of commodity production is expected to raise profitability. But whether there will be any *collective* expression of capitalist class preference will depend on the extent of internal differentiation amongst capitalists and whether the class as a whole is experiencing the difficulties of over-accumulation.

The third set of public expenditures relate to the 'socially necessary' public services required, in varying *forms*, in all social formations.[34] These cannot all be reduced to zero-sum conflicts of specific and antagonistic class interests. For whilst any social order confers benefits *asymmetrically* to the individuals involved, and the reproduction of a capitalist social order reproduces capitalist dominance, almost all individuals not subjected to direct repression will prefer the reproduction of even asymmetric social order to the production of disorder and insecurity for themselves. The 'socially necessary' public externalities are, generally, subject to conflicts over form, extent and application but, precisely because they are *in some form* socially necessary, it is difficult to reduce them wholly to class oppositions—quite apart from the problems of identifying collective behaviour on the part of entire social classes, or attributing individual behaviour that is socially disruptive for some segments of society to class causation. As this set of public externalities includes all the repressive activities of the state, some of which are used against agents seeking to alter the class-relations (or particular aspects or consequences of them) they also involve collective class-struggles over the structural identity of the social formation. In this the modalities of state action become strategic resources in the struggle itself, with both the institutional forms and agent-composition of the state as objects of the strategies. The issue in such collective class struggles, where a given form of the state and its agents is both a strategic instrument in the struggle and the object of direct organized class conflict on the part of opposed classes, is the feasibility or not of the social reproduction of a given social formation itself and goes beyond an analysis of the role of the state in social reproduction.

Even apart from periods of revolutionary class struggle, this third set of public externalities (which involve negative externalities for some) are likely to grow with the increasing socialization of social action. When individual and collective agents are becoming increasingly interdependent and thus intentionally or otherwise producing negative external effects, the state, as the most result-effective, and in the long-run, most economical, and eventually most successful agent of collective action will increase this component of its activities, minimally in the form of regulatory legislation. This entails a certain growth of state expenditure and state activity (requiring growing public employment) along with the rising levels and extent of the socialization of social action. Some capitalists will enjoy indirect positive public externalities owing to the growth of public purchase of commodities this entails, and the whole class will benefit from the state's growing ability to repress individual or collective attempts to alter the social order. As the public externalities in this set are not, under the current market forms, marketable (i.e. not easily convertible into divisible and excludable private goods), there will be no strategic reason for state withdrawal from such expenditures and activities in order to promote capitalist social reproduction.

These different kinds of public externalities are the result of varying strategic responses to different aspects of the historical process of social reproduction and cannot be centrally planned at any given time in a capitalist social formation. Given the possibility of public borrowing, deficit financing, and the state's control over the money supply, there is no *necessary and immediate* constraint on public expenditure at any given time. The state's agents *qua* public administrators or governing politicians are not necessarily identical with members of a particular social class, and have an autonomous range of *strategic* choice, subject to both social reproduction and re-election considerations, which are made under uncertainty regarding the choices of other inter-dependent agents. In these circumstances there is no immediate barrier or sanction against 'over-production' of positive public externalities in capitalist social formations beyond that necessary for social reproduction of a capitalist social formation. In particular the state, as a non-capitalist agent, does not face the sanction of the realization of produced value in markets which capitalists do. There is no analogue of the 'law of value' regulating the conditions for successful reproduction of the state. The strategic drift will lead to a tendency for total public expenditure to rise.[35] But since the state, as a superstructural institution, is not in command of the production conditions in a capitalist economy, it can finance and materially support its activities only through raising taxes, creation of fiat money and the diversion of labour-power and other productive forces from the capitalist 'economic structure'. This will produce unintentional negative public externalities, imposing costs differentially on different segments of the population, in the form of inflation, the experience of rising tax rates, and possibly a disjunction between maximizing profits and maximizing output in the capitalist economy, especially under conditions of monopoly capital.[36] Precisely because the state is not an agent in the social relations of production it is not one of the terms in the class relations of a capitalist social formation. Consequently the incidence of taxes on the one hand and the second kind of positive public externalities on the other hand will be distributed unequally over the population but not in clearly class-related ways. In fact, so long as public externalities or capitalists remain substantial and the ability to shift corporate profit taxes on to consumers is effective, the financing of public externalities may be largely through intra-class transfers, primarily amongst the salaried population. When the negative public externalities noted earlier are experienced by a large portion of the population there will be cross-class or class-neutral collective demand for 'cut-backs' in public expenditure. If the analysis presented here has any merit the 'cut-backs' are mainly possible in the second set of public externalities and this may be insufficient to stem the drift toward rising public expenditure, especially if the public externalities for the capitalist class has to grow in order to reproduce the capitalist organization of production. The state as the non-capitalist collective agent for the reproduction of a class-structured social formation is caught between undermining expanded capitalist production or undermining its own role as the agent for non-capitalist collective benefits. This exhibits the incapacity of capitalist social formations to indefinitely expand both the capitalist economy and the non-capitalist welfare state.

These negative public externalities produced by the interaction of state activities and capitalist economy are new emergent effects, and the ascription of responsibility for them to identifiable, individual agents is both meaningless and impossible. They should be viewed as a novel type of social 'contradiction' to be juxtaposed to those analyzed by Marx in his study of capitalist dynamics *without the state*. These may be regarded as the contradictions of the social reproduction of capitalist social formations (including the state as an agency as distinct from the contradictions of the capitalist 'economic structure' (or base) with its reproduced class contradictions between capitalists and workers on the one hand and the contradictions of capitalist competition on the other.

This provides the currently most fruitful access to an analysis of the new forms of crisis involving inflation, stable or rising unemployment, low or negative growth, struggles over public expenditure, and 'de-industrialization', in the developed capitalist social formations. The object of this theoretical outline has been to provide an initiation into an *extended* Marxist analysis of the role of the state in this process. The extension lies in the explicit recognition of collective action, including that of classes, as a problem rather than a given; of the role of the state as a non-capitalist producer of public externalities; and of the super-structural locus of the state with its agents endowed, like other human agents, with strategic choice constrained by the reproduction requirements of the 'economic structure'.[37]

Notes and References

1. Two very useful attempts at reconstructing the ideas of Marx and Engels are Bob Jessop, *The Capitalist State* (Martin Robertson, Oxford, 1982) Ch. 1; and Kazem Radjavi, *La Dictature du Prolétariat et le Dépérissement de l'Etat de Marx a Lénine* (Anthropos, Paris, 1975).
2. A sympathetic discussion of the latter trend is in Jessop, *The Capitalist State*, Chapter 4.
3. Jessop, *The Capitalist State*.
4. The classic work is William Baumol, *Welfare Economics and the Theory of the State* (Harvard University Press, Cambridge, Mass., 1952, 2nd edition 1965).
5. This understanding of systemic contradictions is promoted by Jon Elster, *Logic and Society* (John Wiley, New York, 1978), and Raymond Boudon, *The Logic of Social Analysis* (Routledge and Kegan Paul, London 1981) Ch. 4, and in *Effects Pervers et Ordre Social*, (P.U.F., Paris, 1977; 2nd ed. 1979) Chapters II and V.
6. Various works are available analyzing the growth of state activities as a function of electoral and public choice considerations, eg. T. E. Borcherding, (ed.), *Budgets and Bureaucrats: The Sources of Government Growth* (Duke University Press, Durham, N.C., 1977); A. Breton, *The Economic Theory of Representative Government* (Aldine Publishing Co., Chicago, 1974); and in a Marxist frame similar to that adopted here: Arun Bose, *Political Paradoxes and Puzzles* (Oxford University Press, London, 1977).
7. For further details and discussion of the neo-classical economists' analysis of public goods and public choice see J. M. Buchanan, *The Demand and Supply of Public Goods* (Rand McNally and Co., Chicago, 1968) and *The Limits of Liberty: Between Anarchy and Leviathan* (University of Chicago Press, Chicago, 1975). Both works are primarily prescriptive and normative rather than seeking to explain historical developments and both assume the individualist starting point where distinct individuals have independent and autonomous preference functions.
8. A recent presentation of such analyses is D. K. Whynes and R. A. Bowles, *The Economic Theory of the State* (Martin Robertson, Oxford, 1981).
9. An excellent though little noticed work, which invites assimilation into a broader Marxist theory, showing the collective sub-optimality of a four-way strategic inter-action between politicians, bureaucrats, consumers and

business is Randall Bartlett, *Economic Foundations of Political Power* (Free Press, New York, 1973). A sustained criticism of theories of the state as an instrument for the realization of the 'general interest' is in Andre Vianès, *La Raison Economique d'Etat* (Presses Universitaires de Lyon, Lyon, 1980). I must acknowledge a profound debt to this excellent book, especially with regard to the concept of positive public externality used in this paper. However, Vianès tends to a system-functional explanation and implicitly treats the state's regulatory role as competent and successful. This paper rejects these claims.

10. Pareto-optimality is a concept of an optimal state which obtains when no one can be made any better-off without at least one person being made worse-off. Pareto applied a similar criterion only to market transactions but it has now been applied to discussions of collective social welfare. Such an extension implies that market relations are paradigmatic for all social relations, and the present version of the criterion rules out inter-personal comparisons as an argument in individual utility functions.

11. The best recent discussion is G. A. Cohen, *Marx's Theory of History: A Defense* (Princeton University Press, 1978), Chapters IX and X.

12. Ibid. For a rather less tidy exposition see E. O. Wright, *Class Structure and Income Determination* (Academic Press, New York 1979), Chapters 1 and 2. For a rigorous development of a theory of economic exploitation more generally applicable than the Marxist theory see John Roemer, *A General Theory of Exploitation and Class* (Harvard University Press, 1982).

13. This judgment has usually informed sociologists' discussion of the relation of Max Weber to Karl Marx and has now resurfaced, in another form, in some feminist critiques of Marxian theory.

14. Wright, *Class Structure*, Chapters 5, 8 and 9.

15. This understanding of Marx's theory based on intentional strategic behaviour and unintended collective outcomes owes much to Jon Elster *Logic and Society*, and *Making Sense of Marx* (forthcoming); John Roemer, *A General Theory*; and G. A. Cohen, *Marx's Theory*. They are not themselves always in agreement on particular issues and none of them is responsible for the errors and confusions of this paper.

16. The best re-analysis of the base and superstructure distinction and relationship is that provided by Cohen, *Marx's Theory*, Chapters III and IV.

17. The understanding informing this chapter is, again, dependent on Cohen, *Marx's Theory*, Chapter II, pp. 55-62. However, Cohen analyses the assessment of *levels* of development of the productive forces but not the issue of their increasing *socialization*. Both dimensions are necessary in Marxist analysis. A useful discussion of growing socialization of the productive forces is in P. Boccara, *et al*, *Capitalisme Monopoliste d'Etat* (Editions Sociales, Paris, 1971), Volume 1, Chapter 2.

18. See the paper by Bob Russell in this volume, and his 'The Politics of Labour Force Reproduction: Funding Canada's Social Wage

1917-1946' in *Studies in Political Economy*, No. 14 (1984).

19. This issue is discussed in (to cite only two of many examples) Bob Jessop, 'Capitalism and Democracy: The Best Possible Political Shell?' in G. Littlejohn et al. (eds), *Power and the State* (Croom Helm, London, 1978); and Samuel Bowles and Herbert Gintis, 'The Crisis of Liberal Democratic Capitalism: The Case of the United States', *Politics and Society*, Vol. II, 1 (1982).

20. Cohen, *Marx's Theory*, interprets historical materialism, *as Marx presented it*, as a diachronic functional explanation invoking hypothetical conditional laws. But it is possible, I think, to sustain Marx's substantive claims on the basis of strategic interaction with intentional actions and unintentional consequences.

21. The analysis and description of the processes exhibiting this dialectical unity of invariance and change in social reproduction is the central concern of Yves Barel, *La Réproduction Sociale* (Editions Anthropos, Paris, 1973), especially pp. 204-362, which includes an incisive critique of E. Balibar's 'structuralist' presentation of historical materialism.

22. The exacerbation of 'contradictions' resulting from the activities of the state has been stressed by the French theorists of state-monopoly capitalism. The incidence of such counter-productive emergent effects, it can be argued, is independent of the validity of the particular explanation given by SMC theorists of the state's involvement in directly productive activities.

23. For the 'free-rider' problem and the collective action problems of privileged and latent groups, see Mancur Olson, *The Logic of Collective Action*, (Harvard University Press, Cambridge, Mass., 1965) *passim*, and Russell Hardin, *Collective Action* (Johns Hopkins University Press, Baltimore, 1982), passim.

24. The structural equivalence of the collective benefit problem for latent groups and the prisoner's dilemma is argued by R. Hardin, *Collective Action*, Chapter 2. On the relation of weak Pareto-optimality to Pareto's own views see Brian Barry and Russell Hardin (eds.), *Rational Man and Irrational Society?* (Sage Publications, Beverly Hills, California, 1982), pp. 137-145.

25. Which is not to imply that such interlocks are not possible. They are an empirical contingency and may be viewed as a relatively sure means of getting the interests of capitalists or sub-groups of them defended during decision-making in state institutions.

26. It should be noted, to avoid misunderstanding, that the theory of state-monopoly capitalism as developed in France is a theory of a phase of the capitalist economy and not a theory of the state in capitalist social formations. Its object is what we have termed the 'economic structure' with regard to which, in the current phase, it claims an indispensable role of the state in the reproduction of the economic structure. It does not claim to provide a full analysis of the role of the state as a distinct set of institutions and agents.

27. Karl Marx, *Grundrisse* (Penguin Books, Harmondsworth, Middlesex, 1973) pp. 529-533.

28. This withdrawl of the state and re-commodification in housing is discussed in P. Bandyopadhyay, 'The State, Private Capital and Housing in the Paris

Region', *Science and Society*, Volume XLVIII (1984); and in Michael Harloe, 'The Recommodification of Housing' in M. Harloe and E. Lebas (eds.), *City, Class and Capital* (Edward Arnold, London, 1981).

29. The most systematic presentation of this judgement, along with an original though unconvincing theory of capitalist crisis, is in Boccara *et al.*, *Le Capitalisme*.

30. The role of dominance in inter-capitalist relations is accorded a central place in the non-equilibrium economics of Francois Perroux, *Unites Actives et Mathematiques Nouvelles* (Dunod, Paris, 1975).

31. This line of argument on intra-capitalist differentation is found in Raymond Courbis, *Compétitivité et Croissance en Economie Concurrencée* (2 Volumes, Dunod, Paris, 1975).

32. R. Boyer and J. Mistral, *Accumulation, Inflation, Crises* (P.U.F., Paris, 1978).

33. A detailed and almost exhaustive breakdown of the components of public expenditure in France over the period 1872-1971, along with an historical analysis of the diverse forces and circumstances accounting for both expansion and contraction in particular components, is provided by C. Andre and R. Delorme, *L'Evolution des Dépenses Publiques en Longue Periode et le Role de l'Etat en France (1872-1971): Une Interprétation*, 2 Volumes, (Centre d'Etudes Prospectives d'Economie Mathematique Appliquées a la Planification, Paris, 1980). The work is now available in more accessible form as *L'Etat et l'Economie* (Editions du Seuil, Paris, 1983). The authors demonstrate that any explanation addressing aggregate public expenditures will miss the significance of contradictory and varying trends revealed by disaggregaton into components, and as such will be inadequate explanations.

34. The idea of 'socially necessary' activities of the state comes from Jessop, *Marx's Theory*. In this paper the category includes the production of internal order which is necessarily class-biased, owing to the structure of property-rights, in a class-structured social formation.

35. This use of the concept of 'strategic drift' was develoed by Lucien Monnier, *Capitaux Publics et Stratégie de l'Etat* (P.U.F., Paris, 1978) but is being used here in a generalized sense to encompass all state activities including those activities strategically chosen to realize the electoral reproduction of the government.

36. A number of recent studies have explored the economic basis of these developments. A Marxist example is A. Lipietz, *Crise et Inflation, Pourquoi?* (Maspero, Paris, 1979); a non-Marxist and controversial example is R. Bacon and W. Eltis, *Britain's Economic Problem* (Macmillan, London, 1976, 2nd edition, 1978).

37. A recent paper addressing, in part, some of the same issues as this chapter but from a non-Marxist background is Ken Judge, 'The Growth and Decline of Social Expenditure', in Alan Walker (ed.), *Public Expenditure and Social Policy* (Heinemann Educational Books, London, 1982). The contrast between Marxist and liberal background assumptions and theoretical claims is discussed with great clarity by C. G. Pickvance, 'The State and Collective Consumption', *State Intervention II* (The Open University Press, Milton Keynes, 1982).

PART III

CLASS AND SOCIAL REPRODUCTION

8

FAMILY, CLASS AND STATE IN WOMEN'S ACCESS TO ABORTION AND DAY CARE: THE CASE OF THE UNITED STATES

Susan Mann

Introduction

This chapter examines aspects of the reproduction of labour power which are much closer to the popular and more narrow usage of the term reproduction by examining certain issues which are related to reproductive freedom or a woman's right to choose when and if she wants to bear a child. Since it is not possible to cover all the issues included under the concept of reproductive freedom, the focus of this chapter will be specifically on social class differences in access to abortion and day care in the United States over the last century. The issues of access to abortion and day care were chosen not only because they work towards different ends, preventing or fostering childbirth respectively, but also because they constitute two of the most critical reproductive issues facing women today.

Within the United States' national political arena, abortion has been pointed to as the most effective single issue used to mobilize a new right-wing backlash to the women's movement and to divide the longstanding Democratic Party sympathies of many Catholic and ethnic groups.[1] In turn, abortion is one of the few contemporary social issues in the United States where political tactics have included the overt use of terror and violence as a means of reaching political goals. Abortion clinics and Planned Parenthood offices have reported cases of arson, fire bombings, kidnap threats and vandalism, all in the name of 'pro-life'.[2] Despite these anti-abortion initiatives, public support for abortion has steadily increased over the last decade.[3] However, the continued passage of legislation to restrict federal Medicaid funding of abortions, and the persistent attempts to pass a constitutional amendment to prohibit abortion suggest that access to abortion continues to be a critical issue facing American women.

Along with abortion, the availability of child care has also become an increasingly critical concern for American women. While child-rearing has traditionally been viewed as a private or family responsi-bility rather than a public concern, marked changes in the nature of American families in recent decades have made this view less tenable. The most striking change has been the increasing entry of women with preschool children into the labour force. In the last three decades, the labour force participation of mothers with children under six has more than tripled.⁴ Since the majority of these women work out of economic necessity rather than choice, fewer and fewer American women have been able to be full-time mothers whether they want to or not. This development, coupled with the rise in divorce rates and the increase in single-parent households, undermines the viability of home-provided childcare for many families.⁵

While the demand for universal day care has been a major thrust of the contemporary women's movement, day care is often not in-cluded in feminist definitions of reproductive freedom.⁶ Rather, most discussions focus on ways women can prevent or control birth and, hence, on ways women can choose *not* to have children. This focus is very one-sided, however, since substantive reproductive freedom also involves the establishment of an adequate social environment in which a woman is able to *choose* to bear a child without sacrificing her own ability to fully and equally participate in the larger society.

With these concerns in mind, we begin by providing a discussion of our theoretical conceptualization of these issues and then move on to provide a history of social class differences in access to abortion and day care in the United States over the last century.

The Reproduction of Labour Power

My theoretical conceptualization of the issues of reproductive freedom relies on Wally Seccombe's recent pathbreaking analysis of the sphere of reproduction.⁷ I agree with Seccombe that orthodox Marxism has tended to reduce the field of production to the production of material goods (i.e., the production of the means of subsistence and of the means of production) and, hence, has overlooked the various ways in which the production of labour power has occurred historically on both a day-to-day and a generational basis. This serious omission in orthodox accounts is surprising since such Marxist analyses are predicated on the basic assumption that labour power is the source of all value. Thus, as paradoxical as it may seem, the very commodity which provides the basis for capitalist accumulation—value creating labour power—has not been analyzed adequately in terms of its own production and reproduction.

Moreover, the production and reproduction of labour power falls primarily on the shoulders of women in most societies, given the relegation of most aspects of childbearing, childrearing and housework to women. Consequently, as Seccombe points out, it is not surprising that orthodox Marxism has often been criticized for being 'gender blind' and hence unable to adequately explain the oppression of women.[8] As a consequence of these shortcomings in orthodox Marxist analyses, Seccombe calls for and begins an analysis of how the production and reproduction of labour power is socially established under different modes of production and in historically specific ways.

The production and reproduction of labour power has four distinct moments. At the individual level, there is the generational replacement of individuals through procreation, childrearing and socialization, as well as the day-to-day renewal of the labouring capacity of existing workers through domestic labour and the consumption of the means of subsistence. This long and short-run reproduction of labour power takes place largely within the confines of isolated and privatized households which are organized in a non-capitalist fashion.[9] In a previous article, Emily Blumenfeld and I have suggested some of the reasons for this non-capitalist production and reproduction of labour power in terms of structural obstacles to the capitalist penetration of domestic labour and childrearing.[10] In turn, some of the problems which arise from the non-capitalist production of labour power within a capitalist social formation—such as the economic inefficiency, sexual inequality, and family conflict often associated with isolated and privatized domestic labour—are discussed.[11]

At the collective or class level, the reproduction of labour power is usually the responsibility of the state and is undertaken through a mixture of hegemony and force. This includes, on the one hand, the reproduction and maintenance of the family or household as a social institution, which as demonstrated by other essays in this volume, is secured by state policies, such as redistributional welfare tax programs, child benefits, various unemployment, accident and health schemes, and state control over access to birth control and abortion. On the one hand, in order to standardize the quality of individual labour power in the face of the various particularities of individual families, the state has also historically taken over a number of former household tasks, through the creation of compulsory social services such as education, or in the case of social 'deviants,' mental institutions and prisons.[12]

While this triumvirate of household, economy and state constitute the productive and reproductive moments of capitalist society considered as a totality, I am specifically interested in how these three spheres historically intersect in the United States to provide for the generational replacement of labour power in terms of (a) limiting and shaping fertility in the case of abortion; and (b) providing for alternative forms of childcare and socialization in the case of day care.

Moreover, I am interested not only in *how* this control over reproductive freedom is established and maintained over time, but also in
who controls access to these aspects of reproductive freedom and
whether such control differs by social class.

Access to reproductive freedom affects all women and, hence, is
an issue which cuts across class lines. However, issues of social class
have repeatedly influenced and shaped the history of women's access
to abortion and day care as regards both differential class access to
these rights and factors which precipitated federal and state interventions on these issues. To date, the evidence of the influence of social
class on access to these reproductive rights is scattered in a number
of different books and articles. One purpose of this chapter, then, is
to synthesize this information by focusing specifically on social class.
In turn, these brief histories are presented not to argue the primacy
of class over sex, but rather to examine the relationship between class
oppression and sexual oppression and hence to provide a better understanding of various reproductive issues which have historically divided
women.

Social Class and Access to Abortion

Recent work by James Mohr (1978) and Rosalind Petchesky
(1984) provide systematic accounts of the development of abortion
legislation in the United States.[13] Mohr focuses on an analysis of the
nineteenth century, whereas Petchesky ties together Mohr's analysis
with later developments in the twentieth century. While these studies
address different issues and concerns as regards this reproductive right,
they also provide some significant insights into the relationship between social class and access to abortion. I shall incorporate these
insights about social class effects into my analysis and supplement
them with material from other sources.

According to these histories, prior to the 1820s, no state had
enacted any legislation on the subject of abortion. Rather, common law
attitudes prevailed and the practice of abortion was viewed as legitimate
up until the time of 'quickening' or the first perception of fetal movement by the woman. The rise of a campaign to criminalize abortion
was in part a response to demographic changes in the fertility rates
of American women. The absence of adequate demographic data for
the nineteenth century makes it difficult to discuss these changes with
much precision. However, the available data do indicate a long-term
decline in fertility from 1810 to 1940. For example, between 1800 and
1900 the total white fertility rate was virtually cut in half from 7.04
to 3.56—a decline which was most apparent among native-born white
Americans in the upper and upper-middle classes.[14] Table 8.1 provides

data on the completed family size of white women aged 45 to 49 in 1910 according to the major occupational group of their husbands. These data indicate an inverse relationship between social class and family size, with more well-to-do families having fewer children both in urban and rural areas.

TABLE 8.1

Completed Family Size of White Population, by Major Occupational Group of Husband and Place of Residence, United States, 1910

Major Occupational Group	1910 Family size[a]	
	Urban	Rural-Farm
Professional, technical, and kindred workers	2.8	4.3
Managers, officials, and proprietors, except farm	3.3	4.8
Clerical, sales, and kindred workers	3.1	4.7
Craftsmen, foremen, and kindred workers	4.0	5.2
Operatives and kindred workers	4.1	5.6
Service workers, including private household	3.9	b
Labourers, except farm and mine	4.8	5.5
Farmers and farm managers	4.2	5.6
Farm labourers and foremen	4.4	5.1

[a] Children ever born to native, white women aged 45-49 years, married once, whose husbands were still living with them at the time of the census.

[b] Rates are not shown when there were fewer than 1,200 women.

Source: Wilson H. Grabill, Clyde V. Kiser, and Pascal K. Whelpton, *The Fertility of American Women* (Wiley, New York, 1975), Table 54.

Class differences in family size can in part be explained by unequal class access to control over reproduction. However, a larger family size is often associated with a lower standard of living and the increased necessity of relying on child labour to supplement family incomes. The absence of child labour laws in many states in the late-nineteenth century fostered this practice and comparative data on families of different classes and ethnic groups suggests that poor and immigrant children were more likely to work to support their families, particularly in cases where the father was unemployed or ill.[15]

The decline in the birth rates of upper- and middle-class women during this era is often associated with urbanization, industrialization and the increase in the standard of living of these classes. However, these factors are not sufficient explanations because of the declining fertility rates also found in rural and frontier areas. In turn, Petchesky's reliance on the prevalence of a 'cult of motherhood' with its prescriptions for a relatively chaste, spiritual and asexual 'ladylike' life to explain why upper- and middle-class women in both urban and rural areas tried to control their fertility is also unsatisfactory since ideologies which glorify motherhood have been used at other times and in other places to foster increased, rather than reduced, birth rates.[16] However, there is agreement on the fact that the perception and publicity regarding the increased use of abortion to control birth during this era precipitated an organized backlash to these developments.

The major force behind the campaign to criminalize abortion in nineteenth century America was not the clergy, as might be expected, but rather certified physicians (i.e., physicians who had received a medical degree). In fact, the protestant and catholic clergy never played a central role in the anti-abortion campaign during this period, despite attempts by medical doctors to recruit them.[17] The leadership of doctors in the anti-abortion campaign can be explained on both economic and ideological grounds.

In terms of economic interests, this campaign was part of a concerted effort to monopolize the market in women's health concerns, and outlawing abortion was linked to the struggle to exclude lay practitioners such as lay healers, midwives and folk doctors from health care.[18] On the one hand, since women were excluded from medical schools at this time, male certified physicians were worried that if female midwives were allowed to attend to medical concerns such as abortion or childbirth, then women, including upper- and middle-class women, might turn to these female lay practitioners for other illnesses. On the other hand, the lay practitioners, both male and female, provided effective competition for the services of the certified physicians because, by and large, there were no substantial differences in the quality or competence of their respective techniques and knowledge prior to the breakthroughs in medicine which occurred during the Civil

War. Comparisons of their respective practices suggest that both were equally primitive; indeed, at times, the trial and error methods of the lay practitioners proved less damaging than the misguided theories which characterized certified medicine.[19]

The victory of the certified physicians in establishing anti-abortion legislation thus reflects the victory both of patriarchal interests, in terms of male professionals gaining hegemony over female lay practitioners, and of particular class interests, since the majority of lay practitioners, both male and female, were primarily poor or working-class people who could not afford medical training. In turn, the clientele of these lay practitioners also tended to come from the lower classes and hence access to health care was most severely restricted for poor people.

On the ideological level, social class issues also helped certified doctors to mobilize support for their anti-abortion campaign. Their claims regarding the increased use of abortion by middle- and upper-class women conjured up fears of racial, ethnic and class 'suicide' for the dominant white population—fears which increased public support for anti-abortion legislation.[20] In turn, as a number of writers have pointed out, these fears were cultivated and buttressed in scientific guise by the rise and development of the eugenics movement in the early decades of the twentieth century. Utilizing newly developed quantitative measures such as the census and intelligence tests, eugenicists argued for fertility control as means of reducing the number of 'inferior' and 'unfit' persons.[21] That this movement coincided with large waves of immigration into the United States, as well as the internal migration of many southern blacks to northern cities is no coincidence.

These racist and class-biased views were embraced by many upper- and middle-class women, including many prominent feminists of the era. For example, feminists such as Julia Ward Howe, Ida Husted Harper and Margaret Sanger accepted such notions of racial and class suicide.[22] In turn, those feminists who advocated birth control often did so using class-based distinctions whereby control over fertility was viewed as a right for the well-to-do, but a duty for the poor. Thus, as Linda Gordon has argued, these feminists separated themselves from lower-class women by maintaining a class-based distinction between reproductive freedom—the control by individuals of their *own* reproduction, and population control—the control by elites of the reproduction of others.[23]

However, the majority of feminists in the nineteenth and early twentieth centuries did not support either abortion or birth control, and instead advocated voluntary motherhood or a wife's right to abstain from sexual intercourse. While today, their anti-abortion position clearly appears anti-feminist, at that time this position was at least theoretically consistent with these feminists' emphasis on gaining political rights and respect for women by highlighting the more humane values women held as a result of their nurturing roles. Since abortion and birth control were viewed as interfering with women's roles as mothers and nurturers, these women did not support these reproductive rights.[24]

Given these racial, class and ethnic divisions it is not surprising that the certified physicians were successful in enacting legislation to criminalize abortion. By 1880, thirty four states and territories had outlawed abortion or revised existing statutes to make their laws more prohibitive.[25] The legislation enacted in the nineteenth century, while occasionally rewritten or rephrased, changed little for almost a century. Hence, for much of the twentieth century, most states allowed abortion only in particular cases where the woman's life was in danger.[26]

The illegal status of abortion during three-quarters of the twentieth century makes it very difficult to obtain sound data on the extent of abortion practices. From clinic and hospital reports we do know that women were having abortions. For example, patient records from the Birth Control Clinical Research Bureau in New York for the period from 1925-1929 indicate that over half of the women admitted (5,010 out of 9,760) had at least one abortion, and the average for all of these women was 2.23 abortions. Whether these abortions were self-induced, or legally or illegally assisted, is not known, but it is reported that more than two-thirds of the abortions were admitted to have been intentionally induced. Over 80 per cent of the women admitted to the clinic during this time period were from poor or working-class families. The records, however, do not provide sufficient information to establish the extent of differential access to abortion by social class.[27]

Data on abortion-related deaths can provide some indication of differential class access to safe abortions. As late as the 1960s, criminal abortions were still a major cause of maternal deaths. For example, illegal abortions accounted for over one third of maternal deaths in metropolitan New York in 1961 and in the state of California in 1964. In each of these cases, criminal abortion accounted for a disproportionately high number of maternal deaths among poor women.[28]

That indigent women were less able to obtain safe abortions is also suggested by data on access to therapeutic abortions. While legally doctors were only supposed to allow therapeutic abortions for severe medical or psychological problems, studies indicate that the major factor associated with doctors' recommending therapeutic abortions was the socio-economic status of the patient.[29] That is, doctors were more likely to recommend therapeutic abortions for women with high socio-economic status, despite the fact that poor women were less likely to be able to support a child. Studies of physicians attitudes towards abortion during this pre-legal era explain this phenomenon by arguing that doctors were more likely to empathize with women from a class background similar to their own, to service women whom they knew from interpersonal contacts, and/or to service women whom they knew could pay the medical fees. As one observer noted, 'the difference between having an abortion or not was the difference between having one to three hundred dollars and knowing the right person, or being without funds and the right contacts'.[30]

Along with studies of physicians attitudes, another major method of studying class differences in access to therapeutic abortions prior to the legalization of abortion is to compare the number of therapeutic abortions recommended to ward patients with those recommended to private patients. Here the ward versus private patient distinction is taken to reflect differences in social class under the assumption that ward patients were unable to afford the greater privacy and better facilities provided to private patients. A summary of such studies shows definite patterns in differential class access to therapeutic abortions. In the 1940s, when the majority of therapeutic abortions were performed primarily for physical health reasons, the incidence among ward and private patients was similar. In the 1950s, when psychiatric reasons began to account for more therapeutic abortions, the incidence for private patients rose to twice that of ward patients. In the 1960s, when the number of therapeutic abortions given for psychiatric and fetal reasons rose sharply, the incidence for private patients soared to more than twenty times that for ward patients.[31]

These class differences in access to therapeutic abortions cannot be explained by differences in the physical and psychological health of the groups compared. Indeed, if the restrictive abortion laws had been applied in a non-discriminatory fashion, we would expect to find a greater number of therapeutic abortions among the poor. This would follow because poverty contributes to and correlates with poorer physical health and a higher incidence of mental illness and acute mental stress.[32] Instead, the patterns found in comparisons of ward and private patients suggests that the more doctors had discretionary power over recommending therapeutic abortion, the more likely there was to be class discrimination. Indeed, such findings on differential class access to therapeutic abortions were used as arguments for the legalisation of abortion in the United States. However, these empirically-based arguments had to await major structural and demographic changes in the American family before they became effective in changing United States abortion legislation.

As Petchesky points out, a number of factors coalesced in the post-World War Two era to increase the need for control over childbirth. Among these factors were the gains women made in terms of both higher education and their increased participation in the labour force. College enrollment among women ages 16 to 34 increased by 57 per cent for white women and 112 per cent for black women during the 1960s and 1970s.[33] These post-war decades also witnessed a substantial increase in women's employment outside of the home, mainly as a result of inflation and economic necessity. For example, the number of married women working outside of the home doubled from 25 percent of all married women in 1950 to 50 per cent in 1980. Employed mothers with children aged five or under increased fourfold from 11.9 per cent in 1950 to 44.1 per cent in 1980.[34] For these wives and mothers such employment outside of the home increased their need for control over reproduction.

For single women, gains in employment and education resulted in an overall shift towards later marriages and the postponement of childbirth. For example, in 1980, 50 per cent of all women 20 to 24 years of age were never married as contrasted to only 28.4 per cent in 1960.[35] This postponement coupled with a reduction in the average age at the onset of menstruation due to improvements in health and nutrition extended the time-span of pre-marital sexual activity for these young women and, hence, increased the need for birth control and abortion.[36]

Alongside these changes in the position of women, the concerns of the federal government with population control also shifted. The rise of the United States as a major world power following the Second World War and its increased military and economic interests in the Third World fostered government strategy to use population control as a means of maintaining 'political stability' in these underdeveloped countries.[37] On the domestic front, these concerns were also heightened by the continuing migration of blacks to northern cities, the growth in the militancy of the Civil Rights movement, and the effect these developments had on breaking up traditional voting blocks in many northern and midwestern cities.[38] Hence, as Petchesky argues, racist ideologies of overpopulation again surfaced and contributed to a shift in state policies on control over fertility both nationally and internationally. From this analysis, it is not surprising that, while from the 1930s through the 1950s the U.S. federal government carefully avoided any involvement in family planning programs, during the 1960s it substantially increased involvement in and funding of such programs at home and abroad.[39]

In the 1960s, the medical profession also had to contend with developments somewhat similar to those which had sparked the nineteenth century anti-abortion campaign. That is, as the demand for abortion increased, so did alternative structures directed towards servicing this demand. The growth of feminist self-help movements, particularly in the areas of prenatal care, childbirth and control over reproduction, the development of underground networks for abortion referral and information, and the increased pressure put on the American Medical Association by the burgeoning feminist movement, all contributed to a growing awareness among doctors of the benefits of legalizing abortion, both in terms of public health and safety and in terms of maintaining their control over these spheres of reproduction.[40] Moreover, unlike the nineteenth century, when the alternative lay practitioners presented comparable care as effective competition, by the 1960s, the legitimacy of the medical profession was well established. Consequently, doctors did not have to engage in direct confrontation with these alternative groups, but instead, could simply extend their control over the areas of medical care serviced by these groups.

These factors combined to produce a major victory for reproductive rights in the 1973 Supreme Court decision, Roe v. Wade; here the Court ruled that states could neither prohibit nor interfere with woman's right to choose abortion in the first tri-mester of pregnancy. After this time, states could establish regulations to protect maternal health and could prohibit abortion after the second tri-mester except in cases where maternal health or life were in danger. Further liberalization of abortion legislation occurred in 1976 and 1983. These included laws which removed requirements for obtaining a husband's consent for abortion, for obtaining parental consent in the case of 'mature' minors, and for having abortions performed in hospitals in the first and second tri-mesters, thus providing greater access to abortion for many women.[41]

However, even with these victories, the lack of adequate facilities and obstructionist state laws prevented many women from obtaining desired abortions. For example, some state laws continued to require both special licensing fees for abortion clinics and performing physicians, and the notification of parents in the case of minors and husbands in the case of married women. In turn, the geographic skew in the availability of abortion facilities and the ability of publicly-funded hospitals to refuse to perform abortions resulted in limited access to abortion, particularly for rural women. Moreover, some states provided no Medicaid funding for abortions even before the passage of federal legislation restricting such funding, and consequently, many poor women were denied access to abortion because of prohibitive costs.[42]

A severe blow to abortion rights came in 1977 with the passage of the Hyde Amendment which prohibited the use of *federal* Medicaid funds for abortion. New versions of the Hyde Amendment are voted on each year and currently this act prevents federal Medicaid funds from being used except in cases of rape, incest or where the woman's life is in danger. The effect of this legislation is to deny many of America's poorest women—welfare recipients—equal access to safe, medical abortions. As one observer remarked, these laws essentially tell women that they cannot have an abortion, 'not because it is illegal or unconstitutional, but because they are poor.'[43]

It is not possible to measure exactly how many women have been denied abortions because of the Hyde Amendment. A recent study by the Center for Disease Control found that 20 per cent of Medicaid-eligible women desiring abortions were unable to obtain abortions after the cut-off; these findings generally confirm earlier studies.[44] However, for those poor women who did obtain money for an abortion, it should be remembered that they often did so by taking funds out of meager food or rent budgets. In 1977 it was estimated that the average cost of an abortion was equivalent to the average welfare family's food budget for three months, and this suggests rather severe economic deprivation for those who obtained abortions after the cut-off of federal assistance.[45]

The passage of the Hyde Amendment is clearly a setback for poor women. Nevertheless, opponents of abortion are continuing their fight to limit access to abortion by introducing even more prohibitive legislation. Right to life organizations are currently lobbying for the passage of a Human Life Amendment which would in effect establish that from the moment of conception a fertilized egg is a 'person'. This amendment would not only make abortion illegal since it would be tantamount to murder, but it would also prohibit the use of certain birth control devices such as IUDs which act to inhibit the implantation of a fertilized egg.

Notably, the contemporary women's movement, while still largely middle and upper-middle class in composition and, hence, largely unaffected by the Hyde Amendment, has continued to oppose these restrictive proposals. For example, many local, state and national women's organizations targeted access to abortion as their major issue in 1983.[46] This contrasts favourably with their predecessors in the nineteenth and early twentieth centuries whose feminist demands failed to fuse the interests of women of different classes.

So far, I have documented how class discrimination has shaped abortion policy in the United States from the earliest enactment of anti-abortion legislation to the present. I now turn to an examination of the history of differential class access to day care. It will then be possible to draw some parallels between the roles of family, class and state in the development of these two aspects of reproductive freedom.

Social Class and Access to Day Care

Margaret O'Brien Steinfels' *Who's Minding the Children?* (1973)

provides one of the most comprehensive analyses of the development of day care in the United States.[47] Like the histories of abortion mentioned earlier, Steinfels' work addresses a broad range of issues related to the rise and development of day care including the role of social class. This section of the chapter relies heavily on her insights into the role of social class, supplementing and updating her analysis with material from other sources.

In the United States, day care developed in the mid-nineteenth century primarily as a response to urbanization and industrialization which forced many women out of the home and into the factory. Children of these working women were often left in care of siblings or on their own, and stories abound of children being locked in apartments or tied to bedposts while their parents worked.[48] This situation of apparent social disorganization proved fertile ground for philanthropic intervention and often wealthy women organized day nurseries for the care of the children of working women.

Alongside the introduction of these day nurseries, Kindergartens were established in the United States at approximately the same time period. Originally this form of day care was started by emigres from the 1848 German Revolution and later spread to English-speaking communities.[49] However, it is important to note that there were major differences between the Kindergartens and the day nurseries. The former were primarily concerned with education, while the latter focused on custodial care. Moveover, because the day nurseries were directed towards servicing the needs of working mothers, they were open long hours and accepted infants and toddlers, as well as older children. In contrast, the Kindergartens operated on a more part-time basis and catered primarily to pre-school children, reflecting the different needs and desires of their middle-class clientele. The separation between these two types of child care was not always rigid, but generally the Kindergarten movement resulted in the establishment of private nursery schools for the well-to-do, while the day nurseries or day cares were established as relief agencies for the poor.[50] We shall focus on the history of the day nurseries rather than the Kindergartens, since the absence of accessible child care for women employed outside of the home places more severe constraints on reproductive freedom.

The first day nursery in the United States was opened in Boston in 1838 to provide child care for the employed wives and widows of seamen. Later, in 1854, New York Hospital established its Nursery for the Children of Poor Women which was primarily for working women. The Civil War further stimulated the growth of day care for war widows and women who worked in hospitals and factories. However, the greatest expansion of day care in the nineteenth century took place in the 1880s and 1890s largely as a result of the massive influx of immigrants.[51] As mentioned earlier, these immigrants were more likely to have a larger number of children, in part because they relied on the labour of older children to supplement family incomes. Moreover, contrary to popular belief, these immigrant families were less likely to live in extended families than native-born Americans and, consequently, were less able to utilize the help of other relatives in child care.[52]

TABLE 8.2

Composition of Female Labour Force by Marital Status, United States, 1890-1970

	Percentage of Female Civilian Labour Force by Marital Status		
Year	Single	Married	Widowed/Divorced
1890	68.2	13.9	17.9
1900	66.2	15.4	18.4
1910	60.2	24.7	15.0
1920	—	—	—
1930	53.9	28.9	17.2
1940	49.0	35.9	15.0
1950	31.6	52.1	16.3
1960	24.0	59.9	16.1
1970	22.3	63.4	14.3

Source: US Bureau of the Census, *Historical Statistics of the United States, Colonial Times to 1970* (U.S. Government Printing Office, Washington, DC, 1975), p. 133.

The composition of the female labour force in the late nineteenth and early twentieth centuries contrasts sharply with the situation in recent years. As Table 8.2 illustrates, from 1890 through the early decades of the twentieth century, married women made up only a small percentage of the female civilian labour force. If we assume that married women were more likely than single women to have children and, hence, to require day care services, it is not surprising that these early day nurseries tended to be run as private charities, rather than as businesses as is the case today. In turn, the data from 1890 and 1900 show a large percentage of widowed and divorced women in the labour force as contrasted to later decades, and indeed these women constituted a major group serviced by these early day cares.

Due consideration should be given to the efforts of the wealthy philanthropists who were responsible for organizing the day nurseries. In the face of little or no public funding, these private charities often provided a vital service to working women. In turn, many of the wealthy patrons were sincerely concerned about the plight of poor and often neglected children. Nevertheless, the advantages these wealthy women received from their services and the class-discriminatory abuses of the early day nurseries should not be overlooked. Many of these wealthy women knew little about child care since they left their own children in the care of nannies or domestic servants. Yet this had little consequence for their suitability for board membership.[53] Indeed, sitting on the board of a day nursery was a prestigious and coveted position, and seats and reopenings on the board were jealously guarded. Moreover, the wealthy women only served as board members and, in fact, hired poor women at low wages to actually run the day cares. The staff usually worked long hours, often beginning at six in the morning and seldom ending until nine at night, and at times employees were looking after as many as sixty children.[54]

Many day nurseries also provided employment services for the mothers of the day care children. These services were used as mechanisms of social control over the poor since mothers who were temporarily unemployed or working part-time were sometimes forced to take a job under the threat of the permanent withdrawal of child care services. In turn, the type of work these day nurseries encouraged—domestic labour—was an underpaid and menial occupation which in the late 1800s and early 1900s suffered from chronic labour shortages. Consequently, these employment services benefitted well-to-do women by providing a solution to the so-called 'middle-class dilemma' of the time—the servant shortage.[55]

Another way in which day nurseries acted as mechanisms of social control over the poor was related to their role in the inculcation of upper- and middle-class values. Of particular concern to many philanthropists was the belief that the poor and immigrant children constituted a 'dangerous class' which, in the absence of 'proper' upbringing, would swell the ranks of ruffians and criminals.[56] In turn, the 'Americanization' of immigrant children was viewed as an essential element in the task of developing the 'right' kind of citizen.[57] Consequently, along with the physical care of the children, the day nurseries showed an equally strong concern for teaching moral values, orderliness and manners. Yet, while interested in inculcating middle-class values, there was generally less interest in providing these children with the requisite skills to actually move up the social ladder. Rather, the skills taught tended to be skills viewed as appropriate for lower-class occupations. As one nursery reported:

> All of the children of suitable age are employed by turns in performing different parts of the housework . . . thus affording them an excellent opportunity of becoming fitted for servants or future housekeepers.[58]

Despite abuses and shortcomings, these early day nurseries run by wealthy philanthropists had a number of important features which were later undermined by the increasing professionalization of the day care personnel. Throughout the 1920s and 1930s the day nurseries attracted professional workers who were critical of the custodial emphasis of the early centers.[59] While the skills and training of these professional nursery workers undoubtedly raised the educational focus and quality of day care, their entrance into the field acted to significantly change day care from a service for working mothers to a social welfare-oriented institution. The early philanthropists, despite their critical attitudes towards the poor, had nonetheless recognized that *external* factors such as poverty, industrialization and immigration forced many women to work, thus presenting these women with crises as regards to child care. In contrast, however, the professional nursery workers tended to locate the problems which generated the need for child care as *internal* to the family, viewing the existence of such need as evidence of a maladjusted or pathological family life.[60]

As a result, the social welfare emphasis led to more selective and restrictive eligibility requirements and families were screened to determine whether they were suitably 'in need of help'. Thus, not only were mothers who placed their children in day care labelled as 'neglectful or inadequate' mothers, but also day care was stigmatized as a form of child care associated with maladjusted families—views which have unfortunately persisted among many Americans up until the present. Moreover, as the result of these new professional definitions, the expansion and contraction of day care during the 1920s occurred without any particular reference to the needs of working women.[61]

Another negative consequence of professionalization was that the care of infants and toddlers by persons other than the mother came to be viewed as inappropriate. On the ideological level, this view was buttressed by the theories of childrearing acquired by day care professionals as part of their training, theories based on the scientific studies of the period which tended to stress the advantages of home rearing.[62] While the relative merits of home rearing and day care for child development are still being debated, the fact remains that during the 1920s, as well as today, many young children were left in unsatisfactory conditions because their parents did not have the economic freedom to choose between outside employment or staying home to rear their children.[63]

In practice, moreover, the professional child care workers neither desired nor were they prepared to take care of infants and toddlers. On the one hand, such care involved menial tasks which were not viewed as making sufficient use of their educational training.[64] On the other hand, professionals balked at working the long hours necessary to meet the needs of lower-class women who worked. As one nursery worker reported:

> We in the Day Nursery world rejoiced as one by one attendants were replaced by these trained teachers. However, various problems cropped up immediately. At first, the teachers would not work all day. Only after years of struggle did they consent to remain even seven or eight hours in shifts to cover the whole schedule . . .[65]

In terms of time, the professionals also viewed the day nurseries as only a temporary expedient until the 'maladjusted' families could be rehabilitated and the mother restored to her 'rightful' place in the home.[66] Thus, the professionalization of day care entailed bias against the working class since the needs of women who had to work on a permanent basis were not recognized or served.

By contemporary standards this view of the importance of women being in the home as a prerequisite to a normal, as opposed to a pathological, family life would also be considered evidence of an anti-feminist bias. However, as noted earlier, the majority of feminists in the nineteenth and early twentieth centuries idealized women's roles as mothers and nurturers and, hence, had little to say about day care. Charlotte Perkins Gilman, who criticized the negative effects of isolation on homebound mothers and emphasized the advantages of day care, appears to have been a lone advocate of this reproductive right.[67]

The federal government shared the views of the professional child care worker on the advantages of home rearing. The first White House Conference on Children and Youth in 1909 urged home rearing and recommended mother's pensions as a substitute for day nurseries. By 1913, twenty states had enacted laws providing pensions to indigent women.[68] Ideologically, this policy reinforced the view that women's place was in the home; in practice, however, it also had a number of negative effects. First, like the contemporary demand for 'wages for housewives', the policy reinforced the privatization and isolation of women's work. Second, it was a subtle mechanism of ostensible support for women which failed to recognize the importance of women's full and equal participation in the larger political and economic spheres of society. Finally, the pension payments were often so inadequate that mothers continued to work, while day nurseries struggled without benefit of government support.[69]

It took the Great Depression and World War Two to generate crises on a national level sufficient to force the federal government into providing funds for day care. In 1933 federal funds for the development and expansion of day care were made available for the first time under the Federal Economic Recovery Act and the Works Progress Administration (WPA). Within four years the WPA had established 1,900 nurseries caring for approximately 40,000 children.[70] While the primary purpose of WPA day care was to provide jobs for unemployed teachers, clerical workers, janitors, and other support staff, the WPA nurseries were identified as educational services and provided excellent health, nutritional and educational care.[71] As the American economy slowly recovered in the late 1930s, federal funding for day care was removed, but only for a brief period of time.

The entry of the United States into World War Two and the consequent necessity for large numbers of women to replace male workers recruited into the armed forces resulted in the resurrection of the WPA nurseries. In 1941, under the Lanham Act, federal and state matched funds for day care were provided to service the needs of these working mothers. By the end of the war, day nurseries had been established in forty-seven states and serviced approximately 1.5 million children.[72] While the Lanham day care centers have been criticized for discriminating against Blacks and for providing services to only about 40 per cent of the children in actual need of care, these centers still marked the most extensive state supported day care program ever seen in the history of the United States.[73]

With the end of the war, federal day care funds were withdrawn by 1946 and day care provision declined in all but a few states where coalitions of parents and child care workers were successful in resisting their demise.[74] As a result of the withdrawal of federal funds more than one million children were left without day care despite the fact that many women continued to work. In 1950, there were 4.6 million women employed as compared to only 1.5 million in 1940. Moreover, after World War Two, for the first time in American history, *married* women made up more than 50 per cent of the female civilian labour force (See Table 8.2). By 1959, five times as many women were employed as before the War, with day care facilities available for only 2.4 per cent of their children.[75]

With substantial numbers of women in the labour force needing child care services, organizations such as the Children's Bureau and the Women's Bureau of the Department of Labor continued to place pressure on the federal government to provide some day care assistance. In an effort to placate these demands while simultaneously avoiding the large expenditures required to directly fund such day care, Congress passed legislation in 1954 which provided income tax deductions for child care expenses—the child tax credits.[76]

Yet despite both the war-time recognition that day care was essential to women employed outside of the home and the significant increase in the labour participation of women in the decades following World War Two, the social welfare view of day care remained intact. As late as 1960, the Child Welfare League of America still defined the day care child as a child who had a 'family problem'.[77] Throughout the 1960s, virtually all of the federal legislation which provided public funds for day care was restricted to poor and underprivileged children. In part this can be explained by the fact that this legislation was generated as a specific response to the Civil Rights Movement, rather than to the needs of working women in general. In turn, since the absence of child care was a major reason why many women on welfare could not seek employment, such day care programs fitted well with the government's interest in reducing the welfare rolls.[78]

Day care legislation passed in the 1960s included various amendments to the Social Security Act which provided income maintenance funds for the child care of welfare recipients and women in work training programs, as well as the Head Start program established in 1964 which provided compensatory education to disadvantaged children. These programs provided a much-needed service to poor families. However, the vast majority of working families were excluded from eligibility and even as late as 1982 Head Start only served 25 per cent of those eligible.[79] Moreover, while Head Start has been lauded for its educational focus and quality, it operates only on a part-day basis and, hence, does not serve the needs of women who work full-time.[80]

By the late 1960s, the feminist movement, unlike its nineteenth century predecessor, challenged the assumption that day care was merely a welfare service and stressed that child care should be available to all employed mothers. This movement was still largely comprised of middle-class women, who recognized that taking time off for child care was often damaging to their prospects for career employment. Despite the fact that the career prospects of these upper- and middle-class women often entailed lifestyles, job autonomy and prestige which were qualitatively different from the job prospects of lower-class women, their child care needs were not substantially different. Consequently, these feminist demands cut across class lines.[81]

This shift in middle-class concerns was accompanied by a substantial increase in the number of scientific studies documenting the benefits of day care for child development, and was in contrast to the scientific literature hailing the virtues of home rearing which had dominated the 1920s.[82] In turn, professional social workers and child care workers who were schooled in some of this new literature and who often required child care to continue their own career employment rejected the views of their early twentieth century predecessors and moved to the forefront of advocacy for day care.[83]

Towards the end of the 1960s, a coalition of groups representing the women's movement, professional child care workers, child development experts, organized labour, and the civil rights community joined with many senators and representatives to make recommendations for a federally-funded, comprehensive, day care system. This lobbying resulted in the Comprehensive Child Development Act of 1971 which provided federal funds for the creation and expansion of day care, where services would be provided free of charge to welfare recipients and available on a graduated fee scale to middle-income families.[84] The most innovative aspect of this legislation was its extension of federal assistance to non-poor families. Support for this legislation was buttressed by an earlier White House Conference on Children in 1970 which selected access to day care as the most serious problem confronting American families.[85]

However, as in the case of abortion, right-wing groups mobilized to fight this legislation. These groups, which included the American Conservation Union, Moral Majority, Christian Voice, and Phyllis Schlafly's Eagle Forum, were well-organized, and they co-ordinated their lobbying and fund-raising efforts.[86] Nevertheless, the Comprehensive Child Development Act passed both the House and the Senate in 1971, only to be vetoed by President Nixon in December of that year.

Echoing the sentiments of the right-wing groups, Nixon declared that the Act was 'the most radical piece of legislation to emerge from the 92nd Congress' and he claimed that such legislation would lead to a breakdown of the American family, diminishing both parental authority and involvement in childrearing. In turn, by arguing that this legislation should be rejected because it sided with a 'communal approach' to childrearing over a 'family-centered approach', Nixon subtly reinforced right-wing propaganda that day care would 'Sovietize' American children.[87]

The presidential veto was unexpected since Secretary Elliott

Richardson had been working closely with senators and representatives in drawing up the legislation and he was supposedly representing the Nixon administration's position in these negotiations.[88] On the one hand, this presidential reversal in policy may have been an amelioratory response to the political mobilization of right-wing critics, particularly given the need at the time to mitigate conservative criticisms of Nixon's detente with Communist China.[89] On the other hand, the rampant growth of inflation in the 1970s, coupled with escalating military expenditures associated with the Vietnam War, may have heightened the nation's fears of introducing additional government expenditures on such an extensive and controversial social service program as day care.[90]

Indeed, in terms of economic costs to the government, the issues of abortion and day care are very different. The legalization of abortion resulted in very few economic costs. In fact, the federal Medicaid funding of abortions prior to 1977 actually reduced rather than increased federal expenditures. For example, in 1977 after the passage of the Hyde Amendment, Department of Health, Education and Welfare officials estimated that the government would pay between $450 million and $565 million for medical care and public assistance for the unwanted births of Medicaid-eligible women during their first year, as compared to $50 million spent in 1975 for Medicaid-eligible abortions.[91] In contrast, the estimated costs of providing day care under the Comprehensive Child Development Act were significantly higher, involving a projected $2 billion dollars in additional federal expenditures.[92]

Since 1971, the majority of new day care legislation has met with repeated legislative defeats. These defeats have served to splinter the earlier coalition of pro-day care groups and have resulted in little significant change in the availability of publicly funded day care.[93] In turn, existing government programs have a number of deficiencies. As already noted, the more welfare-oriented day care programs service only a small percentage of their eligible clientele. Aside from these restrictive, welfare-oriented programs, the only major programs available to families are the child tax credits and the day care provisions under Title XX benefits of the Social Security Act.

Title XX benefits were designated to provide day care services free of charge or on a sliding fee scale to *both* poor and moderate income families. However, as of 1979, half of the states had eligibility cut-off points which were below a lower income family budget and only 28 states had sliding fee scales, thus in effect removing a large number of low to moderate income families from these services.[94] The child tax credits, which provide income tax deductions for a percentage of annual child care expenses, are ostensibly available to *all* families.

TABLE 8.3

Average Differences Between Private and Public Day Care Centers, United States, 1976-1977

Category	Private	Public
Children		
Size of class	17	19
Staff		
Number	4	8
Adult/child ratio	1:8	1:6
Teacher education	14 years	14 years
Teachers trained in child development	44%	66%
Teachers' experience in day care	5 years	4 years
Teachers' time in present center	2 years	3 years
Parents		
Participation as volunteers	12%	45%
Decisions on policy	12%	61%
Cost (in 1978)	$1300	$2500
Ratings		
Superior	1%	10%
Good	15%	28%
Fair	35%	51%
Poor	50%	11%
Other Services	—	Screening, testing, immunization, social work, transportation, referral to other agencies.

Source: Alison Clarke-Stewart, *Daycare* (Harvard University Press, Cambridge, Massachusetts, 1982), p. 55.

However, in practice, this program has been shown to benefit primarily upper-middle-class families. Lower-class families whose tax liabilities could not match the credit, or whose incomes were too low to be able to afford day care even with the nominal credit, received few benefits. Consequently, it is not surprising that in 1977, two-thirds of all child tax credits went to families whose incomes were above the national median income.[95] In sum, the major group ignored by all of these programs are those families whose incomes are above the poverty line, but below the national median income.[96]

Despite the lack of strong government support for day care, between 1970 and 1979, there was more than a 30 per cent increase in day care center enrollment in the United States, with more than a 70 per cent increase in enrollment for children under two years of age.[97] Most of this increase was due to the increase in private, commercial day care centers where the quality of care and facilities varies immensely.[98] Yet despite the increasing demand for day care and the fact that private day care is the primary form fulfilling this need, the conservatives who claim to be the guardians of the American family continue to argue against public day care.

This is particularly ironic since studies have shown that, on average, public day care provides higher quality care than does private day care.[99] Table 8.3 provides a comparison of the average facilities in public day care centers as contrasted to private day care centers for the years 1976-1977. These data indicate that while the costs of public day care are clearly higher on average, in terms of adult/child ratios, teacher training in child development, evaluations of the quality of care, and parental involvement in day care, public day care centers are far better on average than private centers.

Such contradictions in the 'pro-family' position of conservatives have to be addressed if there is to be a greater consensus on the value and need for day care in the United States. My conclusion begins by examining how the patterns and similarities found in the histories of abortion and day care in the United States call into question the views of these conservative critics.

Conclusion

Contemporary critics of reproductive freedom often portray demands for abortion and day care as choices individuals make where egotistic concerns for self take priority over concerns for others—namely children and family relations. As such, contemporary feminists are viewed as undermining the family and contributing to a deterioration of childrearing and nurturing roles in their pursuit of self-interest and self-achievement.[100] This view sets up a false polarization between feminism and the family; moreover, it is based on an ahistorical and individualistic analysis which ignores how social-structural factors shape and constrain individual choices.

The histories of abortion and day care in the United States sketched above have illustrated how social-structural changes have influenced concerns and attitudes over family limitation and demands for alternative forms of child care. Not only were these structural changes beyond the control of any single individual or family, but also they created new concerns with the quality of family life which in turn have shaped particular demands about day care and abortion.

In the mid-nineteenth century, increased concern with family limitation, particularly by middle-class women, was related to urbanization, industrialization, and the subsequent increase in the standard of living of this class. In turn, urbanization and industrialization placed far greater constraints on the family life of lower-class women. Unlike agriculture, which often utilized family labour and forged a closer connection between home and work, industrialization forced poor and working-class women out of the home and into the factory. This created new problems of child care and an increased interest in family limitation, particularly after the introduction of child labour legislation. Since these women worked out of economic necessity rather than choice, using day nurseries and attempting to limit family size were important means for ensuring that their existing families could better survive in the world in which they lived.

Other structural factors which shaped the histories of access to abortion and day care include the massive influx of immigration into the U.S. and the poverty engendered by rapid industrialization. These developments were particularly evident in the ways in which racist and class-based ideologies fostered the acceptance of population control policies and day care in some segments of the well-to-do classes. Fear of 'race suicide' fueled support for anti-abortion legislation, while fear of the 'dangerous' lower classes also pervaded the motives of wealthy philanthropists who established day nurseries to provide 'proper' moral upbringing for poor and immigrant children.

During the twentieth century, structural factors were again the most significient factors shaping the expansion and contraction of day care. The Depression and World War Two saw the greatest expansion of day care in America, while government attempts to get women back into the home in the post-war era influenced its contraction. Despite these attempts, the increased entry of women into the labour force in recent decades has been a primary structural factor which has brought together the interests of both middle- and working-class women around the issue of greater access to abortion and day care. Moreover, the increase in the labour force participation of women was generally not a question of *individual* choice, but one of economic necessity brought about by inflation, the increase in divorce rates and the growth in single-parent households.

Another similarity between the histories of day care and abortion in the United States is reflected in the impact of professionalization. The professionalization of medical personnel and child care workers led to an anti-working class and anti-feminist bias in the provision of these reproductive rights. The professionalization of medicine was integrally related to the establishment of anti-abortion legislation and served to remove lower-class personnel from this field of employment. This in effect restricted access of all women to medically-assisted abortions and was particularly restrictive to poor women since this group had the least contact with certified physicians. Similarly, the professionalization of day care workers removed lower-class personnel from this field of employment and severely restricted access to day care by shifting the orientation of day nurseries from that of providing a service to all working women to that of a rehabilitation agency for 'maladjusted families.' In turn, professionals in both fields idealized motherhood and stressed that women's proper place was in the home, thus further neglecting the needs of women who worked outside of the home.

The role of the feminist movement was also very similar in both cases. The feminist movement of the nineteenth and early twentieth centuries did little to contest the view of professionals. Rather, the vast majority of feminists emphasized the positive aspects of women's roles as mothers and nurturers and advocated neither abortion nor day care. Here they were manifesting their own middle-class positions and aspirations which were quite distinct from those of poorer women who had to work to survive. In contrast, the contemporary feminist movement, while still largely middle class in composition, has supported abortion and day care as a right for all women.

Contemporary feminists have been joined by physicians and professional child care workers who, unlike their predecessors, are also now in the forefront of demanding access to these rights. This shift in the politics of these middle-class groups manifests a shift in occupational interests and concerns. That is, interests in career employment for themselves or for their spouses have increased the needs for greater control over reproduction and for greater access to adequate child care facilities. Moreover, now that the legitimacy of these professions is well established, the increased availability of abortion and day care serves occupational interests, providing employment opportunities and control in these fields.

The histories of abortion and day care have also shown how unequal access to these rights has been a perennial feature of American society. Access to quality day care has historically been the prerogative of middle- and upper-class women; and, indeed, the educationally-oriented, but part-time, child care provided by Kindergartens and private nursery schools was really only affordable and convenient to these better-off classes. In contrast, the early day nurseries, which largely serviced working mothers, provided custodial forms of care. The later welfare-oriented, professionally run day care centers, while improving the quality of available care, were so restrictive that they excluded many families in need of their services. In turn, current government-funded day care programs are similarly restricted to poor and disadvantaged families while the child tax credits service and benefit mainly the well-to-do.

Socio-economic status appears to have been the major factor affecting access to medically safe abortions. Prior to the legalization of abortion in America, poor women were discriminated against in terms of access to therapeutic abortions. After abortion was legalized, there was only a four year period when reasonable access to abortion was generally available to all women. Once the Hyde Amendment was passed, poor women once again became discriminated against as regards this reproductive right and this situation continues today.

In sum, while abortion and child care facilities have historically been most accessible to middle- and upper-class women, contemporary federal legislation on these issues differs in terms of class discrimination. Today abortion legislation is most punitive towards America's poorest women—welfare recipients. Federal day care legislation is most restrictive for those families whose incomes fall above the poverty line but below the national median income i.e., the lower income level of the working class. However, both as regards abortion and day care, even this unequal and limited access is currently under attack by right-wing groups who, under the guise of 'protecting' the family, have politically mobilized to push for further restrictions on reproductive freedom.

It would appear that the state's role in the expansion and contraction of access to abortion and day care was largely in response to the demands of the middle class. When this class, in particular the professional segment, had its interests awakened or threatened, the state often took action. Exceptions to this pattern include national crises which affected all classes, as was the case during the Depression and World War Two, or direct confrontation in the form of social movements, which maintained day care after the war in certain cities. These patterns indicate the class discriminatory nature of government intervention, as well as the absence of sufficient political mobilization by the poor and the working class to assert their rights on the issues of abortion and day care. Moreover, since these reproductive rights affect all women, the patterns also reflect the class-specific issues which have historically divided women of different classes. Fortunately, in recent years, structural changes in American society have fused the interests of middle-class, poor and working-class women on basic reproductive issues. This situation at least allows for the possibility of the emergence of broad-based coalitions, coalitions which can confront existing right-wing opposition to abortion and day care and which can extend reproductive freedoms for all women in contemporary America.

Notes and References

1. Flo Conway and Jim Siegelman, *Holy Terror: The Fundamentalist War on America's Freedoms in Religion, Politics, and our Private Lives* (Doubleday, New York, 1982), p. 101.
2. Ibid., p. 104.
3. Ibid.
4. Richard R. Ruopp and Jeffrey Travers, 'Janus Faced Day Care: Perspectives on Quality and Cost' in E. Zigler and E. Gordon (eds.), *Day Care: Scientific and Social Policy Issues* (Auburn House, Boston, 1982), p. 77.
5. Carlfred B. Broderick, *Marriage and the Family*, 2nd edition (Prentice-Hall, Engelwood Cliffs, New Jersey, 1984), p. 13.
6. See for example Nadean Bishop, 'Abortion: The Controversial Choice' in J. Freeman (ed.), *Women: A Feminist Perspective* (Mayfield, Palo Alto, California, 1976), p. 64; and Gloria Steinhem, *Outrageous Acts and Everyday Rebellions* (Holt, Rinehart and Winston, New York, 1983), p. 151.
7. Wally Seccombe, 'Marxism and Demography' in this volume; and his 'Domestic Labour and the Working-class Household' in B. Fox (ed.), *Hidden in the Household: Women's Domestic Labour Under Capitalism* (The Women's Press, Toronto, 1980), pp. 25-99.
8. Seccombe, 'Marxism and Demography.' For a discussion of various criticisms of Marxist-feminist analyses see Lise Vogel, 'Marxism and Socialist-Feminist Theory: A Decade of Debate', *Current Perspectives in Social Theory*, 2 (1981), pp. 221-223.
9. Emily Blumenfeld and Susan Mann, 'Domestic Labour and the Reproduction of Labour Power: Towards an Analysis of Women, the Family, and Class', in Fox, *Hidden in the Household*, pp. 277-283.
10. Ibid., pp. 290-302.
11. Ibid., pp. 270-273.
12. Ibid., pp. 271-272.
13. James C. Mohr, *Abortion in America: The Origins and Evolution of National Policy* (Oxford University Press, New York, 1978), Rosalind Pollack Petchesky, *Abortion and Woman's Choice: The State, Sexuality, and Reproductive Freedom* (Longman, New York, 1984).
14. Petchesky, *Abortion and Woman's Choice*, p. 73.
15. Claudia Goldin, 'Household and Market Production of Families in a Late Nineteenth Century American City', *Explorations in Economic History*, No. 16 (1979), pp. 115-117.

16. Petchesky, *Abortion and Woman's Choice*, p. 75. For other examples where the glorification of motherhood has been used to increase birth rates, see Anna Davin, 'Imperialism and Motherhood' *History Workshop*, No. 5 (1973), and Leon Trotsky, 'Thermidor in the Family', *Women and the Family* (Pathfinder, New York, 1973).

17. Petchesky, *Abortion and Woman's Choice*, p. 80.

18. Mohr, *Abortion in America*, pp. 31, 256-257.

19. Jacobi Abraham, 'The Best Means of Combatting Infant Mortality', *Journal of the American Medical Association*, 58 (1912), p. 7. Louis S. Reed, 'Midwives, Chiropodists and Optometrists: Their Place In Medical Care', Committee on the Costs of Medical Care, Publication No. 15 (The University of Chicago Press, Chicago, 1932), pp. 20-21.

20. Petchesky, *Abortion and Woman's Choice*, pp. 78-79.

21. Ibid., pp. 84-89. See also Angela Davis, *Women, Race and Class* (Random House, New York, 1981), p. 209; and Allan Chase, *The Legacy of Malthus: The Social Costs of the New Scientific Racism* (University of Illinois Press, Urbana, Illinois, 1980), pp. 12-17.

22. Davis, *Women, Race and Class*, pp. 210-215.

23. Linda Gordon, *Woman's Body, Woman's Right: Birth Control in America* (Penguin, New York, 1976), p. 158.

24. For a discussion of why the early feminist movement did not support abortion see Linda Gordon, 'Why Nineteenth Century Feminists did not Support "Birth Control" and Twentieth Century Feminists Do', in B. Thorne (ed.), *Rethinking the Family: Some Feminist Questions* (Longmans, New York, 1982), pp. 45-46.

25. Mohr, *Abortion in America*, pp. 200, 204, 239.

26. Harold Rosen, 'Psychiatric Implications of Abortion: A Case Study in Social Hypocrisy', in D.T. Smith (ed.), *Abortion and the Law* (Western Reserve University Press, Cleveland, 1967), p. 87.

27. Marie E. Kopp, *Birth Control in Practice* (Arno Press, New York, 1972), pp. 57, 61, 72-73.

28. Kenneth R. Niswander, 'Medical Abortion Practices in the United States', in Smith, *Abortion and the Law*, p. 39.

29. Ibid., pp. 49, 51. See also Rosen, 'Psychiatric Implications of Abortion', p. 87 and Petchesky, *Abortion and Woman's Choice*, pp. 158-159.

30. Rosen, 'Psychiatric Implications of Abortion', p. 89.

31. Niswander, 'Medical Abortion Practices', p. 53.

32. *Plaintiffs Statements of Fact on Issues Other Than Religion* (McRae v Harris) 491 F. Supp. 630 ed. NY (1980).

33. Petchesky, *Abortion and Woman's Choice*, p. 115.

34. Broderick, *Marriage and the Family*, p. 17.

35. Petchesky, *Abortion and Woman's Choice*, p. 110.

36. Ibid., p. 144.

37. Ibid., p. 119.

38. Ibid., pp. 119-120. See also Thomas B. Littlewood, *The Politics of Population Control* (University of Notre Dame Press, Notre Dame, 1977), pp. 10-11, 21-22.

39. Petchesky, *Abortion and Woman's Choice*, pp. 116-118.

40. Ibid., pp. 125-132.

41. Nadean Bishop, 'Abortion: The Controversial Choice', pp. 68-71. For changes in abortion legislation in 1983 see *The Times-Picayune/The States Item*, New Orleans, Louisiana, June 16, 1983, Section 1, pp. 1 and 4.

42. Nadean Bishop, 'Abortion: The Controversial Choice', pp. 71-75. See also The Alan Guttmacher Institute, *Abortion: Need, Services and Policies: Louisiana* (Alan Guttmacher Institute, New York, 1979), p. 18; and The Alan Guttmacher Institute *Abortions and the Poor: Private Morality, Public Responsibility* (Alan Guttmacher Institute, New York, 1979), p. 13.

43. Alan Guttmacher Institute, *Abortions and the Poor*, p. 10.

44. Jean V. Hardisty, *American Civil Liberties Union Speakers Manual on Abortion* (American Civil Liberties Union, Chicago, 1982), p. 21.

45. Alan Guttmacher Institute, *Abortions and the Poor*, p. 28.

46. Tacie Dejanikus, 'Abortion Strategies for 1983', *Off Our Backs*, XII, January (1983), p. 10.

47. Margaret O'Brien Steinfels, *Who's Minding the Children? The History and Politics of Day Care in America* (Simon and Schuster, New York, 1973).

48. Virginia Kerr, 'One Step Forward—Two Steps Back: Child Care's Long American History', In Pamela Roby (ed.), *Child Care, Who Cares?: Foreign and Domestic Infant and Early Childhood Policies* (Basic Books, New York, 1973), p. 158.

49. Steinfels, *Who's Minding the Children?*, pp. 36-37.

50. Ibid., p. 37. See also Ethel S. Beer, *Working Mothers and the Day Nursery* (Whiteside, New York, 1957), pp. 19-26 for a more detailed discussion of some of the differences between Kindergartens and day nurseries.

51. Accounts of these early day cares can be found in a number of sources. See for example Steinfels, *Who's Minding the Children?*, p. 36 and Rosalyn Baxandall, 'Who Shall Care for Our Children? The History and Development of Day Care in the United States', in Jo Freeman (ed.), *Feminist Perspectives* (Mayfield, Palo Alto, California, 1979), p. 442.

52. Goldin, 'Household and Market Production of Families', pp. 113-114.

53. Beer, *Working Mothers and the Day Nursery*, p. 94.

54. Steinfels, *Who's Minding the Children?*, p. 46.

55. Ibid., p. 43. For a similar analysis of early day care centers in Canada see Patricia Vandebelt Schulz, 'Day Care in Canada: 1850-1962', in K.G. Ross (ed.), *Good Day Care* (The Women's Press, Toronto, 1978), p. 141.

56. Steinfels, *Who's Minding the Children?*, pp. 38-39.

57. Kerr, 'One Step Forward', p. 159.

58. Greta G. Fein and Alison Clarke-Stewart, *Day Care in Context* (John Wiley and Sons, New York, 1973), p. 15.

59. Steinfels, *Who's Minding the Children?*, p. 57.

60. Ibid., pp. 61-62.

61. Ibid., pp. 62-63.

62. Ibid., pp. 55-56.

63. Ibid., pp. 55-56 and 65-66. For contemporary debates over the advantages and disadvantages of day care see Anne Robertson, 'Day care and Children's Responsiveness to Adults', in Zigler and Gordon, *Day Care:*

Scientific and Social Policy Issues, pp. 152-173.

64. Ibid., p. 58. For a more detailed discussion of this problem see Beer, *Working Mothers and the Day Nursery*, pp. 23-24.
65. Steinfels, *Who's Minding the Children?*, p. 58.
66. Ibid., pp. 61-63.
67. Kerr, 'One Step Forward', p. 160. Charlotte Perkins Gilman's discussion of the advantages of day care and the negative effects of isolated, domestic labour on women can be found in her book *The Home: Its Work and Influence* (Source Book Press, New York, 1970).
68. Kerr, 'One Step Forward', p. 160.
69. Ibid. See also Steinfels, *Who's Minding the Children?*, pp. 51-52.
70. Kerr, 'One Step Forward', p. 162.
71. Ibid.
72. Steinfels, *Who's Minding the Children?*, p. 67.
73. Kerr, 'One Step Forward', p. 163. See also, Evelyn Moore, 'Day Care: A Black Perspective', in Zigler and Gordon, *Day Care: Scientific and Social Policy Issues*, p. 421.
74. Kerr, 'One Step Forward', pp. 165-166. Here Kerr discusses how public protests were successful in maintaining day care centers in California and New York City after World War Two.
75. Ibid., pp. 166-167.
76. John R. Nelson, Jr., 'The Politics of Federal Day Care Regulation', Zigler and Gordon, *Day Care: Scientific and Social Policy Issues*, p. 269.
77. Steinfels, *Who's Minding the Children?*, p. 72.
78. Ibid., p. 77.
79. Moore, 'Day Care: A Black Perspective', pp. 422-424. See also Baxandall, 'Who Shall Care?', pp. 445-446.
80. Alison Clarke-Stewart, *Daycare* (Harvard University Press, Cambridge, 1982), p. 34.
81. Steinfels, *Who's Minding the Children?*, p. 87.
82. Ibid., pp. 84-85. See also Rochelle Paul Wortis, 'The Acceptance of the Concept of the Maternal Role by Behavioral Scientists: Its Effects on Women', in A. Skolnick and J. Skolnick (eds.), *Intimacy, Family and Society* (Little, Brown and Co., Boston, 1974), p. 372, and Anne Robertson, 'Day Care and Children's Responsiveness to Adults', pp. 152-173.
83. Edward Zigler and Jody Goodman, 'The Battle for Day Care in America: A View from the Trenches', in Zigler and Gordon, *Day Care: Scientific and Social Policy Issues*, p. 347.
84. Rochelle Beck, 'Beyond The Stalemate in Child Care Public Policy', in Zigler and Gordon, *Day Care: Scientific and Social Policy Issues*, p. 308.
85. Zigler and Goodman, 'The Battle for Day Care', p. 339.
86. Beck, 'Beyond the Stalemate', p. 309.
87. Zigler and Goodman, 'The Battle for Day Care', pp. 344-345. For a copy of Nixon's response to the Senate see Stevanne Auerback, *Confronting the Child Care Crisis* (Beacon Press, Boston, 1979), pp. 91-94.
88. Zigler and Goodman, 'The Battle for Day Care', pp. 344-345.
89. Ibid., p. 345.
90. Beck, 'Beyond the Stalemate', p. 307.
91. Bishop, 'Abortion: The Controversial Choice', p. 75.

92. Auerbach, *Confronting the Child Care Crisis*, p. 93.
93. Beck, 'Beyond the Stalemate', pp. 308-309.
94. W. Fary Winget, 'The Dilemma of Affordable Child Care', in Zigler and E. Gordon, *Day Care: Scientific and Social Policy Issues*, p. 360.
95. Moore, 'Day Care: A Black Perspective', p. 431.
96. Beck, 'Beyond the Stalemate', p. 320.
97. Clarke-Stewart, *Daycare*, p. 35.
98. Ibid.
99. Ibid., pp. 53-58.
100. See for example Christopher Lasch, *Haven in a Heartless World: The Family Besieged* (Basic Books, New York, 1979), pp. xvi-xvii. For a discussion of some of the contradictions of feminism regarding individualism and right-wing opposition to this, see Linda Gordon, 'Why Nineteenth-Century Feminists Did Not Support "Birth Control" ', pp. 50-51.

9

THE 'NORMING' OF THE WORKING DAY

Rudy Fichtenbaum and Gordon Welty

The concept of state monopoly capitalism has become well established in contemporary Marxist thought. This concept was introduced by Lenin during World War One to indicate the circumstance where the bourgeois state was required overtly to intervene in the economy in order to secure the reproduction of the social formation.[1] On the one hand, this meant that the concept of the 'night-watchman' state which had been theorized for the preceding stage of competitive capitalism had been transcended. On the other hand, this meant that the centralization and concentration of capital reflected in the development of oligopoly corresponded to a social form wherein 'society'—apart from the 'state'—clearly could not reproduce itself. This suggested the possibility, if not the necessity, of the further development of state planning, planning which would be an index of the demise of capitalism.

This overt and comprehensive state intervention was prefigured in the nineteenth century struggle over the length of the working day. In that instance, pursuit of particularistic interests by individual capitals came to threaten the reproduction of labour power and thus the reproduction of the social form itself. Thereupon the 'liberal' state, representative of capital in general and its interests, intervened to regulate the length of the working day and other working conditions. According to the Marxist view, the struggle over the length of the working day had two major implications: first, since the particular interests of capitals were ultimately contradictory and thus politically irreconcilable, it was unlikely that capitalism could ever 'stabilize' itself; and second, another class, whose particularistic interests could, and indeed must harmonize—whose interests could actually constitute the general interest—was required to establish another social order which could stabilize itself. That other class, the working class, participated in the nineteenth century struggle over the length of the working day both directly, in the form of Chartist and other agitation, and various work actions—and indirectly, since it had not yet secured the franchise.

The struggle over the length of the working day and, more broadly, the 'norming' of the working day is thus of signal interest as a prefigure and even a model of state monopoly capitalism. It thereby gives a rich illustration of the alternatives for working class political action. This topic also illustrates the dialectic of 'necessity' and 'freedom'—the bourgeois state of necessity pursuing the interests of capital in general and regulating the length of the working day, while the working class was emancipating itself and also pursuing the regulation of the working day and other working conditions. Finally, this struggle is of topical interest as well, given recent demands by the working class for a shorter working week with no cut in pay as a response to the current economic crisis.

In this chapter we start by providing a general discussion of social reproduction within the capitalist mode of production. Then we turn our attention to the background of the writing of Chapter X of Volume 1 of *Capital*, where Marx addresses the establishment of the length of the working day. Next, we provide a close reading of the text of Chapter X itself. Finally, we examine some implications of Marx's analysis for the world-wide struggle for a normal working day. In an Appendix, we have included two illustrative misreadings of Chapter X as well as a critique, which highlights the importance of close attention to Marx's text. We have also included in the Appendix some references to the neoclassical economists' writings on the topic of the length of the working day.

The Reproduction of Social Relations and the Length of the Working Day

The struggle over the length of the working day is at least as old as capitalism. In preceding social formations the length of the working day was an object of less contention because those modes of production were driven by different economic laws. Primitive society, for instance, was essentially a subsistence economy where goods were produced for use rather than for exchange and the length of the working day was governed by need and by nature.[2] The material conditions for the rise of society which moves in its social antagonisms (i.e. class society in the generic sense) emerge when (a) the direct producers of a society systematically produce a surplus product (i.e. more than is required for the reproduction of the society's labour power in the long run); when (b) that surplus product is appropriated by nonlabourers (the 'exploiters'); and when (c) a portion of that appropriated surplus is utilized to reproduce the 'exploitative' or antagonistic relationship itself. Within the pre-capitalistic and antagonistic social formations (for example those of ancient slavery or medieval feudalism) the length of the working day was still determined by nature. Even though the surplus product of the slaves and serfs was appropriated by the slave masters and the feudal lords, these social formations were based on production for use; the absence of markets for labour power, in particular, meant that the total commodification of social life in these social forms could not occur.[3] One is struck by the emphasis on the quality of the working day, rather than quantitative considerations, when one reads the didactic writings of the ancient social forms such as Hesiod's 'Works and Days,' dating from the eighth century B.C. However, with the development of commodity production and the emergence of capitalism the length of the working day became a major issue in the class struggle.

The Uniqueness of Capitalist Social Reproduction

Unlike previous social formations, production for exchange is characteristic of capitalism. As a society which moves in its social antagonisms, the form which the surplus product assumes under the regime of capital is the value form, called *surplus value*, which is the value which is created in that portion of the working day which remains after the labour time necessary for the production of the average daily means of subsistence. Here it should be noted that 'subsistence' is not intended in the literal sense, but rather, as we shall see, in the sense of being socially and historically conditioned. The value of labour power, unlike other commodities, has a social, cultural and historical moment.

The basic dynamic of the capitalist mode of production is the generation and appropriation of surplus value. Indeed, surplus value emerges as an economic category only with the development of capitalist commodity production. Thus, production under capitalism must satisfy two conditions: (1) the product must be useful to someone other than the direct producer so that commodity exchange will take place; and (2) the value of the product must be greater than the sum of values used in its production, so that surplus value is generated. Taken together, these two conditions of capitalist production make the length of the working day problematic. Consider the first condition. In order to enter the labour market, the labourer must have something useful to sell, viz. labour power. But this presupposes that the labourer on the average has enough necessary labour time to reproduce the value of the means of subsistence, and also enough non-labouring time to recreate the labour power. As Marx has put it, during work, 'a definite quantity of human muscle, nerve, brain, etc. is wasted and these require to be restored.'[4] This process of restoration of human energy or force will be actualized only if labour power sells at or above its value. This process of restoration of labour power is a necessary condition for the reproduction of the entire capitalist mode production. As for the second condition, to the capitalist in his drive for maximum profits, labour power is useful only if it generates surplus value. Indeed, the capitalistic usefulness of labour is directly related to the amount of surplus value it generates. Thus, the conditions for the maximization of surplus value are met only if labour power sells at or below its value. And the maximization of surplus value is also a necessary condition for the reproduction of capitalism.

These conditions are jointly fulfilled only if labour power sells at its value, i.e. on the average and in the long run neither above nor below its value. However, this outcome is problematic in several regards. In the first place, there are contradictions of capitalism which derive from the anarchy of capitalist production. It is in the interest of each individual capitalist to force the sale of labour power *below* its value; the interest of capital in general, however, requires that it sell *at* its value. Thus, there is a fundamental necessity for coordinating the disparate interests of particular capitalists. This necessity is obscured by the doctrine of the 'Invisible Hand'.[5] In the second place, problems arise because the value of labour power uniquely among all commodities includes 'an historical and moral element'.[6] Even if the necessity of coordination could be resolved, say through the regulatory action of the bourgeois state, the problems of assessing the historically and materially specific value of homogeneous labour power, *hic et nunc*, cannot be ignored.[7]

Wage labour is the predominant and essential element of production under capitalism. Wages are paid to workers in exchange for their ability to work, for their labour power. The value of the commodity labour power is determined, like that of all other commodities, by the labour time which is socially necessary to produce (and in the case of labour power, to *reproduce*) that commodity. Because of the prolonged maturation period of humans, the reproductive labour time which is socially necessary for the immature labourer must be credited to the wage-labouring parent(s); hence the value of labour power includes an element above and beyond that socially necessary for the reproduction of this or that particular adult labourer.[8] If one member of a working class 'nuclear family' is employed, the value of that one person's wage-labour will, on the average and in the long run, equal the labour time which is socially necessary to reproduce that one's own labour power, as well as that socially necessary to reproduce at least three more labourers.[9] If two members of such a family are employed, the value of either one's wage-labour will equal the labour time which is socially necessary to reproduce one's labour power, as well as that socially necessary to reproduce at least another labourer.[10]

A labour market tactic of the capitalist is thereby obvious—periodically to force the sale of labour power below its value, creating pressure on the 'unemployed' adult in the working class 'nuclear family' to enter the labour market. This tactic, in turn, has had two consequences. On the one hand, it has resulted in increased class struggle as the working class resists the decline in its 'standard of living'. This class struggle can intensify into class conflict which threatens the very process of reproduction of the capitalist mode of production. Such class conflict has compelled the state, even where it does not provide representation for the working class, to intervene with regulatory relief on behalf of the interests of capital in general which in effect benefits the working class. On the other hand, such a tactic of particular capitalists has disturbed the domestic arrangements of the working class 'nuclear family', generating what sociologists have come to call 'social problems' which again can threaten the reproduction of the capitalist mode of production. Thereby capital in general, through the mediation of the bourgeois state, is finally compelled to intervene with 'social welfare' legislation. As we shall see, the struggle over the length of the working day was and remains just such a class struggle, involving both regulatory relief and welfare legislation.

Capitalism is essentially a relationship between wage labour and objectified labour (i.e. it is class society in the specific sense). One side of the social antagonism has just been considered, that of living labour or wage labour. Considered from the other side, the capitalist in addition to buying labour power at or below value can do one of two further things to increase surplus value: (1) introduce new technology which will increase productivity, thereby reducing the time socially necessary for the reproduction of labour power, or (2) lengthen the working day. The introduction of new technology is a continuing but uneven process under capitalism. Unlike the fantasy world of the neoclassical economists, the actual capitalist does not have at his disposal a 'menu' consisting of an infinite number of technologies. The actual world is more accurately characterized by the realities of industrial espionage, technological monopolies, etc. which are suggestive of the desperately limited number of technologies available for introduction into the production process at any given time. But the laws of capitalist production demand an increase of surplus value; hence each capitalist is pressured to lengthen the working day as well as to adopt new technologies. Of course there is an interaction between the changing technology and the changing length of the working day which provides the latter with its material base. For instance, the development of large-scale manufacturing, bringing hundreds of workers together in a small area, and the invention of the gas burning lamp by W.

Murdock in 1792 permitted the capitalists to lengthen the working day in unprecedented fashion.[11]

Like most of the essential characteristics of capitalism, the lengthening of the working day manifests itself as a tendency which is subject to certain countervailing influences. The main counteracting influence in this case is the struggle of the working class against overwork and hence against the lengthening of the working day. In addition, a preeminent social and historical factor which conditions the value of labour power is the development of the forces of production. Their development permits the rise of the working class standard of living, even within the limitations of bourgeois society. It does so by lowering the value of the commodities which constitute the average daily means of subsistence. This development thereby 'permits' the rise of the working class standard of living. As the working class fights for this higher standard of living, one of the crucial terrains of this contestation is that of the length of the working day. The reproduction of labour power permits a continual rise in the working class standard of living, a requirement which contradicts the essence of capitalism, the production of surplus value.

Marx's Exploration into Social Reproduction: The Length of the Working Day

Establishing the partition between surplus value and variable capital is problematic within the terms of capitalism. The magnitude of variable capital—the value of labour power—must be large enough to permit the social reproduction of the labour force, yet not occupy the whole workday. This means that labour power must be sold at its value, at least in the long term. At the same time, the magnitude of surplus value will be as large as possible, spurred on by the intrinsic tendencies of capitalist production. This problem tends to find its resolution throughout the history of capitalism. It is resolved for mature capitalism by the development of the 'normal' working day, through the political process which Marx called the 'norming' (Normierung) of the working day. This process is discussed in Chapter X of *Capital*.

The text of Chapter X is not without its difficulties. On the one hand, there are several considerations regarding Marx's intention in writing this chapter. On the other hand, there are issues of its reception. We will focus our attention here on the issues of intention, both personal and dialectical.

On February 10, 1866, Marx wrote a letter to Engels regarding the first volume of *Capital*, indicating that he had 'expanded the historical part on the "working day," which lay outside the original plan.'[12] This is clearly suggestive of intentions. It seems that Marx originally did not plan to include a chapter on the working day in *Capital*. This is corroborated when we examine the earliest of the economic notebooks which Marx had compiled in preparation for the writing of *Capital*. The *Grundrisse* includes Marx's notebooks from late 1857 and early 1858. It is clear that he understood the distinction between absolute and relative surplus labour time in the late 1850s.[13] But his focus was on relative surplus labour time, the decrease in the portion of the working day required for necessary labour, and strikingly so. Notebook 3 and the first pages of Notebook 4 address the growth of surplus value accruing to a growth in productive forces. Within this lengthy discussion of relative surplus labour time are sprinkled no more than a couple of comments about the growth of surplus value accruing to the lengthening of the working day. Symptomatically, Marx notes at one point that the working day of capitalism does not respect the night, noting that 'this discussion belongs in the Chapter on Wages'.[14] Again, this is strongly suggestive of Marx's intentions.

Thus, Marx was not only highlighting relative rather than absolute surplus labour time in the late 1850s, but seems to have intended to relegate such discussion as there was to be of the latter concept to a chapter which was to be placed at a much later point in the text. At this preparatory stage in his analysis, Marx seems to have been more concerned about conceptualizing the role of machinery, science, etc. in mature capitalism than in the gradual development of capitalism itself. Such concern would explain his stress on relative rather than absolute surplus labour time because it would presuppose that the length of the working day had been standardized. Marx makes two observations in the *Grundrisse* which tend to corroborate this view. First, he says that the development of capital is directly related to the growth of productive forces necessary to effect any change in surplus value. This is because the smaller the portion of the working day allotted to necessary labour, the less can the growth of productive forces diminish necessary labour.[15] A few pages later, Marx notes the converse of this 'boundary effect', namely that the magnitude of surplus labour time is directly related to the difficulty of realizing an absolute increase in labour time, i.e. an elongation of the working day.[16] However, this focus in Marx's studies, which emphasized relative rather than absolute surplus labour time, was not to remain unchanged.

By early 1863, Marx seems to have begun to revise his original plans for the first volume of *Capital*. This is evident in the economic notebooks he had begun compiling after he had published the *Contribution to the Critique of Political Economy* in 1859. The *Theories of Surplus Value* includes Marx's notebooks from 1861 through early 1863. In Notebook 18, compiled towards the end of that period, Marx provided an outline for a text to be entitled 'Production Process of

Capital,' which, it will be recalled, was to become the sub-title of Book I of *Capital*. Moreover, of the proposed nine parts in the outline, the first six correspond fairly well to the published contents of the first volume of *Capital*.[17] Specifically, the third part of the outline corresponds quite closely to Part Three of *Capital* as it was published, focusing on absolute surplus value; part 3(d) was proposed to address the 'Struggle for the Normal Working Day.' Lastly, all of this was to precede a proposed fourth part on relative surplus value. Thus, Marx's intentions were changing, more in accord with his published results.

Yet differences seem to remain between Marx's intentions in 1863 and the first volume of *Capital*. In 1863, for example, he still speaks of topics, such as the value of services, which 'belong to the Chapter on Wages'.[18] Here is reference to a study of wages which was never completed. Can this be reconciled? We believe so. In Part 6 of *Capital*, entitled 'Wages' and clearly *not* the proposed 'Chapter on Wages', Marx indicated that 'Wages . . . take many forms'; he continues 'An exposition of all these forms, however, belongs to the special study of wage-labour, not therefore to this work' (p. 543). Thus in 1867 Marx still recognized a distinction between the contents of *Capital*, which has only to address 'the two fundamental forms' of wages, and that of a 'special study of wage-labour', which would address all the forms. Moreover, in Chapter XVII of *Capital*, Marx indicates the terms of a theory of wage determination (p. 519, also 559). This theory would include the following determinants: (1) the length of the working day; (2) the normal intensity of labour; (3) the productiveness of labour; as well as (4) 'the value of the necessaries of life habitually required by the average labourer'; (5) the expenses of developing the labour power to maturity (which as was noted above is to be credited to the value of the labour power of the parent(s)); and (6) the 'natural diversity' of labour power, i.e. the differences between the sexes and between age cohorts. Moreover, (7) there is the difference between simple and complex labour power (p. 198). Marx excluded the last three of these determinants from the discussion in the first volume of *Capital*; this further corroborates the argument that he intended to pursue the theory of wage determination in a subsequent study. Thus, Marx could have intended in 1863 to include the discussion of absolute surplus value and the length of the working day in *Capital*, and still have recognized that the theory of wages could not be addressed at a theoretically appropriate level of specification in that most general volume.

There are still other, more personal considerations which may bear on the text. Marx himself suggested in his February 10, 1866 letter to Engels that his illness in early 1866 had left him too weak for any kind of substantial theorizing; while disabled he occupied himself with the historical account included in Chapter X. Some of Marx's biographers have taken the linkage of his state of health and the content of *Capital* very seriously.[19] Marx modestly went on to say that this chapter was but an updating of Engels' *Condition of the Working Class in England* of 1845.[20] It will be recalled that Engels sought in that book to describe and to some extent analyze the living and working conditions of the English working class, where proletarian conditions existed in their 'classicial form.' Knowledge of these conditions was indispensable, he asserted, both to provide a grounding for socialist theory and to permit a definitive critique of utopian schemes.[21] Engels' book begins with a chapter on the development of capitalism and the rise of the proletariat in England. A chapter follows on the correlative 'centralization' of property and population.[22] Engels next provides a long chapter on the Great Towns, which is one of the earliest and still one of the great urban ethnographies. Next comes a chapter on Competition, which includes a rudimentary theory of wage determination as well as a theory of the 'reserve army of the unemployed'—the 'surplus' population in the business cycle.[23] Following a brief chapter on Irish immigration, Engels summarizes his findings on the overall condition of the proletariat in a long chapter entitled 'Results,' one of the earliest studies of what is today called 'social problems.'

Then Engels turns from the general to the more particular, addressing one chapter to the topic of Factory Hands (in the industries regulated by the various Factory Acts) including therein much material on the length of the working day, and another chapter to the remaining branches of industry.[24] Engels' discussion of these two portions of the labour force cumulates in a chapter on Labour Movements. Engels completes his book with chapters on the extra-urban working class—one on the Mining Proletariat and another on the Agricultural Proletariat—and a final chapter on the response of the bourgeoisie. This book is certainly one of the great, albeit early, works in the tradition of historical materialism.

In his letter of February 10, 1866, Marx recommended that Engels consider a second edition of that book. He was of the opinion that Engels could easily prepare the new edition, since only the *Children's Employment Commission Reports*, the *Factory Reports*, and the *Public Health Reports* were scientifically acceptable, and Engels was already quite familiar with these sources.

Thus, there is some reason to believe that the length of the working day and the associated issue of absolute surplus value were originally not to receive the attention which Marx bestows upon them in Chapter X, and that they were certainly not to be attended to so early in *Capital*.

Personal intentions aside, there is a logic inherent in *Capital* which imposes itself upon the text. The dialectical deduction of the categories of capital seems to require the explicit presentation of absolute value and the length of the working day. It will be recalled that the first volume of *Capital* is constituted by eight parts. Each part represents a major dialectical deduction. The dialectics of the initial five parts are directly relevant to this essay. Part One presents the dialectic of commodities (pp. 35-145). One commodity has the peculiar characteristic that it exchanges directly against all the rest; this necessitates the deduction of the universal commodity, money. Part Two presents the exchange of commodities at value (pp. 146-176). Another commodity has the peculiar characteristic that it generates self-expanding value; this necessitates the deduction of that special commodity, labour power. Part Three presents the labour process as it generates the necessary as well as the surplus portion of the labour product (pp. 177-311). Capitalism characteristically strives to enlarge the surplus portion. But this striving can move in two directions: the labour product, hence its surplus portion, can be enlarged by lengthening the working day, or else by intensifying labour and enhancing its productivity. The dialectical deduction of this characteristic of capitalism thus requires the determination of one of the alternatives in the resolution of the other.

It is abstractly conceivable that the intensity and productivity of labour would be determined, after which the length of the working day would be deduced. But Marx was quick to note that the intensity and productivity of labour is only limited by the development of the productive forces, while the length of the working day is 'naturally' limited. Indeed, as was suggested before, the limitation of the length of the working day may have been *so* natural that Marx was initially prepared to take it as predetermined. Further, such an abstract programme, determining initially the intensity and productivity of labour and then deducing the length of the working day, would overlook Hegel's distinction between extensive magnitude (Quantum) and intensive magnitude (Grad).[25] In any case, the correct dialectical deduction initially determines the length of the working day; once that is established, the striving of capitalism for more and more surplus value will necessarily turn to the intensification of labour and the enhancement of its productivity. Thus relative surplus value is dialectically deduced from the very restriction of absolute surplus value, and is presented in Part Four of volume one (pp. 312-507). Finally, Part Five presents the completed dialectics of surplus value, before turning, as already noted, to the elements of a theory of wages (pp. 508-534). These are the dialectics of the unity and difference of absolute and relative surplus value.

On the one side, Marx points out that the extension of labour time and the intensification of labour become contradictory at a certain nodal point of capitalist development (p. 409). Surplus value is thereafter differentiated. On the other side, Marx comments that 'any distinction between absolute and relative surplus value appears illusory.' This is because relative surplus value prolongs the working day beyond necessary labour time, hence has an absolute (extensive) moment. Likewise, absolute surplus value necessitates increased labour productivity so that necessary labour time can be shorter than the working day, hence it has a relative (intensive) moment (p. 511). Thus, surplus value is unitary.

We can now conclude this discussion. Whatever the theoretical preconceptions and practical obstacles with which Marx had to deal as he was engaged in the studies preparatory for *Capital*, his thought had matured by the time of writing the first volume to the point where Chapter X had become an integral part of the complex dialectic of the whole.

Even if the issues surrounding the development of the theory of absolute surplus value had been resolved, Chapter X of *Capital* has also suffered a number of misreadings. As might be expected in the cases of undialectical readings of *Capital*, some of the misreadings have been one-sidedly formalist: some have been just as one-sidedly empiricist. We have appended an example and critique of each, one due to Michio Morishima and one due to Edwin West. Such misreadings of Chapter X strongly invite, if not demand, our careful attention to the text.

The Regulation of Reproduction: The Working Day

In this part of the essay, we endeavor to provide a close reading of the text of Chapter X of *Capital*. As Blaug has informed us, 'one can never be certain that one has understood [Marx] until one has taken the trouble to translate his thoughts into one's own words.'[26] Such a reading discloses that the content of the chapter is four-fold. First, it provides further refinement of Marx's terminology and the framework of the analysis of capitalist production. Next, it indicates how unregulated capitalism tends towards the super-exploitation and ultimate destruction of labour power. Then, Marx turns to the historical struggle for the normal working day in England. From this discussion we derive Marx's model of the process of 'norming' the working day. Finally, Marx considers the implications for other countries of the English Ten-Hour Day movement.

Section 1, of Chapter X, addressing the 'Limits of the Working Day,' presents some definitions and analysis. The working day under the regime of capital has two parts—the part necessary for the production of the average daily means of subsistence, and the *surplus* part. The ratio of surplus/necessary working time is the rate of surplus value or *rate of exploitation*. As Marx observes, 'the rate of surplus value alone would not give us the extent of the working day' (p. 232).

The length of the working day varies within certain limits. The *maximum* limit is established by the necessity of non-labouring time for replenishing the organism, as well as for the cultural needs of humans. Under the regime of capital, of course, the *minimum* limit of the working day must exceed the necessary working time so that surplus labour generates surplus value; beyond this, the minimum limit is indeterminate. As Marx points out, 'both these limiting conditions are of a very elastic nature and allow the greatest latitude. So we find working-days of 8, 10, 12, 14, 16, 18 hours, i.e. of the most different lengths' (p. 232).

Capital seeks to maximize the working time of its employees, while labour seeks to expend only so much labour power as can be replenished by its earnings. There is no unique economic settlement of the bilateral relation between capital and labour, a conclusion which has been popularized by F.Y. Edgeworth.[27] Marx concludes this section by commenting that 'in the history of capitalist production, the determination of what is a working-day presents itself as the result of a struggle, a struggle between collective capital [Gesamtkapitalisten], i.e. the class of capitalists, and collective labour [Gesamtarbeiter] i.e. the working class' (p. 235).

Section 2 on the 'Greed for Surplus Labour' considers the intrinsic tendency of capitalism to lengthen the working day. While surplus labour is characteristic of many pre-capitalist forms, its maximization is the particular object of capital. This tendency is illustrated by a comparison of the corveé labour system of nineteenth century Roumania with the wage labour system of contemporaneous England. In the pre-capitalist form such as Roumania, legislation such as the Réglement Organique of 1831 sought to enlarge surplus labour. In the more mature capitalist form, by contrast, legislation such as the Factory Act of 1833 in Britain sought to regulate the excessive lengthening of the working day and the extreme abuses of child labour. Even so, capitalists manipulated the regulations to extend time even a few precious minutes a day.

But little else than regulation availed to limit these extensions and abuses. Marx points out that business crises may interrupt production and shorten the working week. But what we have come to call 'compulsory overtime' lengthens the working day for those employees not laid off (p. 241). Marx concludes Section 2 by reemphasizing that 'labour' is a collective term: 'The worker is . . . nothing more than personified labour-time.' And he notes that capitalism considers labourers in just this sense (p. 243; cf. also pp. 233, 264).

Having illustrated capitalism's tendency to lengthen the working day despite regulation, Marx turns in Section 3 to capitalism's tendencies when untrammeled. He recounts evidence, much of it official, of almost incredible overwork and abusive conditions of labour in eight industries: lacemaking, the pottery industry, the matchmaking, wallpaper and bakery industries, the millinery industry, the blacksmith trade and agriculture.[28] It is important to notice that these discussions do *not* depend upon interindustry comparisons of rates of surplus value, wage levels, etc. The general theory has not been sufficiently specified at this point in *Capital* to permit such comparisons. This is rather an institutional discussion of the effects of nonregulation, on the length of the working day, to be compared with the effects of state intervention.

Section 4 treats the 'Relay System' and 'Day and Night Work'. Today we refer to the Relay System as the 'Shift System'. Capital strives to operate at full capacity hence strives for round-the-clock production. This, conjoined to capitalism's tendency to lengthen the working day, tends to restrict possible lengths of the working day to proportional parts, e.g. 12 hours, 8 hours, 6 hours, etc. Capitalists in the nineteenth century seriously considered only the first of those possible lengths. The resulting twelve-hour working day proved quite destructive of labouring youth. This was especially true of those on the night shift.[29]

In Section 5 on Early Modern Laws for the Extension of the Working Day, Marx begins to discuss the struggle for the normal working day. He commences this section by reiterating that when capitalism lengthens the working day in its insatiable search for surplus value, it thereby raises the reproduction costs i.e., the value of labour power. Not only is a 'normal working day' in the interest of labourers but also 'It would seem therefore that the interest of capital itself points in the direction of a normal working day' (p. 266). However, the anarchy of capitalist production tends in the other direction. The conjunction of greed for surplus value plus the perception of an excess population turns capital (dem Kapitalisten im Allgemeinen) towards the squandering of the health of labourers, unless capital comes under some form of societal control (pp. 269-270).

Again, Marx notes that 'the establishment of a normal working day is the result of centuries of struggle between capitalist and labourer'. He continues that 'the history of this struggle shows two opposed tendencies' (p. 270). Immature capitalism had used state power to lengthen the working day as well as to 'free' labour from its own subsistence economy from fourteenth to mid-eighteenth century England. By contrast, the state begins to impose restrictions on the length of the working day for mature capitalism in England around the middle of the nineteenth century. The magnitude of the lengthening under immature capitalism 'approximately coincides' with the magnitude of the shortening under mature capitalism (p. 271).

This permits us to introduce the first moment of Marx's model of the process of the 'norming' of the working day. The length of the working day, T, at time t is a function of the length of the working day in the preceding period, $T(t-1)$, plus an increment, $C(t)$ which is an index of the maturity of capitalism at time t. Thus we have:

$$T(t) = T(t-1) + C(t)$$

where C is positive for all t's between 1400 and 1750 (the epoch of immature capitalism), is approximately equal to zero between 1750 and 1800, and is negative between 1800 and 1860 (the epoch of competitive capitalism).[30] If it is thought necessary to establish additional sub-periods in the development of capitalism, they can be introduced into the equation and will imply that C assumes different values through its positive range (corresponding to Goldstone's sub-periods 'A' and 'B') as well as through its negative range. Finally, any phases within the periods can similarly be introduced.[31]

Returning to Marx's historical account in Section 5, the Statute of Labourers of 1349 initiated a series of English statutes which lengthened and regulated the working day in the interest of extending absolute surplus labour time. This epoch of increasing and state-promoted industrial control over labour culminates in a 'House of Terror' which takes 'the shape of a gigantic "Workshop" for the industrial worker himself. It is called the Factory' (p. 277). This section closes with a striking evocation of the extreme control which maturing capitalism tends to establish over labour, an extreme which is also utterly deviant from the normal working day.

Section 6 continues the discussion of the Struggle for the Normal Working Day, reviewing the history of the English Factory Acts between 1833 and 1864. The maturing of capital implies the maturing of its labour. The resistance of labour to the excesses of capitalism's extension of the working day and to its other abuses at first secured only nominal concessions, such as the Factory Acts of 1819, 1825, and 1831. Finally, the Factory Act of 1833 established 'a normal working day' for cotton, wool, flax (linen), and silk factories. Engels has already discussed the background and passage of this Act in some detail.[32] For his part, Marx focuses upon the eight-hour day which was required for children under thirteen years of age. This regulation was included in the Act of 1833 due to fear for the very existence of the working class in the face of capitalism's untrammeled abuse of child labour.[33] In his legislative history of the Act of 1833, Marx recounts how the Whig government, under pressure from the manufacturers, proposed but failed to limit the eight-hour day to children under twelve years of age. This point about the lobbying efforts of capital is symptomatic of the history of the Factory Acts. As Marx put it, 'nothing is more characteristic of the Spirit of Capital than the history of the English Factory Acts' (p. 279).

By 1844, the combined pressure of the gentry—seeking revenge for the Free Traders' repeal of the Corn Laws—and the Chartists was sufficient to force the passage of a new Factory Act which placed adult women under protection, limiting their working day to twelve hours. After listing some of the details of these Factory Acts, Marx continues that 'these minutiae which . . . regulate by stroke of the clock the times, limits, pauses of work, were not at all the products of Parliamentary fancy. They developed gradually out of circumstances as natural laws of the modern mode of production. Their formulation, official recognition, and proclamation by the State, were the result of a long struggle of classes' (p. 283). Of course, such regulations, themselves the outcome of class struggle, acted dialectically back upon the ongoing class struggle. As Marx points out, 'one of their first consequences was that in practice the working-day of the adult males in factories became subject to the same limitations, since in most processes of production the cooperation of the children, young children, and women is indispensable' (p. 283). The conjunction of Factory Acts and the exigencies of modern industrial production created new norms. 'On the whole, therefore, during the period from 1844 to 1847 the twelve-hour working day became general and uniform in all branches of industry under the Factory Act' (p. 283).

With Chartism and the Ten-Hours agitation at their peak, a new Factory Act was passed in 1847, restricting the working day of youth and women to ten hours, effective May 1, 1848. As Engels recounted it a few years later, since these labourers and children are 'the decisive categories of workers in the factories, the necessary consequence was that the factories were able to work only ten hours daily.'[34] Marx now recounts the lobby efforts of capital against this legislation. The manufactures initially attempted to reduce wages by at least 25 per cent under the pretext of the reduced working day. Then they sought to enlist the factory workers to agitate for repeal of the 1847 Act (p. 284). He mentions three examples of the lobby efforts of the capitalists.

First, the manufacturers prepared petitions for workers to sign, complaining about the consequences of the Act. The petitioners later testified that their signatures were extorted from them. Next, the manufacturers declared in the name of labour that it was the factory inspectors, and not the workers, who wanted the Ten-Hour Day. Marx continues that 'this manoeuvre also failed. Factory Inspector Leonard Horner conducted in his own person, and through his sub-inspectors, many examinations of witnesses in the factories of Lancashire. About 70% of the workers [Arbeiter] examined declared in favour of ten hours, a much smaller percentage in favour of eleven [hours], and an altogether insignificant minority for the old twelve hours.'[35] Finally, the manufacturers obliged adult males to work overtime, then publicized this as evidence of the workers' desires. Many of these overtime workers, when examined by Horner, indicated that 'they would much prefer working ten hours for less wages, but they had no choice' (p. 285). In each of these examples of capitalism's lobby efforts against the Act of 1847, the point of the evidence which Marx adduces is that 'neither lies, bribery nor threats were spared in this attempt' (p. 284). As Engels had commented on the manufacturers response to the Act of 1844, 'they have used every honorable and dishonorable means against this dreaded measure'.[36] Exhorted signatures invalidate a petition and signatures were extorted. The vast majority of working men ('about 70%') reported that they wanted the Ten-Hour Day—whether or not the factory inspectors also wanted the shorter working day. Finally, *compulsory* overtime provides no evidence for working men's desires for a shorter working day.

Marx concludes that the 'campaign of Capital thus came to grief, and the Ten Hours Act came into force May 1, 1848' (p. 285). But that did not mean the end of class struggle. Engels has provided some contemporary documentation of this in his article on 'The Ten Hours Question', published in the *Democratic Review* in 1850, which he amplified upon in 'The English Ten Hours Bill' for the *Neue Rheinische Zeitung: Politische-okonomische Revue*, also in 1850.[37] Marx goes on to indicate the ups and downs of the class struggle well into the 1860s, and the resultant variation in the regulation of the working day. He sums up this section by noting the societal consequences of the establishment of the normal working day in England. 'The Principle had triumphed with its victory in those great branches of industry which form the most characteristic creation of the modern mode of production. Their wonderful development from 1853 to 1860, hand-in-hand with the physical and moral regeneration of the factory workers, struck the most purblind' (p. 295). These observations echo those Marx had already expressed in late 1864 in his 'Inaugural Address of the Working Men's International Association'.

Here we can introduce the second and concluding moment of Marx's model of the process of the regulating of the working day. The length of the working day by regulation, T, at point in time t is a function of three elements: the length of the working day by regulation in the preceeding period, T(t − 1), the balance of forces in the class struggle, S, at time t, and the already introduced index of the maturity of capitalism, C, at time t. Thus we have:

$$T(t) = S(t) \, T(t - 1) + C(t)$$

where C(t) takes the values noted in the preceeding equation and the value of S(t) approaches or drops below –1 as class struggle intensifies and approaches zero or becomes positive as class struggle moderates. Thus S can be taken as an index of interclass harmony. We can conclude that:

A *uniform* working day tends to be established where

$$0 > S(t) > -1; \; t = 1, 2, 3, \ldots$$

A *normal* working day tends to be established where

$$\sum_{1400} C(t) = 0; \; t = 1, 2, 3, \ldots$$

The uniformity and the norming of the working day are thus mathematically independent, reflecting the independence of the two aspects—class struggle and the maturity of capitalism—in social reality.

There are time periods and social forms where the working day is of uniform but abnormal length; an example would be a Fascist regime. There are also time periods and social forms where the working days tend to be, on the average, of normal length, but they are not uniform; examples would be provided by settler colonies which have a racially fragmented working class or societies which are in an acutely revolutionary phase. In the first of these cases of the normal working day, the index of interclass harmony tends to be high and even positive due to false consciousness and racist collaboration of elements of the working class with their capitalist exploiters. In the second case, the index of interclass harmony tends to fall below –1, suggesting the imminent collapse of the regime.

In the 7th and concluding section of Chapter X, Marx completes his study of the struggle for the normal working day in England by examining the implications of this struggle for other countries. He makes two major points by way of generalization. First, the excesses of capitalism's exploitation of labour commence in those industries where capitalism initially creates the modern mode of production; then the excesses follow the development of capitalism into the remaining industries. Societal regulation follows in the train of capitalism's excesses, hence factory regulation and the limitation of the working day initially seem to be 'exceptional legislation'. With capitalism's conquest of all of English industry by the middle of the nineteenth century, the scope of factory legislation comes to be extended as well, resulting in the 'triumph in Principle' of the normal working day. Second, the history of the struggle for the normal working day indicates that the isolated labourer has no power of resistance to the excesses capitalism. The struggle for the normal working day is collective, an element of the 'protracted civil war' between the classes. The necessity of collective action pertains to groups of labourers as well as to individual workers.

Whenever the working class is divided, as in the antebellum United States by slavery and racism, its struggle will be paralyzed. As Marx put it: 'Labour cannot emancipate itself in the white skin where in the black it is branded' (p. 301).

Thereupon Marx concludes this section as well as the chapter on the working day with a stirring call to action: 'The labourers must put their heads together and, as a class, compel the passing of a law, an all-powerful social barrier that shall prevent the very workers from selling, by voluntary contract with Capital, themselves and their families into slavery and death' (p. 302). One theoretical implication of such a 'legally limited' and normal working day has already been noted. Such an 'all-powerful social barrier' to labour's imprudent disposition of its vital powers is no less a barrier to capitalism's extension of the working day; it restricts the expansion of *absolute* surplus value. Capital must thereby find another means for its insatiable drive for self-expansion. Thus, the dialectical deduction of the subsequent category of *Capital*, that of *relative* surplus value.[38]

Implications of Marx's Analysis of the Norming of the Working Day

In Chapter X Marx discussed the struggle for the 'norming' of the working day which occurred in England during the early and middle parts of the nineteenth century. In this section we will show that similar struggles were being carried out in other countries; this provides some evidence of the salience of Marx and Engels' original analysis. Furthermore, we point out that the struggle for a shorter working day almost always began at the shop level, usually in the form of strikes, but was not generally successful until the working class was able to force the state to act.

The struggle for a short working day began during the late part of the eighteenth and the early part of the nineteenth centuries. Between 1825-27 there was a series of strikes by French workers in Paris, Marseilles, Commentry, Toulon, Ulm, and Saint Cantin. In Rouen the spinners went on strike in 1830. A major issue in most of these strikes was the demand by workers for a shorter working day.[39] Between 1830 and 1844, according to the Swiss historian Aguet, there were 382 strikes in France and many of these included demands about the length of the working day.[40]

The struggle for a shorter work day in the United States has a long history. It begins with the carpenters in Philadelphia who struck for a shorter work day in 1791. In the 1820s strikers began demanding a ten hour day as evidenced by the strikes of the Boston carpenters in 1825 and the Philadelphia general strike of 1827 which was started by the workers on the Schuylkill River coal wharves, demanding higher wages and a ten hour day.[41] Furthermore, in the four years between 1833 and 1837 there were 168 strikes in the United States and 26 were for a ten hour day.[42] By 1862, Canadian trade unions were also assisting each other in strikes for shorter working hours.[43]

Similar struggles took place in Germany, Italy, Spain, Sweden and Russia, principally in the latter half of the nineteenth century. In these countries the industrial revolution occurred at a later date which explains why the strike movement did not emerge as early as it did in France, Britain and the United States. In addition, strike movements emerged in Australia, Chile, Cuba, Brazil, and China. Almost all of these strikes put forward economic demands and prominent among these was the demand for the shortening or at least the preservation of the length of the former working day.[44]

The early strike movement was thus characterized by spontaneous action on the part of workers to win certain economic demands, including the demand for a shorter working day. Later this spontaneity was transformed into more organized forms of struggle with the development of the trade union movement. As the class struggle began to take on more organized forms workers began to realize that there were limits to what could be won through the struggle of workers at the shop level. Thus, the working class turned to political struggle using strikes and other forms of protest to force the bourgeois state to pass legislation to further workers' economic demands. Initially, the political struggle for the shorter working day emerged as a struggle to shorten the working day for women and children. For example, in Paterson, New Jersey, children in the textile mills went on strike in July 1835 to reduce the working day to 11 hours and 9 hours on Saturday. During this strike the parents of the striking children formed the 'Paterson Association for the Protection of the Working Classes of Paterson', and they called for the support of workers in neighbouring towns.[45] As a result of these types of struggles, laws limiting the working day to ten hours were passed in New Hampshire, Pennsylvania, Maine, Rhode Island, California, Ohio, and Connecticut between 1847 and 1855.[46] Similar struggles took place in Great Britain leading to the passage of the Factory Acts and in Russia a massive strike movement in 1896 forced the government to pass a Factory Law limiting the working day to eleven and a half hours in 1897.[47] In speaking of the significance of this particular law Lenin wrote: 'The significance of the new factory law lies, on the one hand . . . in its having been *won* from the police government by the united and class-conscious workers . . . On the other hand . . . it necessarily and inevitably *gives a fresh impetus* to the Russian working class movement.' He continued: 'It will provide a splendid, convenient, and *lawful* opportunity for the workers to present their *demands*, to uphold their *interpretation of the law* . . . to press for more favourable terms when concluding *new agreements* on overtime, and to press for *higher pay*, so that the reduction of the working day may really benefit the workers . . .'[48]

All these experiences suggest that the struggle for the shorter work day and for the 'norming' of the work day is an integral part of class struggle. In addition, the history of the struggle for the shorter work day reveals that the working class must advance and fight for this demand as a political demand if it is to be successful.

Conclusion

This chapter shows that the struggle over the length of the working day as an element in the struggle over the conditions of social reproduction is a reflection of the basic contradiction of capitalism, namely the social production of commodities by the working class and the private appropriation of those commodities by the capitalist class. The 'laws of motion' of capitalism are subject neither to the desires of capitalists nor workers. Rather they are the outcome of a mode of production based on antagonistic social relations, and it is this essential feature which dictates the terms of the struggle over the length of the working day. The capitalist class strives continually to lengthen the working day. However, this drive is opposed by the working class whose standard of living is determined by the class struggle in relation to the degree of development of the forces of production. The dynamics of social development, as worked out by Marx and Engels, contend that history is directional, whereby higher socioeconomic formations replace the lower forms. It is this 'directionality' which influences the nature and the eventual outcome of the struggle over the length of the working day.

This means that the 'norming' of the working day and those aspects of reproduction which are covered under the normal working day is the outcome of the class struggle which occurs within bounds set by social and historical terms. Thus, the struggle for shorter hours initially manifested itself as a struggle within the boundaries of a particular country at a particular time. However, these bounds were soon transcended since the very process of the development of capitalism tended toward an internationalization of production. The 'norming' of the working day in one country had an effect on other countries such that it is possible to detect a tendency towards the 'norming' of the working day for the international working class.

The initial struggle for the shorter working day occurred spontaneously. However, in many countries this spontaneity crystallized in the development of trade unions which in turn struggled with individual capitalists or groups of capitalists over basic economic questions which included the length of the working day. In many instances the working class quickly learned that even such militant and determined struggle as exemplified by the early strike movements was insufficient. Gains made in one shop or with one capitalist could quickly be negated by capitalist competition if not by changes in economic conditions. Thus, the class struggle could not remain at the level of a single shop or at the individual enterprise level, but rather had to enter the terrain of political struggle where the working class, as a class, challenged the entire capitalist class. In fact, this tendency is central to political struggle under capitalism.

Thus, the working class in many countries quickly realized that to win a shorter workday it would have to win a concession from the entire capitalist class and that this necessitated political action to bring pressure on the state. The role of the struggle in the local shop, the struggle with the individual capitalist was thus gradually transformed. It served to pressure the capitalist into acquiescing to political concessions at a societal level. If the working class was strong enough to win concessions at the individual shop level then these particular capitalists could only protect their interests by pressing all capitalists to make the same concessions. Here it is important to note that this political struggle, taking place within the context of the bourgeois state, did not require that the working class be enfranchised or have its representatives elected to office, although for the working class this is clearly a desirable goal. Even under the difficult conditions of political dictatorship the working class is sometimes able to carry on political struggle. Indeed, in the early struggles for the shorter workday workers could not vote and had no representatives in legislative bodies, but nonetheless the capitalist class was forced to shorten the working day through legislation and state regulation.

Today the working class is under a new and intensified attack and this attack is an expression of the qualitative deepening of the general crisis of capitalism. Through a series of austerity programs in Britain, the United States and elsewhere, this attack attempts to lower the standard of living of the working class. To a degree the capitalist class has succeeded in obtaining certain concessions from the working class by using the reserve army of the unemployed as a lever against those who are employed. The threat of unemployment has caused workers to make concessions regarding wages and benefits and has led to the lengthening of the working day through the use of both 'voluntary' and compulsory overtime. In this context the campaign for a shorter working day remains as crucial an element of the class struggle as it was over one hundred years ago when Marx wrote his chapter on the working day.

Appendix

As we observed above, the text of Chapter X is not without its difficulties, and we have addressed Marx's changing intentions and the maturing of his thought regarding the significance of absolute surplus labour time in the social reproduction of capitalism in an attempt to clarify some of these difficulties. But some of the difficulties regarding Chapter X seem to lie in the 'reception' of the text, rather than its 'creation'.

In his 'Ontologie', Georg Lukács has discussed the 'speculative conceptions' of formalist thinking and the 'merely notational ideas' of empiricism which are symptomatic of much of bourgeois thought; as has been suggested elsewhere, both lead ultimately to abstractly inchoate terminology and conceptualization.[49] In this Appendix we will briefly consider examples of each, before turning to the neoclassical economists' discussion of the 'norming' of the working day. In the writings of the neoclassicists, it will be evident that they concurred with Marx on this point if on no other.

A Formalist Misreading of Chapter X

In Michio Morishima's well-known neoclassical book, *Marx's Economics*, we find an example of a formalist misreading of Chapter X. As we shall see, Morishima confuses the abstract and the concrete in his discussion of the rate of exploitation and the length of the working day.[50] He correctly defines the rate of exploitation (e) as the ratio of unpaid labour $(T - \wedge B)$ to paid labour $(\wedge B)$. He supposes that the rate of exploitation across industries must be equal, i.e. $e(i) = e(j)$ for all industries (i,j), and he concludes that equal rates of exploitation imply a uniform length of the working day, $T(i) = T(j)$.[51] However, this formalist analysis confounds the abstract and the concrete.

Marx makes clear as he defines the rate of exploitation in Volume 1 of *Capital* that he is working at a fairly high level of abstraction, i.e. defining the rate of exploitation as a relationship between two classes. At such a level of abstraction, more concrete determinations such as the distinction of the gender of the labourer, or the heterogeneity of labour cannot be made (p. 198). Likewise, a distinction cannot be made between industries; instead, the rate of exploitation across industries is *identical*, i.e. $e(i) \equiv e(j)$, and the length of the working day is also taken as being equal across the economy.

At the level of the more concrete, by contrast, the specification by industry of rates of exploitation $[e(i), e(j)]$ extends not only to the length of the working day $[T(i), T(j)]$ but to variable capital as well $[V(i), V(j)]$. Marx has indicated that labour power can be sold above its value (p. 519) and 'in actual practice' can be sold below its value as well (p. 314, also p. 527). Thus we have:

$$\{ T(i) > T(j) \} \longrightarrow \{ V(i) > V(j) \} \ v \{ e(i) > e(j) \} \ v \{ [V(i) > V(j)] \ \& \ [e(i) > e(j)] \}$$

Algebraically, such an equation with two unknowns is indeterminate; as Marx would have put it, for the level of the concrete, labour's tendency to migrate between industries due to shorter hours would be cancelled out by its mobility due to lower wages. This is a circumstance where 'the price of labour power and the degree of its exploitation cease to be commensurable quantities' (p. 527).

Thus, on his own terms Morishima must maintain his formalist analysis either at the level of the abstract or else at the level of the concrete; he cannot confound the two levels. At the first level, determinations by industry cannot be made; at the second, they can be made, but no determinate argument follows. Trapped in the terms of traditional logic, Morishima cannot undertake the requisite dialectical deduction. According to Marx's well-known 'Method of Political Economy', science necessarily advances from the abstract to the concrete. As John Weeks has put it in his critique of Morishima, 'the societal rate of surplus value [must be] established prior to considering many capitals'.[52] Commencing as he does with the particulars, trapped as he is in the terms of the traditional logic, Morishima's formalist analysis finally shades over into empiricism.[53]

An Empiricist Misreading of Chapter X

Edwin West's recent article in the *Journal of Political Economy* provides a straightforward example of an empiricist misreading of Chapter X.[54] West follows Mark Blaug in supposing that the empirical testing of hypotheses is the *sine qua non* of scientificity.[55] The methodological merits of such Popperian positivism have been noted elsewhere[56] and in any case it is no substitute for theorizing. Unfortunately, West gives no indication that he understands that theorizing is a precondition of hypothesis testing. He presents several hypotheses regarding the length of the working day:[57]

(1) The labour supply schedule has an elasticity of −1, i.e. it is a 'backward-bending labour supply curve'.
(2) The variance in hours of the working day will be almost negligible.
(3) The length of the working day rises during the slump in the business cycle and falls during the boom.
(4) The length of the working day will increase with the accumulation of capital.

On the one hand, hypotheses 1, 2, and 4 are not derived from Marx's writings at all. The first is due to Robert Eagly; West acknowledges that this hypothesis is 'Eagly's version of Marx's reasoning'.[58] The second hypothesis is due to Morishima, as we have already noted. The fourth is due to West's conflating of two distinct propositions advanced by Fred Gottheil; West suggests that this hypothesis 'has been drawn from Marx's argument' but might better have said it was spun from West's own imagination.[59] As we have already observed, Marx held that the length of the working day would be *normed* with the development of capitalism, and this norming would tend both to *shorten* the average length of the working day and to make them of uniform length.

On the other hand, West's 'tests' of these hypotheses, to whomever they are properly attributed and from whatever theory they are validly deduced, can charitably be described as nothing but sophomoric. Regarding hypothesis 1: The supposition that the elasticity of labour supply is −1 stems from a misinterpretation of Marx. Eagly assumes that the value of labour power is fixed at the subsistence level. Thus when wages rise, hours must decline so that the labourers remain at subsistence. However, this ignores Marx's clear statement (see our footnote 6), that the value of labour power includes a social, cultural and historical element.

Regarding hypothesis 2: West supposes that a 95 per cent confidence interval of $9.73 < \mu < 11.54$ hours shows that the 'spread' of the mean hours of work (around the length of the Ten Hour Day) is 'still significant'.[60] The problem, however, is that of the comparison of the variances of the lengths of the working day through time. This problem cannot be addressed through the use of cross-sectional data.

Regarding hypothesis 3: West supposes that the lengthening of the working day during the slump in the business cycle is disproved by 'the reduction in the length of the average work week' as though days and weeks were the same.[61] Such evidence as is available, for instance Hopkins' reappraisal of working hours and conditions in the Industrial Revolution, suggests that 'hours were notoriously long' in the English metal-working industries such as the nail-making industry, for example, and the hours were 'especially long when trade was depressed. Thus, in 1812 a working day might stretch to 16 or even 18 hours . . .'[62] As West acknowledges, Hopkins used 'evidence that was accessible to Marx'.[63] On the contrary, the evidence which West adduces, namely that of the NBER Business Cycle Indicators, is confounded by issues of time-and-a-half pay for overtime, benefits, etc. which were unknown in the nineteenth century.

Regarding hypothesis 4: West supposes that Joseph Zeisel's study of changes in the length of the work week during the past century bears on the question of the length of the working day. Zeisel's 'systematic facts' do indicate that the length of the work week on the average declined from 66-70 hours per week in 1850 to 44 hours per week in 1940, to 40 hours per week in 1956.[64] This is precisely what Marx and Engels anticipated in their support for the Ten Hour and later the Eight Hour movements.

West concludes his argument by stating that 'the results of (his article) have at least as serious implications for Marx's labour theory as those connected with the famous 'great contradiction' that Böhm-Bawerk attempted to demonstrate' and that 'the substance of discussion has [clearly] been far from trivial'.[65]

So here we have it: misreadings of Chapter X of *Capital* of the first magnitude. However, when we turn to the neoclassical economists themselves we find a rather different understanding of the issue of the length of the working day.

The Neoclassicists on the 'Norming' of the Working Day

William Stanley Jevons held that 'a free labourer . . . will cease to labour just at the point where the pain becomes equal to the pleasure gained . . .'[66] This proposition contradicts the concept of the norming of the working day, since Marx holds that the length of the working day does not depend upon the sentiments of the worker. It is a testament to the accuracy of Marx's analysis that, with few exceptions such as Chayanov,[67] the neoclassical economists since Jevons' time have tended to concur with Marx's point. Böhm-Bawerk, for example, pointed out that the burden of labour can be varied in two ways, by varying the *extension* of the working day and by varying the *intensity* of labour.[68] The 'debate' on this issue between Böhm-Bawerk on the one hand, and Edgeworth and his 'English and American colleagues' on the other hand, focussed on the empirical relevance rather than the formal validity of Jevons' proposition. As Böhm-Bawerk puts it, 'this rule [of Jevons] has no wider application than is justified by the assumption upon which it is based; namely, that the labourer is entirely free to determine how long he will continue his daily labour'. He continues that 'in most branches of production the labourer is not free to determine the length of his working day'. Böhm-Bawerk concludes, and this should be stressed, that 'the hours of labour are fixed more or less by custom or law'.[69]

Alfred Marshall did have his points of disagreement with Böhm-Bawerk. But the two can only be read as concurring on the issue of the norming of the working day. When discussing the extension of the working day, Marshall held that 'if [the labourer] has to work with others, the length of his day's work is often fixed for him'.[70] Finally, George Stigler discusses 'Hours of Work' under the heading 'Wages Under Competition', hence is addressing the topic of Jevons' 'free labourer' in contrast, say, to the unionized labour discussed under the heading 'Noncompetitive Wages'.[71] Stigler cannot be read as promoting a model of worker's choice of the length of the working day; instead his terms specify only a model of *alternative norms* of hours of work. Stigler's discussion is not only restricted to the latter, but to a model of *relatively uniform* hours of work as well. 'It will remain true that anyone whose tastes differ greatly from those of his fellows will be compelled to pay a substantial price [by way of choices of work] to behave differently.'[72] Thus, even the neoclassical economists appear to concur with the notion of the 'norming' of the working day.

Notes and References

1. See, for instance, V. I. Lenin *Collected Works* (Progress Publishers, Moscow, 1964), Volume 25, p. 357.
2. Marshall Sahlins, 'La première société d'abondance', *Les Temps Modernes*, No. 268 (1968), pp. 641-680.
3. G.E.M. de Ste. Croix, *Class Struggle in the Ancient Greek World* (Cornell University Press, Ithaca, NY, 1981).
4. Karl Marx *Capital* (International Publishers, New York, 1967), Volume I, p. 171. As Emmett has observed, this might better be expressed as 'a definite quantity of energy or force from human muscle . . . is wasted and this requires to be restored'; Wm. Henry Emmett, *The Marxian Economic*

Handbook and Glossary (International Publishers, New York, 1925), p. 15, also pp. 132-3, note.

5. For comments on this doctrine ranging across the political spectrum, see Wilhelm Röpke, *A Humane Economy* (Henry Regnery Company, Chicago, 1960), p. 137 ff.; and Raymond Williams, *The Sociology of Culture* (Schocken Books, New York, 1982), p. 101 ff.

6. Marx, *Capital*, Volume 1, p. 171. All subsequent references to this volume of *Capital* will be cited parenthetically in the text, for instance as (p. 171).

7. These tend to be strategic rather than the merely empirical or technical problems discussed by Hayek in his critique of post-capitalist society; see Friedrich A. Hayek, *Collectivist Economic Planning* (George Routledge and Sons, London, 1935).

8. In *Capital* Marx explicitly recognized that such an element would 'enter into the determination of the value of labour power' (p. 519, also p. 559). Richard Cantillon had discussed this as early as his *Essai* of 1755.

9. This is the so-called 'family wage,' where the labour power of the 'unemployed' adult as well as the immature replacements must be provided for in the value of the labour power of the employed. The qualification 'at least' accommodates the element of risk in human reproduction.

10. This is the so-called 'dual career family', where the sum of the values of the labour power is equal to that of the 'family wage'.

11. B. N. Ponomarev *et al*, *The International Working Class Movement* (Progress Publishers, Moscow, 1980), Volume 1, p. 180.

12. Karl Marx and Frederick Engels, *Werke* (Dietz Verlag, Berlin, 1965), Bd. 31, S. 174.

13. Karl Marx, *Grundrisse*, in Marx and Engels, *Werke*, Bd. 42, S. 276; absolute and relative surplus value are discussed at S. 321-22.

14. Marx and Engels, *Werke*, Bd. 42, S. 254.

15. Ibid., S. 258-59.

16. Ibid., S. 262.

17. Karl Marx, *Theories of Surplus Value* (Foreign Languages Publishing House, Moscow, 1963), Part I, p. 401.

18. Ibid., p. 392.

19. Robert Payne, *Marx* (Simon and Schuster, New York, 1968), pp. 348-49.

20. Karl Marx and Frederick Engels, *Collected Works* (International Publishers, New York, 1975), Volume 4, p. 297 ff; see also Steven Marcus, *Engels, Manchester, and the Working Class* (Random House, New York, 1974).

21. Marx and Engels, *Collected Works*, Volume 4, p. 302.

22. Mark Blaug, *A Methodological Appraisal of Marxian Economics* (North-Holland, Amsterdam, 1980), p. 43 informs us that this concept is 'found in John Stuart Mill', although the *Principles of Political Economy* was not published until 1848.

23. Blaug, *Methodological Appraisal of Marxian Economics*, pp. 43-44 observes that the concept of the business cycle, too, was found in Mill.

24. The significance of Engels' distinction between 'factory hands' and workers in the other branches of industry has recently been emphasized by Hopkins in his reappraisal of working conditions during the Industrial Revolution; see Eric Hopkins 'Working Hours and Conditions During the Industrial Revolution', *Economic History Review*, Volume 35 (1982), pp. 52-66. This

article points out the irregularity of the working day in those industries not yet absorbed into the 'factory system'.

25. G.W.F. Hegel, *Werke* (Suhrkamp Verlag, Frankfurt am Main, 1970), Bd. 8, S. 216 ff.

26. Blaug, *Methodological Appraisal of Marxian Economics*, p. 1.

27. Francis Y. Edgeworth, *Mathematical Psychics* (C. Kegan Paul & Co., London, 1881), p. 29 ff.

28. See also Marx and Engels *Collected Works*, Volume 4, pp. 481-500, and pp. 548-561. Regarding agriculture, Joseph Zeisel, 'The Workweek in American Industry: 1850-1956,' *Monthly Labor Review*, Volume 81 (1958), p. 25, pp. 27-28, has documented the uniformly much longer work week here when compared to all other occupations, from 1850 up to 1956.

29. See also Marx and Engels, *Collected Works*, Volume 4, p. 444.

30. This periodization corresponds to that of Jack Goldstone 'A New Historical Materialism', *Contemporary Sociology*, Volume 12, No. 5 (1983), pp. 487-90, which periodizes the account given in E. A. Wrigley and R. S. Shofield, *The Population History of England: 1541-1871* (Harvard University Press, Cambridge, Mass. 1981.) Goldstone finds a 'Preindustrial' period up to 1751, and 'Early Industrial' period from 1751 to 1816, and an 'Industrial' period after 1819. The difference between the commencement of the final periods is due to Goldstone's inclusion of the Napoleonic era in his 'Early Industrial' period.

31. This points to Marx's demographic insight that 'every special historical mode of production has its own special laws of population, historically valid within its limits alone'. *Capital*, Volume I, p. 632; see also Engels' letter to Lange, March 29, 1865, in *Werke*, Bd. 31, S. 466-67.

32. Marx and Engels, *Collected Works*, Volume 4, pp. 442-44; 460-462.

33. See also Zeisel, 'The Workweek in American Industry', p. 25.

34. Marx and Engels, *Collected Works*, Volume 10, p. 297.

35. It should be noted here that both context—(the lobbying efforts Marx is recounting addressed the desirability of a Ten-Hour Day for adult males)—and the text itself—(in a footnote to the cited sentence Marx indicates that 'adult male labourers were examined')—require that 'workpeople' or 'Arbeiter' be read in the masculine gender. Edwin West, 'Marx's Hypotheses on the Length of the Working Day', *Journal of Political Economy*, Volume 91, no. 2, pp. 266-281, fails to observe this and hence incorrectly accuses Marx of misrepresenting Horner's survey results.

36. Marx and Engels, *Collected Works*, Volume 4, p. 465.

37. See Marx and Engels, *Collected Works*, Volume 10, pp. 271-76 and pp. 288-300.

38. Emmett, *Marxian Economic Handbook*, p. 155, also p. 238, has suggested that Chapter XI of *Capital*, which completes Part 3 and is thus interposed between Chapter X and Part 4, in fact 'constitutes an appendix to this part'.

39. Ponomarev *et al*, *International Working Class Movement*, Volume I, p. 200.

40. Ibid., p. 201.

41. Philip Foner, *A History of the Labor Movement in the United States* (International Publishers, New York, 1975), Volume I, pp. 115-17.

42. Ponomarev *et al*, *International Working Class Movement*, Volume 1, p.

203.

43. Steven Langdon, 'The Emergence of the Canadian Working Class Movement, 1845-75', *Journal of Canadian Studies*, Volume 8, no. 2 (1973).

44. Ponomarev et al, *International Working Class Movement*, Volume 1, p. 209.

45. Foner, *History of the Labor Movement in the United States*, Volume I, p. 111.

46. Labor Research Association, *History of the Shorter Workday* (International Publishers, New York, 1942), p. 13.

47. Lenin, *Collected Works*, Volume 2, p. 271.

48. Ibid., pp. 302-03.

49. G. Welty, 'Marx, Engels, and 'Anti-Dühring', *Political Studies*, Volume 31 (1983), p. 293.

50. Michio Morishima, *Marx's Economics* (Cambridge University Press, Cambridge, 1973), p. 47 ff.

51. Ibid., p. 52.

52. John Weeks, *Capital and Exploitation* (Princeton University Press, Princeton, NJ 1981), p. 67.

53. Ibid., p. 71.

54. West, 'Marx's Hypotheses'.

55. Blaug, *Methodological Appraisal of Marxian Economics*, Chapter 2.

56. G. Welty, 'Giffen's Paradox and Falsifiability', *Weltwirtschaftliches Archiv*, Bd. 107, Heft 1 (1971), S. 139-46. See also Igor Naletov, *Alternatives to Positivism* (Progress Publishers, Moscow, 1984).

57. See West, 'Marx's Hypotheses', p. 271, p. 272, p. 278, and p. 278, respectively.

58. Robert Eagly, *The Structures of Classical Economic Theory* (Oxford University Press, London, 1974), p. 106; see West 'Marx's Hypotheses', p. 276.

59. Fred Gottheil, *Marx's Economic Predictions* (Northwestern University Press, Evanston, 1966), p. 34, also pp. 194-95; see also West, 'Marx's Hypotheses', p. 278.

60. West, 'Marx's Hypotheses', p. 267.

61. Ibid., p. 278.

62. Eric Hopkins, 'Working Hours and Conditions During the Industrial Revolution', *Economic History Review*, Volume 35 (1982), p. 61.

63. West 'Marx's Hypotheses', p. 279.

64. Zeisel, 'The Workweek in American Industry', p. 24.

65. West, 'Marx's Hypotheses', pp. 279-80.

66. William Stanley Jevons, *The Theory of Political Economy* (Penguin Books Harmondsworth, 1970), p. 194.

67. Alexander V. Chayanov, *The Theory of Peasant Economy*, (Richard D. Irwin, Inc., Homewood, Illinois, 1966), p. xvii and p. 81.

68. Eugen Böhm-Bawerk, *Capital and Interest* (Libertarian Press, South Holland, Illinois, 1959), Volume 2, p. 178.

69. Eugen Böhm-Bawerk, 'The Ultimate Standard of Value', *Annals of the American Academy of Political and Social Science*, Volume 5, no. 2 (1894), p. 23.

70. Alfred Marshall, *Principles of Economics*, 8th edn (Macmillian, London, 1920), p. 438.

71. George J. Stigler, *The Theory of Price*, 3rd edn (Macmillian, New York, 1966), pp. 263-70.
72. Ibid., p. 265.

PART IV

CONTRADICTIONS IN SOCIAL REPRODUCTION UNDER CAPITALISM

10

RETIREMENT PENSIONS: REINFORCED EXPLOITATION

James Stafford

The intention of this chapter is to describe the effects of private retirement pensions from a critical perspective that focuses on their implications for social reproduction. The popular characterization of such pensions is one of beneficence wherein pension plans are seen as a reflection of the largesse of employers who match employee contributions to help them prevail in their retirement years. Pensions are thus perceived as a form of benevolent paternalism wherein, although employees are required to make contributions, it is in their own long term interest to do so.

There is truth in the argument that workers benefit from pensions because they would not otherwise accumulate savings to the same extent; but other hidden truths about pensions need to be exposed. Deductions from the worker's paycheck are held in trust for long periods, sometimes 30 to 40 years, during which time they are used to further the interests of capital and to reinforce the rate of exploitation of workers. They also operate to stabilize and fragment the work force, thus camouflaging the class struggle and muting the efforts of labour to gain power and raise wages.

The following section will provide an outline of the theoretical framework embodied in this chapter. The class struggle and the structure of capitalism lead to a crisis of accumulation and a need to reinforce the exploitation of labour by capital. This results in certain policies adopted by capital to maintain its dominant position, one of which is the utilization of pensions to increase accumulation and control the labour force.

The second section provides an historical account of the rise of pensions in Canada and of the circumstances leading to their prominence. The advent of public pensions was a crucial part of the rise of the welfare state whereas the first private pension schemes were introduced as a means of cutting out less competent, but loyal workers.

The introduction of pension terms into union-management negotiations half a century later caused considerable manipulations on the
part of management to turn such concessions to its own advantage.

The third section places pension plans within the theoretical
framework described in the first section. Examples are presented to
support the argument that pension plans, although they benefit most
individual recipients, are a form of reinforced exploitation because they
add to the accumulation of capital and fragment the labour force. An
important effect of pension schemes is to subdue and stabilize the
labour force, guaranteeing skilled, docile workers for capital. The final
section of this chapter traces the implications of private pensions. The
impending demographic squeeze on pension plans will further ex-
acerbate the class struggle and the crisis of accumulation in Western
industrial societies.

Theoretical Framework

The nature of capitalism is inherently antagonistic. The concentration of ownership of the means of production in the hands of a few
leads to the division of society into two classes: owners and workers.
Antagonism arises from the conflict of interest between the two classes.
Capitalists receive income from their ownership of capital while
workers gain their sustenance through the sale of their labour power,
their sole significant economic possession, in the marketplace.

The fact that the two classes own separate and distinct factors
of production is not in itself sufficient reason to generate conflict.
However, in the case of the capitalist economic system, the purpose
of production is to create commodities for exchange and through this
activity to create value. The total mass of value created in a society
can be expressed as:

$$VA = V + SV$$

where VA = total mass of value (which is total abstract labour)
       V = value of labour power
       SV = surplus value

This formula represents the capitalist wage relation which is the fundamental relation defining the capitalist mode of production.[1] Simple as
it is, the formula reveals the inherent conflict between labour and
capital because an increase in V which accrues to labour requires a
decrease in SV which is appropriated by capital (assuming that VA
is constant). Of course, increases in the components of VA are not
necessary if all parties are satisfied with their share, but this is unlikely
under most circumstances and is impossible under competitive capi-

talism. The obvious alternative is to increase both components of the total created value. Since value is created in the labour process, the two possible ways to increase VA include lengthening the working day and increasing the intensification of labour. The first alternative would allow greater productivity without altering the labour process, while the second involves changes in the labour process without lengthening the work period. The latter can be achieved by means of reorganization, mechanization and acceleration of the pace of production.

The manipulation of the labour process by capital is resisted by labour. Longer working days cut into the workers' own time, so incremental increases in the working day, and consequent wage increases, eventually reach levels of diminishing returns in the perspective of labour, thus escalating the struggle between the two classes. Capitalists then turn their attention to the intensification of the labour process in order to gain a larger surplus value. Once again this meets with resistance as worker autonomy is eroded and greater strains are placed on the social reproduction of labour.

Once the limits to absolute surplus value are approached the alternative is to increase relative surplus value, i.e. to increase surplus value at the expense of wages by increasing the technical composition of capital.[2] Replacing labour with machines alters the relationship between capital, labour, and the productive forces such as scale of enterprise and organization of the labour process. It creates new conditions and erects new barriers between the two classes. In the long term the introduction of technology increases productivity and pays for itself, but in the short term the profits it generates do not meet the additional expenses, and profits are reduced.[3]

This crisis of declining rates of profit puts additional pressure on capital to maintain increasing demand for commodities. Wages are raised to achieve this end, but productivity must be expanded to meet the higher wage bill. Thus capitalists find themselves in the contradictory position of continually undermining the long term profitability of machines by replacing them with new machines before the amortization period of the old machines is reached. In this way, constant capital is devalued, exacerbating the crisis of falling profits. Competitive firms can survive only by increasing in size to increase their control of the market and to take advantage of economies of scale. Capitalist competition leads to monopoly capitalism because smaller firms do not have the amount of capital needed to replace obsolete fixed capital and to pay interest on large sums of borrowed money. This vicious circle of monopoly pricing, technological innovation and devaluation of constant capital puts pressure on firms to increase the share of surplus value by decreasing that of wages.

Reinforced Exploitation

The tendency of the rate of profit to fall puts pressure on the capitalist and the state to create structures that will support or increase the prevailing rate of profit, some of which have been relatively effective. Castells suggests that profits are bolstered by an interlocking set of practices that include increasing the rate of exploitation of labour, cheapening the elements of constant capital, enhancing demand for commodities, fragmenting the capital sector and encouraging state intervention.[4] We will elaborate on the first of these—the increase in the rate of exploitation of labour—because the rise of private pensions in industrial societies can be identified as a component of this process.

The concept of exploitation has generated much dialogue in recent years as social scientists discuss alternative definitions and implications.[5] For present purposes, the Marxian perspective is taken whereby exploitation is a covariant of surplus value. Marx specified that the degree of exploitation of labour by capitalists is equal to the rate of the surplus value extracted.[6] Since the rate of surplus value derives from the ratio of surplus value (SV) to wages (V), it follows that when $SV \neq 0$, exploitation exists, and that for any given value of V, the degree of exploitation will vary directly with SV. Thus any procedure used to increase or consolidate surplus value is also one which increases or ensures exploitation.

Marx intended exploitation to apply to the process whereby labour is consumed by the capitalist at a wage rate which is less than the value of the commodity produced by that labour. The conflict arising from blatant efforts to increase exploitation has led capital to pursue less direct procedures that reinforce exploitation.[7] Two examples of this approach are the fragmentation of labour and the redistribution of wages.

Wages are redistributed by means of taxation, monopoly pricing and forced savings for health insurance and pensions. Marx predicted this procedure when he stated that:

> [Consumer goods production] has this advantage over [capital goods production], that its labourers have to buy back from it the commodities produced by themselves . . . Every industrial country (for example, Britain and the U.S.A.) furnishes the most tangible proofs of the way in which this advantage may be exploited—by paying nominally the normal wages but grabbing, alias stealing, back part of them without an equivalent in commodities.[8]

Pension deductions are a case in point. They are deducted from wages with the expectation that full value will be repaid upon retirement. But in the interim the money is used to augment surplus value and thus to increase the level of exploitation.

The second procedure considered here as a means to reinforce exploitation is the fragmentation of labour, a process that has its roots in the capitalist struggle for profits as well as in the class struggle between capital and labour. Labour is fragmented by numerous regulations and processes, an example of which is the multitude of pension plans available to certain workers, and the absence of these for others.

Inter-capitalist competition leads to monopoly capitalism as individual owners convert accumulated capital to economies of scale to further augment accumulation. The crisis of falling rates of profit resulting in the devaluation of capital by monopolies allows them to realize profit rates that are greater than small, marginal firms. The marginal sector is consequently not able to provide employees with the same level of wages and security as the monopoly sector. Thus, fragmentation of capital leads to fragmentation of labour.[9]

The second root of labour fragmentation is the class struggle which has led to efforts by capital to control and manipulate labour. Rather than being located in an open market place where it competes for wages on a universalistic scale, labour finds itself operating within a series of discrete, segmented markets. Each market is separated from others by hierarchical constraints and each can be distinguished from others by internal regulations and dynamics. The returns of a member of the labour force are dependent on the labour segment in which he or she is located rather than upon the supply and demand for skills and qualifications that have been assembled. The voice of labour is thus muted by internal divisions and squabbles.

The theory of labour market segmentation arose in the context of the American 'war on poverty' when researchers discovered that increasing experience, training and education of blacks, chicanos and women did not reduce the proportions of these populations who were unemployed or employed in marginal activities. The precise boundaries of these segments have not been established. The original scheme included two segments but this has evolved into three segments: primary, subordinate primary, and secondary.[10] The primary labour market includes medium and high-ranking jobs in large, profitable firms. Occupations in the subordinate primary sector include lower level positions in these large firms while the secondary labour market consists of jobs in small, marginal firms.

The three labour markets are distinguished in terms of labour processes, remuneration, security, and opportunities for upward mobility. Those in the secondary labour market receive lower marginal returns for increments of training, experience or skills. Employer-employee relations are more authoritarian and capricious with little protection from dismissal for workers in this segment.[11] The subordinate primary sector consists of the traditional industrial and lower level clerical occupations. Jobs are repetitive and routinized, but pay is better and job security is greater than in the secondary sector on account of the prevalence of unions.[12] The third sector is labelled 'independent primary', and consists of professional, skilled and administrative positions. Persons in this sector realize greater returns for experience and training and receive the highest wages and the greatest job security among the three sectors.

Much more research is needed to refine the conceptualization of these segments. There is considerable debate as to the number of segments to be identified, the way they should be distinguished, and the permeability of their boundaries. Although women, blacks and ethnic minorities are predominantly located in the secondary labour market, evidence suggests that the nature of their markets differ.[13] Thus, subsectors may be introduced to help explain variations in the labour process within each of the various sectors.

The class nature of the capitalist system, especially in regards to the commodification of labour, requires the exercise of controls over labour in order to ensure accumulation. Direct supervision is the prototype of control. The employer observes the employee's performance and dismisses or punishes him or her if it is unsatisfactory. Accumulation has resulted in economies of scale in the production process; this leads to problems because direct control is no longer possible. Loss of direct control means that the capitalist employer cannot be assured that labour will apply itself to the extent necessary to realize profits. This condition generates a need for other forms of control, the manifestation of which becomes an essential part of the labour process experienced by workers. Consequently, the three segments of labour discussed above can be characterized by three forms of control.[14] In the secondary sector control is direct. The employee in a small firm works under the scrutiny of the person who pays him or her. In a larger firm, work is monitored by a foreman who acts as the agent of the capitalist. Hiring and dismissal is frequent because the nature of the work requires little training and because the employer knows that a large reserve labour force is available from which to choose replacements. Efforts on the part of capital to encourage loyalty and stability are less profitable than ensuring that turnover of workers is not encumbered by state or union regulations. This is accomplished by organizing the labour process so that few skills are necessary, thus guaranteeing ease of replacement for the employer and lack of commitment for the employee. Such fluidity also works in the interest of the capitalist in that it allows adjustment of labour force size to meet the needs of the market. In many marginal firms in this sector, such freedom to manipulate work force size is necessary in order for the firm to survive.

The form of control that dominates in the primary subordinate sector is that of technology. Not only does technology reduce the dependency of capital on labour, but it enhances its control over labour. Direct control is not necessary because the speed of the assembly line process dictates the productivity of the employee. This form of control is not without its contradictions. The agglomeration of machines necessitates the agglomeration of workers on a large shop floor which increases their sense of dependency and vulnerability. Thus in these types of industrial occupations, unionization has arisen. Unions pattern their demands after the benefits and structures of the dominant primary sector, so that in addition to higher wages and shorter hours, workers gain the security of seniority systems, minimum workplace health and safety standards, and health and welfare benefits packages. These gains have been balanced by concessions granted to management of further mechanization and higher levels of output.

Ironically, unionization has contributed controls on this sector in addition to those enforced by machines. Union regulations relating income and security to seniority place further pressure on the employee to remain on the job and to struggle for higher positions in spite of any negative attitudes towards his employment. The longer the worker remains with the firm, the greater sacrifice in terms of wages, pension benefits, and job security is involved if the individual wishes to move from one firm to another.

The recent growth of corporate capitalism with its bureaucratic scale and elaborate chains of command has necessitated forms of control characteristic of the primary labour market segment.[15] The nature of the labour process is such that the dominant modes of control are not effective here, although high technology appears to be gaining in-roads into this sector and will exercise considerable control in the coming decades. Until it does, capital must deal with a skilled, expensive labour force which does not produce tangible, concrete items. However, the bureaucratic framework itself acts as a system of control. The tasks of each position in a bureaucracy are specified as are lines of communication and authority. All positions are assigned rights and responsibilities in hierarchical fashion so that the potential success of an actor is measured by movement up succeeding niches in the bureaucracy.

The crucial problem in controlling the labour force in this sector is to motivate achievement and loyalty. This is attained through long term benefits and a carefully graded system of standards and procedures. Fulfillment of one's duties in a status leads to promotion to a higher status and an accompanying increase in monetary rewards, authority and long term benefits which are closely tied to income and experience. Movement up the bureaucratic ladder places the employee in a more comfortable office, provides access to greater resources and gives increased flexibility in the way private and public life is conducted. The holiday period is lengthened and the health and pension benefit package becomes more generous. Thus, bureaucratic employees commit themselves to the goals of the firm in order to further their own careers.

Historical Rise of Private Pensions

Pensions have existed throughout recorded history for the purpose of rewarding lengthy, loyal or noteworthy service. Hilton documents payments known as pensions paid out annually by parish churches in thirteenth century England.[16] A general rule of the Worcester Cathedral Priory required a peasant who took over a half-yardland holding of his mother's to provide her with free lodging and annual payments consisting of twelve bushels of rye, four bushels of barley and one bushel of oats.[17]

In 1825 Charles Lamb described the circumstances under which he received his pension after 33 years of service with the East India Company:

> . . . just as I was about quitting my desk to go home (it might be about 8 o'clock), I received an awful summons to attend the presence of the whole assembled firm in the formidable back parlour. I thought, now my time is surely come, I have done for myself, I am going to be told that they have no longer occasion for me.[18]

A few minutes later Lamb learned that his employment was terminated as of that minute, but that he would receive a monthly pension amounting to two-thirds of his wages, a prospect that had not crossed his mind. His trepidation and subsequent elation reveals that the practice of doling out company pensions was unusual and was done at the sole discretion of the owner or manager of the firm.

Before continuing with a description of the rise of private pensions in North America, we briefly recount the development of the main sources of support for the elderly, which were friendly societies and public pensions which originated in Western Europe. This diversion is necessary to appreciate the context within which private pensions developed, a context in which such pensions were sponsored for purposes other than the welfare of recipients of such payments.

The rise of capitalism emasculated the traditional systems of family and community support of the elderly. The landless proletariat could no longer provide lodging or daily rations from their gardens. The need for a replacement of this function was partly filled by the rise of friendly societies in England in the second half of the nineteenth century. These societies were working men's clubs formed to provide sickness and death benefits to their members. But membership lasted a lifetime, so that as the lifespan increased by two and a half years in that period, friendly societies found their benefits functioning to an increasing extent as old age pensions. Although they first opposed trade union pressure on Parliament to institute old age pensions for fear that contributions to such a program would reduce those to friendly society coffers, the continued drain of funds to support the elderly caused them to support the plan when it was finally introduced.[19]

Public pension plans were in operation in several countries before Britain's came into effect. Bryden lists France as the first country to provide a pension for an occupational group, seamen, in 1791.[20] Bismarck introduced the first universal pension for all wage earners and low-paid salary workers in 1889 in Germany. Denmark is acknowledged as providing the first means-tested universal plan for all citizens in 1891. A similar plan was adopted by New Zealand in 1898, by Australia and Great Britain in 1908, and by Sweden in 1913.

The first universal means-tested plan in North America was introduced by Newfoundland in 1911. Before that, the Canadian Government had legislated a voluntary annuities plan in 1908 which provided a vehicle for retirement savings for those who wanted and could afford to use it. Needless to say, it was not a successful venture. The Canadian Old Age Pension Act was put into effect in 1927. It required a means test for those over 70 who had to meet a number of criteria with respect to citizenship, residency and marital status. This act and its ensuing amendments held until 1951 when universal old age pensions were legislated for those over 70 years of age, and old age assistance based on need was provided for anyone between the ages of 65 and 70.

The United States lagged far behind other industrial nations in providing public pensions for its elderly. Although the first state pensions were introduced in 1915, they were inadequate in provision and limited in coverage. Legislation made families responsible for their indigent parents, while elderly paupers with no relatives were relegated to almshouses.[21] Pressure on the government for a universal pension system came from three sources: The United Mine Workers of America, the American Association for Labor Legislation, and the Fraternal Order of Eagles, which was a descendent of the British friendly society.[22] Their efforts were resisted until the Depression which rendered over 50 per cent of the elderly unemployed and caused the collapse of company and union pension plans. In 1935 the Social Security Act was passed which established a compulsory plan covering the entire work force, financed by a payroll tax and paying benefits according to the amount contributed.

The first private retirement pension plans in North America were introduced by railway companies in the last quarter of the nineteenth century. Why this industry should be first is an interesting question. Railways were the prototypical industry in early capitalist expansion. With their wide, geographical scope they required bureaucratic organization and control, rational planning, specialized workers, mechanization and efficiency.

When a depression struck North America in the 1870s, railways and other industries cut wages and laid off thousands of workers. This action contrasting with continued high dividends to capitalists holding railway stock led to the violent railway strikes of 1877. Riots, destruction of railway property, clashes with federal troops and loss of life ensued along with widespread criticism of the railways by the press and public. In this context the problem of worker control and public relations was uppermost in the minds of railway officials. Theirs was a skilled labour force working in an industry in which accidents were common and litigation costly. The need to disengage older, loyal workers because of slower reflexes or past injuries in the context of public antipathy required tact and diplomacy. The solution was to introduce company pension plans that could be used to rid the company of such workers without raising the ire of the public.

The first private plan in North America was established in 1874 for employees of the Grand Trunk Railway of Canada with a charter from the Canadian parliament.[23] The terms of the plan were surprisingly similar to those of present day plans, and represent an anomaly from most of the United States plans which quickly followed. Employees made contributions equal to two and a half per cent of salary and received benefits based on years of service and final salary. It differed from virtually all other nineteenth-century plans in that payment of benefits was not contingent on incapacitation.

The second plan, initiated a year later by the American Express Company, was more typical of the plans which followed. This was a non-contributory plan providing benefits to those employees of twenty or more years of service, at least 60 years of age, who were permanently incapacitated. Further to these criteria, benefits were paid only upon recommendation by the general manager and approval by the executive committee of the board of directors.

The number of pension plans increased rapidly in the following years, especially in the railway industry, where 39 per cent of United States employees and 74 per cent of Canadian employees were covered in 1908.[24] Coverage in the Canadian railway industry increased to 90 per cent in 1923 when the government railway system was formed.

A major weakness of most of the early plans was that they were financed on a pay-as-you-go system. When the Great Depression of the 1930s eliminated company profits, most of the pension plans were terminated. Revival came during the Second World War after American government regulations restricted wage increases and levied a heavy tax on excess corporate profit.[25] The improvement of employee fringe benefits was encouraged, and company pension fund contributions, which were tax deductible, came to be seen as mutually beneficial to both capital and labour.

John L. Lewis and the United Mine Workers of America were the first to push for pensions and were instrumental in bringing this type of benefit to the forefront of union-employee negotiations.[26] The UMW strike in 1946 led to government intervention, and ultimately to the establishment of a pension fund financed by employers at five cents a ton of mined coal. The steel industry struck successfully for pensions in 1949, the same year that the United Automobile Workers under Walter Reuther signed the first two pension agreements in the automobile industry with Ford Motor Company and Chrysler Corporation. The efforts of these larger unions resulted eventually in an increase in pension coverage in private industry from about 20 per cent in 1950 to about 50 per cent by the 1970s in the USA.[27]

Private Pensions as Reinforced Exploitation

The prevalence of private pension plans increased significantly during two periods: first, at the turn of the century when welfare capitalism was used to control labour, and second, in the post-World War Two period when forces of expansion led to new efforts to increase accumulation. In the first period pensions were used to reinforce exploitation by controlling the labour force while the purpose in the second period was to redirect wages in two directions. Wages were redistributed over time by means of forced savings to support the retired workers and thus allow capitalists to use surplus value for purposes of accumulation. In addition, while savings were being held until the time of retirement, they were recycled back to capitalist coffers and used to counteract declining profits.

Pensions as Forms of Control

The inherent tendency under capitalism toward concentration and monopolization has led to growth and mergers of all firms that survive. This trend first began to dominate the North American economy in the latter part of the nineteenth century when, for example, the McCormick Harvester Machine Company employed 1,400 workers in 1884 and expanded to 4,000 in 1899. Other firms, such as Edison and Pullman employed 10,000 and 14,500 in 1893.[28] Firms in Canada were also expanding. In 1900, the Montreal Cotton Company employed 3,000 mill hands at Valleyfield, Quebec, the Dominion Iron and Steel Company employed 2,500 men at Sydney, Cape Breton Island, while the Canadian Pacific Railroad, Canada's largest employer, had to deal with 35,000 employees across the country.[29]

As size increased, direct supervision of the labour force by the owner became impossible. Control which had formerly been achieved by means of direct sanctions and personal empathy was eroded and was replaced by a hierarchical chain of command. But as structures became more complex and tasks more specialized, the control and discipline of the work force became increasingly problematic. The crisis of control that erupted is reflected in the incidence of strikes and violence in the late nineteenth century.

Out of the conflict evolved a system of welfare capitalism designed to inculcate loyalty and obedience among the work force. Firms provided health and recreational services, as well as insurance, profit-sharing and pension plans. These increased the expenses of the firm in some cases, although usually the costs were transferred to the workers through payroll deductions. Most firms considered any additional expenses worthwhile if the result was a dedicated, stable labour force.

The potential of retirement pensions to control workers first became apparent to the state and was often the reason why state pensions themselves were inaugerated. Evidence of this function appears in statements by Bismarck, who is credited with introducing the first national pension scheme in Germany and who argued that such a plan would pacify poorly paid workers and increase their stake in the social order.[30] He is quoted as stating that:

> I will consider it a great advantage when we have 700,000 small pensioners drawing their annuities from the state, especially if they belong to those classes who otherwise do not have much to lose by an upheaval and erroneously believe they can actually gain much by it.[31]

A similar justification for pensions in Sweden was presented by Adolf Hedin in his Riksdag motion in 1884 for the government to investigate ways of providing workers with accident and old age insurance. His motion argued that the benefits accruing from pensions would include the discouragement of revolutionary activity and support of the existing social structure by the majority of the working population.[32]

The introduction of the various pension schemes in Canada was preceded by the usual debates about advantages and disadvantages. One of the arguments in support of the extension of public pensions was that they would encourage loyalty towards the capitalist system among the workers:

This is why I suggest it would be unwise to criticize any reform or any government that brings about social security in our own country, because if there is one way of preventing the communist form of government, it will not be by the institution of rules and regulations saying that the communist party is outlawed or that it should be driven underground, but rather by bringing to the masses in this country the means that will give them a decent standard of living. In this way they will not be tempted to have recourse to communism.[33]

Fourteen years later the same concern is voiced in debating a different pension plan:

I hope sir, that while we are discussing this bill in the broadest sense of the word we will realize that it is not coming to grips with the basic question of poverty in Canada, which is something most social legislation should and can do. I hope that we shall realize that we must put an end to poverty in the midst of plenty. Otherwise, sir, what will our answer be to communism abroad?[34]

Capitalists saw pensions as a vehicle by which to achieve similar effects on their own labour forces. Thus, the private pension plans of the CPR and Canadian National Railroad inaugurated in 1903 and 1904 respectively, included clauses specifying that any employee participating in a strike would forfeit pension rights accrued prior to the date of the strike. The CNR took the liberty to make the effect of this clause retroactive, so that the maintenance of waymen who participated in the strike of 1899 were deprived of all credits accumulated before that date although the pension terms were drawn up five years later.[35]

The discouragement of strikes was one of several reasons for introducing private pensions. International Harvester instituted a variety of welfare programs shortly after the turn of the century. Cyrus McCormick supported the incorporation of a Benefit Association and Pension Plan in the company welfare program for purposes of improving public image and forestalling antitrust legislation as well as gaining worker control.[36] Colliers Magazine had charged Harvester with irresponsibility in regard to injured workers, while the United States government was investigating it for violating antitrust laws. The company image was of concern to McCormick who was engaged in public fund raising connected with the United States presidential election of 1908. Harvester employees knew that the welfare package was a reward for not joining a union. Written into the terms of the pension plan was a stipulation that pension benefits and even contributions would be forfeited by any person dismissed by the company for gross misconduct.³⁷

The Harvester pension plan was administered by company officials who were responsible for setting, revising and interpreting the terms. Virtually all companies followed this procedure to ensure themselves of discretionary powers over their pension plan. For example, the terms of the pension plan of the Grand Trunk Railroad, introduced in 1908 to replace an earlier one, stipulated that members of the Pension Committee were nominated at the 'pleasure' of the Board.³⁸ The first members of the Committee were the Second Vice President, the Third Vice President, the Fourth Vice President, the General Solicitor and the General Transportation Manager. Some of the rules of the plan that are most blatant in their allocation of discretionary powers include:

5. Subject as aforesaid and as hereinafter expressed the Pension Committee shall have power:

   To make and enforce rules and regulations for the efficient operation of the Pension Department;

   To determine the eligibility of Employees to receive Pension allowances;

   To fix the amount of such allowances; and

   To prescribe the conditions under which such allowances may be granted;

8. The Pension Committee shall have power under special circumstances to retire an Employee prior to his reaching the age limited by Article 7, and any Employee after the age of 60 years with not less than 20 years continuous service claiming to be unfitted by reason of permanent physical or mental disability from following his usual or any other suitable employment in the Company's service be retired if the Company's Chief Medical Officer shall certify to such disability as aforesaid.

14. No Employee who sues the Company for damages on account of personal injuries sustained by him in the course of his service will have any claim for pension or allowance under these Rules.

19. The Pension Committee may also withhold permanently or temporarily the payment of any pension or allowance in case of any misconduct on the part of the recipient of the same of any action on his part inimical to the interests of the Company.³⁹

Employees suffered a serious disadvantage in bargaining with management under these terms, particularly if they were approaching retirement or had made contributions to the plan for a long period of time. Any activity construed as 'inimical to the interests of the Company' could be considered grounds for dismissal with consequent loss of pension contributions as well as benefits. Labour's position was weakened by the fact that all interpretations and definitions were in the hands of management.

The transparency of pension plans as a form of worker control reduced their effectiveness to achieve this end. Gradually, state regulations, union pressure and management manipulation resulted in changes that better camouflage the control function of pension plans. Examination of present day pension terms reveals the powerful effect of pensions to maintain worker loyalty and to discourage mobility to other firms. Contributions to pension plans are compulsory. Until recent years, companies were under no obligation to return pension contributions to employees who did not stay with the company until normal retirement age. Horror stories abound of workers being terminated after a lifetime of service without pension benefits because they stopped working for the company before reaching age 65. Reasons for these terminations might be company closure or illness, but nevertheless the results were deprivation of benefits for the worker.

Recent government legislation in Canada has required that employees' pension benefits be locked in after a period of time and/or a minimum age of the employee, often ten years service and/or 45 years of age. This reduces the effect of hindering worker mobility but it does influence those who are over age 45 and who have less than ten years service with a firm. Similarly, workers who are within ten years of retirement are not likely to entertain the thought of changing jobs. Such mobility would reduce pensions that are based on length of service and final average salary.

In spite of the veil drawn over the function of welfare programs, capital was not able to achieve its objective of control of the labour force. Even the most generous welfare program does not hide the inequities in the struggle between the two classes. The rise of monopolies and the conflict with labour has led capital to fragment the labour force in an effort to consolidate its power. As was mentioned earlier, different styles of control have strengthened the fragmentation. Pension plans are one aspect of bureaucratic control and therefore play a more important role in maintaining loyalty and stability in the independent primary sector than in the other two. The subordinate primary sector, with the aid of union negotiations, has obtained pension plans but the terms of their plans are not as generous as are those of the independent sector. Workers in the secondary sector do not have the power to negotiate industrial welfare programs and most depend on universal state pensions when they retire. Thus, workers in the various segments are not only divided by different working conditions, types of control and levels of consumption, but they are also fragmented by the diverse living standards which they can anticipate after retirement. We shall elaborate on this aspect of labour segmentation with reference to a study of pension plans undertaken recently by the author.[40]

Inequalities in pension benefits examined in the study are the result of two sets of factors: first, the formula for deriving benefits favours independent primary workers; and second, formulas in pension plans of independent primary workers are more generous than those in plans for income earners in the other sectors. In the first case, we must examine the structure of the formula while in the second we must compare terms in the different formulas.

Pension benefit formulas are usually based on income and length of service while contributions are based on income. Thus a typical formula may require the employee to contribute four per cent of earnings to the pension fund and allow benefits based on one and a half per cent of the average of the final five years' salary multiplied by the number of years of service. Thus a person with final average earnings of $40,000 will receive twice the pension of someone with $20,000 final average earnings if they have equal lengths of service. Of course, the higher wage earner made twice the contributions of the other so we are tempted to see this as a fair compensation.

The most appropriate method of comparing unequal pensions involves the calculation of 'the net present value of future benefits'.[41] According to this method, future benefits are discounted at the market rate to their present value which is then compared with the present value of the contribution. For a simplified example, we can compare two persons who contribute $100 and $200 this year and receive $120 and $240 respectively next year. At a market rate of five per cent, $120 is discounted to $114.29 while $240 is discounted to $228.57. Thus the net present values of the two benefits are $14.29 and $28.57 even though the rates of return are equal. So long as the market rate is less than the rate of return—and it usually is—those with higher salaries will realize greater net present values of pension benefits.

The second form of inequity occurs when a company administers more than one pension plan. Each plan covers a limited cluster of occupations such as shop workers, office staff and management. Comparisons of these plans are often difficult because the inequities are camouflaged by the ways the terms are articulated. For example, the plan covering salaried employees of a mining company uses a formula to calculate benefits which is the sum of A and B where:

$$A \ = \ 1.75 \text{ per cent} \times Y_1 \ (S\text{---}\$1,800)$$
$$B \ = \ 1.75 \text{ per cent} \times Y_2 \ S\text{---}Z$$

where $Y_1 \ =$ number of years of pensionable service before January 1, 1982

$Y_2 \ =$ number of years of pensionable service after January 1, 1982

$S \ =$ average of best five years' salary

$Z \ =$ 1/70 of the Canadian Pension Plan benefit for each year of credited service after January 1, 1982

All contributions to the fund come from the company.

A railway company uses the following formula to calculate monthly pension benefits:

$$(A + B) \ X + C \ (Y)$$

Where A and B apply to the period after 1965 and C applies to earlier years.

$A \ =$ 1.3 per cent of that portion of average monthly salary in the best five years which is below the C.P.P. ceiling

$B \ =$ 2.0 per cent of the same average salary which is in excess of the Canadian Pension Plan ceiling

$X \ =$ number of years of service since 1965

$C \ =$ 2.0 per cent of average monthly salary in the best five years prior to 1966

$Y \ =$ number of years of service prior to 1966

There is a 35-year maximum benefit accrual period.

Members contribute 4.42 per cent of income up to the Canadian Pension Plan ceiling and six per cent of income that exceeds the ceiling.

In spite of difficulties in making these comparisons, we can sense inequities when we note the data on earnings and pensions aggregated by labour market sector collected by Stafford and White presented in Table 10.1.[42]

TABLE 10.1

Earnings and Pensions
By Labour Market Segment

Labour Market Segment	Average years of service	Average earnings, final year	Average monthly pension
Independent primary	31	$29,228	$870
Subordinate primary	30	$23,522	$645
Secondary	19	$20,279	$127

These data reflect earnings, service and pensions among those who are retiring *with pensions*, and should not be construed as representing averages for all workers in the three sectors.

In order to make valid comparisons of pension income in the three labour market sectors, Stafford and White standardized career earnings and length of service, and obtained the following results presented in Table 10.2.[43]

TABLE 10.2

Payroll Deductions and Pensions
By Labour Market Segment

Labour Market Segment	Per Cent Payroll Deduction	Monthly Pension
Independent primary	4.2	$836
Subordinate primary	4.3	$763
Secondary	3.9	$333

In clearing away the confusion of terms in the pension plans we find that subordinate primary workers lose a larger proportion of their wages in contributions to their pension plan than independent primary workers, yet they receive $73 per month less in pension benefits. Workers in the secondary sector who are fortunate enough to be covered by a pension plan receive 60 per cent less than independent primary sector workers even though their contributions to the plan are only marginally less. Thus fragmentation of the labour force is supported by various pension plans and exploitation is reinforced.

Pensions as Redistribution of Wages

The argument made in this section is that private pensions reinforce exploitation by transferring part of wages back to capital to be used for accumulation. Pension fund contributions come from payroll deductions and company contributions. In many cases, all contributions to the fund come from the company without a deduction from the worker's wage. An important point is that all pension fund contributions, whether they come from the employer or the employee are really deferred wages belonging to the employee.

Empirical evidence supports this argument because unions will sometimes negotiate for increased pensions *in lieu* of higher wages. Further evidence is found in surveys which show an inverse association between pension benefits and wage levels. Courts of law share the view that pensions are a form of wage when they have ruled that recalcitrant firms must include the pension scheme as a negotiable item in contract deliberations with unions.

Moving to a theoretical level, Brittain finds stronger support for classifying pension fund contributions as deferred wages.[44] He makes the case that neoclassical economics allocates all pension fund contributions to the worker. It does this by means of marginal productivity theory which presents a rational competitive world of employers hiring employees until the additional wage equals the marginal value of the product. If a universal tax, such as a pension contribution, is imposed on the employers, the marginal value product is reduced with a consequent potential to cut back on the number of employees. The result is a reduction in wages because employees have no opportunities for alternative employment given the universality of the tax.

However, marginal productivity theory does not rule out alternative ways of conceptualizing pension fund contributions. For example, it is possible that a universal tax may lead to price increases rather than lower wages, or to a substitution of leisure for wages, thus reducing the supply of labour at a constant wage. Brittain acknowledges these possibilities and attempts an argument under less restrictive assumptions. Assuming that the employer wants cost minimization, he will react to an employee-related tax, whether it is a tax on the employee or on the employer, as if it is part of the total wage package. Brittain examines the effect of such a tax under all possible cases of elasticity of the supply and demand for labour. He finds that in every plausible case labour bears the effect of a tax on the employee and on the employer.

Given the variety of evidence in support of the claim that employer contributions to private pension funds are the property of employees, many authors have deplored the total lack of control exercised by employees over such plans.[45] Administration of pension plans are usually in the hands of employers while use of the funds is determined by a few managers in financial institutions.

Canadian pension plan regulations do not allow a group of employees to independently institute a registered pension plan. The employer must be a party of the plan. Regulations require that an administrator be appointed, which normally is the company, although it can be a trust company or a group of individuals. The company then chooses a funding agency which is an insurance company or a trust company to manage the funds.

Pension plan funds represent a considerable force in the markets of the advanced capitalist countries. In Canada, it is estimated that these funds make up 95 per cent of the $7 billion in market values held by insurance companies.[46] The growth of pension fund assets in Canada has been phenomenal. Their estimated values from 1970 to 1981 are presented in Table 10.3.[47]

TABLE 10.3

Pension Fund Assets, Canada, 1970-81
(Billions of Dollars)

	1970	1980	1981
Insurance Companies	4	14	15
Trustees	11	51	60
Other	1	1	1
Total	16	66	76

Much larger amounts of these funds have accumulated in the United States. Rifkin and Barber estimate that public and private pension funds total more than $500 billion which is greater than the combined gross national products of the United Kingdom and France.[48] Increasing percentages of these funds have been directed towards the stock market. Peter Drucker estimates that by 1985 pension funds in the United States will own more than half of the equity capital of United States business.[49] Calvert notes similar trends in Canada where 70 per cent to 80 per cent of new capital needed by industry will come from private pension funds during the decade to 1985.[50]

The important question is whether these large scale investments benefit labour from whose pockets the money is taken. In the past corporate profits were the primary source of new capital investment. As profits dwindled, it became necessary to turn to outside sources since the rate of return on such investments was so low that investors were withdrawing rather than investing their money. From 1972 to 1975, the number of persons with investments in the stock market declined by 22 per cent.[51] The primary reason for this loss of investors was a drop in investment return from 10 per cent in 1965 to 5.4 per cent in 1973.[52]

While returns on stock market investments were in decline, the cost of living increased 65 per cent from 1964 to 1974. During that period $100 billion in pension funds were used to purchase stocks, causing Epstein to argue that pension funds were being used by capital to prop up a faltering market. Rifkin and Barber suggest that the selection of investments for pension funds has undermined the welfare of labour.[53] American banks have invested unionized pension funds in non-unionized industries. Funds from northeastern United States industries have been used to bolster industries outside the region, especially in the sunbelt states. This has depleted capital stock in the industrialized areas, leading to unemployment and forced migration of labour from that area.

Epstein goes so far as to say that pension funds are being used to cover the malaise of capitalism. He blames the declining returns of corporate investments on an industrial system that has become 'centralized, unresponsive and mandarin, wasteful, dangerous, and beyond human scale'.[54]

Implications

Capital introduced private pensions to instill loyalty in its work force and to combat the crisis of accumulation. In the short run, both of these goals have been furthered. The terms written into earlier pensions discouraged workers from going on strike, forming unions or even from making statements that management might define as being contrary to company interests. The increased accumulation of capital is realized in the diversion of billions of dollars of workers' wages into stocks, bonds and the real estate markets.

In the longer perspective private pension plans have simply postponed the inevitable crisis in control of labour and decline in profits. The most important external factor in this crisis is the changing demographic structure. For example, the number of persons 65 years of age and over in Canada will almost double, from 2.3 million in 1981 to 4.1 million in 2011. But the impact of this increment will be dwarfed by the increase in the number of elderly after the year 2011 when the post-World War Two baby boom cohort begins to reach age 65.[55]

The shift in age structure is already creating problems for capital because of the consequent demand for more of the total income to go toward wages. Capital established a wage differential associated with age as part of its efforts to instill loyalty in the labour force. Indeed, this is even more effective than pensions because younger workers are more aware of wage increments than of pension terms. As the labour force ages, this tactic is returning to haunt capital which must pay out more if age-related wage differentials are to be continued.

The increasing wage bill will squeeze profits which will suffer further losses when the demographic bulge begins to enter the retirement phase. At that point age-associated wages will combine with an increased demand for pensions to squeeze profits even further. Capital will attempt to alleviate strains induced by wages in a number of ways: reducing wages among older age groups, increasing the size of deductions from payroll checks, reducing hours of work among older workers and enforcing earlier retirement. None of these policies will meet the approval of labour.

As the size of the retired population increases, pension funds that had been growing will start to diminish, depriving capital of monies which it has badly needed for investment. The solutions chosen in this case will be to reduce pension benefits below what had been promised and increase payroll deductions for pension contributions. Both responses will increase discontent among the workers. Ultimately, present pension plan policies will lead to an increased class struggle and a further shortage of accumulation for capital.

Notes and References

1. Michael Aglietta, *A Theory of Capitalist Regulation* (NLB, London, 1979), p. 45.
2. Manuel Castells, *The Economic Crisis and American Society* (Princeton University Press, Princeton, 1980), pp. 49-51.
3. Ibid.
4. Ibid., pp. 58-75.
5. For recent debates on Marxian and other interpretations of exploitation, see G.A. Cohen, 'The Labor Theory of Value and the Concept of Exploitation', *Philosophy & Public Affairs*, Volume 8, no. 4 (1979); John E. Roemer, 'Property Relations vs. Surplus Value in Marxian Exploitation', *Philosophy & Public Affairs*, Volume 11, no. 4 (1982); Glenn Yago and Kathleen Blee, 'The Political Economy of Exploitation: A Revison', *The Insurgent Sociologist*, Volume XI, no. 2 (1982); Nancy Holmstrom, 'Marx and Cohen on Exploitation and the Labor Theory of Value', *Inquiry*, Volume 26, no. 3 (1983); Bob Russell, 'Revising Political Economy: Critical Comments on Blee and Yago', *The Insurgent Sociologist*, Volume 11, no. 4 (1983).
6. Karl Marx, *Capital*, Volume I (Random House, New York, 1906), p. 241.
7. The term 'reinforcement of exploitation' comes from Castells, *The Economic Crisis*, p. 61.
8. Karl Marx, *Capital*, Volume II (Progress Publishers, Moscow, 1967), pp. 512-513.
9. Castells, *The Economic Crisis*, p. 68.
10. Richard Edwards, *Contested Terrain: The Transformation of the Workplace in the Twentieth Century* (Basic Books, New York, 1979).
11. Don Clairmont, Richard Apostle, and Reinhard Kreckel, 'The Segmentation Perspective as a Middle-range Conceptualization in Sociology', *The Canadian Journal of Sociology*, Volume I, no. 3 (1983).
12. Edwards, *Contested Terrain*, p. 171.
13. Harry V. Herman, 'Immigrant Culture and Occupational Choice,' paper presented at the annual meetings of the Canadian Sociology and Anthropology Association, Saskatoon, 1979; Peter S. Li, 'Chinese Immigrants on the Canadian Prairie', *The Canadian Review of Sociology and Anthropology*, Volume 19, no. 4 (1982); Graham S. Lowe, 'Women, Work and the Office: the Feminization of Clerical Occupations in Canada, 1901-1931, *The Canadian Journal of Sociology*, Volume 5, no. 4 (1980); Ruth Milkman, 'Female Factory Labour and Industrial Structure: Control and Conflict over "Women's Place" in Auto and Electrical Manufacturing', *Politics & Society*, Volume 12, no. 2 (1983).
14. Edwards, *Contested Terrain*, pp. 177-183.

15. Wallace Clement, *The Canadian Corporate Elite*, (McClelland and Stewart, Toronto, 1975) for a description of the rise of corporate capitalism.
16. R.H. Hilton, *A Medieval Society: The West Midlands at the End of the Thirteenth Century* (Cambridge University Press, Cambridge, 1983), p. 32.
17. Ibid., p. 111.
18. *The Works of Charles Lamb*, Volume III (Pafraets Book Company, Troy, New York, n.d.), p. 79.
19. Bentley B. Gilbert, 'The Decay of Nineteenth Century Provident Institutions and the Coming of Old Age Pensions in Great Britain', *Economic History Review*, Series 2, Volume 17, no. 3 (1965).
20. Kenneth Bryden, *Old Age Pensions and Policy Making in Canada* (McGill-Queen's University Press, Montreal, 1974).
21. Laura Katz Olson, *The Political Economy of Aging* (Columbia University Press, New York, 1982), p. 39.
22. Louise Leotta, 'Abraham Epstein and the Movement for Old Age Security', *Labour History*, Volume 16, no. 3 (1975), p. 359.
23. Murray Webb Latimer, *Industrial Pension Systems in the United States and Canada*, Volume I (Industrial Relations Counselors, 1932), p. 20.
24. Ibid., p. 21.
25. William C. Greenough and Francis P. King, *Pension Plans and Public Policy* (Columbia University Press, New York, 1976), p. 43.
26. Ibid., p. 44.
27. Ibid., p. 114.
28. Edwards, *Contested Terrain*, pp. 27, 28.
29. Canada Department of Labour, *The Labour Gazette*, Volume 1 (King's Printer, Ottawa, October, 1900), pp. 101, 223; M. Riebenack, *Railway Provident Institutions* (Pennsylvania Railroad Company, Philadelphia, 1905), p. 149.
30. Gaston Rimlinger, *Welfare Policy and Industrialization in Europe, America, and Russia* (John Wiley and Sons, Toronto, 1971).
31. Ibid., p. 121.
32. Hugh Heclo, *Modern Social Politics in Britain and Sweden: From Relief to Income Maintenance* (Yale University Press, New Haven, 1974), p. 180.
33. Canada House of Commons, *Debates of the House of Commons* (Government of Canada, Ottawa, 1951), p. 1332.
34. Canada House of Commons, *Debate of the House of Commons* (Government of Canada, Ottawa, 1965), p. 11643.
35. Canada House of Commons, *Debates of the House of Commons* (Government of Canada, Ottawa, 1925), p. 4929-4931.
36. Robert Ozanne, *A Century of Labor—Management Relations at McCormick and International Harvester* (The University of Wisconsin Press, Madison, 1967), pp. 80-85.
37. Canada Department of Labour, *The Labour Gazette*, Volume 9, 1909, p. 745.
38. Ibid., Volume 8, 1908, pp. 995.
39. Ibid., p. 996.
40. James Stafford and Betty White, 'Pensions, Policies and Perceptions: Retirement in Six Major Industries in Northwestern Ontario', report submitted to Labour Canada, 1983.

41. J.E. Pesando and S.A. Rea, Jr., *Public and Private Pensions in Canada: An Economic Analysis* (Ontario Economic Council Research Studies #9, University of Toronto Press, Toronto, 1977), pp. 95-99.
42. Stafford and White, 'Pensions, Policies and Perceptions', Table 3B.
43. Ibid., Table 3C.
44. John A. Brittain, 'The Incidence of Social Security Payroll Taxes', *American Economic Review*, Volume 61, pp. 110-125.
45. Geoffrey Calvert, 'Contrasting Economic Impact of OASDI and Private Pension Plans' in Dan M. McGill (ed.), *Social Security and Private Pension Plans: Competitive or Complementary?* (Richard D. Irwin Inc., Homewood, Illinois, 1977); Jeremy Rifkin and Randy Barber, *The North Will Rise Again: Pensions, Politics and Power in the 1980's* (Beacon Press, Boston, 1978); John F. Myles, 'Pensions, Power and Profits: The Political Economy of Old Age Security in Canada', paper presented at the annual meetings of the Canadian Sociology and Anthropology Association, Saskatoon, June, 1979.
46. Statistics Canada, *Trusteed Pension Plans: Financial Statistics*, 1981, Catalogue 74—201 (Supply and Services, Ottawa, 1983), p. vi.
47. Ibid., p. vii.
48. Rifkin and Barber, *The North Will Rise Again*, p. 84.
49. Peter Drucker, 'Pension Fund Socialism', *The Public Interest*, Volume 42 (1976), p. 8.
50. Geoffrey Calvert, *Pensions and Survival: The Coming Crisis of Money and Retirement* (Financial Post, Toronto, 1977), pp. 42,44.
51. Rifkin and Barber, *The North Will Rise Again*, p. 252, n. 10.
52. Jason Epstein, 'Capitalism and Socialism: Declining Returns', *The New York Review of Books*, Volume 23, no. 2 (1977), p. 37.
53. Rifkin and Barber, *The North Will Rise Again*, pp. 83-124.
54. Epstein, 'Capitalism and Socialism', p. 37.
55. Frank T. Denton and Byron G. Spencer, 'Population Aging and Future Health Costs in Canada', *Canadian Public Policy*, Volume 9, no. 2 (1983).

11

THE CRISIS OF THE STATE AND THE STATE OF THE CRISIS: THE CANADIAN WELFARE EXPERIENCE

Bob Russell

Introduction

One of the more striking aspects of the current capitalist crisis is the centrality of the state and political issues in its development. Ideologically, this is reflected in the common perception that state policy may no longer be part of the solution (as it was during the 1930s, for example) but instead part of the problem which besets the advanced industrial economies in the 1980s. Thus approximately fifty years after it was consolidated as a mainstay of capitalism, the welfare state, and the regime of social reproduction that was premised upon it, is in serious danger of dismemberment.[1] For this reason, the object of this concluding essay is to turn to an examination of the contradictory effects of state intervention in social reproduction, precisely as a means of understanding the dynamics of the current crisis. Underpinning this analysis is the argument that important elements of the crisis are prepared in the state apparatus and through the fulfillment of state-regulated reproduction processes.[2] Obviously, crisis is not an intended result of state activity. Rather it follows from the juxtaposition of private accumulation on the one hand, and socialized forms of reproduction on the other.[3]

Before proceeding further some clarifications are in order. By social reproduction, and following other authors in this collection, I refer specifically to the reproduction of labour power in the narrow sense of the term, as daily and intergenerational labour force renewal, and the reproduction of labour power in its specifically capitalist guise as wage labour and hence the reconstitution of the broad social relationship which is the defining feature of the capitalist mode of production. Under the auspices of the modern state this takes place through the extension of social wages—the system of state expenditures on public goods and income transfer payments that are destined

309

for the on-going maintenance and renewal of capitalist labour supplies. In turn, the production of a social wage ensemble by the state is prefixed by the partial socialization of wage income through modern income and social security tax measures.[4] Reproduction by means of the social wage form is thus the reciprocal product of wage levels that are in advance of minimum subsistence levels, and which thereby permit a partial socialization, and levels of wage employment that are capable of generating adequate revenue resources for transformation into a social wage. Once these conditions have been fulfilled, such a regime permits many of the costs associated with reproduction to be externalized from the sphere of private production to the public domain of state finances.

Secondly, by the term crisis I refer to a persistent decline in the rate of capital accumulation. Such contractions represent periodic events in the history of capitalism.[5] They often delineate major 'watersheds' in the history of capitalist production through the transformations which they generate as the conditions for renewed accumulation (i.e. economic recovery). The consolidation of welfare state practices composed of stabilization policies geared towards full employment and a comprehensive social wage factor can be seen as just such a transformation emerging from the crisis of the 1930s. It is important, however, to recognize that such modalities of crisis resolution are significant not only in determining the specific traits of the next phase of accumulation, but also in setting the limits to its expansion. Just such a claim can be advanced with respect to state interventions into social reproduction. While the broadening of state mandates following the 1930s served to constitute a new chapter in the history of capitalism, the limits to this mode of expansion are being increasingly approximated. How can this turning point be depicted?

With the introduction of social wages and their Keynesian prerequisites as the refurbished basis for a renewal of capitalist accumulation, the contradiction between the production of surplus value and the reproduction of the necessary preconditions for its production is fully manifested in the public sphere. Whereas previously the costs associated with the reproduction of labour power had been externalized to an 'arm's length' relationship with respect to capital in such institutions as the household, with the incorporation of a social wage function into the state apparatus this is no longer the case.[6] Antagonisms between the standards of class reproduction on the one hand and the rate of accumulation on the other which were previously registered as chronic household deficits, as in the analyses provided by Dickinson and Wayne, come to assume an immediate politico-economic form once proletarianization is subsumed under welfare state aegis.[7] More specifically, through the extension of social wages, extra-market support in the form of state pensions, unemployment insurance, family allowances and subsidized consumption is administered to designated sections of the working population. Such support, however, must ultimately confront the dominant logic of market society. This relational contestation between market and extra-market forces within the public sector is one of the principle features of the current crisis. On the one hand, it is registered as a crisis of the welfare state, whereby the state is continually pressed in the direction of employing capitalist forms of organization and calculation but in the pursuit of socially defined objectives. The fiscal crisis of the state and demands for government cutbacks are only manifestations of this antinomy. On the other hand, such tensions are reflected in the broader economic crisis, important dimensions of which are prepared in the state sector as disproportionalities between the production of public and private goods. This scenario, it should be noted, is in marked contrast to previous crises which have impinged upon the state from the realm of civil society, thereby rendering state intervention a real possibility in subsequent transformations. Thus, it is possible to concur with Bandyopadhyay who argues that there is no overarching rationale for viewing the state as a privileged sphere of contradiction.[8] At the same time, however, in the current era of capitalist development, the state through its role in social reproduction actually does serve as a formative centre and 'lightening rod' for many of the symptoms associated with the contemporary economic malaise.

These themes constitute the object of study in the analysis of the welfare state which follows. For convenience they are mapped out in Figure 11.1. Here social wage provision is carried out through major distributive and productive functions that are engaged in by the state. Underlying the former are the major intra-class, intertemporal revenue transfers that are effected on behalf of individual households. As outlined in greater detail below, these funds are subject not only to the political process of transformation into a social wage through various programs of social insurance, but also to generalized economic pressures for valorization into loan capital. With respect to production functions, resources are committed for the creation of public goods by the state which entails the establishment of implicit exchange ratios with commodities produced in the private sector. However, these ratios may be deemed unsatisfactory or disproportionate and result in a call for cutbacks in state productive functions. While this is the specific manifestation of the crisis which attaches itself to public goods supply, state transfer programs have been subject to processes of devalorization which have appeared as fiscal crises and demands for tax revision. Implicit then in the model is the localization of the crisis in the different realms of social wage production.

This critical analysis should not, however, be taken as lending support to the currently fashionable supply-side doctrines. According

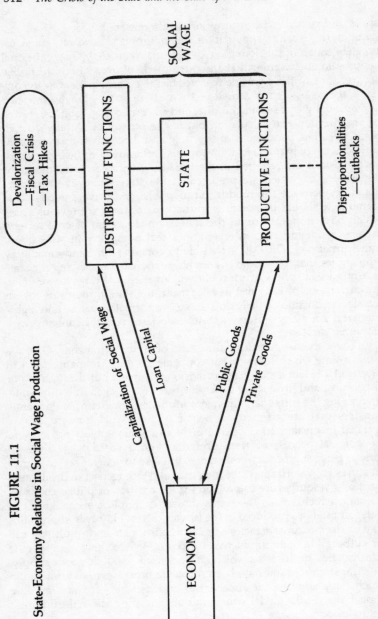

FIGURE 11.1

State-Economy Relations in Social Wage Production

to these theories, the expansion of state welfare activities siphons resources away from the production of market output so that inevitably 'productive sectors have become too small for what is required of them'.[9] Such approaches, by assuming the unproductiveness of state economic activity, actually contain their conclusions in their initial assumptions. They are premised upon an all too-rigid dichotomy between productive and unproductive labour, which in admitting to no exceptions, harkens back to Adam Smith and his Physiocratic predecessors.[10] Furthermore, given the current extent of excess capacity of both physical plant and labour supplies in the developed capitalist economies, the investment 'crowding out' effects that are attributed to state social policies have few empirical referents. In short, it is much more realistic to examine the unequal development between reproductive and productive spheres than it is to make *a priori* assumptions concerning labour that is employed in the public sector.

The analysis presented here bears far greater affinity to the significant investigations that have previously been launched by O'Connor and Gough[11], while at the same time attempting to proceed beyond the limitations of these earlier works. Thus, while Gough assumes a crisis and is principally interested with its effects on the future of the welfare state, the task of this paper is to provide a diagnostic account of the crisis and its origins within the welfare state. Coinciding with this objective and with the overall level of importance of social wage expenditures in state budgets, the focus of this analysis is on the state and reproduction rather than on the broader accumulation and legitimation functions that the capitalist state has always carried with it. This difference in emphasis requires a different set of concepts than those which have been deployed by O'Connor. In particular, it is necessary to distinguish as above between the actual expenditure of resources by the state in the *production* of specific use-values that enter into reproduction, (e.g. subsidized consumption) and the *redistribution* of values that have already been produced and which also constitute a significant proportion of the social wage (e.g. transfer payments). In O'Connor's analysis these items are subsumed under the accumulation/legitimation typology without undergoing any additional development in respect to their effects on the costs of reproducing capitalist relations of production.[12] It is precisely this latter question, however, which is at the crux of the crisis.

In the following sections the different aspects of state social wage production are examined both as they pertain to the specific crisis of the contemporary welfare state and to the larger crisis that confronts capitalist production. The data which is presented in this study was collected from an earlier investigation of the social wage

question in Canada. Although manifesting certain national specificities, the Canadian state can be taken as a fair representation
of an advanced welfare state. While the trends which are enumerated below thus refer to a particular national example, the forces
which have given rise to them are operant across the developed
capitalist world.

The Canadian Welfare State: Fiscal Crisis In The Social Wage Funds

State interventions directed towards the reproduction and commodification of labour power involve two partially autonomous processes, or expenditure outlays. First, with the proceeds from tax revenues (largely socialized increments of wage income appropriated by
the state) direct revenue transfers are made to social wage recipients.
In each instance, receipt of state payments is premised upon a contractual obligation between the individual income earner or citizen and the
state as a form of social insurance against the exigencies of capitalist
accumulation, including those which are brought on by the practices
of ageism and the absence of full-employment rights. As a social
insurance such monies are often composed of special ear-marked tax
contributions credited to separate social wage account funds from
which designated payments are made.

A second component of state revenues are designated for expenditure on social capital (both constant and variable) through which a
variety of public goods enter into the reproduction process. The list
here is potentially quite long and consists not only of the production
of use-values which by their nature must be consumed collectively (as
the normative school in the public finance literature would have it[13])
but also of necessary goods and services which cannot be *profitably*
extended to all sectors of society (e.g. education and health facilities).

Table 11.1 provides the necessary breakdown of the social
wage into its two constituents of production and distributive functions. Significantly, public goods production is almost completely
dominated by health and education functions, which collectively
account for over 50 per cent of total social wage costs. The
provision of these services chiefly entails expenditures on the
wages of state employees combined with physical inputs, and only
secondarily direct transfers of income to households. The remaining state programs consist almost entirely of income transfers. In
some cases where such funds are delineated from general state
accounts, administrative staffs are employed to oversee the dis-

bursement of benefits (e.g. Canada Pension Plan). Otherwise, such programs simply utilize the general administrative apparatus of the state and are not recorded as separate employers.

TABLE 11.1

Breakdown of State Social Wage Expenditures, Canada, 1978

	% Resource Expenditures	% Transfer Expenditures	% of Total Reproductive Expenditures
Education	28.0	7.2	35.2
Health	27.8	0.5	28.3
Canada/Quebec Pension Plan	1.5	4.2	5.7
Old Age Security	—	12.8	12.8
Unemployment Insurance	0.7	10.4	11.1
Family Allowance	—	5.3	5.3
Workman's Compensation	0.4	1.8	2.2
Total	**58.4**	**42.2**	**100**

Source: Statistics Canada, *Consolidated Government Finance* (Supply and Services, Ottawa, 1978), Cat. #68-202.

Each of these elements of social wage provision is subject to different dynamics and thus carries diverse implications with it. State transfer expenditures such as unemployment insurance or pension funds represent a reallocation of revenue *via* an operative fiscal system as in the above mentioned instances, for example, from the employed to the unemployed, or from the active labour force to dependent elements in the population. As revenue transfers the payments do not embody the creation of any new or additional value. Nonetheless, this is no reason for ignoring the importance of such expenditures. For in supporting the commodity status of labour power, through the social assignment of exchange-values to individual households, the creation and administration of social wage transfer funds such as the pension plans or the unemployment insurance funds does denote a massive reallocation of resources in the economy. This is particularly evident when the development of such reserves is carried out by 'accumulation' as opposed to 'pay-as-you-go' techniques, as was the case in Canada.[14]

Such funds then constitute a vast financial reservoir that is available to the state in the course of mediating individual consumption practices.

A number of social wage expenses, characterized by uncertain future liabilities such as unemployent or long-term but distant expenditures (e.g. pensions) are particularly amendable to 'accumulation' techniques, whereby large deposits are built up from special earmarked revenues in anticipation of future claims. Since the total capacity of such funds are not usually drawn upon at any singular moment, the balance of such accounts are available to the state on a continuing basis. While such savings could be deployed in a variety of ways, in practice their use has been almost entirely devoted to the refunding of state debt. As Table 11.2 illustrates, the increasing dependence of governments on loans contracted from these funds over a short space of time is one of the more remarkable aspects of contemporary public finance.

TABLE 11.2

Funds Invested by Canada and Quebec Pension Plans in Financing Government Debt

(% of Total Government Debt)

1965-66	0.3
1966-67	5.9
1967-68	10.9
1968-69	15.3
1969-70	19.4
1970-71	23.2
1971-72	26.1
1972-73	28.6
1973-74	30.9
1974-75	32.3
1975-76	31.6
1976-77	30.6

Source: Statistics Canada, *Social Security: National Programs* (Information Canada, Ottawa, 1976 and 1978) Cat. #86-201.

There are two aspects to this development. Prior to the advent of the social wage, state finances were formally dependent upon tax revenues and loans from personal savings (both domestic and foreign). Whenever tax receipts fell short of expenditures, the state would have to enter the open market and bid competitively for loan capital, using future tax obligations as collateral for public borrowing. The direct taxation of wage income and the centralization of these revenues in special social wage accounts for future expenditures opens up an alternate possibility, that of borrowing on tax revenues which have *already been received and allocated*. No longer reliant on the vagaries of private lenders, state administrators were able to go directly to social wage accounts and borrow from them; moreover in most cases funds were borrowed at substantially below market rates of interest (e.g. the Canada Pension Plan).[15]

The extension of state financing to include not only borrowing on private savings secured with future tax receipts, but additionally to calls on tax revenues already collected and set aside for designated purposes is not without important implications for the future of the welfare state. When state authorities borrow on the private loan market, certificates that stand for the taxing power of the state are issued to creditors in exchange for loan capital. From the perspective of the creditors, investment in state issues is identical to the advancement of money capital for any other undertaking; it is carried out as a source of gain, rather than as a means of saving or hoarding. Because of this, state certificates are tradeable. As a form of money capital, it is therefore only necessary that the state, at any given time, possess sufficient revenues with respect to its debt as are required to ensure interest payments at rates which are acceptable to its creditors. Although sinking funds were originally established for this purpose the most significant and revolutionary aspect of capitalist state finances is the creation of permanently-funded state debt. As implied by the terms, the noteworthy feature here is that state debt is permanently refunded regardless of the fact that the principle debt is never discharged.

The contemporary practice of borrowing on state social wage accounts differs from this procedure in vital aspects. Social wage trust funds do not exist as a source of profit for owners of money capital or for fund contributors, but rather as a means of reproduction through which wage income may be spread out over the life span of the wage-earner and the wage dependent household. It is thus absolutely necessary that such funds be reconstituted in all of their integrity as the demand upon them occasions. Now, the interesting question in respect to social wage funds and state transfer expenditures in the current conjuncture revolves around the problem of whether such reserves can be recomposed to meet future social wage payments as they have been contractually delimited. Part of the answer, of course, lies in the use to which the state places such borrowed funds. If they directly or indirectly increase social productivity, then the raising of additional tax revenues to cover the principle of such borrowing plus interest payments should not be problematical.

Traditionally, this was the situation when states mobilized for warfare, and in fact it was the demands of modern warfare which first gave rise to the practice of revolving public debt. In a war economy, the state becomes the single largest customer of private industry and provides an assured market for new output. Capital investment and employment levels rise quickly in response to new earning potentials, while the income which is generated provides assured tax revenues with which interest on the war debt can be met. Generally speaking, deficit spending in a period of full employment is unproblematic from the point of view of financing debt, although its effects in undermining price stability is another matter of concern.

Conditions are very different during periods of economic deflation and it may be for this reason that we have only witnessed the concentrated application of Keynesian techniques at the outset of long waves of economic expansion.[16] During serious economic recessions, on the other hand, additions to state debt through public borrowing can erode 'business confidence' while placing the state in direct competition with private industry for loan capital especially in the early stages of a downturn when credit facilities are in short supply. Coterminous tax increases, whether on wage incomes or profit revenues in order to finance larger state expenditures are largely self-negating under such conditions. With the onset of generalized recessionary traits the conversion of social wage accounts into public loan capital has emerged as a specific crisis in the provision of social insurance. The actual outcome, however, will to a large extent be determined by the use to which such borrowing has been placed and specifically whether or not it contributes to the restoration of social productivity. Only if this is the case will additional tax revenues be available for the purpose of compressing debts in the social wage accounts.

Unfortunately, it is seldom possible to track the uses to which loans on social wage accounts have been placed, for once such funds are appropriated they are usually married to the general revenue accounts of the state. Customarily, in the Canadian context at least, these revenues have been utilized in the production of social capital although there is still a wide range of discretion available in their deployment. In some instances they have been made available to state enterprises in the energy, communications and industrial development fields.[17] Throughout the 1970s there was an identifiable shift away from social capital projects involving social welfare expenditures and their replacement with investments in direct aid of accumulative investment. For instance, undertakings such as highway, bridge and water and sewage facilities which accounted for 37.8 per cent of the province of Ontario's capital expenditures in 1972-73 had risen to 58.2 per cent by the 1980-81 fiscal year while health and education outlays declined from 32.1 to 10.7 per cent over the same period.[18] In some of these instances social wage funds are clearly being used to subsidize the accumulation of capital through the production of delimited sets of social use-values. To what effect and with what effects on social reproduction though still remains indeterminate. In fact at this point it is more instructive to place the social wage question in a wider historical context, beginning with the now established fact of the portability of social wages into domestic loan capital.

The Future Of Social Security

Already there has been a partial rehearsal of the existent contradictions between the socialization of reproduction through the extension of a system of substitute wages on the one hand, and privatized accumulation on the other with the operation of unemployment insurance. Here, certain contingencies arising from the operation of the Canadian state's plan can be taken as providing an omen for future social wage development.

In 1971 the Canadian Unemployment Insurance Act was revamped for the first time since its introduction thirty years earlier. Although accompanied by a great deal of fanfare, including the publication of a 'White Paper' prior to debate on the bill, very little in the way of rationale was provided for the new Act by either state spokespersons or other analysts. A glimpse at the Unemployment Insurance Account (Table 11.3) furnishes much of the missing information. Despite the acquisition of considerable reserves during World War Two when unemployment insurance was first launched in Canada, as well as in the immediate post-war years, by 1970, just when the world economic downturn was beginning to gather momentum and calls on the fund were expected to be large, the prospects of the fund remaining solvent were slim indeed. The essence of the new insurance proposals that were brought forward consisted of a unique blend of punitive and atoning measures. For the first time claimants of unemployment insurance benefits were required to attend mandatory interviews at Commission offices for maintenance of eligibility. This extension in surveillance was combined with the raising of wage income ceilings on which weekly premiums were paid, as well as with the extension of coverage to an additional 1.6 million workers (virtually covering the entire wage labour force) which permitted a significant increase in benefit levels as well as an extension of the contribution base.[19]

TABLE 11.3

Unemployment Insurance Fund Account
(in millions of Canadian dollars)

	Current Surplus/Deficit*	Balance of Account
1942	425.7	114.0
1943	325.4	190.3
1944	138.0	268.1
1945	248.5	317.9
1946	55.6	372.8
1947	82.9	455.8
1948	80.5	536.4
1949	53.4	589.9
1950	84.6	674.5
1951	108.2	782.8
1952	74.4	857.3
1953	30.2	887.5
1954	−41.2	846.2
1955	13.1	859.4
1956	18.9	878.4
1957	−134.2	744.2
1958	−244.3	499.8
1959	−133.9	365.8
1960	−181.2	184.6
1961	−118.0	66.5
1962	−56.9	9.6
1963	−8.8	0.87
1964	39.6	40.4
1965	100.9	141.4
1966	116.7	258.2
1967	44.4	302.6
1968	79.6	382.3
1969	75.8	479.7
1970	−134.5	323.6
1971	−286.6	36.8
1972	−59.	−22.
1973	−38.	−60.
1974	−40.	−100.1
1975	−67.	−167.0

*Current surplus/deficit includes payment of benefits, and purchase of securities collections and interest income and income from sale of assets.

Source: Government of Canada, *Public Accounts of Canada* (Supply and Services, Ottawa 1945-1975).

Perhaps the most interesting feature of the new plan, however, were the financing arrangements. Previously, the state had contributed 20 per cent to a 40-40-20 tripartite scheme which included employers and workers. Under the new provisions, labour and capital would each contribute 50 per cent of total contributions until the unemployment rate reached 4 per cent. At this level of unemployment, which is usually defined as optimal in contemporary capitalist economies, a system of extended benefits would be triggered, financed totally out of state contributions (i.e. general revenues). The counterpart of this massive increase in state participation through general revenue expenditures was the termination of a separate unemployment insurance trust fund. Henceforth, unemployment insurance was simply another entry in the general accounts of the state. This 'reorganization' was, of course, a tacit admission of the bankruptcy of the old scheme, although at the time this appears to have gone unnoticed.[20] As the unemployment wage fund went further into debt, loans that had been made to the federal government were called in, and the fund quickly moved from the status of creditor to the state to the position of taking out loans on its own accord. This no doubt contributed to the mushrooming federal budget deficit that appeared in the early 1970s as well as to the disbanding of the fund and its merger with general state revenues.

Two points emerge from this brief review of unemployment insurance expenditures. First, no method of financing such schemes is inviolable to the exigencies of capitalist accumulation. Although the 'accumulation' method of social wage funding does provide a cushion for social insurance assets, sizeable reserves can dwindle over a short period of time. This tendency is made all the more marked when generalized stagflationary pressures are brought to bear on the real value of social wage reserves. When this occurs, programs such as unemployment insurance undergo a *de facto* conversion from 'accumulation' to 'pay-as-you-go' principles.[21] Increasing pressure on general state revenues follow directly from this and are exacerbated by the large scale non-public borrowing on such funds, while the careful principles of bureaucratic control upon which the original social wage transfers were constructed are further undermined. In this case, the dissipation of social wage accounts such as the unemployment insurance fund does point to a major weakness, or to the fragility of social security systems in a wage economy. The mode of organizing public accounts and in particular the conversion of social wage deposits into loan capital and state debt increases the impact of the crisis on the welfare state.

Placing the issue in perspective, however, it should be noted that the sums involved in the unemployment insurance account pale by comparison with those of the largest social wage transfers—the public pensions. The extent to which these monies have been made the object of public finance has already been described in Table 11.2. At the same time, pension plans differ quantitatively from unemployment allowances in that the period of claim on the fund is normally much longer than is the case with unemployment insurance (i.e. a matter of years rather than weeks or months). It therefore follows, for example, that in the case of the Canada Pension Plan, this element of the social wage complex will not be rescued with the same degree of alacrity as was unemployment insurance—in effect by a simple appeal to the general revenues of the state. Turning towards general state budgets as a source of refunding retirement pensions is increasingly problematic simply by virtue of the magnitude of the sums involved in any rescue mission. In other words, it is far from certain that, even if the political 'will' were present, the fiscal resources of the state could measure up to the lengthy commitment involved in balancing this major social wage entitlement. State documents now elude to as much:

> A continuation of the present borrowing structure with the monies in a fully funded Canada Pension Plan would not be in the best interest of the people ... (sic). It (Royal Commission on the Status of Pensions) considers that only when monies are borrowed in the money market, at market rates, with payment guaranteed by the tax base and with scheduled repayments can there be any meaningful restraint on government borrowing. It is significant that no one suggested to the Commission that the provinces be obliged to pay back the capital sums already borrowed from the Canada Pension Plan fund. In fact it may be that some provinces would be hard pressed to do so.[22]

The dilemma faced by the Canadian state with respect to these funds is visibly graphed in Figure 11.2 which examines the largest such resource, the Canada Pension Plan. Up until 1985, the situation will devolve as is illustrated for the 1982-83 fiscal year. Revenues from payroll taxes exceed expenditures paid out by $0.6 billion. Together with the interest that is due, but will be loaned back out ($2.2 billion) new loans from the fund totalling $3.7 billion are made. Total trust balances which stood at $21.5 billion at the beginning of the year will amount to $24.3 billion by the end.

These practices, which have existed since contributory pensions came into existence in 1966, will only be altered when expenditures begin to exceed current contributions; a situation which is expected to arise around 1985 (designated 'Critical Year I'). At this point, authorities will have to start calling some of the interest payments due in order to cover the imbalance between contributions and expenditures, while the remainder of the interest generated by the plan will continue to be reloaned. Initially, such interest repayments will be

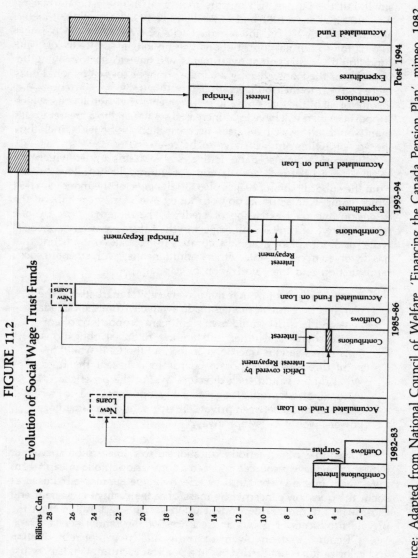

FIGURE 11.2

Evolution of Social Wage Trust Funds

Source: Adapted from National Council of Welfare, 'Financing the Canada Pension Plan', mimeo, 1982.

small, but the burden will quickly mount, with one estimate placing it at $300 million in 1986 and $1.7 billion by 1990.[23] Shortly thereafter, at 'Critical Year II', full interest paybacks of over $2 billion per year in addition to normal contributions will no longer suffice to keep the fund liquid. At this point governments will have to start repaying the principle of the loans, thereby adding a strain of several billion dollars more per year to their budgets. *In lieu* of this unlikely occurence,—i.e. if some or all of the loans have to be forgiven—the payroll taxes which support the plan will have to be increased sooner and to a greater extent than would otherwise have been necessary, or else benefits, including the age of retirement will have to be re-evaluated.[24]

This unfolding scenario indicates the strains under which the social wage trust funds are currently operating. They follow directly from the subordination of such plans to the logic of the money market which compels the valorization of money into money capital and the extension and over-extension of credit.[25] The remarks made by one representative of capital with respect to the future conversion of social wage funds into money capital accurately reflects the contradiction that has devolved upon the state with its simultaneous involvement in social reproduction and the valorization of capital:

> Even if invested through the private capital markets . . . the plan (i.e. investment monies made available from the Canada Pension Plan-BR) would own significant proportions of corporate shares and other outstanding financial obligations. This raises serious questions as to how the CPP would appoint directors to corporate boards to represent the fund. What duties would such directors owe to the beneficiaries? Whose interests would they ostensibly represent . . . The lines of demarcation between private enterprise and parliamentary powers would be swept away.[26]

Of course, other 'serious' questions also remain to be answered. When social wage resources undergo a conversion into loan capital for investment in state debt can they effectively be guaranteed? Posed as such, the question concerns the mass of wage earners in society and those who are directly dependent upon social wages rather than the private producers of goods and services or the rentier social strata.

Of course, state involvement in the dual circuits of reproduction and valorization is not carried out in a political vacuum. While pressure for a revision of social security taxes, possibly combined with calls for a more restrictive application of eligibility rules can be expected to compensate for the partial but inevitable loan defalcations on the social security account, an increasing awareness on the part of labour of the stakes involved in the social wage question is also becoming apparent.

Thus, the funding and use of social wage resources will become a much more important public issue in the near future.[27] When this occurs, the traditional range of trade union concerns with the state, which up until now have primarily focused on employment related issues, will have been significantly extended.

From Civil Servant To State Worker: Recent Trends In Public Goods Production

As previously noted, the transfer expenditures examined in the last section account for only a part, and indeed the smaller part, of total social wage expenses. As a producer of goods and services that enter directly into the reproduction of the wage economy the state faces other immediate paradoxes. In order to pursue the issues involved here it is necessary to examine more thoroughly the processes of social reproduction that are carried out by the state.

In supplying use-values that enter into the reconstitution and renewal of capitalist relations of production, state agencies are charged with the organization of specific labour processes. This involves bringing together the labouring powers of workers employed by the state and the technical requirements of production that are necessary for the delivery of a certain limited range of use-values. Thus, alongside the general growth in state expenditures on reproduction there has been a specific expansion in the number of state employees, which is documented in Table 11.4. Most noteworthy is the expansion of employment in the health and education sectors (between 300 and 500 per cent in the post World War II period) as compared with the growth of employment in the private sector (95.8 per cent over the same period). Of equal significance is the proportion of new jobs created in the public sector. In 1974, for example, fully one-fifth of all new employment was in the state sector, while in previous years this figure has risen to over one-third of all new employment.

Given this massive extension in the public sector, it nevertheless remains difficult to specify the economic effects that follow from it. Deductively, it is consistent with the political economy tradition to treat state reproductive employment in a manner akin to workers who are employed in the sphere of commodity circulation.[28] That is, while such workers are not employed in the production of surplus value, they are nonetheless exploited within their own labour processes, and as a result of this exploitation their labours reduce the costs of production for capital as a whole. Thus, while not strictly speaking a value-producing labour, the expenditure of labour on public goods production does influence the value of surplus value-producing labour in the private sector. At least this is the burden which reproductive labour

TABLE 11.4

State Employment Growth in Canada, 1946-1974

	Total Number of Government All New Workers	New Government Workers as % of Workers	Total Number of Education All New Workers	New Education Workers as % of Workers	Total Number of Hospital Workers	New Hospital Workers as % of All New Workers
1946	278,368	13.1	70,840	5.3	6,822	5.9
1951	334,840	22.0	93,563	7.5	93,725	8.3
1956	442,402	36.3	130,286	10.4	134,320	12.4
1961	613,100	18.3	179,171	9.8	192,391	6.8
1966	814,044	28.4	286,764	11.2	266,930	5.0
1971	1,077,207	10.3	390,960	2.1	313,005	2.6
1974	1,186,067	20.3	413,045	7.7	340,608	6.1
Growth 1946-1974	326.1		483.1		399.3	

Source: Hugh Armstrong, 'The Labour Force and State Workers in Canada' in Leo Panitch (ed.), *The Canadian State*, (University of Toronto Press, Toronto, 1977), Tables 2-5.

is given to bear in this essay and it is because of this that employment in social wage production is so important.

In practice it is a much more formidable job to locate the efficacy of state services in reducing the costs of social reproduction. Generally, this is because empirical referents of the type used in studying macro-economic trends in the private sector are not available. Indeed, not only is there a dearth of information that would be useful in studying the political economy of reproduction in the state sector, but in many instances, the methodological problems of developing useful indicators have not (or cannot) even be posed. For example, in the absence of an equivalent to the 'value added' concept, how can the productivity of workers engaged in social reproduction be measured or compared to the performance of workers in the traditional spheres of labour activity?[29]

TABLE 11.5

Annual Percentage Base Wage Increases in Private and State Reproductive Sectors, Canada 1967-1977

	Private	Health, Education & Welfare	General Government*
1967	7.8	9.4	9.5
1968	8.1	10.0	7.2
1969	8.6	6.9	8.3
1970	8.6	8.9	8.3
1971	8.0	8.4	7.6
1972	9.2	6.5	8.1
1973	10.1	10.2	10.6
1974	14.4	17.8	14.2
1975	14.4	21.3	17.3
1976	9.3	10.2	11.2
1977	7.1	6.8	8.5
Average			
1967-77	9.6	10.6	10.0
1973-77	11.1	13.3	12.3

*Includes various government utilities.

Source: Calculated from R. Bird *et al*, *The Growth of Public Employ-ment in Canada* (Butterworth, Toronto, 1979) Table 5.1.

While such issues do complicate the analysis of state resource expenditures, it is still possible to isolate some of the major trends that have characterized such outlays. It is evident, for example, that the costs of employing reproductive labour have undergone a significant increase in recent years. This is apparent when the earnings of state workers are compared with private sector incomes. As indicated in Table 11.5, wage increases in the public sector have consistently outstripped those in the private sector from the late 1960s.

Although overall differences in wage growth have been marginal, they have tended to increase throughout the 1970s, with the largest wage gains being registered in the health, education, and welfare employments. The significance of these trends can only be adduced from examining relative wage costs over a longer time frame. Such a perspective is provided in Table 11.6, which arrays average real median wages in the education sector against mean wages in manufacturing employment. Limitations in the original data force us to rely on these two statistical measures with the result that incomes generated in manufacturing vis-a-vis those in the education series are somewhat understated throughout. Nonetheless, a distinct picture emerges over time. The wages of education workers lagged behind those in private industry until the boom in state educational expenditures in the late 1950s. From 1958, however, the series 'cross over' and a widening gap emerges between wage levels in this sphere of public goods production and in manufacturing industry.

No opprobrium need be attached to this movement, in the sense that 'overpaid' state workers are to blame for the crisis of the welfare state. Indeed, this would represent a complete misreading of the data insofar as a movement towards rough wage parities is to be expected, while significant discrepancies between sectors can only be viewed as anomalous in a modern labour market setting. Rather the *relative* growth in the wages of state service workers is the product of a number of interrelated factors that hinge upon the vast centralization of reproduction processes which has occurred under state auspices in the post-1945 period. This movement, which entails a partial rationalization of delivery systems includes such diverse measures as the nationalization of hospitals and their inclusion in the system of government accounts, and the regionalization of the education system. State employment is thus subject to pressures which eventuate in the growing socialization of labour as expressed not only in the greater number of workers entering employment with various governments and agencies, but also by their grouping in larger and larger units of production. Mirroring these conditions is the growth in organization amongst state workers, a development which commences only as late as the 1960s, but which by the next decade has already produced several novel traits on the political landscape. Measures of effective strike ratios, trade

TABLE 11.6

Real Wages and Salaries in Manufacturing & Education, in 1971 Canadian Dollars

	Education	Manufacturing
1937	2364	3036
1938	2333	3011
1939	2376	3080
1940	2312	3171
1941	2248	3233
1942	2481	3430
1943	2507	3655
1944	2731	3756
1945	2911	3689
1946	3130	3561
1947	3345	3650
1948	3237	3639
1949	3308	3726
1950	3350	3827
1951	3424	3864
1952	3638	4091
1953	3858	4333
1954	4086	4422
1955	4286	4590
1956	4479	4785
1957	4766	4871
1958	5029	4985
1959	5364	5110
1960	5566	5292
1961	5747	5385
1962	5812	5639
1963	5977	5768
1964	6193	5935
1965	6391	6105
1966	6604	6267
1967	7482	6421
1968	7153	6642
1969	7555	6866

Source: Statistics Canada, *General Review of the Manufacturing Industries of Canada* (Information Canada, Ottawa, 1971), Table 1; Statistics Canada, *Salaries & Qualifications of Teachers in Public Elementary & Secondary Schools* (Information Canada, Ottawa, 1956 & 1969), Table 7; Statistics Canada, *National Income & Expenditure Accounts* (Information Canada, Ottawa, 1976) Table 7.

union growth, etc. all point to the newly-acquired militancy of state employees.[30] Indeed, the period between 1968 and 1976 is reminiscent of the rapid and militant growth of industrial trade unionism in Canada between 1937 and 1946, only this time around the issue was the proletarianization of reproductive functions rather than the deskilling of industrial occupations.[31]

As a result of these new pressures emanating from the state sector, wages have become an increasingly significant element in the total costs of providing reproductive services. This is reflected in Table 11.7, where the evolution of capital/labour ratios are examined for public and private spheres respectively. Here—and *contrary to the general laws of capitalist production*—the price component of capital stock in the total cost price of education and health services exhibits an interesting tendency to decline over the thirty years for which data is available. Conversely, the proportional cost element of wages increases. As Table 11.7 makes clear, this is precisely the opposite of the general movement in capital/labour ratios in manufacturing industry and we might add to capitalist industry as a whole, where increasing capital/labour ratios are normally identified with the rising organic composition of capital and intensified productivity. In other words, labour costs relative to the private sector have been increasing in the social sphere of reproduction, while technological development and utilization has lagged behind. Given the trajectory that is depicted in Table 11.7, where the capital/labour ratio has declined by 50 per cent in the education sector and by 70 per cent in the labour-intensive health care field, compared to an increase of 52 per cent in manufacturing industry, it is accurate to infer a relative decline in the productivity of those public sector activities that are charged with the commodification of labour power.

This, however, is symptomatic not of the unproductiveness of state workers, but rather of a developing *disproportionality* between reproductive and productive labours. Thus, while social wage production subsidises the costs of reproduction, the steady increase of labour costs and labour/capital ratios in this arena erodes the potential savings for capital that accrue from externalizing the costs of reproduction onto a state authority. Potential savings which are derived from the production of social use-values are diminished as the costs of these services mount over time and with respect to commodities in general.

When this occurs the partisan demand for 'public economizing' (i.e. cutbacks) is not long in following. In this case, however, it is not a crisis of the welfare state *ex nihilo* that is being addressed, but rather a crisis of relations between the social reproduction of the dominant wage labour-capital relation on the one hand and the primacy of its constituent feature, the accumulation of exchange-value on the other. As a result of this, a resolution to the crisis and the form it might assume is not at all obvious. A continuation of the crackdown on public

TABLE 11.7

Ratio of Capital Stock to Wages, Selected Areas, Canada 1950-1978

	Manufacturing	Education	Hospitals
1950	4.2	10.2	8.4
1955	5.8	9.3	6.9
1960	5.5	6.6	5.4
1965	5.6	5.7	4.2
1970	5.8	4.9	3.0
1974	5.8	5.5	1.6
1978	6.4	5.1	2.5

Source: Statistics Canada, *Fixed Capital Flows and Stocks* (Supply and Services, Ottawa: various years). Revenue Canada, *Taxation Statistics* (Supply and Services, Ottawa: various years). Statistics Canada, *General Review of Manufacturing Industries in Canada* (Supply and Services, Ottawa: 1961, 1977). Statistics Canada, *Hospital Statistics* (Information Canada, Ottawa: various years).

sector workers through the continuation of selective income policies and limitations on the right to strike is likely, but the success of such policies will in part depend upon the organizational strength of state workers.[32] While more extensive cutbacks remain another option, it is important to note that thus far they have been brought to bear largely on the discretionary welfare programs that are intended for the poor rather than on the larger social wage entitlements that cover working class reproduction. The possibilities for underfunding the production of public goods also appear constricted over the long run, given the absence of real alternatives such as returning the provision of such functions to the household. Attacking the problem of sectoral disproportionalities from the other end of the spectrum through the introduction of labour saving technologies also promises to yield uncertain results at best. This follows from the service-oriented nature of many social wage functions, which is only an expression of the ultimate dominance of use-value over exchange-value relations in the social reproduction process.

Conclusions

In the preceding sections the two major forms of state intervention into social reproduction have been analyzed with respect to the current crisis. The outcomes of intervention, the evolving fiscal crisis in the social wage transfer funds, and the growing disproportionalities between the costs of reproduction and those of production pose unwieldy challenges to the contemporary capitalist state. It would, of course, be erroneous to interpret these developments as evidence that the state is adverse to a reversal of current trends or that it is locked into a position of strategic drift. As previously noted, efforts at obtaining 'economic rationalities' through state restraint is only one harsh reminder of the urgency which is attached to this project. On the other hand, the present conjuncture is not just a case of disproportionality in the classical sense as between different departments of capitalist production. Rather, it is the contemporary manifestation of the contradiction between reproduction and accumulation, between labour and capital.

This contradiction between the maintenance and reproduction of a labour force and the valorization of capital has attained a new saliency, however, precisely because it has become a political issue subject to regulation by the state in its dual role as guarantor of class property and overseer of social reproduction. Due to the fact that the state has now become a major element in social reproduction through its organization of the social wage, the conflicting exigencies of capitalist production can no longer be expunged from the political-economic system of capitalism, or isolated at individual points of production or consumption in enterprises or households. For this reason, the crisis assumes not only an economic form, but also a political and a social component, with the state at the centre of the ensuing social disaggregation. Hence, the following impasse: state intervention in the circuit of reproduction (through the regulation it imposes on the value of labour power) directly intercedes with the functioning of private capital. This critical mediation is only accomplished by incorporating capitalist forms of (re)productive organization and calculation into the reproduction process. Concretely, we have seen this assume the form of capitalizing social wage funds in respect to distributive functions, and in the exploitation of wage labour and the rationalization of labour processes in the outlay of production expenditures. Out of these relationships flow the pressures which are continually brought to bear on the public economy for cost accountability. Under given conditions these constraints which constantly assail state intervention into social reproduction are registered as a crisis of the welfare state. This, however, is at best a partial, symptomatic picture.

For at the same time, the object of social wage policy—human labour power—is not strictly speaking a commodity production, nor is the state simply an enterprise for the renewal of labouring skills.[33] In other words, social reproduction under capitalist state auspices entails the extensive utilization of *wage labour* and *money capital* in a *non-commodity* production. This represents the essential contradiction of social wage creation as well as the particular dilemma of the modern welfare state. Social reproduction with its disposal over wage labour and social wage reserves consistently confronts the dominant logic and limitations of capitalist market production, without, however, being able to conform to these parameters, or to alter them significantly. In the foregoing, we have seen this expressed in social wage funds which cannot be incorporated into the state's permanent debt structures, or assimilated to state accumulation functions without thoroughly undermining the fiscal principles and discipline which guided the formation of such programs. Analogously, the production of goods and services by the state which subsidize the costs of reproduction are partly immune from the normal laws of capitalist accumulation despite the utilization of wage labour on a considerable scale.[34] In both cases the results impact upon the unfettered accumulation of capital: in one instance as the accumulation and eventual devalorization of money capital in the state sector as deficit social wage funds; and in the other instance as disproportionalities between the costs of reproduction and production.

Thus, while the accumulation of capital circumscribes the objectives and content of state social policy, the production of a social wage introduces major political determinants into the ongoing accumulaton of capital. Currently, it is on the political terrain where market and extra-market (social) forces contend with one another. While this now assumes the explicit form of economic disorder it is only the most recent expression of the fundamental antagonisms between capitalist production and human need.

Notes and References

1. F. Piven and R. Cloward, *The New Class War* (Pantheon, New York, 1982).
2. Another recent work which stresses the linkages between state welfare interventions and ensuing crisis tendencies is S. Bowles and H. Gintis, 'The Crisis of Liberal Democratic Capitalism', *Politics and Society*, Vol. 11, No. 1 (1982).
   Also see the essays by Bandypadhyay and Stafford in this volume for analyses that develop a complimentary position.
3. For the definitive article that makes the distinction between accumulation and social reproduction refer to C. Meillassoux, 'From Reproduction to

Production', *Economy and Society*, Vol. 1, No. 1 (1972).

4. For an analysis of capitalist taxation and contemporary revenue inputs into social wage production see B. Russell, 'The Politics of Labour Force Reproduction: Funding Canada's Social Wage', *Studies in Political Economy*, No. 14 (1984).

5. My approach to capitalist crises has been influenced by the important essays of G. Arrighi and I. Wallerstein in S. Amin et al. (eds), *Dynamics of Global Crisis* (Monthly Review Press, New York, 1983).

6. For a complete treatment of the household and its role in social reproduction see the collected essays in B. Fox (ed.), *Hidden In the Household* (Women's Press, Toronto, 1980).

7. See the papers by J. Dickinson and J. Wayne in this volume.

8. Bandyopdhyay, 'Theoretical Approaches to the State and Social Reproduction', in this volume.

9. R. Bacon and W. Eltis, *Britain's Economic Problem* (Macmillan, London, 1978).

10. According to the eighteenth-century French Physiocratic school of economists, only the agrarian sector of production was capable of producing an economic surplus. Adam Smith was cognizant of the shortcomings of this position and duly extended the definition of productive labour to any activity that eventuated in the creation of a 'vendable commodity which lasts for some time at least after that labour is past'. This definition excluded both the production of services, as well as use-values that were not produced as commodities. A. Smith, *The Wealth of Nations* (Random House, New York, 1965), p. 315.

11. I. Gough, *The Political Economy of the Welfare State* (Macmillan, London, 1980); J. O'Connor, *The Fiscal Crisis of the State* (St. Martin's, New York, 1973).

12. Such confusion is periodically exhibited in *Fiscal Crisis* pp. 161, 211, where it is unclear, for example, whether social consumption expenditures (i.e. outlays on the social wage) and the taxes used to fund them reduce or increase the costs of purchasing labour power. For a more elaborate critique see H. Mosley, 'Monopoly Capital and the State', *Review of Radical Political Economics*, Vol. 11, No. 1 (1979).

13. R. Musgrave, *Public Finance in Theory and Practice* (McGraw-Hill, New York, 1976); P. Samuelson, 'A Diagramatic Exposition of a Theory of Public Expenditures', *Review of Economic Statistics* (1955). Ironically, the category of goods that best fits the public finance case, that of true collective consumables is of diminishing importance relative to total state outlays. Concurrently, locating state expenditures solely in terms of specific use-value attributes as does the normative school of public finance while abstracting from the social relations that are bound up in their production is bound to result in distortions in their analysis.

14. Social insurance trust funds may be operated in accordance with two funding principles. 'Accumulation' techniques, as the name suggests, implies the accumulation of large reserves through special social security taxes. For a number of decades fund revenues exceed expenditures and the system embodies an element of income redistribution between current contributors and recipients. 'Pay-as-you-go' techniques, on the other hand, do not

countenance a build-up of funds. Revenues are set only to meet current obligations.

15. J. Tomlinson also treats the issue of public borrowing in his papers, 'Why Was There Never a 'Keynesian Revolution' in Economic Policy? *Economy and Society*, Vol. 10, No. 1 (1981) and 'The 'Economics of Politics' and Public Expenditure', *Economy and Society*, Vol. 10, No. 4 (1981). While Tomlinson examines obstacles to public borrowing (the 'gilt strike'), paradoxically he does not account for them, nor does he examine the public finances of social wage borrowing.

16. Also see K. Schott, 'The Rise of Keynesian Economics', *Economy and Society*, Vol. 11, No. 3 (1982), and J. Tomlinson, 'Where Do Economic Policy Objectives Come From', *Economy and Society*, Vol. 12, No. 1 (1983).

17. Advisory Committee of the Canada Pension Plan, 'The Rate of Return on the Investment Fund of the Canada Pension Plan', mimeo (1975), p. 7.

18. Ontario, Ministry of Treasury and Economics, *Ontario Budget* (Ontario Government, Toronto, 1978; 1980).

19. By the measures of the 1971 Act, unemployment insurance benefits were raised to equal 66.6% of normal wage earnings.

20. Indeed, in the hundreds of pages of debate on the new Unemployment Insurance Act, only one mention concerning the restructuring of the fund is to be found. Dominion of Canada, *Debates, House of Commons* (Queen's Printer, Ottawa, 1971).

21. This much was admitted by the Minister who tabled the new Unemployment Insurance Act. 'The idea is for the whole plan to finance itself as it goes along. Periodically, once a year . . . we will adjust the rates according to the experience of the past year . . . the government will absorb the extraordinary cost features of the plan which come into effect at the 4 per cent level'. Ibid., p. 5143.

22. Ontario, *Royal Commission on the Status of Pensions in Ontario*, Vol. V, p. 97.

23. National Council of Welfare, 'Financing the Canada Pension Plan', mimeo, 1982, p. 13.

24. Given the contractual nature of substitute wages between citizens and state, more onerous rate schedules are a more distinct possibility than are cutbacks in this area of the social wage.

25. Suzanne de Brunhoff tends to gloss over such problems, viewing the welfare state as a solution to the problem of proletarian reproduction. Hence she argues that 'the management of a part of the value of labour power could not be taken over by either capitalist or workers; if one side or the other attempted to do so it ran the risk of adopting practices associated with class interests, which would contradict the goals of welfare and social security (as would occur, for example, if employers used funds for financial speculation . . .) (sic). The bourgeois state . . . could directly manage or impose a framework of managerial institutions so that the "general interest" of the reproduction of capital would prevail over those of the two antagonistic classes'. S. de Brunhoff, *The State, Capital, and Economic Policy* (Pluto, London, 1978).

26. Toronto Stock Exchange, *Brief to the Royal Commission on the Status of Pensions in Ontario* (Brief no. 219, Ontario Archives).

27. By way of example, the Canadian Union of Public Employees has recently gone on record as advocating that 'the public money accumulated through the fully funded Canada Pension Plan and public employee pension funds, instead of being used to finance the investment requirements of the private corporate sector, would instead be used in the public interest to: 1) Repatriate the Canadian economy by directly purchasing the outstanding equity interest of foreign owned or controlled corporations and to: 2) Pursue an industrial strategy by indirect C/QPP (Canada/Quebec Pension Plan—BR) public employee pension fund investment in the industrial sector through Federal and Provincial Crown Corporations', Canadian Union of Public Employees, *Brief to the Royal Commission on the Status of Pensions in Ontario*, Dec. 1977 (Brief no. 101, Ontario Archives).

28. K. Marx, *Capital* Volume II (Progress Publishers, Moscow, 1971), Section 1.

29. In ordinary commodity production productivity is measurable by virtue of the homogeneity of the output which itself is a function of engineered quality control systems. No such analogue exists in the realm of 'human services' as it is overseen by the state. For a further discussion of these issues see D. Daly (ed.), *Research on Productivity of Relevance to Canada* (Social Science Federation of Canada, Ottawa, 1983), Section B.

30. The organization of state workers has proven to be the most expansive arena of trade unionism in recent years. Thus, of the 16 unions in Canada with 50,000 or more members in 1981, 5 were state employee organizations and of these 3 were in the top 5 largest unions. Similarly, an examination of effective strike ratios between public and private spheres, (defined as the number of workers on strike in a given sector/total number of workers in that sector) demonstrates the growing synchronization between the two series with disputes in the state sector attaining relative parity with strikes in private industry in 4 years and greater relative significance in another 4 years between 1967 and 1980. Labour Canada, *Directory of Labour Organization in Canada* (Supply and Services, Ottawa, 1981); Canada, Dept. of National Revenue, *Taxation Statistics* (Supply and Services, Ottawa, various years) and Canada, Dept. of Labour, *Strikes and Lockouts in Canada* (Supply and Services, Ottawa, various years).

31. For keen insights into the development of state trade unionism see the extensive interview conducted with J-C Parrot, President of the Canadian Union of Postal Workers in 'Jean-Claude Parrot: An Interview', *Studies in Political Economy*, No. 11 (1983).

32. For an analysis of the new era in state labour policy refer to L. Panitch and D. Swartz, 'Towards Permanent Exceptionalism'. *Labour/Le Travail*, No. 13 (1984).

33. This raises an essential distinction: While the social existence of labour power is only verified through its commodity status in capitalist society, labour power is not produced and marketed as a commodity by the state. To quote Polanyi, it is a 'fictitious commodity'. K. Polanyi, *The Great Transformation* (Beacon Hill, Boston, 1965). It is ultimately this 'fictitious' quality that gives rise to the contradictions in the sphere of reproduction that have been discussed above.

34. Industrial relations experts are also partially aware of this contradiction as

witnessed in the following observation: 'Governments face fewer economic constraints in collective bargaining than employers in the private sector. Wage policy is not tied to a profit position or strict capacity to pay. A government does not measure the productivity of its services and it will not close down if it operates at a deficit . . . However, while the profit-loss criterion is usually absent in determining wage policy in the public sector, a government cannot ignore the pattern-setting effect of negotiated settlement with its own employees and their repercussions on the economy as a whole. . . . A government also faces particular constraints as the guardian of the public purse and the elected representative of the people'. Goldenberg, *Public Service Bargaining* (Industrial Relations Centre, Queen's University, Kingston, 1973), p. 13.

Notes on Contributors

Pradeep Bandyopadhyay, educated at Calcutta, Oxford and Manchester Universities, currently teaches sociology and comparative development at Trent University, Peterborough, Ontario. He has written and researched in Marxian political economy, development-planning, urban analysis and the philosophy of science. He has contributed to *The Value Controversy* (New Left Books, London, 1981) and to various journals including *Science and Society* and *The International Journal of Urban and Regional Research.*

James Dickinson teaches in the Department of Sociology at Rider College, Lawrenceville, New Jersey. He received a B.A. from the University of Kent in England, an M.A. from the American University, Washington, D.C. and Ph.d. from the University of Toronto. He has written and published on economic development, agriculture and the state, and social policy. He is currently working on a comparative study of the welfare state.

Rudy Fichtenbaum is Associate Professor of Economics at Wright State University in Dayton, Ohio. Dr. Fichtenbaum's publications have appeared in the *Review of Social Economy*, *The Forum for Social Economics*, *Growth and Change*, *Review of Regional Studies*, *Urban Affairs Quarterly* and *Journal of Behavioral Economics.*

Susan Mann received a Ph.d. in sociology from the University of Toronto. She currently teaches in the Department of Sociology at the University of New Orleans, Louisiana. Her main interests are in the areas of social theory, women's studies and uneven rural development. She has contributed to *Hidden in The Household: Women's Domestic Labour under Capitalism* (Women's Press, Toronto, 1980), *The Journal of Peasant Studies* and *Rural Sociology.*

Bob Russell graduated with a Ph.d. in sociology from the State University of New York at Binghamton. He has previously published in *Studies in Political Economy* and *The Insurgent Sociologist.* Currently he teaches in the Department of Sociology at the University of Saskatchewan in Saskatoon and is engaged in research on the state, industrial relations and social wage programs in Canada.

Wally Seccombe received a Ph.d. in sociology from the University of Toronto in 1982. Currently he is teaching in the Department of Sociology at the Ontario Institute for Studies in Education, Toronto. He has importantly contributed to the domestic labour debate and his publications include 'The Housewife and her Labour under Capitalism' (New Left Review, 1973) and two chapters in *Hidden in the House World: Women's Domestic Labour under Capitalism* (Women's Press, Toronto, 1980). His major work, *Family Forms and Modes of Production*, will be published by New Left Books in 1985.

James Stafford received a B.A., B. Ed., M.Ed. and Ph.D. at the University of Alberta. He has taught and administered in schools in Alberta and Tanzania. He is presently Associate Professor of Sociology at Lakehead University, Ontario where he pursues research interests in labour migration and the welfare of the elderly.

Jane Ursel currently teaches in the Sociology Department at the University of Manitoba, Winnipeg. In addition to her historical and theoretical work on women, the family and social policy she is also interested in policy impact studies. Most recently she has contributed to the evaluation of wife abuse programs in Manitoba.

Jack Wayne is Associate Professor in the Department of Sociology, University of Toronto where he pursues studies on development and the political economy of modern capitalism. His other recent writing has focused on colonialism and imperialism, and he has published on this topic in *Studies in Political Economy*. At present he is completing a book on the scramble for Africa by the European powers in the late nineteenth century.

Gordon Welty received his doctorate from the University of Pittsburgh in 1974. He is currently Associate Professor of Sociology and Communications at Wright State University in Dayton, Ohio. His recent publications have appeared in *Political Studies*, *Dialectics and Humanism* and *Filosofskaia Nauki*.

Eli Zaretsky is Adjunct Professor of History at San Francisco State University and Professor at the Wright Institute, Berkeley, California. He is the author of the widely-known and much-translated *Capitalism, the Family and Personal Life* (Harper and Row, New York, 1976) and has edited a new abridgement of William I. Thomas and Florian Znaniecki's *The Polish Peasant in Europe and America* (University of Illinois Press, Urbana, 1984).